UNITED WE STAND
Pre WW II-Chronicles of the Italian Colony of Stamford

Anthony Socci

CASA LAGO PRESS
NEW FAIRFIELD, CT

Diaspora
Volume 3

As "diaspora" is the dispersion or spread of people from their original homeland, this book series takes its name in the intellectual spirit of willful dispersion of subject matter and thought. It is dedicated to publishing those studies that in various and sundry ways either speak to or offer new methods of analysis of the Italian diaspora.

The publication of this book has bene made possible through a generous grant from an anonymous donor who wishes not to be identified but urges others to donate to historical and cultural studies.

COVER PHOTO, FRONT: Vetriolo Grocery store (Virginia Cavanna Vetriolo and Quintino Vetriolo). Photo Courtesy of Vetriolo Family.

COVER PHOTO, BACK: Charles Pasquale Esposito — Convicted and sentenced to hang for murder. His cause united many Italian organizations in defense of Esposito and prevented his hanging. He was pardoned and released after eighteen years in prison. Image Courtesy of Stamford Advocate Archives.

COVER DESIGN: Ed LoPresti

ISBN 978-1-955995-07-8
Library of Congress Control Number: Available upon request

CASA LAGO PRESS
New Fairfield, CT

To my mother and father, who had the courage, and foresight to leave their homeland in search of better opportunities not only for themselves but also for their future descendants, I am proud of what you accomplished and am eternally grateful. Thank you for teaching me to not only admire and respect America but also Italy, Italians, and their culture.

CONTENTS

ACKNOWLEDGMENTS

Our communities are made a better place thanks to people who envision an improved future not only for themselves and their contemporaries but also for those that will come after. First, I must thank all those Italians who came before who stood united and worked hard to improve their lives and in doing so, managed through their trailblazing to advance the lives of the entire community (Italian and Non-Italian) here in Stamford and in all of America. *Grazie di cuore!* I will attempt to tell your story, do it justice, and preserve it for future generations.

Writing a book is more difficult than I could have imagined, but infinitely more rewarding. A world of information and history was revealed to me during my research that has forever impacted me, and I hope the readers of this book. This compilation of Stamford Italian American history would not exist if not for the contributions of many thoughtful and supportive people. Thank you to all the staff at the Stamford History Center, especially Ron Marcus (without whom this book would not have been possible) for your encouragement and generosity in sharing your time and historical knowledge, but also to Dan Burke, Rick Lewis, and Kathleen O'Farrell.

I must also acknowledge Italian American researchers Kim Harke Shushon and Mario Toglia whose assistance has been invaluable.

Thank you to my Chicago connections Deryck Nevelstraum and James Lucca. Thank you to Debra Emery. Thank you to the following descendants of Italian Americans who were so generous during my research: Dr. Dennis Barone, Rosemarie and Emmanuale Blosio, Attorney Michael J. Cantore, Rick Castiglione, Theresa Conetta Cucco, Tony Coviello, Philip Giordano, Elaine Vacca Kanelias, Richard Morris, JoAnn Napoletano Dipanni, Nancy Lazzaro Fekete, Mary Lou Rinaldi, Attorney Peter J. Somma Jr., Patricia Scalzi, Dr. Anthony Julian Tamburri, and Rosemary Vacca.

Thanks to the local social club members who were so helpful: Franco and Angelo Raus of the Minturnese Social Club, Teodoro Melchionno of the San Manghese Social Club, and Anthony Ferraro of the Società Mutuo Soccoroso Gravinese and the Italian Center of Stamford.

Lastly, I must acknowledge you, the reader. Thank you for being curious and spending your time learning about the past. For those of you with Italian-American roots, I have attempted to cover as much as I could, but of course, I could not capture everything. I hope this will inspire you to do your own research and continue the work to document our history. It is also my wish that it triggers a re-engagement in your culture and a reclaiming of pride among our community; not solely from the lens of the past but in terms of what it means to be Italian today. Your ancestors have always been there in plain sight, waiting for you to discover them. For those that are not Italian, I hope you take away a better appreciation not only for what the Italian culture has given us here in Stamford, but also the long and difficult journey Italians traversed here, and that you recognize similarities in your own background that engender empathy with not only the immigrants of the past but for other citizens of the city.

I hope that all the love that came my way during the time this project unfolded, from those of you whether mentioned above or not radiates back out to the readers of this history.

PROLOGUE

"Nescire autem quid antequam natus sis acciderit, id est semper esse puerum."— Marcus Tullius Cicero.(Not to know what happened before one was born is always to be a child.)

One need only look to the skyline and infrastructure of the city to understand the most visible and omnipresent contributions Italian contractors, architects, and laborers have made to Stamford. However, the impact of Italians does not stop there, look deeper and you will find that they have made many other important contributions to their adopted land. They excelled in many areas, despite obstacles thrown their way. It is likely that the reader is one of the citizens of the city who has pizza, pasta, or some other Italian cuisine at least once a week. As a worker, you enjoy workplace protections fought for and earned by those long ago, including Italian workers. You enjoy public policies and entitlements introduced by Italian American politicians in the city. You enjoy the benefits of public health administration pioneered by Italian Americans in the city. Many parks in the city have connections to Italian Americans. Many of the homegrown sports heroes from Stamford have an Italian American background. Italians contributed several Mayors, representatives, and city board members. Many popular local businesses have Italian American owners. Italians have contributed much to local Arts as well. Italians have influenced every aspect of Stamford society, including religion, business, sports, and entertainment to name a few. It can be said with certainty that Stamford has been made a better place by the contributions of Italian Americans. Of course, not only the Italians have contributed to Stamford; but this is a history of Stamford Italians and as such the discussion is confined accordingly.

Many are likely asking why we should compile a history of Stamford Italians who lived so long ago. What does this have to do with me? Who cares? The most important reason is that they merit acknowledgment for their contributions to not only Italian-Americans living in the city today (currently about 15.2% of the population)[1] but to Stamford itself and all of its citizens whatever their ethnic background. These generations of Italian Americans have helped shape our society and steer the course of our history, and they did it all while carrying on their regular jobs and maintaining their families. Foremost on their minds was elevating not only the existing "Italian Colony" but future generations as well. They formed a plan, stood united and executed it to perfection. They did it by navigating a language different than their first

[1] usa.com/rank/connecticut-state--italian-as-first-ancestry-population-percentage—city-rank. htm (2022).

language, in the face of bias, and with limited resources. What do you do when you have limited resources? You become creative! I don't like to generalize (especially when speaking about a diverse group such as the Italians), but this is probably one of the most important of all Italian traits. For instance, Italians may have not invented pasta, nor were tomatoes or potatoes indigenous to the Italian peninsula; but they certainly put their spin on these simple ingredients with amazing results confirmed by the gastronomic admiration of people all over the world.

Beyond their worthiness and to be selfish, the recording and preservation of the Italian American history and experience in Stamford is important to all of us. History can give us not only a sense of belonging to a given political, social, and geographical area, but a sense of shared human achievement. Everyone makes some kind of a contribution, either negative or positive, to the progress of civilization that, taken collectively, has meaning. Without recording this local history, it is very likely that this meaning would become lost. If we do not document and save it for the future, no one else will or worse someone could alter it to serve their own purposes. Often, we do not realize the important impact that this documentation has until it is too late. I will not let this happen. Italian Americans have now gotten to a point where their cultural differences are much more widely accepted (for instance pizza is one of the most favorite foods not only in the U.S. but the world) and have become so assimilated that we are more worried about retaining our ethnicity and customs. Documentation is key here as well.

It is vital as well to honor those that came before and as some say, "upon whose shoulders we stand," to acknowledge that we didn't get to where we are by ourselves, while we express gratitude for their contributions. Drawing on our forbearers' courage and principles can help us lead in the future, applying lessons learned.

This history is a compilation of Stamford Italian-American historical events in summarized format and includes names and dates of the participants where applicable. The periods covered in this history are from the 1860s to 1941 (pre-WW II). When you read their stories, I think you will be as inspired as I was. For me, it was impossible to not feel empathy for some of the people whose stories are told here, and I wish I could answer all the questions left open from the primary sources used.

While most of the history is factual and based on primary sources, there are personal stories and recollections that Italians generously shared with me that are interspersed throughout. Of course, I had to interpret and read into some of the written primary sources, sometimes written over a hundred and forty years ago, but attempted to speculate appropriately based on existing facts, backed up by references without whitewashing this history. I included the good and bad, in order to provide a more realistic and complete history. I believe it is important to understand that much as we might dislike it, life is not entirely black or white; in fact, there are many shades of gray in between. Our heroes most likely have some imperfections, and we need to appreciate this without discounting any of their important accomplishments.

There were several challenges in doing this research. One is the matter of the scale of the number of immigrants coming into Stamford. The size of the group makes it hard to draw conclusions about the collective community. It is important to realize how diverse Italian Americans are and how complicated it is to generalize (even with respect to Italians in Stamford). Impacts of local culture, social status, education and training, and degrees to which bias affects individuals vary within the community. This is true also for those not in the Italian community; as such, there of course was a diversity of reactions to Italians that arrived.

The second issue is the lack of written evidence handed down by Italians themselves, often because of illiteracy, and difficulties in mastering a new language. I have used various resources to gather information from official records, newspaper accounts, and documents published by Italians. Unfortunately, it has been a long time and sometimes the scent of the trail is lost and a complete chronical is not possible.

Often in Stamford Italian American writings, they refer to the Italian community as the "Italian Colony." This was terminology commonly used in the late 19th Century and early 20th Century. One of the definitions of "colony" is a group of people of one nationality or ethnic group living in a foreign city or country.

To give perspective of when Italians first came, and then how their numbers increased over time, here are some numbers on Italian immigration to the United States from 1880 to 1914:[2]

IMMIGRATION FROM ITALY TO U.S.

YEARS	
1880-1889	267,660
1890 – 1899	603,791
1900-1909	2,154,611
1910-1914	<u>1,265,535</u>
Total	4,291,597

---

[2] Stephen Puleo (1994). Betty Boyd Caroli, 33, 38.

Italians immigrated to many other countries at this time as well, resulting in the largest voluntary mass migration from a single country in history. The impact was widely felt even here in Stamford. Eventually, the sheer numbers became overwhelming in America and led to the passage of The Immigration Act of 1924, which limited the number of immigrants allowed entry into the United States through a national origins quota. This law was largely enacted to slow the number of Italians entering the country.

Between 1900 and 1910, Italian immigration hit its peak in Stamford, which became one of Connecticut's fastest-growing cities. The population grew by fifty-three percent. The number of manufacturing companies increased from 49 to 86, fueled by the growing labor force (Toglia, 288). Concurrent with the explosion of Italian immigrants and the resulting bias, the new residents contended with many events during this period, including a world war, the outbreak of the Spanish Flu epidemic, and The Depression. Yet, they were determined to make Stamford their home, to elevate the Italian Colony, and to become a valuable and indispensable part of Stamford society. How did they do it?

CHAPTER 1

First Italian Americans in Stamford

Chi cerca, trova.
(Seek and ye shall find)

It is always best to start at the beginning of the story. There is much interest in who the first Italian in Stamford was. Based on oral history, it has been reported that the first Italian American in Stamford was John Geronimo. Italian American history in Stamford parallels much of what we know about the pattern of Italian American immigration in the whole of the United States. If in fact John Geronimo and his family were the first Italians in Stamford, the origins of the first Italians in Stamford mirror that of the first Italian in the Americas, as the Geronimos haled from the same region of present-day Italy as Columbus did, Genoa.

John Gironimi (later Geronimo) was born in Genoa in 1844.[1] Still other variations of the last name exist depending on what the source is; Gironni is found in the 1880 United States Federal Census, Gerolomo and Giaromini in Stamford information directories, Geronimeein Stamford land records, and DiGiralamo in newspaper reports. The spelling of Italian names some-times changed after families immigrated to the United States, which makes tracing people more difficult. This was a common occurrence while research-ing this book. Often this happened because of illiteracy or because immi-grants found their names were hard to spell or pronounce to American eyes and ears, so they were simplified, or they simply wanted to fit in better. Some-times the person writing the name spelled it the way it sounded to them. The story that names were changed at Ellis Island, however, is not actually true (names were provided on the ship manifests from the land of origin) and is not relevant in this case as Ellis Island was not open until 1892.

Geronimo emigrated to the U.S. around 1855-1860 and reportedly en-listed in the Union Army and served under General Sherman. I was unable to verify this through military records. He settled in Hoboken, NJ, and was married there in 1868.[3] He brought his family (his wife Rosalind and children (Anthony, Peter, James, and John) to Stamford in 1877. More children fol-lowed while they lived in Stamford. In 1880, they lived at 12 North Pacific Street.[4] Many of the addresses listed in this history no longer exist, for they

---

[1] Findagrave.com, Darien, St. John's cemetery.
[3] Stamford Advocate, December 18, 1976, 5.
[4] 1880 US Census.

were removed as part of urban renewal and the construction of Interstate 95. For many years, John kept a peanut stand on the north side of the former Town Hall. This was followed by the ice cream business (from his wagon). He later introduced the first steam-powered ice cream maker and sold the product wholesale to local stores.[5] Stamford land records show that he purchased land in 1885 bordering the Mill River. His obituary indicates that a poor child with only a nickel got just as much ice cream as one fortunate enough to possess a dime. He died from the effects of two strokes at his home at Number 2 North Street on November 16, 1915.[6] Rosalind died at their home about a year later at 63 from complications of diabetes. She was also born in Genoa. They had nine children; Anthony, Charles, William, Peter, John, George, Anna, Louise and Madeline.[7]

Their cape-style house built in 1910 on North Street still exists and has a beautiful stone porch that one can imagine the family sitting on during the summer months while listening to the babbling waters of the Mill River as they passed the house. It is a short walk from here to the Italian Catholic parish, Sacred Heart Church, but unfortunately, Mr. and Mrs. Geronimo died before the church (so important to local Italian Americans) was built. I am sure they would have been happy with the church. There is more on the history of the church and its importance to Italians in Chapter 5.

However, it is important not to rely solely on oral accounts. Verification through documented evidence provides a more dependable testimony. Research of census records leads us to the conclusion that there were at least nine other residents of Stamford who were born in Italy that predate the Geronimo family's appearance in the town. The first Stamford residents born in Italy appear in the 1860-1870 United States Federal census. The first Italian-born resident was Joseph Shamish, who was 25 years old in 1860 (born 1835). He was a farm laborer on the farm of Alfred Hoyt.[8] I was unable to find any other vital or immigration records for this name (either in Stamford or elsewhere).

More Italian-born residents joined and are found in the 1870 census. Sopha Guerber, born in 1842 in Italy was the governess of the Quintard family. Edward A. Quintard was the first president of the Stamford Water Company. Projects for this company would later bring many Italian laborers to Stamford; some of whom would settle there. Saretha E. Williams was born in Italy in 1868 to James and Fanny Williams; presumably, Mr. Williams's business brought the

---

[5] Felicity Hoffecker, 16.
[6] Stamford Advocate, November 17, 1915, 1.
[7] Stamford Advocate, November 27, 1916.
[8] 1860 Federal Census.

family to Italy where Saretha was born (his occupation was listed as banded warehouse) as both of her parents were born in New York. Therefore, it appears that Saretha although born in Italy, was really American. Lastly, in the 1870 Census, there is a reference to the Altriche (Altrocchi) family, which appears to be a well-to-do family. In the household, there was Domico (Domenico) a fifty-six year old retired music teacher born in Italy, his thirty-seven year old spouse Pauline (daughter of a wealthy businessman), and their children Nicola (age 19), Marretta (age 18), Lucia (age 15), and Jiavanno (Giovanni, age 11). There are three other persons in the household (possibly borders), one of whom is listed as a servant (Mary Toben). I have found a reference that Domenico was born in Lodi, Lombardy in 1814. He was a musician and composer who had studied with Gaetano Donizetti (Italian composer of over seventy operas). He was banished by the Austrian government in 1839. The family was affiliated with the Episcopal Church. I find no other reference to this family in Stamford after this census except for Nicola. Nicola married Anna Gertrude Humphrey (daughter of Dr. Humphrey) on June 26, 1874 in Stamford. Nicola attended Harvard University, graduating in 1876. He studied law in the office of the Hon. C. G. Childs, United States district attorney for Connecticut at Stamford, Connecticut. Nicola and Anna had a daughter Pauline. Unfortunately, Anna died in 1879; a service was held at St. John's and the burial at Woodland Cemetery. Domenico died in August of 1879, in Viareggio, Italy. Lucia died at age twenty-two in Florence, Italy. Since there is no evidence of other family members beyond the 1870 census, it is likely they moved back to Italy; except for Nicola who attended university and was married in Stamford. Nicola later died at age forty-four in Florence, Italy in 1894 and probably left Stamford because his wife had passed away. In 1879, the Stamford directory lists John Venini, a cabinetmaker who lived opposite of the train depot. There is an obituary for a cabinetmaker John Vanine in 1893 that is likely the same person. He was employed at the Collender factory. He died in Bridgeport Hospital, having been sent there the previous spring after an attack of the grip (influenza). He was a member of the Cornet Band, was 63, spoke five languages, and was a veteran of a few European wars.[9] The same directory also lists an ice cream maker named B. Metti who lived at Pacific St. near Cottage St.

Census records do not include either Joseph Shamish, or Sopha Guerber after the 1860 and 1870 censuses; it is possible that they returned to Italy. Between 1820 and 1870, fewer than 25,000 Italian immigrants came to the U.S. and most of these were from northern Italy.[10] Based on the surnames of

[9] Stamford Advocate 8/9/1893 1; Stamford Advocate 1/10/1879 p2, 1870 Census, Harvard School Catalogs 1765-1935.
[10] Library of Congress, classroom materials/immigration/Italian/early-arrivals.

the two it is likely they came from Northern Italy. They likely came through Castle Garden, on the southern tip of Manhattan, the first immigrant processing station. I was not able to find immigration records to verify this.

It has been reported that the first Italian American-born citizen of Stamford was Maria Crucia Laurio, born June 14, 1887 (and baptized July 3, 1887). However, I was able to find documentation that Pauline Hemenway Altrocchi (daughter of Nicola Altrocchi and named after her grandmother) was born on June 4th, 1875 in Stamford, thereby making her the first Italian American birth verified for Stamford. Charles Geronimo (the family rumored to be the first in Stamford) was born in Stamford on July 5, 1886; Charles, therefore, is among the first Italian Americans born in Stamford. The documentation for Geronimo was a death certificate; I was not able to verify this with birth documentation.[11]

Italian American cultural identity is complicated. "Italy" was not unified as a country until 1861 (furthermore, some regions that comprise Italy now were not unified until after that date). Local and regional identities were stronger than the common Italian nationality identity at that point. Italian immigrants in America created communities based on the same local or regional identity they shared in Italy. While this did occur later in Stamford, the early organizations were not based solely on regions, likely because there was not a critical mass of immigrants from specific regions. As such, they banded together recognizing that greater numbers resulted in more easily obtaining bargaining power and representation. With time, after their numbers grew, organizations began to become more regionally based.

Most migration occurred because the Italians had to, not because they wanted to. A combination of economic, political, geographic and health-related forces pushed much of the population to the brink of starvation and made life nearly unbearable for the remainder.[12] One of the causes of migration was the stagnation of Italian agriculture, caused by lower priced imported wheat and rice. Another was a dramatic loss of income caused by increased taxes for infrastructure projects of the newly unified country and the lowering of tariffs on products of foreign countries.[13] In the 1870s, southern peasants had to pay up to 90% of their crops in taxes. Concurrently, vineyards were

---

[11] Stamford Advocate 6/30/1991, Illinois US Death Index 1916-1947, Sacred Heart Church Golden Jubilee booklet 1973, Ancestry Library family tree of Stella Altrocchi.
[12] Puleo, Stephen, "From Italy to Boston's North End: Italian Immigration and Settlement, 1890-1910" (1994). Graduate Masters Theses. Paper 154.
[13] Piccoli, G. (2014). Italian Immigration in the United States (Master's thesis, Duquesne University). Retrieved from https://dsc.duq.edu/etd/1044.

devastated by disease. In 1910, Mount Etna erupted and killed many people[14]. This led to political and social unrest and the mass exodus of many impoverished Italians. During the first phase of Italy's Diasporas, before 1880, peasants and workers were leaving primarily from northern regions (particularly from Piedmont and Veneto).

From 1880 to 1930, this led to what has been called by the historians "la grande migrazione" (the great migration) out of Italy. More than 17 million Italians left their country. This was the largest voluntary mass migration in history. The great migration involved all the Italian regions. Italian immigration in the United States registered a steady increase from 1881; by the end of the century, more than 700,000 Italians had landed in American ports. From 1901 to 1914, there was a staggering rise, with an average of more than 238,000 Italian immigrants per year. The migration rate from southern regions surpassed the migration rate from northern regions only after 1890.[15]

There is a part of Italian immigration that is particular to the ethnic group. In the first intense phase (from 1880 to 1914), four out of five immigrants were males and 50% of them returned to Italy (they were called "ritornati"). That means that a large part of them was made up of seasonal migrants who did not show interest in integrating into the American society, acquiring citizenship, and learning the English language.[16] This could very well explain why Mr. Shamish, the Altrocchi family and Ms. Grueber did not appear on later census records; they too may have been "ritornati."

The phenomenon of return migration was more widespread among Italians than any other immigrant group. There were two types of return migrants. Seasonal workers came to America, returned to Italy in the winter, and were referred to as "birds of passage." The other group repatriated to Italy permanently, often unable to bridge the cultural gap between the peasant life in Italy and the faster-paced lifestyle in America.[17] As many as $1.5 million of these immigrants eventually returned permanently to Italy between 1900 and 1914. The Italian love for family and homeland was a powerful force pulling them back. My grandfather, Antonio Vitti was in the second group. He immigrated to Stamford in 1906, aboard the S.S. Konig Albert in

[14] Puleo, Stephen, "From Italy to Boston's North End: Italian Immigration and Settlement, 1890-1910" (1994). Graduate Masters Theses. Paper 154, page 4.

[15] Piccoli, G. (2014). Italian Immigration in the United States (Master's thesis, Duquesne University). Retrieved from https://dsc.duq.edu/etd/1044, page 10.

[16] Piccoli, G. (2014). Italian Immigration in the United States (Master's thesis, Duquesne University). Retrieved from https://dsc.duq.edu/etd/1044, page 20.

[17] Puleo, Stephen, "From Italy to Boston's North End: Italian Immigration and Settlement, 1890-1910" (1994). Graduate Masters Theses. Paper 154, page 5.

September, and worked as an ice harvester on the Mill River in Stamford (before refrigerators were in homes, iceboxes were used). This was difficult and dangerous work. He often recounted how his hands were stiff and locked in position as he went to sleep each night. He was not happy in Stamford and returned to Italy after a short time. This did not prevent most of his children from eventually immigrating to Stamford. Return migration kept many Italian communities in the United States from stabilizing and developing politically and economically until around 1914.[18] Stamford seemed to have fared better in this regard, as the Italian community started to show signs of permanency prior to this, as will be demonstrated in the following chapters.

Again, the Italian American experience is complicated due to the diversity of Italians. We will see that some of the immigrants who came with skills or were fairer skinned were likely received better by other residents in America (including Stamford) and therefore transitioning into American life may have been more appealing and a more welcoming environment. The sheer number of immigrants may have affected their treatment as well (i.e. once the numbers of immigrants sored, resentment increased due to competition for resources, and their treatment declined further).

In general, for Italian immigrants, family well-being was more important than personal goals. Actually, roles in the family and personal decisions were subordinated to the family's goals. For example, boys had to work even at very young ages in order to increase the family's income; instead, daughters remained home to take care of younger children and perform cleaning and cooking duties. In Italian communities, a lower percentage of females worked outside the home. Sometimes, economic necessities required that women work outside the home. Being part of a specific ethnic group influenced job choices and opportunities. Thus, Italian women were employed less as domestics than Scandinavian or Northern European women. This was due to cultural reasons as well as ethnic bias.[19] Ms. Grueber, the governess for the Quintard family, likely from the North may have escaped some of this bias based on her skin shade.

There are other residents on the 1880 census and therefore at the same time as the Geronimo family. George and Mary Rosasco were born in Italy and emigrated to the U.S. Their daughter Laura was born in New York. They lived at 12 Canal Street. There was no occupation listed for George on the census. Petro Operando was 35 in 1880 and lived on 239 Gay Street (the street no longer exists, the Stamford Mall is situated on the location). He was

---

[18] Puleo, Stephen, "From Italy to Boston's North End: Italian Immigration and Settlement, 1890-1910" (1994). Graduate Masters Theses. Paper 154, page 5.
[19] Stamford Advocate 3/12/2003.

single and an ice cream peddler. Fauflean (Faustino or Folstine in other sources) and Louisa Bird Deangeline (DeAngelis in other sources) lived at 301 Waterside. They moved from New York City where they were listed in the 1870 Census as the Deanglen family. The family consists of head of household (Folstine), his wife Louisa, and children Franiesks (Francis), James and Jacka. Louisa was born in England. Faustino is listed as a cabinetmaker. Records show that Faustino and Louisa Dangelo arrived from Germany in 1865 aboard the Peruvian and Faustino was listed as a German. However, in all later documentation he is identified as Italian born. On the 1880 Census Faustino was listed as a billiard table maker and was born in Italy. Their son Francis worked at the billiards factory at age 14 (child labor was common). It is likely that they worked at the Collender Billiard Co.. The H.W. Collender Co. was the leading billiard manufacturer in the country, employing 200 persons in 1881. The factory was destroyed by fire on the night of February 14, 1883, at an estimated loss of $200,000, Collender rebuilt and opened as the Collender Wood Working Co. in 1885. Shortly thereafter, the firm merged, forming the Brunswick-Balke-Collender Co., and the manufacturing of tables was discontinued at the Stamford factory.[20] Their other sons were James and Henrico. Henrico was handicapped likely the result of a broken spine. Louisa died sometime after the 1880 census, and Faustino remarried in 1887. His second wife was the widow Mary Heiser Foulds. It appears that Faustino adopted two of her children Charles and Mary. Unfortunately, it appears that the second marriage did not last, and discord was reported in the Advocate in 1898. Faustino, Francis, James, Joseph, and Henry are listed in the Stamford directory from 1887 through 1901. Faustino is listed as moving to New York in 1901, and it appears his sons eventually moved as well. Faustino died at 63 in Stamford Hospital on April 27, 1904.[21] Henrico died in 1935.

John Zinnine was 32 in 1880 and lived at 239 Gay Street and was employed as a cabinetmaker. Phinelo Pasquirao was born in 1845 in Italy. He was also a cabinetmaker and lived at 239 Gay Street in Stamford in 1880.[22] I was not able to find additional references to these immigrants; it would appear that they moved on to areas other than Stamford or were "ritornati."

Boyd's 1881-1882 directory of Fairfield County lists the following Italians living and or working in Stamford: Arnise, a carpenter at 24 Gay St., Rev. Antonio Arrighi at 29 Myrtle Ave. (discussed further in chapter 5), Forstean

---

[20] Stamford Industry Down the Years, Stamford Advocate Tercentenary Edition, 1941, 62; Keeler, Manufacturing Interests, 988-89; Stamford City Directory, 1889-90, 48; D. Hamilton Hurd, History of Fairfield County, Connecticut (Philadelphia: J.W. Lewis & Co., 1881), 718.
[21] *Stamford Advocate* 4/28/1904. 3.
[22] 1880 US Census.

Deangli (Fausteen Deangelis), a cabinet maker at Orchard St., Fernando De-Silva on Stillwater Ave., John Giaromini (John Geronimo), a fruit vendor at Main, Atlantic and Canal Sts., Joseph Lepra, a bricklayer at E. Meadow St. and Railroad Ave., Eugene Rusco, a carpenter at 47 Franklin St. John Venini, a cabinet maker at Pacific St., and Railroad Ave., and Frank Vite, a carpenter at Strawberry Hill Ave.

John Franklin was born in Italy in 1851, made his home in Stamford at Cove Road near Willis Avenue,[23] and worked as a laborer. He was married to Mary who was born in Germany. Mr. Franklin's life in Stamford was not entirely a happy one and he experienced some misfortune. It appears that Mary passed away and Mr. Franklin became a bachelor once again. However, in 1896 he confided in his friend Mr. Louis Rotunno (who owned a shoe shop on William Street) that he would like to get married. Because of Franklin's age and what is described as an "unprepossessing appearance", he found it difficult to find a bride. Mr. Rotunno was happy to assist him. Rotunno indicated that he traveled to Italy and returned with "Signorina Rotunno" (his "sister") as the intended bride. Franklin was overjoyed and purchased a diamond ring and they were married in September.

Immediately after the wedding, Rotunno presented Franklin with a claim of expenses incurred while procuring his wife amounting to $35. Mr. Franklin willingly paid. Who wouldn't? It was such a small price to pay for companionship and to experience happiness once again. Two days later, the newly Mrs. Franklin left her husband and returned to her "brothers" house. The reason she gave for leaving was that Franklin was too old for her (apparently his money was the correct age though). Mr. Franklin made several attempts at obtaining his wife's return. After a final appeal at Rotunno's shop for the return of his wife, the two were involved in a fight and were arrested.[24] Franklin was arraigned on three counts, assault and battery, breach of peace and threatening and quarreling.[25]

Rotunno testified that Franklin threatened to kill him and Franklin's wife, dragged him outside the store and struck him in the head with a shoe hammer. Dr. Bohannan, who attended Rotunno after the incident testified that the bruises could have been inflicted by striking a stone in falling. Milkman Harry Buttery (actual name) was on William Street and saw the incident. He saw Franklin "rap" him upon the head. Mr. Dann close by took the hammer away and Franklin picked up Rotunno and slammed him down several times.

---

[23] Stamford Directory 1893-1894.
[24] Stamford Advocate, November 17, 1896.
[25] Stamford Advocate, November 23, 1896.

Franklin's side of the story indicates that Mrs. Franklin (before the marriage) wanted him to secure her for debt. He paid her $25 in cash to pay her debts. More details came out during the trial.[26] The principal evidence was a letter written (but not signed by Mr. Rotunno in Italian and translated by Tony Palo (one of the early Italian-American leaders in Stamford discussed later in Chapter 3): "My Dear Wife: Go to bed, because I am going to New York with Maria, because Maria, she don't want to stay with her husband, but she wants to stay with me. She said her husband, he was old, and he wasn't any good for her. Also, Maria said she don't want her husband to go after her, because she will have him arrested." Rotunno admitted that he did not travel to New York but wrote the letter to avoid trouble with Franklin.

Upon cross-examination, Franklin indicated that he had only used his fists upon Rotunno during their fight and only to defend himself. His testimony indicates that he lived in the country since 1870, and in Stamford for 18 years (i.e. since 1878, which seems to be a year after the Geronimo family immigrated to Stamford) during which he was only arrested one other time for discharging a gun on a Sunday. Unfortunately, The Advocate does not report the outcome of the trial. Franklin later dropped the separate charges on his ex-wife Maria.[27]

The story does not stop there, however. It turns out that Rotunno and Mrs. Franklin ran away together to Jersey City, Elizabeth, and then to Providence Rhode Island, where Mrs. Rotunno found them and had them arrested. They served six and a half months in jail.

Franklin divorced his wife. Two years later, she returned to Franklin's home. Rotunno came looking for Mrs. Franklin, however, Mrs. Rotunno had tipped off both the Franklin's and the police. A shootout occurred between Rotunno and the police, however, Rotunno escaped.[28] He was later caught but was released with no charges.[29]

There was a claim that the first Italian family in Stamford was actually the Triacca family. The family-owned a soap factory on the west side in 1865. In 1881, Charles Triacca lived at 43 Elm Street, and Mary and Peter Triacca, his parents lived at 36 Henry Street. However, it turned out that Mary was born in Ireland and Peter in Germany.[30] The last name could possibly be of Italian origin, but technically, they were not Italian, but likely part of the Italian diaspora. Interestingly, Charles Triacca was later killed by a train while

---

[26] Stamford Advocate, November 24, 1896.
[27] Stamford Advocate, April 3, 1897.
[28] Stamford Advocate, March 12, 1898.
[29] Stamford Advocate, March 14, 1898.
[30] Ibid 1/8/1985, 9/13/1984,1880 U.S. Census, 1900 US Census.

walking home, and his son Frank, years later had both legs amputated after getting run over by a train in Stamford. Early on, trains presented a safety hazard in Stamford, as discussed in Chapter 2.[31]

I could find no other mention of the other early Italians to come to Stamford mentioned above (other than Mr. Franklin, Nicola Altrocchi, John Vanine, and the Geronimo Family), either in census records, or news accounts. Therefore, it appears that lore is true to a great extent, for the Geronimo family, although not the first to live in Stamford, was in the early group of immigrants to Stamford that actually planted their roots here. For the rest of the early residents, it is likely that many of them returned to Italy after accumulating money, or as has been the case for Stamford for a long time, they came for work and moved on in search of work elsewhere.

Though the Italians were living and working in the first, second, and third wards (West Stamford) of Stamford, the West Side would become most identified with Italians. The 1982 Historic West Main Street study by The Historic Neighborhood Preservation Program indicates that the first Italian permanent resident of the West Side was blacksmith Gaetano Capas (probably Clapes), who settled on Stillwater Ave. in 1889. The community quickly spread out from here to include Finney Lane, Liberty Street, and Spruce Street, by 1900 and numbered 80 Italian families or ten percent of the population. By 1920, the Italian Colony increased to over 700 families, more than half of the area's population. The Italian population was responsible for the West Side's most rapid growth, constructing most of the buildings in the area after 1900. Many of these houses were brick, stone, or stucco and very characteristic of Italian-American neighborhoods in general. The shopping district along West Main Street between Greenwich Avenue and Spruce Street reached its fullest development after WWI, becoming a "Little Italy", with all but 2 of its 27 businesses owned and managed by Italians. There were eight grocery stores, four saloons, two barbers, two tailors, and two confectionaries. There were over one hundred apartments, mostly occupied by Italians, located over or behind the business fronts. See Appendix J for a walking tour of Italian-built structures in the area.

Many more Italians would follow, and the Italian-American population of Stamford would explode, forever changing not only Stamford's skyline, but also its political, religious, commerce, and culture. This transition was not always smooth and for the early immigrants, as we will see in the next chapter, life was hard.

---

[31] Ibid 6/3/1903, 5/11/1903, 4/8/1903, 4/7/1903, 4/6/1903, 4/3/1903, 12/23/1895, 8/28/1894, 8/27/1894.

CHAPTER 2
Early Emigrant Experience in Stamford

"Every immigrant who comes here should be required within five years to learn English or leave the country."
—Theodore Roosevelt 1913

The early Italian immigrant experience is complex and blanket generalities would not provide an accurate picture of life for all Italians. It is not sufficient to note only that bias occurred, and that life was hard. The Italians are a diverse group and the degree of treatment or mistreatment from other groups and general well-being may have depended upon the immigrant's occupation, politics, religion, or even their complexion. It is obvious that bias occurred, however, it is important to note that there were non-Italians who assisted and treated Italians well; these interactions just do not sell newspapers. Therefore, it is worth mentioning that newspaper accounts mostly cover one aspect of the Italian American experience. As a result, it is harder to paint a complete picture of the immigrant experience through contemporary documentation. The local newspaper documents many circumstances of bias, poor working conditions, and mistreatment. As documented later in this chapter in the Pasquale Esposito case, bias in court could cost you your life. Though a minority of the reporting, some newspaper articles actually treated some of the immigrants with higher social status (because of occupation, inter-marriage, or complexion) almost as socialites and reported on their comings and goings. We will see that some articles recognized Italian American achievements and were complimentary. Early on, Italians could not rely on organizations that protected rights in the U.S. as they were barred entry into most organizations. They soon learned they had to band together to obtain the rights that others enjoyed in America. As Italian joined together working to improve their image and the language barrier was overcome, local Italians' experience within the non-Italian society got better over time.

Imagine the strength and faith it would take to leave your homeland, customs, family, and friends, risking your life traveling across an ocean to a land you had never been to, with a language, culture, cuisine, and religious practice different from your own. Most immigrants traveling between the 1880s and early 1900s traveled in steerage aboard steamboats that took ten to twelve days to reach their destination. This was a huge improvement over earlier boat travel that would take months. However, it still was not an altogether pleasant experience. An undercover investigation in 1908 for the Immigration Commission of the U.S. Congress concluded that: "disgusting, demoralizing and revolting conditions generally prevailed in transatlantic steerage." To add insult to the injury experienced under subpar traveling conditions, and the trauma of leaving all they knew behind, immigrants would then arrive in America and discover that they were not welcome by the locals.

For decades, Italian communities lived on the fringe of American society. Italian immigrants were living in the "slums" (enclaves portrayed by urban decline, run-down buildings, dirt, poverty, and violence). Their way of life and surroundings reinforced prejudices against them. Discrimination and prejudice were so strong that racist notions against Italian immigrants became exaggerated, and movies or newspapers constantly misrepresented Italian immigrants. Numerous accounts of bias in the Stamford Advocate are noted in this history.

Sometimes there were extremely violent acts against them. On March 14, 1891, the first mass lynching by a mob in the U.S. occurred against Italians in New Orleans. Eleven Italian immigrants (eight of whom had American citizenship at the time they were killed) were lynched by an angry mob numbering in the thousands. This was the result of the assassination of a police chief. A witness reported that when the dying police chief was asked who did this, he responded "dagoes." None of the eleven were convicted and the mob decided to take justice into its own hands. In 1892, President Harrison, in response to the lynching and reaction to it created Columbus Day. This is one of the many reasons that the holiday has become important to Italian Americans. It took until Friday, April 12, 2019, for the City of New Orleans to make an official proclamation of apology to Italian Americans. The amount and breadth of this prejudice is beyond the scope of this history, for further information on this one can find many resources discussing the topic: including the dissertation by Stephen Puleo in the bibliography. Other than the mass lynching, there is no reason to believe the experience in Stamford was dramatically different from experiences elsewhere in America. Even without computers and social media news travels quickly, Italians in Stamford would have been well aware of what occurred in New Orleans and throughout America, and from that lens, they would have navigated through life in Stamford.

Stamford was a farming community until the railroad reached it in the 1840s. Once it became part of the railroad line, the town grew in size and began to add industries.[1] As industry grew so did the draw of immigrants looking for jobs. The earliest Italian immigrants were mostly from Northern Italy and/or were skilled tradesmen. The early immigrants described in Chapter 1 (e.g. cabinetmakers, and billiard table makers, etc.) demonstrate this.

---

[1] Britannica.com Stamford, CT.

Many Italians who ended up in Stamford came to America to work on the Brooklyn Bridge. Work on the bridge began in 1869 and was completed in 1883. The first large influx of Italians came about 1884, with the end of the Brooklyn Bridge construction and the commencement of a sewer contract in Stamford.[2] These young, hard-working men were "specialists" in trades not existing in America yet. Their last names included: Corbo, Clapes, DiPreta, Laureno, Tamburri and Vacca. They came from Settefrati, Picinisco and Roccasecca if they were stonecutters (DiPreta, Tamburri, Vacca) or from Avigliano if they were blacksmiths, like the Clapes and Corbos. Michele (Michael) Laureno, an Italian American contractor engaged many of them to work on the Stamford Reservoir when they were done with the Brooklyn Bridge.[3] About a decade later, the number of Italian immigrants into Stamford would increase again as the railroad widened and they changed the grade of its main line.[4] Later on, the type of Italian immigrant would change as most immigrants were coming from the South and were unskilled laborers.

Early on Italians were eager for work and a chance at a better life in America. In 1886, an "employment wanted" ad was taken out in the Stamford Advocate by Italians seeking jobs: "For a number of Italian men and boys. Willing to work at any labor. Some of them good farmers and gardeners and competent as coachmen, valets, stablemen, etc. A bright Italian boy of 15, willing to work at anything, wants a place where he can support himself and learn English. Please leave word at T. Halloran's, junction Pacific Street and Railroad Ave."[5]

In the Italian Center's history of Italians in Stamford, Pittaro (an early Italian American leader discussed later in Chapter 3) writes about the Italian American experience in Stamford and confirms that much of the negative experience in America was also encountered in Stamford: "Before 1883 emigrants in the city, with few exceptions, did not have fixed accommodations, usually worked on temporary jobs, and were subject to insults and violence based on race."[6] For the average Stamford Italian of this time working conditions were hard, and dangerous. Living conditions were often dangerous as well.

Some of the new workers may have even been brought to the Stamford area as part of the "padrone" system. The padrone (which means boss in Italian) system was a contract labor system. A padrone often controlled the wages, contracts, and food supply of the immigrants under their authority. They often

---

[2] Felicity Hoffecker, *The Stamford Weekly*.. 16 "Our Italian Citizens: Stamford's Ethnic Groups."

[3] *Stamford Advocate* 10/13/1980. P. 11.

[4] Felicity Hoffecker, *The Stamford Weekly*. 16 "Our Italian Citizens: Stamford's Ethnic Groups."

[5] Stamford Advocate 7/30/1886.

[6] "Twenty Five Years of Progress 1910-1935," The Italian Institute Inc. Stamford, CT.

(not always) victimized their own countryman. Many Italian immigrants found themselves toiling for low pay in unhealthy working conditions. At the turn of the 20th century, southern Italian immigrants were among the lowest-paid workers in the United States. Child labor was common (as discussed, one of the first Stamford immigrants Francis DeAngelis worked in a factory at 14), and even small children often went to work in factories, mines, and farms, or sold newspapers on city streets (there are personal stories of Stamford Italian newsboys in this history). The padrone system, despite its many injustices, was not eradicated until the middle of the 20th century.[7] The padrone system did exist in Stamford. An article in The Advocate describes a high-risk explosive job for the Stamford Water Company with an Italian padrone. It does not shed light on the abuses of the system though, and merely states "an Italian padrone in his fatherly dealings with those who are his charge."[8]

Many citizens of Stamford were taken aback by the influx of Italians settling on Pacific Street and the West End. They were different. They did not have a language in common with other immigrants (the Irish spoke English). They had different customs (e.g., they paraded ancestral home patron saints around, which some saw as idol worship, ate different things, etc.). What a difference time makes, originally ridiculed for what they ate and their traditions; things like pasta and pizza are so popular now and now non-Italians have become more knowledgeable about Italian customs and traditions. Obviously, these differences combined with resentment fostered by having to share limited resources among more residents and the lack of education and understanding of these new people encourage prejudice. Prejudice prevented Italians from joining organizations such as unions. To combat this bias, Italians had to be creative and form their own organizations and request the resources they deserved. Even religious observance became an issue. There is more on this intolerance of diverse religious practice in Chapter 5. The simple act of picking apples off a tree, which was likely common in the old country, landed Mrs. Carmelia Latti, Mrs. Filomena Vitti and Marie Vagnone of Liberty Street in jail after John Rutz caught them with a basket of his apples on his orchards on Palmer's Hill. They were fined $5 each.[9]

The media of the day portrayed Italians as lazy, superstitious, prone to crime, ignorant of the high-minded principles of democracy (ironic in itself, for the ignorance of the Italians' contribution to democratic principles used in the foundation of the United States), and prone to righting personal

---

[7] Library of Congress, classroom materials/immigration/Italian/early-arrivals.
[8] Stamford Advocate 5/28/1903.
[9] Stamford Advocate 9/19/1907, 9/21/1907.

wrongs outside the bounds of traditional American justice.[10] This was no different for Stamford; throughout this Chapter there are numerous accounts reported on by the local paper, The Stamford Advocate that demonstrate the bias Italians encountered in the reporting of events. Again, this is one side of the experience and does not touch on the many daily encounters not leading to newspaper reports.

One Stamford family's story encompasses a two generational transition from the difficult life, and bias of the first generation to better conditions in the next generation. About 1884, Vincenzo "James" Vacca came to Stamford, with a group of stonemasons who were recruited from New York City to build the North Stamford Reservoir. The leader of the stonemason group was Michele Laureno who bought a house at 91 Liberty St. where some of the masons boarded. Mr. Vacca would walk across town from the boarding house to the reservoir each day (about 6.5 miles each way) with a bag of tools on his back. He and other immigrants experienced prejudice, by the older immigrant group, the Irish, who were then living on the west side of Stamford and were not happy with the new arrivals on their turf. Antonio DiPreta and Annunziato Tamburri, were also among the early immigrant masons. Vincenzo's son, Alfonse Vacca was born in the Clark St. home (currently where the Bell St. parking garage is). Vincenzo sent his son Alfonse at three years of age with his wife back to Settefrati, because he wanted his son to be trained and apprenticed to a stonemason there. At age seven, he was duly apprenticed and returned to Stamford with his mother at age nine. He then attended Stamford public schools and later enrolled at the Yale and Towne apprentice school where he studied designing and drawing for four years. Yale and Towne set up the school to ensure they would have a better pool of workers. The applicants had to pass an entrance exam; once passed, the employee had to sign a four-year contract, the first three months of which the employee was on trial to demonstrate their mechanical ability and general efficiency. They were taught arithmetic, algebra, geometry, and trigonometry. Apprentices were also given thorough training in mechanical drawing and instruction in mechanics. Alfonse was paid 10 cents an hour and worked for 55 hours a week. After school, he sometimes mixed mortar for his father and dug ditches. He later enrolled in a two-year architecture course at Pratt Institute in Brooklyn. In 1922, he graduated as a registered architect and opened an office in Stamford. He would later design Boyle Stadium at Stamford High School, which was built under the Works Progress Administration (WPA)

---

[10] Chris Wolf, "A brief history of America's hostility to a previous generation of Mediterranean migrants—Italians" November 26th, 2025, The Trials and Triumphs of New York's Italian Catholic Immigrant community in the Struggle for Equality, "old Cathedral.org."

and is named to the State Register of Historic Places, because of its unique architecture and Depression-era history. He designed it to be able to be flooded during winter to make an ice-skating rink. Lore is that the design was based on a wall from Settefrati. Mr. Vacca was the town architect and one day received a call requesting that the plans for the stadium be provided within a few weeks. He sat for hours at his desk trying to come up with a design to no avail. Instead, he went out to play cards with his friends. In the middle of the game, an image of a wall in Settefrati belonging to a man who owned a parrot in the village came to him. He left the card game right then and went home to work out the plan. He worked all night and completed the design. The structure weighs 1500 tons, it had room for lockers and showers. The seating accommodates 12,000 spectators, all of whom can exit the stadium within 2 and a half minutes. He designed a home for Guy Lombardo and is featured in the September 1945 issue of *Better Homes and Gardens*.[11]

In 1930, Alphonse Vacca unsuccessfully ran for the Democratic nomination for assessor, losing by 57 votes. He was later promised an assistant building inspector post with the city in 1931, but due to a downturn in the economy, he was not hired. Alfonse remained prominent in the Third Ward Italian American Democratic Club.[12] Generation by generation Italian American efforts to elevate themselves were working.

Italian American migration into the Stamford area increased in the 1880s due to railroad work. The following was reported by The Advocate: "Still another gang of Italian laborers reached Stamford on Tuesday morning for the parallel railroad. They were their own baggage smashers, and marched up town heavily loaded with trucks, bundles, pans, kettles, and all kinds of cooking utensils and portable bedding."[13] A group of railroad workers was referred to as a gang, so this was not a reference to illegal activity or a slight of the workers. However, it should be noted that in many of the articles, the protagonists of the reporting are often solely referred to as "The Italian" or "Italians," as they are seemingly not worthy of the effort of elaborating a name for edification or even acknowledging them as an individual persona. In 1888, laborers were working in Glenbrook to connect the line to Noroton, and a "caravansary" was erected where the laborers were housed and fed.[14] There is no real description of the accommodations, but it is likely they were

---

[11] *Gazzetta Settefratese*, Vol I, June 1947, published in Stamford, Ct available on settefrati.net.
[12] Stamford Advocate 9/11/2007, 4/26/1998, 9/13/1930,12/31/1930, 8/13/1931, 9/21/1942, 12/11/1976 p 39. Memories of Alfonse Vacca, oral history told to Kim Sushon, Stamford Advocate 6/27/1911.
[13] Stamford Advocate 2 22 1884.
[14] Stamford Advocate 4/20/1888.

not top-notch, especially by today's standards. A few years later, when the four track rail operations began between Glenbrook and Noroton, Italian laborers began work and a temporary shed was erected to be used as living quarters. The work was difficult, as they were hired to remove ledge rock to make way for the tracks.[15]

In 1892, in Waterside two laborers crossing at Taylors crossing and Atlantic Street were struck by a train while going to work. The men were Fiorante DaRiva and Alberto Ferrero who lived on Pacific Street. One of the men had his leg broken near the ankle. They had not heard the train until it was within a few feet; and were hit by the engine and thrown into the air. People used the crossing often and it was a wonder to the reporter why more people were not injured at this spot. The article reads "It has been suggested that the tracks be enclosed and that persons found trespassing upon the railway company's property be punished, but there is little disposition to do this."[16] Apparently, it had not occurred to anyone that it might be the fault of the railroad for not better securing the area, likely because of the expendability of those crossing.

The Temperance Movement was boosted by the influx of immigrants into the U.S. Many Americans blamed immigrants for crime, political corruption, and fondness for intoxication. Temperance was promoted to immigrants. Some immigrants felt discriminated against because of their culture, others embraced temperance as a path to Americanization. Sometimes proponents of the movement used other methods such as opposing liquor license applications (licensing required public notification in Stamford), pressuring for the enforcement of "illegal sales, and even trolling to find real or fabricated infractions to make the business difficult to maintain."

In 1893, bias was evident in the opposition of a citizen who applied for a license to sell liquor near the Noroton station based on the ready supply of customers (300 Italian laborers working on the tracks), and in the actual reporting of the challenge to the permit. The story reads: "A favorable response to the petition would insure for Noroton and the Soldier's Home, a lively and exciting time for the next two or three years, and would ensure a safe guarantee for a prompt increase of victims from the Home for mutilation and death on the track-possibly helped, now and then, by a stiletto in the hands of an easily excited visitor from the sunny plains of southern Italy."[17] Glenbrook citizens were also against approving a liquor license to Wilbur E. Lewis

---

[15] Stamford Advocate 5/13/1893.
[16] Stamford Advocate 10/31/1892.
[17] Stamford Advocate 5/23/1893.

because the likely customers would be Italian laborers and it would be injurious to the neighborhood; so much so, that ninety-nine percent of Glenbrook residents signed a petition. In defense of his application, Mr. Lewis actually indicated that he would discriminate and not sell liquor to Italians under any circumstances. The article goes on to state that attorneys for the neighborhood stated that there would be 200 to 300 Italians working in the area, and "there is no police protection, during the day as nearly the entire male population is employed elsewhere leaving the place at the mercy of hoodlums."[18]

In addition to limiting liquor licenses, "illegal sales" were also prosecuted, and the reporting again doubles down on bias. There were cases of charging men for liquor sales to Italian railroad workers. In 1893, Mike Laureno (the padrone contractor) of Stamford was acquitted for lack of evidence. The news report indicates: "It is a notorious fact that Italian laborers consume a large quantity of lager beer in the regular course of their everyday life; that bread and beer make up the larger part of their diet."[19] Antonio Corbo of Stamford was not as lucky, as he was fined $5 for sale of liquor. The report not only discusses the case, but also manages to characterize Italians as drunkards, unsociable, and cheap: "The recent prosecutions have frightened the Italian colony considerably, and there will not be so much sold by unlicensed dealers hereafter… it is astonishing how much beer they use. In the wintertime, they drink whiskey-the poorest sort of stuff-but in the summer, beer forms an important part of their diet. It is a rare thing indeed to hear of an Italian being arrested for drunkenness. When they do drink to excess they remain in their apartments or shanties, and when they quarrel they seldom invoke the interference of the law…The Italian laborers are scarcely ever to be seen drinking in saloons except those kept by persons of their own nationality, and even here the American custom of treating does not prevail to any large extent. In the morning, when a gang of laborers is on their way to work, one of them often slips into a saloon and gets his dinner pail full of beer, which he and his companions drink on the street. No class of people drink so much at such a small expense as the Italians, and that they save their money and send a good deal of their savings back to their native land anybody who takes the trouble to inquire at the Stamford banks or the money-order department of the local post-office can readily ascertain."[20] Another article, about imbibing causing trouble in North Stamford where Italian laborers were working on the reservoir appeared in 1900, also indicated that beer is part of the daily diet of the Italian laborers. The problem was not so

---

[18] Stamford Advocate 5/2/1894.
[19] Stamford Advocate 6/12/1893.
[20] Stamford Advocate 6/13/1893.

much the Italian laborers but their influence on the locals who had been in-dulging too freely following the bad example of the Italians. So, in summary, Italians trying to better their lives, working difficult jobs (that no one else wanted to do), under dangerous conditions, could not even during their limited free time have an alcoholic beverage (as other citizens were allowed) but were then deemed responsible for causing bad behavior in the general population.[21]

Italian workers in Stamford were subject to violence just for being Ital-ians. In 1893, a report was made of Italian laborers being accosted at work: "A number of young rowdies who walked the railroad track to Noroton yes-terday came in contact with a gang of Italian laborers who are working on the four-tracking operations in that section. They began to abuse and throw stones at the Italians, who finally became enraged and several of them with knives in their hands rushed at their assailants, who immediately took flight."[22] Italian laborers were definitely losing the propaganda wars at this time; bias was also evident in the Stamford Advocate report about Myrtle Avenue residents being worried about the influx of Italian railroad laborers: "if there is to be a thousand or more Italian laborers in that vicinity they view the situation with alarm."[23]

Another Advocate article not only characterizes Italians but also threat-ens them: "Some of the untamed Italians who swarm about the old house at Crystal Lake, were seen chasing some young girls across the fields in that vicinity, on Sunday afternoon. Had not a Stamford man and two boys come upon the scene as they did, some mischief would have been done, for the girls were crying murder, and running at their best speed. The Italians will have a little war on their hands if this kind of diversion is not stopped.[24]

Some additional brief examples of biased reporting follow. "An Italian, who either jumped or fell from a train passing here at 6:10 Saturday evening, was badly shaken up, and injured internally. He was supposed to belong at Port Chester and was coming to see his brother, who is employed at Mr. Todd's place, down at the shore here. He had better stay in the land of sunny skies, from which the hand-organist hies."[25] "The town is completely over-run with Italian bootblacks."[26] A bootblack is a shoeshine. In the early days of southern

---

[21] Stamford Advocate 7/9/1900.

[22] Stamford Advocate 9/25/1893.

[23] Stamford Advocate 3/12/1906.

[24] Stamford Advocate 5/16/1884.

[25] Stamford Advocate 6/18/1886

[26] Stamford Advocate 2/2/1887

Italian immigration, padroni brought young boys to the United States for shoe-shine and other juvenile menial work.[27] "There are now sixteen barber shops in this town. One of the proprietors is an Italian."[28]

Mistreatment was not just received from non-Italians. Italians sometimes took advantage of other Italians. As previously indicated, many immigrants sent back much of their earnings to Italy. This was the case of many in Stamford as well. In fact, a bar owner Giuseppe Acunto accepted money from Stamford immigrants that he promised he would forward to their relatives. It turns out a lot of this money never reached its intended recipients. Mr. Acunto owned a saloon on 37 Pacific Street. In March 1899, after his wife joined him from Italy, Mr. Acunto went missing. He lived in comfortable circumstances and employed Rosini, a servant girl. He left town, accompanied by Rosini and he left numerous debts behind. He fled after it was discovered by one of his "clients" that Acunto cashed a paycheck with a forged signature and kept the money. He confronted Acunto who became frightened and liquidated all of his stock and left.[29] This seems to be the same Giuseppe Acunto who was president of the Italian Republican Club in 1898.

Caricatures of Italians in the media undoubtedly impacted the perception of Italians by other groups in Stamford. Likely, participants at the following parties had no intent to disparage, and it may be somewhat unfair to analyze the behavior of the people involved with hindsight, however the facts are the facts. It is easy to see that bias against Italians was present. In 1893, a "poverty party" was given, where guests were to wear the oldest clothes each could find. The host, Mr. Davenport wore old patched pants held up with rope. The Austin brothers appeared in Italian laborers' dress.[30] In 1917, someone won second prize (for oddity) dressed as an Italian laborer.[31] Obviously, this occurred during a different time with different standards, but visualize yourself as an Italian trying to better your life and integrate into American society picking up a newspaper and reading this matter of fact account of how other citizens regarded your ethnicity. I am sure you can feel empathy at their plight.

The more frequently Italians took jobs away from other groups, the more opposition grew. In 1893, the following article appears: "It would help the town substantially if the workingmen and merchants of Stamford would combine upon a platform making local application of protection principles. Give

[27] Chain Migration Ethnic Neighborhood Formation and Socials Networks, John S. MacDonald and Leatrice D. MacDonald.
[28] Stamford Advocate 10/4/1889, 4/8/1899.
[29] Stamford Advocate 3/11/1899.
[30] Stamford Advocate 4/29/1893.
[31] Stamford Advocate 4/20/1917.

Stamford workmen and Stamford merchants the preference every time, if you want your town to prosper. Put men in office who are in sympathy with this and you'll never have imported Italian labor here while Stamford workmen are out of a job.[32] Another article reports that Italians are being brought in to work on laying pipe for the sewers in Stamford, while hundreds of idle laborers are in Stamford (who will likely have to be supported by the city). Wooden shanties were erected on the salt meadows east of Canal Street. It was pointed out that the contractor was from out of town and the less money he pays for the labor the greater his profit. The report states "It is possibly too late now to make any change, but it is a pity that when a large public work is being done, an undesirable class of men are imported to do it, while laborers who contribute something of value to the city which pays the bill are standing idly around the streets and suffering for the necessities of life."[33] The laying of pipe was difficult work because without pumps the high tides would make work demanding. The men were obliged to work night and day, whenever there was a low tide, as ditches would fill during high tides. The Italian laborers reportedly dwindled down as they became dissatisfied with the small number of hours, and cold weather.[34]

One article reporting on naturalizations taking place foretells the feared impact upon voting in the city and simultaneously sheds a bad light on "Italians." "There are an exceedingly large number of aliens wishing to swear allegiance to Uncle Sam, but the Italians predominate. From a glance at those in the City Courtroom today, one would suppose the Irish vote and the German vote would be eclipsed this year by that of the Sons of Italy. The Italians themselves know little or nothing about the proceedings of obtaining naturalization papers, but they do just what they are told by the party leaders. Leo Donatel (actually spelled Donatelli, and is one of the early Italian American leaders in Stamford discussed in Chapter 3) was busy all day, ushering his countrymen into the courtroom. One politician from Greenwich came to town with a party of sixty-seven Italians, who appeared very anxious to know what it all meant. They were obliged to wait in the corridor of the Town Hall for some time and made an interesting spectacle. It is said that they will all vote the straight Democratic ticket on the 8th of November. Other nationalities were represented to some extent, but none have turned out in such numbers as the Italians."[35] Contrary to the reporting, if one pays close attention to this list of names, one will see names of Italian Americans who became leaders in the Stamford community, and involved with politics, unionization,

---

[32] Stamford Advocate 10/14/1893.
[33] Stamford Advocate 10/7/1893.
[34] Stamford Advocate 11/11/1893.
[35] Stamford Advocate 10/12/1898o

business, and sports. Notably, the first applicant for naturalization was Rev. Pasquale DeCarlo (another early Italian American Leader discussed in Chapter 3). A list of applicants in 1898 included:[36]

Alphonso Acunto, 29 Manhattan St.
Giuseppe Acunto, 37 Pacific St.
Lorenzo Altieri, 79 Pacific St.
Theodore Argeaneis, 11 Manhattan St.
Giovanni Cangiano 37 Pacific St.
Giuseppe Caperino, 37 Pacific St.
Michele Caputo, 30 Pacific St.
Enrico Carpainni, 44 Pacific St.
Alphonso Casta, 44 Pacific St.
Vincenzo Catino 3 Pearl St.
Pasquale Catino Black Road
Lorenzo Chiapetta 37 Pacific St.
Vito Nicolo Colucci, Finney Lane
Joseph Coppera, 20 Canal St.
James Corbo, Stillwater Ave.
Joseph Corbo, Stillwater Ave.
Giuseppe Crocci, 37 Pacific St.
Antonio Dellarocca, 37 Pacific St.
Leonard Deminno, 17 Canal St.
Vincenzo Dicamillo, 37 Pacific St.
Michael DiPompa, 37 Pacific St.
Antonio Esposito, 18 Railroad Ave.
Francisco Esposito, 37 Pacific St.
John Ferrari, 3 Ludlow Place
Vito Fiorillo, 22 Cottage St.
Sabato Fiorentino, 35 Pacific St.
Andrea Galasso, 11 Pacific St.
Giovanni Galtano, 37 Pacific St.
George Genoneo 56 Cottage Place
Nurianto Giannetri, Stillwater Ave.
Luciano Grasso, 27 Pacific St.
Samuel Grasso, 4 Lee Ave.
James Latte, Finney Lane
Cesare Latte, Finney Lane
Elio Lotte, 37 Pacific St.
Frank T. Loco, Summer and Fifth St.
John Maggi, 44 Pacific St.
Pasquale Morucco, W. Stamford Ave.

Michael Moreno, 78 State St.
Carmine Nastri, 35 Pacific St.
Theodore Ottaviano, 27 Pacific St.
Max Otto, Mission St.
Paul Otto, 1 West St.
Ruciano Ozzella, 5 Pearl St.
Gerardo Palmiere, William St.
Michael Pascarelli, 37 Pacific St.
Marino Passero, Finney Lane
Michael Passero, 37 Pacific St.
Pasquale Pellien, Summer St.
Luigi Piallige (Pellicci?), 20 Stillwater Ave.
Antonio Pieta, 37 Main St.
Leonardo Piacendo, Finney Lane
Frank, Pinonto, 32 Cottage St.
Angelo Pugliano, 37 Pacific St.
Marco Rossi, 37 Pacific St.
Luigi Russo, North & Franklin Sts.
Giuseppe Sandello, 61 Hawthorn St.
John A. Scalzi, State St., William Bldg.
Carmine Sacci, Finney Lane
Cherubino Socci, 124 Atlantic St.
Vincenzo Spagnoli, 44 Pacific St.
Salvatore Sproniero, 37 Pacific St.
Michael Taddone, 37 Pacific St.
Boreto Tamburri, 124 Atlantic Street.
Nunziato Tamburri, 277 Main St.
Francesco Torbora, Stillwater Ave.
Antonio Terenzio, 124 Atlantic St.
Pietro Terenzio, 4 Liberty Place
Ermenegildo Terenzio, 37 Pacific St.
Antonio Urbano, 37 Pacific St.
Capto Urbano, 56 Canal St.
Vincenzo Vacca, 4 Liberty St.
Luciano Vazella, 5 Pearl St.
Salvatore Vergilo 72 Pacific St.
Paul Viggiano, Stillwater Ave.

---

[36] Stamford Advocate 10/21/1898.

George Votto, 57 Meadow St.　　　　　Gennaro Volpe, 12 Ludlow St.
Cesidio Votto, 4 Meadow St.
Filippo Vitti, 37 Pacific St.
Vincenzo Fuda, 37 Pacific St.

In 1900, the Italians among the applicants to the voters' registrars were:[37]

Michael Abbario, Stillwater Ave.
Arrigo Arrigassi, 118 Pacific St.
Raffaele Boccuzzi, Stillwater Ave.
Vincenzo Boccarusso, 93 Pacific St.
Leonardo. Bocchichio
Luigi Buzzeo, Liberty St.
Michele Caputo, 17 Pacific St.
Vito Carlucci, Roxbury
Pasquale Catino, 74 State St.
Vincenzo Catino, Spruce St.
Lorenzo Chiappetti, Liberty St.
Nicola Collini, 19 Manhattan St.
Emiglio Colucci, Stillwater Ave.
Joseph J. Colucci, Finney Lane.
Donato Corbo, Stillwater Ave.
Antonio Di Preta, 30 Pacific St.
Vincenzo Fastiggi, 39 Pacific St.
Pasquale Fortensato, 30 Pacific St.
Vito Fastiggi, 39 Pacific St.
Francesco Frattaroli, Liberty St.
Andrea Galasso, Stillwater Ave.
Rocco Genovese, Liberty St.
Giovanni Gerardi, 35 Pacific St.
Rocco Giuffre, Liberty St.
Salvatore Granese, 65 Hawthorn St.
Elia Latte, 30 Pacific St.
Francesco LaValle, Finney Lane
Antonio Lopiano, Spruce St.
Bernardo Lupinacci, Liberty St.
Carmine Lupinacci, Liberty St.
Caromine Lupinacci, Stillwater Ave.
Carmine Macari, Liberty St.
Joseph Minero, 27 Pacific St.
Benedetto Mallozzi, Spruce St.
Pietro Mangufi, Stillwater Ave.

Andrea Martinelli, Stillwater Ave.
Nicola Massaro, Liberty St.
Vincenzo Moavro, 78West Main St.
Henry Mori, 73 Atlantic St.
Raffaele Ottaviano, Spruce St.
Oscar Otto, 1 West
Marino Passero, 30 Pacific St.
Alvie Palmatier, 4 Atlantic St.
Aerger Parchi, 62 Pacific St.
Vincenzo Pellicci, Stillwater Ave.
Elia Pia, 30 Pacific St.
Raffaele Pia, Liberty St.
Luigi Piacenza, Liberty St.
Joseph Pombi, Chapel St.
Angelo Pugliano, 95 Pacific St.
Geo Rambo, 55 Bedford St.
James Riodi, 30 Pacific St.
Luigi Rosso, 85 Pacific St.
Nudo Salvatore, Finney Lane
Giacomo Sabia, Stillwater Ave.
Cesidio Socci, Liberty St.
Pietro Socci, Liberty St.
Salvatore Spruriero, 7 Spruce St.
Giuseppe Tamburro, 52 Chapel St.
Francesco Tartora, 86 W. Main St.
Bennie Tedesco, 98 State St.
Giovanni Teodora, 21 Pacific St.
Antonio Terenzio, 13 Pacific St.
Giuseppe Tinglese, 32 Pacific St.
Teodoro Uva, Spruce St.
Michele Vaccaro, Stillwater Ave.
Vincenzo Vacca, 10 Clark St.
Michele Venturini, Liberty St.
Raffaele Vitti, Liberty St.
Domenico Vitti, 35 North St.

---

[37] Stamford Advocate 10/19/1900.

Stamford Italians understood that they had to show up at the polls in numbers to obtain proper representation.

Some articles portending to be reporting reinforce outright bias. The title of one such Stamford Advocate article: "A crazy Italian" goes on to indicate "arrested a rather crazy Italian and took him to lockup. It is not known what his full name is, but he goes by the name of Tony...called to Tony's habitation on Cedar Street, where a regular circus was going on, witnessed by an excited crowd. Tony was stripping up the clothing in the house right and left...and Tony threw the knife away and was taken to lockup...His curious demeanor may have been caused by the great heat."[38]

The next article is presented as printed. I can only guess that it was comically published but shows the bias that early Italians had to confront. Imagine how humiliating, demoralizing, and frustrating it must have been to see what the establishment in the city thought of them and their attempts to elevate themselves by joining an educational lecture group. This also helps illustrate the different levels of bias Italian Americans faced depending on their occupation, social status, skin tone, etc. The reporting is told from the point of view of a shoeshine boy who unwillingly ends up at an educational lecture and is written in "broken" English[39]:

Nick Goes To A LECTURE
How an Intellectual Treat Impressed the Shiner Man

Someone gave Nick a ticket the other day, which bad more of a superior tone about it than the average bid, which he picks up once in a while between shines. He tried to swap it for a ticket for the Nelson-Gans fight, by motion pictures, in Realty Hall, but there was emphatically no market for such a trade, for all that Taft was elected. Then he tried a swap that would give him an entree to one of the several vaudevillian performances that are going on nightly in this town, but without success, and finally, when one of his pals told him that a bloke couldn't raise a dog on that bit of paper, Nick was on, even if you may not be, and he decided to see the thing through himself, even if he did have to put on a collar and tie and wear a derby hat. He stuck to 'his resolution to the bitter end, and so it was that the little bootblack spent Friday evening as a patron of the Stamford Scientific Society and heard the illus-

---

[38] Stamford Advocate 7/18/1890
[39] Stamford Advocate 11/9/1908.

trated lecture by Dr. William T. Hornaday, who no doubt in his versatile career as a writer and lecturer, has. had occasion to quote those "to see ourselves as others see us" lines of Bobby Burns.

"Meester," said Nick, "what a you think, l getta the gold breek bad. The bid said eet was to be wha you call eelustrate, but honest. Meester, they handa eet out bad, for they no have one mova de pict' all night. An' everboda' seemed to take eet all right and they try to look as though they un stam, but taka eet from me, Meester Hornaday an' hees whola show woulda gota de hook een three meenits at Tona' Gercu's. I geta een with the teck to the good, and pretta soon vera tall young man, looka vera what you call serious, coma to me. Will he finda me one seat? He look funna man. Ambrogio say eet was fulla dress when I tell him, but I say cet was like the man who disha chowder at Rye Bick at the Etalo-American peecnic las' twentieth Septembair. Ambrogio say I no un'stan' an' eet ees fulla dress and swella to wear. He say Meester Palo own one and wears once. There ees plenta seats, so I say "no thank" and he say to fren all dredda the same. That eet ees treebute to scientifeec societee, that eet ees to reach the Etalian peepul an' hees fren say eet ees treebute and showa how dem'cratic the sience ees to become and how risa up the Etalian peepulees when they getta the chaust. He say he maka note of that and writn lecture on eet. I keepa me trap closed. but eef I spigoty, Meester. I tella tehm to see the Nelson-Gans fight for the real thing. and stopa four flushing in the High School, but mebbe they no un'stan' an'I no spigoty at all, an' try so to look ·wise Iika the rest. Pretta soon the show ees on, an' everboda clapa the hans, and Meester Hornaday bow an' say eet ees a pleasure to look over such a peepul an' everboda clapa hans again. But eet was all plaina picture and no mova at all. Eet was laka Sunday school show at Christmas. that Meester DeCarlo used to give, and eet ees certainly Es kina de block by Tona Geron's vaudeville. Eet was all een one act an' no one to dance een between or to singa schoolday. The man no maka speech but just talka plain. He no spigoty Iika Dr. Sorgi and Charla Rowell ees mucha bettair. Everboda leestin, and seet there just as though eet was -een church. BY an' by he say thees ees all, an' everboda say to everboda eesn't eet to the good to heara such a man. "The show was certainly to the bad, but, Meester how much eet costa to see what Meester Hornaday tell about? Eet was so vera fine country he spigoty of an' eet ees so nota like anything I ever -see. Eet ees pretta much alla same here, an' I lika to go hunta beeg game once myself. I thinka on that all right, an' say, Meester, honest, now has a bootblack gota any chaust?"

In October of 1908 another article from "Nick's" point of view appears, talking about the Mayor's race[40]:

Nick was shining a pair of boots this morning and, as he shined he talked. "Meester," said Nick, "whosa to win? No? You're funna man, Meester. Everyone I shine tella who win. Meester's Pal's customers-they all dress up slick, you know-all say eets over now, and Tuppa ees Mayor again. And Meester Pumpo, he says eet's vera well to have eet so-hedona care so much, but Tuppa, he gets Meester Pumpo play so fine for Meester Fairbanks, eet ees what you call "Hola time in old town," and "Cavedeler Rustican," all een one. Then Jimmy Rinaldi, he come down from west side, and he say eet eess alla Meester Rowell-he no hang a man: he cuta the tax and raisa h---ees what Meester Rinaldi say. An' pretta soon Joe Colucci, he come along. An' he smila me, as he always do-you see Joe Colucci smile, ain't you Meester?- an' he say, "Nick" he say, the dope eet ees for Dr. Ryle-the others will be sella plate. I no just un'stan', but Joe ees awful smart, and he always know which posa win. He flashed de roll, and say eet's sevena five on Ryle, but when he see Jacka Moore come by, he hida de roll, an' say, eet's hard to tell. "But, Meester, ever'one hasa think an' you sure a funna man, no thinka who to win. You see, eet's as I say. Meester Palo's frens, they all ees Tuppa men, and Meester Donatel, too, Jimmy Rinaldi say it canna be so: eet ees piped for Charla Rowell, and I about make up my mind when Joe Colucci flasha d'roll and say, "Put your coin on Ryle; eet ees like taka canda from a babe." An' Meester, can you give a teep? No? You the only man lika that I meet."

An early political figure Romolo D'Aloia wrote the following editorial in 1904 in the Stamford Advocate in response to innuendo surrounding the Italian American community: "I read with surprise the evidence given in a trial in the City Court, as reported in yesterday's Advocate. I can say that an Italian secret society such as was hinted at exists only in the imagination of a very poor mind. The Italian colony of Noroton is composed of laborers, almost ignorant of the rest of the world, seeking only to earn money by their hard work. They don't know what a meeting is, or what a society means, and the evil and trouble, from fighting, knifing and quarrels, are a consequence of card-playing and beer on Sunday. The local laws are very lax about boarding houses, where many Italians crowd into small houses and rooms, sleeping like pigs endangering their health and the city's decency. I know of a boarding house on Pacific Street where, a few days ago, some Italians quarreled over some money stolen. There were so many boarders that an officer fled because of the foul air. That story of an Italian secret society is not a subject for alarm,

---

[40] Stamford Advocate 10/29/1908.

but for laughter. This was in reference to an assault case in Stamford in which, Giuseppe Tisano was charged with assaulting Franke Raffaele with intent to kill. Raffaele alleged that the assault was a result of his refusal to pay $10 to Tisano and Pietro Bove for the privilege of joining a secret society (inferring the mafia, or black hand) about which he could obtain no information in advance. It was alleged that the secret society met in Noroton. Tisano was convicted but during the proceedings on Bove no mention was made of the secret society, and Bove was not convicted. [41]

The events of September 15, 1907 illustrate the bias against Italians, the severe impact bias could have upon a young life, and the need of Italian-Americans to form alliances to stand up for each other. On that Saturday, Vittoria Marsico was found shot dead in the backyard of her boarding cottage on the heavily traveled Boston Post Road in Mianus, Greenwich. Three bullets had been found in her body, two in her skull and one in her left shoulder. There was no sign of a struggle and the shots had been fired within one or two feet of Mrs. Marisco. Three boarders of the landlady, Joseph Chirillo (sometimes spelled Cherillo, or Cherello), Charles Pasquale Esposito and Rocco Pierro were implicated in the shooting and detained by the police.

Initial reports were that Rocco Piero had been angry because the deceased refused to allow him to marry her daughter (Marie) and had shot Mrs. Marisco. Pasquale had mentioned the alleged romance during his questioning. The daughter declared that Piero had never made any proposal of marriage and as far as she knew, he had no such intentions. Marie also testified that Esposito had been in frequent quarrels with her mother about his unpaid board bill. On the day before the murder, Mrs. Marisco said: "If you don't pay me tomorrow, you'll have to pack your things and go." Esposito was charged with the murder.[42]

At the hearing, Chirillo testified that Esposito had told him he had shot and killed Mrs. Marisco over the unpaid bill and wanted Chirillo to go away with him. He said that Esposito told him if they were caught, to say that he was with him all day. Esposito denied this testimony and noted he was with Chirillo at the time of the murder and not at the murder scene.[43]

Charles Pasquale Esposito was 15 when he immigrated to America from Italy in 1905. An uncle and aunt who had no children had sent the passage money for him. After living in Pennsylvania for a while, the three moved to Greenwich in June of 1906. The aunt and uncle in a separate residence and Pasquale at Mrs. Marisco's cottage. In the midsummer off season like many

[41] Stamford Advocate 11/29/1904, p 1, 11/30/1904, 12/12/1904 p 1.
[42] Stamford Advocate 9/21/1906
[43] Stamford Advocate 9/26/1906.

other unskilled laborers, Pasquale was laid off. While he was idle, his boarding bill ran up unpaid.[44]

A jury of twelve were selected. The general line of examination of the prosecution was to find whether the juror had prejudices against capital punishment or circumstantial evidence. The defense was most interested in knowing whether there was prejudice against Italians.

The following circumstantial evidence was presented at trial. Esposito testified that after Mrs. Marisco told him he must pay or leave he went off with Chirillo into the woods and met Rocco Piero. Esposito and Piero roughhoused a bit and, in the scuffle, his wrist was scratched, which caused blood to be on his shirt. He indicated that he did not have a revolver after July 4th. He helped carry out the dead body from the house on a board and thought some of the blood on his shirt might have come from her head. He washed out the bloodstain. He also testified that from the time he left the house in the morning with Chirillo, the latter had not left him. Chirillo testified that at some point he left Pasquale to go to Greenwich for an errand. Deputy Sheriff Ritch of Greenwich indicated that Esposito's shirt was not stained with blood but that there were wet spots on it where Esposito had washed away the blood. Josephine Moretti testified she had cooked meat for him and Chirillo on Thursday before the murder and Esposito stated it was the last time they would be there for he was going to Pennsylvania on Saturday. With this evidence, Esposito was convicted and sentenced to hang.[45]

The first appeal to the State Board of Pardons was denied. Esposito maintained his innocence. This was against advice from counsel that thought he would receive a lesser sentence if he would confess. Esposito was adamant and decided to go to trial instead, and indicated that he would bring disgrace to his family in Italy by making a confession of guilt.[46]

The story galvanized the Stamford Italian community ("The Italian Colony"), the Italian government and other Italians in the state. The local group requesting clemency included the following: V. Pittaro, President of the Società Vittorio Emanuale III, G. Passaro, president of The Società Operaia, G. Maddaloni, president of Società Fra Tommaso Campanella, P. Fortunato, Società Umberto I.F of A, P. Nardozzi, president of the Società Aviglianese, R. Martino president of the Società San Manghese, Doctor A. Sorgi, president of the Società Mazzini, A. Paolini, president of the Unione Muratori, T. Ottaviano, president Unione Manovali, and G. Umile, president of the Club

[44] Stamford Advocate 3/17/1908.
[45] Stamford Advocate 1/10/1907.
[46] Stamford Advocate 6/5/1907, 6/25/1907.

Progessivo.[47] An appeal was made to the Governor Woodruff and he granted a reprieve twice. The last came just at Christmas time. Unfortunately, the Governor's maximum authority was only to defer the hanging, which the second time extended clemency until the end of March of 1908.[48] The final petition from the United Italian societies and clubs of Stamford was as follows:

> We beg your Excellency to do what is in your power to have the death sentence commuted. The condemned young man is a minor and speaks no English. He had no means with which to defend himself, and was convicted upon circumstantial evidence.
>
> Hoping that your Excellency will act before the severe penalty of death has gone into effect. We remain, for the combined societies,
>
> (Signed) G. Maddaloni, V. Pittaro, G. Ferretti, A. Cantore, A. Taddeo, P. Nardozza, G. Umile, R. Martino, T. Ottoviano, R. Natale, G. Passaro, M. A. Toglia, presidents, C. Tamburri, general secretary.

A newspaper account describes Pasquale as "born in the southern part of Italy, at Calabria, which is noted for its large criminal class."[49] The courage of these men to stand up for Pasquale should not be underestimated. They did so at great risk to their reputations and livelihoods. They did so even in the face of bias and an uneven power structure. This is one of the many reasons for which I am honored and inspired by these men of principle and feel that they should be remembered and their stories told.

The Stamford Italian societies were fortunate enough to obtain financial and moral support from the non-Italian community, namely Mrs. Blickensderfer of Stamford. Her brother-in-law was the inventor of the portable typewriter.[50] Mrs. Cecelia Blickensderfer wrote a book titled "The Death Penalty as a Failure" in which she studied several capital case crimes, including Pasquale's case. In her study of the evidence, she made the following observations. Cecelia noted that it would be only a madman who would have shot Mrs. Marisco in plain sight for all to see as they passed on the Post Road (where people were constantly passing in autos, carriages and open trolley cars). She noted that Pasquale had helped carry the body out and as a result got blood on his shirt and that the deceased's brother saw this and demanded that Pasquale be arrested. The other man who was arrested as well, Chirillo,

---

[47] Stamford Advocate 10/18/1907.
[48] Ib Stamford Advocate id 12/26/1907, Bridgeport La Tribuna Del Connecticut, 11/2/1907, 10/19/1907 p4, 11/2/1097 p.4.
[49] Stamford Advocate 1/17/1907.
[50] Stamford Advocate 3/12/2003.

who previously worked as a laborer but now kept a store testified that Pasquale came into his store previous to the shooting and showed a pistol that he was going to use to settle the account. Celia observed that the witness also admitted under cross-examination that he did not warn the widow Marisco (with whom he was friendly) about Pasquale's remarks. Mrs. Blickensderfer summarized, that the state produced the shopkeeper to prove premeditation, and the companion to disprove the alibi. The accused became guilty until proven innocent. There was no eyewitness, no pistol found, no corroboration of Chirillo's story (although this supposedly happened in the middle of a busy general store). She also argues that friends of Pasquale were no doubt also friends of the victim and shopkeeper, and as such would not want to cast any aspersions on the widow, and likely had accounts running with the shopkeeper and could not afford a quarrel with him. The only safety was silence. She also noted a neighbor who overlooks the scene of the crime saw a large man running from the scene (and not the small framed Pasquale). The person was willing to state this but not sign an affidavit.[51] She argued there was sufficient doubt in this case.

Pasquale's lawyer, Attorney Carl Foster presented to the clemency board a petition from the 12 jurors who convicted him, asking for commutation of the sentence, and one from a single juror who said he voted for conviction with reluctance. He also indicated that Mrs. Marisco had a lover, and he would prove that jealousy had caused the murder. With the grace of God, the Clemency Board changed the sentence and commuted it to life in imprisonment on March 23rd, 1908.[52] Pasquale did not give up and petitioned the Board of Pardons in 1913 and 1920.

Fate intervened, and a chance encounter would alter Pasquale's life. Genevieve Cowles a painter, was working on a set of paintings for Christ Church in New Haven. One of the panels was to be entitled "The Prayer of the Prisoner," for which she decided she must have an actual model who was a prisoner and whose face would portray long confinement. She was allowed to select from among the "lifers" her model. Miss Cowles first search was a disappointment, she found no one who fit the mental image she had formed. After hundreds of viewings, she finally came across her model.

There are different accounts of who the model was (Charles Pasquale Esposito, or another man, Gerald Chapman). It is likely, that the model was not Pasquale based on an account by the artist: "In the prison library, I saw a figure bending over a hand-press. He lifted his head, and the expression of

[51] Stamford Advocate 3/17/1908
[52] Stamford Advocate 3/23/1908, 12/9/1918,p. 9, 1/9/1907, p. 2, 6/25/1907 p. 1, 12/26/1907 p 1, 3/23/1908 p. 1, 12/8/1924, p. 3,

his face was as the anguish of darkness. Here was the record of prison life written in flesh! I held out to the man, who I later learned had committed murder for gain, a branch of pure white deutzias blossoms. His face lighted up. It was like sunshine on dark waters." Another account reads: "Every sinew and muscle of his once powerful body, every line on his haggard, ashen face emphasized the great moral lesson she wished her painting to teach. His countenance was deeply shadowed by the despairing prison look and yet through it there shone a softening light from within, a light that told of penitence, of faith, hope and charity persisting in spite of everything." She finished the painting, and Pasquale remained in prison.

Later she wanted to paint a mural for the prison and prisoners. It was at this time that the warden told her of Pasquale's story and that he felt he was innocent. She read every word of the court records and became convinced that the jury based their decisions on illusion and not true facts. She looked up witnesses who testified at the trial and sent abstracts of the record and submitted them to famous authorities for opinions. Chirillo indicated to her that he only implicated Pasquale because the authorities said he would be convicted of the murder if he did not. Among the distinguished authorities she sent the information to were Professor John Dewey of the Department of Philosophy at Columbia University, Spencer Miller, the eminent psychoanalyst of New York City, Dr. George W. Kirchway, perhaps the greatest American criminologist of the time and Dr. Irving Fisher of Yale University. They did not believe he had been proved guilty; for the reason that the two witnesses whose testimony resulted in his conviction were also under suspicion. They thought at worst the charge should have been manslaughter, which was punishable by 15 years (and he had already served 18 years).

When Miss Cowles saw Pasquale, before her last attempt to get him freed she found him carving a beautiful ship, "miniature in size but perfect in detail." He told her, "I call it my "ship of Victory." She sold it and with the proceeds financed her last step in the long fight. With the opinions she had collected she went to the State's attorney and convinced him that Pasquale had not been found guilty beyond a reasonable doubt. Finally, in 1925 after 18 years, Charles Pasquale Esposito walked out of Wethersfield prison penniless, broken in health, but a free man.[53] I was not able to find information on Pasquale after this point and do not know where he went after leaving incarceration. It is disheartening to know that because of prejudice not only Pasquale's freedom was taken away for 18 years of his life, but that because of his age during those

---

[53] Bridgeport Times 5/10/1913 p. 9, 5/21/1920 p. 20, Syracuse Herald, 7/19/1925 p. 16, Times Signal, 8/9/1925, p. 33, Helena Independent, 9/6/1925, p. 24., Project Cantebury, *The Chronicle of Christ Church*, by Deaconess Josephine A. Lyon, New Haven, CT, Quinnipiack Press.

years, he was deprived of many of life's gifts. He was likely not able to fall in love and marry. He was likely not able to have children, or grandchildren and watch them grow up. He was not able to provide, support for the future generations that would have come after him (as was the custom of most Italian immigrants who were content to sacrifice for the benefit of their offspring). He was spared his life, but still so much was taken.

Giuseppe Fuda and Nicodema Imposino did not fare as well a decade earlier. On February 17, 1897, a cold night, with snow still on the ground from the last storm, at approximately 11 pm, a railroad engineer (Mr. M.P. Gates) spotted something up ahead on the eastbound track on his way out of the East Norwalk train station. He was able to stop his train before hitting the object; it was a woman's body. He thought a train had killed her. However, the crew of the freight train once up close saw that the body bore marks of violence, the head gashed as if an axe had been used. There was a wound extending from the crown of the head down to the base of the brain. There were 12 wounds in all in her body. Three of four of them in her back, seemed to have been inflicted with a sharp instrument other than a hatchet. The body was removed and taken back to Norwalk. About the scene were footprints and other indications that a struggle had taken place. The victim's head was covered with wounds, any one of which was sufficient to cause her death. Later, near the scene of the crime the hatchet with which the deed was done was found. No identification was found on the body. In the pocket of her dress was found a dance program. The next day a search for the murderers began.

The body was later identified as Mrs. Fuda. Mr. Fuda was born in Martone, Reggio Calabria, Italy and had been in the country for three years. Imposino came to the house next to him in Stamford, shortly after Fuda arrived. He sent for his wife a year later, they had been married five years. Maria was quite a few years younger than her husband. Fuda knew Imposino; they grew up together in Italy.

It was learned upon inquiry among Stamford Italians that Fuda reported that his wife had suddenly left home, taking with her money belonging to him, and that he had not seen her since. He also indicated that she had slept with him on the night of the murder. These false statements caused suspicion to fall on him. Witnesses saw Fuda, Imposino and Mrs. Fuda (Maria Carmelia) at the Stamford depot early in the evening, and they were seen taking an eastbound train. Additionally, a witness indicated that Fuda came home at 4:30 in the morning the night of the murder, that he had changed his clothing and had gone to New York saying his address would be 96 Mulberry Street (an Italian bank). Officer Nevin, of the Stamford police force reported this to the prosecuting attorney who told him to go to New York to arrest Fuda saying "Get him. We'll arrange about the warrant later. There is no time to lose now." Officer Nevin took Leo Donatelli with him to provide translation services. They ran across an Italian who used to live in Stamford and asked him if he knew where Fuda was. His response was "You tell me what you want him for and I tell you, maybe." Donatelli told him that a railroad train killed Mrs. Fuda and they wanted Fuda to go up to identify her. The man brought them to 112 Mulberry Street where on the top floor in a group of men Fuda was located.

Once back in Stamford, they scraped Fuda's fingernails and took his shoes. The shoes matched the footprints found in the snow at the crime scene. They also learned that Fuda had his belongings packed and intended to set sail for Italy the day he was apprehended.

Imposino was on the run as well and believed to have a hand in the crime. He told a relative he had committed a crime and asked for money to take him to Canada. When the relative ascertained the nature of the crime he notified the police and Imposino was arrested on the train to Buffalo.

The grand jury took a full day to return its verdict that both men should be tried for first-degree murder. Some of the jurors were not satisfied with the evidence against Imposino. For Fuda there was hardly a shadow of a doubt among the jurors. The question as to Imposino was the degree in which he was implicated in the crime, the jurors requested a precise distinction between first and second-degree murder. It was explained that first-degree murder was by poison, lying in wait, premeditated, deliberated, in case of robbery, burglary, injury to the person in which explosives were used with results fatal and several like ways. Murder in the second degree was murder committed in any other way than those mentioned.

Before his trial Fuda stuck to his story that his wife ran away from him and he had nothing to do with her murder. While Imposino adhered to his statement that he was on the bridge on the night of the murder and heard Mrs. Fuda scream, and that Fuda came to him and told him what he had done and threatened to kill him as well if he didn't keep quiet about it. Reporting indicates while incarcerated, and before being charged Fuda was morose, sullen and acted as though there was something weighted heavily on his mind, while Imposino was getting tired of incarceration and was confident that at trial he could prove he was innocent.

The trial of Fuda started in May of 1897. The following testimony was presented. Louis Macri a neighbor in the same house as Fuda testified that Fuda borrowed a file with which to sharpen the hatchet shortly before the murder. He also testified that the morning after the murder, he complained that his wife had taken his money and departed. Fuda was cleanly shaven, and his neck was slightly cut; this he explained was caused by a slip of his razor. Macri indicated that Fuda was quiet and not quarrelsome and that he exhibited love for his wife. Fuda's counsel endeavored to show that Fuda had been in the country only a short time and that Imposino had been in the U.S. for several years and because of this advantage had unusual influence over Fuda. Macri testified that on the night before the murder, he saw Imposino at supper at 7 pm. Imposino complained of feeling ill and stated his intention of going to sleep. On the day, succeeding the crime Impossino remained in bed all day with a fever. He remained there until Saturday night, 3 days after the murder. Giacomo Calve also lived in the same building testified that he saw Fuda sharpening his hatchet with a file. Calve occupied a room adjoining Imposino and in order for the latter to get to his room he had to pass through Calve's room. Calve retired at 9 pm the night of the murder. At that time, Imposino was not in his room, although Macri testified that he retired about 7 pm. Calve was awakened at about 2 or 3 in the morning, by Imposino returning. Lucia Zanga reported an encounter between Fuda and Maria four or five days before her death. At this time, the two quarreled and Fuda struck his wife in the face four or five times. Mrs. Fuda had been working in a factory for several days and Fuda took the money she earned. Mrs. Fuda had demanded her money and this led to the fight. Louis Pannetta testified about playing cards with the couple often, and indicated sometimes there was peace and at other times they acted as though they were crazy. A few days before the murder while playing cards an argument broke out and Fuda took his hatchet and went over to his wife and said: "See here, if you don't behave yourself, I will finish you. I will take you out in the woods and finish you."

Donatelli testified that during interviews after capture, Fuda stated "Who is this Imposino? Perhaps he is the man who took my wife and money." He also offered that Fuda had contradicted himself during interviews first saying he had left his wife on Thursday night and then later stating Friday morning. Later after Imposino was apprehended, Donatelli returned to interview Fuda and told Fuda that Imposino accused Fuda of the murder, and that the police had found his coat and the shoes that fit the footprints in the snow at the murder scene. Fuda explained that he had loaned Imposino the coat and shoes on the night of the murder, he also added that maybe Imposino took the hatchet with him. He also indicated he did not know of Imposino's whereabouts the night of the murder. After Imposino pointed to Fuda and said he was the murder he indicated that he would tell the truth. He said Imposino had ruined the lives of he and his wife. He admitted that his wife had lived a life of shame. He said on the morning of February 17, Imposino and Fuda, accompanied by Salvatore Angioletta, were walking along Main Street near the Methodist Church, when Imposino informed Fuda that another quarrel had occurred between him and Mrs. Fuda, saying " I am tired of her. I have a notion to kill her. If you don't kill her soon, I'll shoot her." Fuda replied he didn't have the courage to do it, to which Imposino replied "Leave that to me. You take her to South Norwalk. Tell her we are going to a show, and when we get there we'll fix her."

Donatelli's testimony of Fuda's statements continued: When they reached South Norwalk, Fuda suggested to get off. Imposino said: "We will go to the next station. This town is too large." When they got to East Norwalk, Imposino said, "We will take a walk." Mrs. Fuda asked "Where are we going?" to which Imposino replied "We will take a walk and then take a trolley car." When they got to a point below the bridge, Imposino said, "Now catch her." He caught her about the waist, threw her over on one side, and then delivered the blow upon her head. She screamed: "Holy Virgin! Holy Virgin!" and to each exclamation, Fuda replied: "Holy Moses! Holy Moses!" Fuda and Imposino than ran up the bank and met on Bridge Street not far from the railroad bridge. While they were walking to East Norwalk, Imposino called Fuda's attention to blood on his coat and told him to cut it out, and it was done. On the way home, Fuda asked what the neighbors would say, and Imposino said: "Tell them that she got up early in the morning and went away with some of my money." They agreed to this, got off the train, and took different routes home.

Fuda's testimony during trial indicated that he did not know that Imposino had evil designs on his wife (even though he had told Donatelli so). He indicated that he was surprised when Imposino told him to catch his wife, and that he thought it was because a freight train was coming. He did not see Imposino strike her and did not remember the words that were used, he was frightened and ran away. He did not attempt to prevent Imposino from injuring his wife and was afraid Imposino would kill him. He wanted the jury to understand that he simply believed the three were going to the theater, after that they would draw a confession from his wife as to the number of times, she had been guilty of misconduct, whereupon he would give her money and send her away. Fuda then declared that while he was confined Donatelli tried to extort property in Italy out of him in exchange for which he told him he could get him off free. He indicated that he declined this offer.

Imposino after understanding Fuda was trying to get off by implicating him, offered to tell the truth as long as he would receive a life sentence instead. This was denied. The first count of jurors indicated that ten jurors were for first-degree murder and two for second. By the second ballot, the two changed their verdict to agree with the others. Fuda was sentenced to hang.

Imposino's trial started shortly after, and the following testimony was presented. Vincenza Papandeca testified that she witnessed Mrs. Fuda pouring a pitcher of water over Imposino's head after he asked for a drink. Vincenzo Ciroonsta heard a conversation about fifteen days before the murder where Imposino threatened Mrs. Fuda if she were to say another thing about his sister he would shoot five shots into her. Francesca Balitte testified that a month before the murder, Mrs. Fuda told Imposino to go play with his sister, to which he replied, "if it was not out of respect for your husband, I would slap your face." Another witness saw Imposino hit Mrs. Fuda with a snowball, to which she responded, "If you don't leave me alone, I will have you arrested." Salvatore Amgidesse indicated that Imposino wandering the streets said he was afraid the police would arrest him.

Imposino's confessions to Donatelli as presented in court were in contrast to Fuda's rendition. He indicated he met Fuda and his wife at the depot in Stamford and accepted his invitation to join them. After getting off in East Norwalk, Fuda asked him to walk up to the road to see if there were tracks so that they could board a car to the destination. While he was standing there, he heard Maria cry "Oh my god you are killing me." Fuda came running up the embankment towards him holding the hatchet. He asked Imposino to keep the secret. The understanding between the two was that neither was to say anything about the murder unless both should be arrested and one of them charged with the crime. In that event, Fuda was to confess. Imposino testified that on the day of the murder Fuda asked him to buy tickets to Norwalk because he thought there was a job opening. He also indicated that he and Maria used harsh words toward each other so that Fuda would not suspect their affair. He stated, "I did not know that she was to be killed. I did not help to kill her. I did not kill her. I should have helped her if I could." Under cross-examination, he gave contradictory statements under the prosecutors questioning. Imposino was also convicted after the jury requested clarification of murder in the first degree and as an accessory. There was an issue with rumors that a juror went to the crime scene on his own to investigate, but this was later dismissed. The newspaper reports indicated that "West Side Stamford Italians" were happy with the verdict and that they believed Imposino was the real murderer.

Fuda provided a confession to Father Flannery the spiritual advisor to both men that was prompted by a desire to repair injury done to Imposino on the witness stand and to make known the true story of his crime. The confession was in Calabrian dialect. Imposino's lawyer and the Italian Consulate requested a reprieve, but the state indicated that it would be useless to present any petition as Fuda's confession only further implicates Imposino.

Imposino indicated that the newspapers did more to convict him than the evidence submitted in trial. He may have been correct. Here are a couple newspaper accounts that exemplify the bias Italians experienced by Stamford media:

> There is a marked contrast between the two men. Fuda is an ordinary Italian laborer, poorly dressed and apparently without wits enough to plan a murder like that of which he is accused. Imposino, on the contrary, is above the ordinary run of Italians in appearance, manner and intellect. He has a rather dark, sallow complexion, not unlike that of a mulatto, and has an easy, self-composed manner. He speaks good English and was fairly well dressed. Contrasting the two men the average individual would come to the conclusion that Imposino is not the really innocent man he pretends. He may not have committed the deed or have witnessed it, as he claims, but there are many who, after having seen both of the prisoners today gave it as their opinion that it was Imposino who planned the murder, and that Fuda carried it out according to his directions.

> The execution of Fuda, and that of Imposino, which is soon to follow, will undoubtedly prove a valuable object lesson to the lawless element in Stamford, and will be especially effective in demonstrating to the disorderly fellow-countrymen of this detestable pair that the Law has a strong arm, and that punishment will surely follow crime. It is no reflection upon the scores of respectable and industrious natives of Italy who have settled in Stamford, to state that many Italians who have come here are ignorant, reckless and depraved. Evidence of that are not wanting in the police records of this city. Until they can be taught the virtues of decency, cleanliness and good behavior in other ways, the community must protect itself by recourse to the Law. Speedy trial and punishment of offenders of every class will do a power of good.

On December 3rd, 1897 Giuseppe Fuda was hung. A heavy weight at the end of the rope fell with a thud, and Fuda's body flew six feet into the air, and quickly dropped four feet. His pulse stopped 9 minutes after the time the weight fell. Two weeks later Imposino would have the same fate. On the day of execution, he said to a deputy: "Tell all the world me no kill Mrs. Fuda, me innocent, me no kill Fuda's wife, Fuda kill. I no know." He could not understand why he was convicted for complicity, when Fuda really did the deed.[54]

In another case that occurred in 1910, there was police overreach. The police noticed Nicholas Tamburri walking on Summer Street with a chicken wrapped in paper. The officers noted that there were chicken thefts lately (not that day) and decided to take the man to the police station. While there they checked his story, (Tamburri actually brought them to the shop where he obtained the chicken) and he indeed purchased the chicken. Mr. Tamburri sued the police for $2,000 for arrest without warrant, and without justification or probable cause.[55] The Italo-American Political and Benevolent Club later took this up. Nicholas lost the suit in 1911; the jury having concluded there was no malice.[56] Nicholas did go on to have a successful contractor business.

Also in 1910, complaints of different treatment with respect to tax assessments was reported in the Advocate: "How different they treat some of our citizens! – for with them sauce for goose is not necessarily sauce for gander. An Italian bought the property of Miss Mary Holly on Stillwater Avenue for $2,700. The assessors valued it at $3,000, or $300 more than he gave for it. James Miller just purchased two lots on Division Street for $1,800, the exact valuation of the property by the assessors. Why is it that one piece of property is valued at just what it sells for, another at more than it sells for, and still others at much less than they sell for? Is this their idea of equaling values?" Quintino Vetriolo appealed to the Superior Court in 1916 and was awarded abatements on two properties he owned.[57]

The facts are indisputable. Italians were among the most discriminated-against immigrant groups to arrive on America's shores. The scope and breadth of this discrimination was remarkable. It ranged from physical mob violence to less overt, yet extremely damaging, discriminatory pronouncements and writings from politicians and journalists and in judicial proceedings, and as shown, was evident in Stamford as well.[58]

---

[54] Stamford Advocate 12/17/1908 p 7, 12/17/1912 p 1, 6/4/1931 p6, 4/27/1900 p 4, 12/6/1897 p 1, 12/4/1897 p 1, 12/3/1897 p 1, 11/27/19897 p 1, 6/30/1897 p 1, 6/28/1897 p1, 6/26/1897 p 1, 3/6/1931 p 6, 3/5/1897 p 1, 3/8/1897 p 1, 3/9/1897 p 1, 3/10/1897 p 1, 5/29/1897 p 1, 6/1/1897 p 1, 6/2/1897 p 1, 6/4/1897 p 1, 6/5/1897 p 1, 6/8/1897 p 1, 6/9/1897 p 1, 6/11/1897 p 1, 6/12/1897 p 1, 6/15/1897 p 1, 6/16/1897 p 1, 6/17/1897 p 1, 6/18/1897 p 1, 6/22/1897 p 1, 6/23/1897 p 1 6/25/1897 p 1 6/26/1897 p 1 6/28/1897 p. 1 12/6/1897 p 1.
[55] Stamford Advocate 6/24/1910, 7/1/1910
[56] Stamford Advocate 7/6/1910, 11/16/1911 p 1.
[57] Stamford Advocate 3/17/1910, 6/17/1916 p 1.
[58] Puleo, Stephen, "From Italy to Boston's North End: Italian Immigration and Settlement, 1890-1910" (1994). Graduate Masters Theses. Paper 154.

At the turn of the century in Connecticut if you were a non-Italian male, you would most likely be employed in "Manufacturing and mechanical pursuits," which accounted for 45% of the jobs. This group would include carpenters, iron and steelworkers, machinists, manufacturers, and painters. An Italian male, however, would most likely be employed in "Domestic and personal services." This group would have included mostly barbers (8% of jobs) and laborers (making up 85% of jobs). "Manufacturing and mechanical pursuits," would make up most of female jobs as well (roughly 45%). This group would have included dressmakers, cotton, silk, woolen or textile mill operatives. Foreign-born woman had an even higher percentage of workers in this category closer to 57%. It is likely that Italian woman were employed in mostly these categories as well. The jobs employing Italians, would have been at the lower end of the pay scale.[59]

Besides contending with prejudice, Italians everyday life in Stamford was often under miserable working conditions. The jobs Italians took in Stamford were difficult and often dangerous and working conditions were not always the best. In fact, many of the jobs they took were jobs not wanted by other residents. The following are brief early reports on the situation. In 1887, Italians were employed to dig ditches to lay pipe to connect North Stamford to lower Stamford for the Stamford Water Company. Between twenty to thirty Italian workers were occupying a single-family home while employed.[60] "Monday afternoon in Finch's drug store, Dr. Darby sewed up the middle finger on the left hand of an Italian who was hurt at the Gasworks. One piece of timber fell while the Italian had his hand on another piece, and the consequence was a bad split in the finger."[61] "The Italian whose leg was crushed near the depot, in the laying of the new gas main is rapidly recovering under the skillful treatment of Dr. R. W. Bohannan."[62]

In May of 1892, Giovanni Rocco Manguse, a twenty-six-year-old, recently married, Italian laborer died from burns suffered while excavating and relaying pipes on Canal Street for the Gas Company. Early reports were that Giovanni carelessly ignited a match in the trench, causing a slight explosion. However, later it was found, (based on Giovanni recounting the event to the attending physician) that a spark, which ignited the gas was caused by Giovanni striking a flinty stone with a tool while digging. Fellow workers, who

[59] Connecticut Occupation Statistics 1900 https://www2.census.gov/library/ publications/decennial/1900/occupations/occupations-part-8.pdf
[60] Stamford Advocate 5/13/1887.
[61] Stamford Advocate 9/13/1989
[62] Stamford Advocate 11/29/1889

denied the match story, corroborated this. The burns were extensive and included his face, neck, hands, and arms. Erysipelas (a common bacteria infection of the skin) quickly set in and proved fatal.[63]

"An Italian laborer, known among his fellow workmen as Joe Mack was fatally hurt by a fall at the new Lawrence-Brown block *("block"* refers to a building*)* on Tuesday. He had just been warning people to keep away from the excavation, when he himself slipped on the edge and fell in. ...unfortunately for him he was at the moment engaged in carrying a heavy stone with both hands....Some grave internal injury was caused by the stone, which resulted in the death of the unfortunate man the same night."[64] In 1909, a piece of apparatus on a derrick in use on the dam work in North Stamford gave way and allowed a big iron bucket full of concrete to drop several feet upon a group of Italian laborers. Tony Delmars and Vito Muchi were hurt so badly they were sent to the hospital. Delmars had a severe concussion. In 1910, when the bread winner of the family, Mr. De Martino of 41 Gay St. was hit and killed by a car, his wife and six children were left to fend for themselves, as Mr. De Martino was not a member of an Italian Society. His fifteen-year-old son had already been working at Yale and Towne, but his salary was not enough to support the entire family so his fourteen-year-old brother Vincenzo was forced to look for work. In 1912, Edward Scaravo employed by the Stamford Street Railroad likely lost an eye as a result of injury. While working, a chisel he was using broke, and it hit his eye. In 1913, Frank Gigliardi, an employee of the Rubber Company in Springdale, almost burned to death. He was carrying a can filled with naphtha into the churn room, where it is placed in churns with rubber and cement, to make a compound that is spread over cloth to make it waterproof. The highly flammable compound was set afire while he was carrying the can. The explosion burned his face and arms and set his clothes on fire. Lyon an engineer in the building tore the burning shirt from his back and extinguished the rest of the burning clothing with a wet cloth.[65]

Banned from admission to existing American Unions, some Italo-Americans formed independent workers' unions. By the early 1900s, there were some attempts by Italian labor movements to improve things. However, these were not always met with success. In 1900, the officers of the State League of Italian Clubs met to form a campaign to have the "shanty" system of housing Italian Laborers abolished in the state. The league included Leo Donatelli of Stamford as secretary. They were seeking to use their political

---

[63] Stamford Advocate 5/18/1892.
[64] Stamford Advocate 6/6/1890.
[65] Stamford Advocate 6/25/1909, 12/2/1910, 4/1/1912, 1/13/1913.

influence to support candidates who would assist in having an act passed that would provide a penalty for placing several hundred Italians in a shanty as was the practice of large New York contractors doing work in the state.[66] Italian laborers putting up a concrete factory building on Henry Street went on strike in 1907 because as reported by the newspaper, they did not like the foreman (who drove them too much).[67] Four alleged ringleaders of the strike were arrested. They were Frank Serafino, a 16-year-old, Frank Sofio, 19, Concesso Palemaro, 30 years old all of 92 Spruce Street, and Raffaele Augustino, 25 years old of 267 Spruce Street. They were charged with breech of peace and intimidation. It was claimed that they induced 100 laborers to stop work and on the following day by force and arms of threat to prevent the laborers from returning to work. The chief of police said that they were guilty of no actual violence, other than to threaten the men. At police headquarters, the men under arrest said (contrary to reporting) they had no issue with the foreman, but objected to the conditions under which they were working. They were doing concrete work and excavating, and much of the work was done while they stood in water up to their knees. Only one of the men arrested wore rubber boots, and those were short-legged. The feet of all were soaking wet, (this event occurred during winter in January).[68] To summarize, four men (two of them teens) prevented one hundred laborers from doing their job, and for merely complaining about having to work in water in the dead of Winter without boots, the four were put in jail by their employers. Obviously, a balance of power had not shifted in the Italian workers' favor. In 1908, masons and Italian laborers on the water works had a grievance about wages and dropped work for a while.[69]

Italian societies met in 1909 in response to Italian laborer grievances with respect to work being done on Halloween Park (now Cummings Park) for the city of Stamford under the contractor William McCabe. The *Advocate* reported: "It is believed that, if the Italians present their grievance, there may be a get-together meeting which will result satisfactorily all around. Mr. McCabe is, of course, under a definite contract with the city, and the latter cannot compel him to do any more than the contract calls for, and he need not make any concessions unless he wishes to. There is a disposition on the part of city officials not to do anything to hamper the contractor, as everybody is anxious to see the park in shape for public use as soon as possible." So much for protecting your constituents, be they undesirables or not.

---

[66] Stamford Advocate 10/4/1900.
[67] Stamford Advocate 1/3/1907.
[68] Stamford Advocate 1/4/1907.
[69] Stamford Advocate 12/10/1908.

In 1910, a labor meeting held by the Central Labor Council of Stamford for local shirtwaist makers caused a stir. Two hundred workers were addressed by Salvatore Ninfo, an organizer from the headquarters of the Shirtwaist Makers' Union in New York City, and by Miss Rebecca Rosen, a striking shirtwaist maker. Edward Collins, president of the Central Labor Union and Joseph Roth, manager of the Roth waist factories also spoke (Mr. Roth without invitation). The union speakers advised that organizing would better their conditions. Mr. Roth attempted to reply but was interrupted and left in disgust, and intimated that if it became necessary to engage union labor, he would close his place and move to New York. In his speech, Ninfo said: "It isn't for us to tell you to strike. We only come over here to tell you girls and men we want you to join the organization. We don't care what your race or your creed is, we want you to join the society which will lead you into better conditions than you have today...Your hell in this world is when you only receive $3 or $4 per week, when you don't get money enough to buy clothing and food for your family. What can a girl do for $3 or $4 per week?" A week later a meeting was held for purposes of signing up workers to the union.[70]

In 1911, Italians could leverage the power of their union, the Italian laborers decided to demand $2 a day for eight hours of work, beginning in May. The masons' helpers demanded $2.75 per day for the same number of hours. However, in that same year laborers working on the Strawberry Hill sewer threatened to strike because the city wouldn't provide boots (a familiar bone of contention). The newspaper reports that the superintendent of public works arrived on the work site to find the Italian workmen sitting along the edge of the hole, smoking when the foreman informed him that they wanted eight pairs of rubber boots. Otherwise, they wanted to work an hour less each day, and they would buy their own boots, or they would just leave the job. The mayor called their bluff and told them they could go ahead and quit. They still continued to work but declared that "the mayor always pretended to be a good friend of the Italians, but that next Election Day they would "show him." The councilmen for the area advised that the city should pay for the boots as that is the custom among contractors (noting that he knew Frank Palmer bought boots for the workers). Apparently, the demand of these Italian workers had been by now acquiesced by most employers. Two weeks later the workers went on strike again, because they did not receive their wages reportedly due to a bank account funding issue. Mayor Rowell stated: "The workmen on the Strawberry Hill sewer struck yesterday; I believe upon the ground that they weren't paid the day before. Some of the

---

[70] Stamford Advocate 1/15/1910, 1/20/1910.

men went to work upon the sewer for the first time yesterday. The men who were dissatisfied forced the others to quit. This is the same gang who struck for rubber boots two weeks ago. Then, as now, a few are the ringleaders and forced the others to quit. What is needed is a man with a strong hand who will handle them with firmness and fairness, but at the same time keep them in their place. To give in once, simply encourages them to the belief that the city will always give in. The Superintendent of Public Works, backed by six councilmen, gave in before and purchased the boots. I have no idea what he will do now, but am of the opinion that it would be better to hire new men at once. I understand that the strikers in both cases were Italians. They seem inclined to try and run the Public Works Department." The workers were understanding that unity among them would bring better conditions for all of them (even if this was an alien concept to the mayor).

In the same year, fifty stonemasons went on strike, for an increase in pay to $4 a day (a fifty-cent increase), in conformity to the wage scale in surrounding towns. The three principal employers of stonemasons in the town were Nicholas Tamburri, Vincenzo "James" Vacca, and Pasquale Terlizzo. Some of the contractors noted that "they would pay a good man all he was worth-$4 or more, but that the Stamford of Stone Masons' Union had very few $4 men in it. A fine of $10 was to be imposed on every man belonging to the union who worked that day. Apparently, not all Italians were for a unified effort; often it depended upon if you were the contractor or laborer. In 1912, work halted at the Stamford Hospital when Italians struck for more pay and better conditions. They did not receive anything and went back to work. The Italian supervisor called Officer Hickey because he thought they might become unruly. Intimidation worked; at the sight of the officer, they indicated they would be back to work the next morning. The contract was with a New York firm, and the supervisor was Joseph Giovanni supervising fifteen Italians who were excavating. Recent rains left the work sight filled with mud, and they thought they should be put to use at another job on the sight until the mud and water receded. In 1913, more than one hundred Italian laborers working for Joseph Christiano, Gregory & Merritt, and other local contractors struck. They demanded an additional 25 cents per day for laborers, 30 cents for rock-breakers, and 35 cents for concrete mixers. The report stated: "Several hundred Italians were parading in the streets this morning, and several complaints were received at police headquarters. They have formed themselves into small bands of twenty or thirty men and are making a canvass of the town. No acts of violence have as yet been committed, but a number of farms and other places where laborers are employed were visited this forenoon and in most cases, the men left off work and joined the strikers. Last

43

evening a meeting was held, where a union was formed, and it was said this morning that more than five hundred Italians signed their names and paid dues. Heretofore the strikers have been receiving $1.75 per day for ten hours of work. They are now demanding $2 per day for nine hours of work." In 1914, Domenico DeLuca of Stamford was injured during a strike in Norwalk when he crossed the picket line to replace strikers in Norwalk. Contractor Benjamin Harris discharged some men at a job in Norwalk, and the remaining workers struck. Harris then hired men from Stamford to fill their places. As the Stamford men were leaving, their truck was ambushed with flying rocks, then fist fighting. Witnesses said the rocks were flying like hail at one time and that some of them were large enough to kill a man. In 1915, five hundred city workers went on strike in Stamford demanding two dollars for eight hours of work and union recognition. Six men were accused of intimidation and were arrested. Those arrested included Frank Galasso, 24 years old, at 75 Spruce St., Galataldo Deneditis, 27, of 9 Rose Park Ave., Daniel Telesco, 35 of 59 Liberty St., Andrew Romenelli, 53 of 49 Liberty St., Vito Plase of 46 Liberty St., and Rocco Fiancione, 38 of 121 Spruce St. Felix D'Allesandro of Mt. Vernon, NY, president of the union, told Chief of Police Brennan that the strike was unauthorized, and would advise the strikers of such. The strikes affected work for the O'Connor Brothers building a factory on Fairfield Ave., West Side work for the Stamford Water Company, the post office on Shippan Point, and a park job near the Methodist Church. The workers had been getting two dollars for a nine-hour day.[71]

Events involving Italian Americans outside of Stamford drew national attention. In 1911, 146 Italian-American women were killed in the "Triangle Shirtwaist Factory" fire in New York City. This tragedy led to work safety measures that we all enjoy today. In 1914, by order of the Democratic Party Woodrow Wilson Administration, the Colorado National Guard burned down a tent city of striking American workers. Two women and eleven children died – all Italian-Americans. These national headlines would have certainly made an impression on Stamford Italians.

While Italian labor was gaining some power, working conditions were still dangerous in Stamford. In 1910, 35-year-old Saverio Grippo lost both of his hands in an accident at the Insulated Wire Mill, (a wire factory) where his hands were caught in machinery and were crushed. He was born in Genzano, Basilicata, Italy and only came to the country about a year earlier, living at 70 Pacific Street. A fund was created for him (administered by Lelio Donatelli) that was estimated to reach $2,000, enough they thought to send him back to

---

[71] Stamford Advocate 4/4/1911, 5/25/1911, 3/19/1912, 4/29/1913, 5/5/1914 p 3, 7/2/1915 p 7, 7/20/1915 p 7, 4/19/1915 p 1.

Italy and for care by his wife and children for the remainder of his life.[72] In the same year, an unnamed Italian laborer was crushed to death while engaged to cut down a tree at Shippan Point. During 1911, Raffaele Nurra was killed when working on the Richmond Hill sewer line, being crushed by earth while trying to climb out of the hole.[73] In 1912, an Italian laborer escaped death from asphyxiation by gas while on the job. John Cannon, Michael Kane and J. Cobara (the Italian), all employees of Stamford Gas and Electric were overcome by gas while working on repairing a leak of the lines on Main and Canal. Cobara was resuscitated, but the other two never recovered consciousness. Cobara dug the ditch, about four feet deep, to reach the pipes. It was dangerous work, and many men were overcome while repairing lines.[74] An Italian laborer working on the East Side sewer excavation was not as lucky. He was fatally injured in a cave in on his first day on the job. His name was not reported.[75] In 1921, Nicola Pavia of 92 Spruce St. lost virtually all sight in his left eye (only 10 percent of vision remained, and little more than light could be seen) when lime got in it during contractor work with the Geneovese Brothers. He was awarded 104 weeks of compensation at the rate of $11.27 a week.[76]

Vincent Vitti of 5 Virgil St. had his hip severely fractured while working at Stamford Rolling Mills on Fairfield Ave. in 1923. He was working on an electric tractor when it suddenly moved forward and pinned him to a wall.[77]

The International Ladies' Garment Workers' Union was begun in Stamford in 1919. In 1926, they picketed the Anna Costume Company on South Pacific Street and Piper & Salerno at Atlantic St. In August of 1926, Angelina Coppola of 38 Fairfield Ave. was arrested for intimidation at picket lines at Piper & Salerno. A total of seven picketers were arrested. In 1934, Josephine Metallo was a member of the union and Minnie Annunziato and Susie Sessa were elected delegates to represent the Stamford Union at the Chicago convention. Other members included: Dora Coperine, Jennie Itri, Sally Arancio, Mollie Gerardi, Josephine Metallo, Jane Centonzi, Susie Sabato, Mary Serino, Una Berlingo, Rose Bruno, and Mary Parisi. In 1935, the union petitioned against Pasquale F. Chiappetta's (owner of the Lindy Dress and Blouse Mfg. Co.) claim of interference by the union of production, stating that there was no justification for working more than 35 hours a week. The union indicated

---

72 Stamford Advocate 7/21/1910, 3/1/1910, 6/7/1910, 6/16/1910.
73 Stamford Advocate 8/23/1910, 3/30/1911, 5/11/1911, 5/31/1911.
74 Stamford Advocate 8/26/1912.
75 Stamford Advocate 6/16/1938.
76 Stamford Advocate 9/20/1921 p 2.
77 Stamford Advocate 4/12/1923 p 1.

that in the last two years, it had collected $3,000 in back wages for workers in Stamford. Members in 1938 included Louise Epifanio, Phillip Saganelli, Michael Lombardo, and Canio Coppola. Mrs. Susan Sessa Franconeri was listed as an officer of the organization in the Stamford directory from 1936 through 1940. In 1940, Minnie Annunziata was chairman, and chosen delegates to the national convention included Lettie Biangone. In 1933, three Stamford manufacturers of women's apparel were fined for violations of state labor laws, including the London Dress Co, the Flossie Dress Co, Italian owned Anna Dress Shop on Fairfield Avenue. London was charged with allowing underage Rose Bonina and Helen Carella to work more than eight hours a day. The Flossie shop was charged with employing a minor without a school certificate, working a minor for more than eight hours in one day, and allowing a minor to work past 6 pm. The Anna Shop was charged with seven violations, including the same as above, and in addition: allowing a woman to work more than 55 hours in one week, more than ten hours a day, allowing work after 10 pm, and failing to post in a conspicuous place the state labor regulations. It was noted however, that the factory conditions with respect to light, heat, etc. were excellent.[78]

In 1939, a live telephone wire electrocuted an Italian laborer Gabriel Malloza (probably Mallozzi). Two bystanders who tried to assist were knocked out by the electric current. Someone who used a rubber coat to protect his hands finally pulled Mallozzi off the wire. Mallozzi fled and was found later, a doctor dressed his left hand, which was burned almost to the bones in several places. In 1937, the Advocate reported that a miracle occurred. Mariano Italiano 45, of Greyrock Pl. was measuring the distance between the high voltage wire and the tracks at the Courtland Ave. viaduct of the New York, New Haven and Hartford Railroad when a jolt of eleven thousand volts of electricity passed through his body and he survived.[79]

Even as late as 1941, working conditions were unsafe. Joseph Gerardi, forty-three of 55 Virgil St. was working at an excavation dig on Erksine Rd. and fell into a ten-foot excavation when the plank of wood he was pushing a wheelbarrow on broke underneath his feet. Joseph's back was broken in the fall and he received fatal internal injuries.[80]

---

[78] Stamford Advocate 4/10/1933 p1 and 8, 7/16/1926 p 2, 8/6/1926 p 1, 9/30/1933 p 8, 9/30/1933 p 1, 10/30/1933 p 1 and 11, 12/15/1933 p 24, 10/15/1934 p 8, 9/27/1935 p 8, 10/3/1935 p 4, 9/30/1935 p 1 and 7, 8/18/1937 p 1 and 8, 3/1/1938 p 9, 5/17/1940 p 8, 4/16/1934 p 3, 4/30/1934 p 8.
[79] Stamford Advocate 7/22/1971 p 4., 9/19/1939.
[80] Stamford Advocate 1/24/1941.

Safety was an issue outside the job as well in Stamford. In June of 1898, at William's Pavilion, John Scalzi was accidently shot and badly wounded. The accident occurred in the lower-level billiard room. Outside there was a shooting gallery. Someone had left a loaded Remington rifle on a pool table that James Reese was going to use. As he picked up the rifle to move it, the gun went off and hit John. The bullet tore and perforated the intestines. John was brought to Stamford hospital where his prospects were grim. In fact, rumors circulated that he was dead. Stamford history would have played out a little different had he not survived. He survived and would go on to compete as a billiard player in Stamford, and then go on to opening a tavern and a widely known business in Stamford, Scalzi's paint store. His sons would become a major league player, and a war honor recipient. Unusual for Italian Americans at that time, John was involved with some social groups whose members were integrated and not entirely Italian American. For instance, he was a member of the Stamford Wheels Club (a bicycle riding group), Romolo Pleasure Club, and the Heptasophs (a fraternal organization).[81]

In 1912, an un-named "Italian" boy who made his living by singing on the street for a few months since being in Stamford was attacked. The boy had limited use of his right leg, and it was said that he was a good singer and had earned enough to keep him in food and clothing by passerbys who would throw coins in his hat. He was only twelve, a newsboy picked him up out of the gutter and aided him to his home on Pacific Street. An "Italian" called Mariano, working as an iceman for William Hoth crushed three toes so badly, he was sent to the hospital by ambulance. There were no laws in place for tenant safety in 1915 when Jennie Centonze, a six-year-old on 325 Pacific Street fell from the second story window of her home. She landed on the tar sidewalk twenty feet below. She suffered a concussion, rendering her unconscious for about half an hour and her nose was broken.[82]

In 1919, Rocco Verderosa in the eighth grade of 39 Greenwood Hill lost his right hand, and several fingers on his left hand, after playing with a stock of dynamite he found at Woodside Park. The dynamite was being used to clear trees in the park. As an adult, he lived with his brother, and worked as a land surveyor and civil engineer. He was married (for the first time) at the age of sixty.[83]

Mary Lou Rinaldi (granddaughter of Francesco (Frank) Saverio LaBella) recounts family lore, which tells of the tragic consequences that dangerous conditions had upon her Aunt Jennie (Frank's daughter) who at the age of four

[81] Stamford Advocate 10/20/1897,6/8/1898, 6/10/1898, 6/14/1898, 3/18/1903.
[82] Stamford Advocate 5/27/1912, 7/18/1912, 8/18/1915.
[83] Stamford Advocate 5/5/1919 p 1, 5/8/1919 p 11, 12/19/1929 p 27.

died after falling into scalding hot water at her home on 44 Liberty Street in 1921. On wash day, a large pot full of hot water was taken off the stove in order to make room to prepare dinner. Jennie inadvertently backed into the pot and fell in. It was the second similar accident occurring in Stamford during the week. The family story is verified by an article in the local newspaper.[84] Boiling laundry was the common method used for washing items that needed heavy disinfection, were hard to clean or had tough stains.

In September of 1908, little Emilio Farascinoe, a thirteen-year-old, of 15 Virgil St. complained to the police about punishment inflicted by school personnel. Claiming the teacher choked him. Superintendent Willard had no comment. The Advocate indicated "It has been found in times past that the teacher has, as a rule, been no more severe than was necessary." 12-year-old Paul Pavia of 92 Spruce Street also took matters into his own hands. On October 28, 1908, he went to police headquarters to complain about unnecessary corporal punishment inflected upon him by his teacher and Principal Stevens. He was in the seventh grade at West Stamford School and was knocking a pen and pencil together when his teacher struck him across the knuckles with a ruler. He laughed in response and was then taken to the principal. While the principal held his legs, the teacher hit him several times with a stick. The Advocate tried to locate Mr. Stevens to get the other side of the story, but he was not available for comment. The teacher declined to say anything about the incident. Had this occurred today, there likely would have been ramifications. Little Paul did have some minor infractions reported by the Advocate. In 1907, he was fined $10 for stealing a pet fox terrier and handing it over to the dogcatcher for a reward. In 1910, he was arraigned in City Court for stealing ice skates from a local store. Little Paul though would grow up to be an active politician and became known as the "Mayor of the West Side," because of his interest and commitment to the Italians in that area. See more on Mr. Pavia and his political career in Chapter 7.[85]

In 1900, the leading causes of death in Connecticut (in order of prevalence) were tuberculosis, apoplexy, heart disease, diarrhea and enteritis, pneumonia, gastritis, cirrhosis of the liver, appendicitis, and Bright's disease and nephritis. Together these accounted for about 55% of the deaths. In Stamford, in 1900 the leading causes of death (accounting for approximately 55% of the deaths) were apoplexy (includes stroke), Bright's disease and nephritis, tuberculosis, heart disease, and pneumonia.[86] There are no separate records

---

[84] Stamford Advocate 2/7/1921.
[85] Stamford Advocate 8/23/1907, 10/28/1908, 12/31/1910, 9/25/1908 p 1.
[86] CDC records 1900 https://www.cdc.gov/nchs/data/vsushistorical/mortstatsh _1900-1904.pdf.

by ethnicity, but one could assume the average Stamford Italian American's death statistics would be similar.

One victim of the 1918 flu epidemic was thirty-one-year-old Lavinia Rabasca Zarrilli. The family story is that Lavinia came from a wealthy family that had arranged a marriage for her. She refused and instead married Isidoro Zarrilli, who took her to America in 1907 at the age of eighteen. They had five children that ranged in age from eleven to two years old when she died. Isidoro could not manage the family by himself, so all but the oldest son stayed with him. The others went to an orphanage. Mr. Zarilli finaly remarried and reunited the family. Lavinia is buried at Woodland Cemetery, where her grave was still drawing the grandchildren that never met her, exhibiting the respective for family that is passed from generation to generation in Italian families.[87]

Before the introduction of penicillin in the 1930s, life could be perilous for patients with simple injuries. In 1906, Mrs. Margaret Candido of Spruce Street, an Italian American, crushed the bones of her legs near the ankle after falling from a rail car. A statement from the Consolidated Railroad of Port Chester indicated Mrs. Candido arose in her seat as the car approached Fairfield Avenue and signaled the conductor to stop, but before the car came to a standstill she brushed past the people in the front seat, broke from the restraining grasp and stepped off the car. Mrs. Candido's family's version states that she asked the conductor three times to stop the car at Spruce Street and that he ran by it and was running past Fairfield Avenue when she became nervous and stepped on the running board, where she lost her balance and stepped off the car. Doctors advised amputation, but the family would not permit the operation, and an attempt was made to bring the bones together and have them knit. Unfortunately, blood poison developed and later lockjaw. Mrs. Candido suffered quite a bit before death. Today antibiotics and a tetanus vaccine would be used to treat the bacteria; sadly, these were developed much later. She left behind a husband and eight children. The funeral was attended by a delegation from the Vittorio Emmanuele Society of which her husband Natale Candido, a barber was a member. I was unable to find out whether the family was able to obtain compensation from the rail company. Unfortunately, to compound the family's misfortunes, Mr. Candido sent his nine-year-old daughter, Teresa, and her brother for a visit to Calabria with his brother and family when a large earthquake hit the Reggio Calabria area. Natale never remarried.[88]

---

[87] *Celebrating the Heritage*, by Mario Toglia Xlibris Publishing p 349, Stamford Advocate 9/26/2009.
[88] Stamford Advocate 9/5/1906, 9/6/1906, 12/31/1908, Us Census 1940, 1930.

In an oral history interview of Dr. Jacob Nemoitin of Stamford, the doctor highlights the impact bias could have on Italians' health in Stamford. Dr. J. Nemoitin was a Jewish physician who served the immigrant community in Stamford, including the Italians. To better serve the Italian community he learned Italian with the help of Father Kelly, Edison cylinder records and Italian medical books, including "Terapia Delle Malattie Dell'Intestino," and "Il Fanciullo III." Phil Giordano recounts that the doctor would serve the immigrant community without worrying about payment and often accepted bartered items in payment. In one story, the physician relates how symptoms of worms were misdiagnosed as meningitis, because doctors were used to treating wealthier patients, who did not have these sorts of issues. The Sabias were given little hope until a colleague, a pharmacist (Dr. Champagne) suggested trying de-worming medication, as he had seen a doctor use in another Italian colony he had worked in. The second story relates to Dr. Nemoitin making a house call in New Canaan because the Italian could not get local doctors to come out to his house. When Doctor Nemoitin asked him why he did not call a local doctor, he told him that he did, but when they initially came out, they saw the child was very sick and might die. During this time, it was highly publicized in New York that a certain Italian man shot the doctor because he did not cure his child. Because of this, at that time doctors were afraid to treat Italian families with serious conditions.[89]

In 1931, the leading causes of death (in order of prevalence) in Connecticut were heart disease, cerebral hemorrhage, nephritis, pneumonia, cancer, and early infancy. Together these accounted for about 50% of the deaths. In Stamford, in 1930 the leading causes of death (accounting for approximately 65% of the deaths) were heart disease, diphtheria and coup, cerebral hemorrhage, gastritis, cirrhosis of the liver, appendicitis, nephritis, and pneumonia.[90] In 1938, a study was performed that recommended that a permanent full-time health director should be hired by Stamford. Dr. J.J. Costanzo took this role on and is discussed Chapter 7. The study indicated that the record high deaths from diphtheria, scarlet fever, whooping cough, and early infancy deaths posed a real challenge. The study also noted that Stamford's birth rate was very low, infant mortality was considerably higher and death of mothers due to factors associated with childbirth were excessive.[91]

Phil Giordano recounts the hard times his family faced due to disease. His parents Egidio (sometimes Eglio, Giglio) and Venere (sometimes Vera),

[89] Stamford Historiy Center biographical information on Dr. Nemoitin, including Oral history of Dr. Nemoitin conducted by Ron Marcus.
[90] CDC Records, https://www.cdc.gov/nchs/data/vsushistorical/morttable_1931-1932.pdf
[91] Community Chest Study for Italian Center 1931

joined other family in Stamford from Gravina, Italy in 1918. They brought first-born Angelo (born in Italy) with them, and soon seven other siblings would follow (Frank, Michael, Ralph, James, Eglio, Bruno (the first Italian American mayor of Stamford), Phil, and Angelina). Egidio started out as a laborer, but later bought a stationary store (that sold newspapers, flowers, etc.) at 6 Bedford St. It was a three-story wooden building close to where McDonald's is today. Mr. Giordano also sold Christmas trees on a vacant lot across the street near the Ferguson library. Unfortunately, Egidio contracted tuberculosis (TB) in the 1930s. Egidio was unable to work; the family had to give up the business and move to a three-family house on Broad St. TB is caused by a bacterium called Mycobacterium tuberculosis. The bacteria usually attack the lungs. Unfortunately, for Mr. Giordano, his daughter Angelina, and countless others streptomycin, a compound that acted against Mycobacterium tuberculosis, was not discovered until the 1940s. The compound was first given to a human patient in November 1949. During the 1930s, patients were isolated and as a result Egidio was sent to a sanitarium in Shelton. He passed away in January of 1937 at 50. Angelina died at 30 from TB. Because of the deaths, the family had to move once again; relocating to 40 Liberty St. Where they lived with Phil's maternal grandmother Felemo Toto. The oldest Angelo assumed the responsibility as head of household as the oldest male. This role eventually fell to the next oldest, Frank when Angelo married and relocated. During his father's illness (and during the Depression) all the siblings had to work. The impact on the family was not just the mourning of family members; the disease had profound effects on the entire family. Money needed to be earned to support the large family. All the siblings worked. Phil started work at age 5, selling newspapers. His route was on Bedford and Main Streets. At that time, he was attending Center School (which was located where Macy's and the Mall are currently). He would deliver papers in the morning (365 days a year even in the dead of winter) and then attend school. After school, he would deliver the Stamford advocate, which was an afternoon edition. Newspaper boys would have to pay two cents per paper and sell them for three. They were not allowed to return unsold papers, so they had to make sure they sold every paper they had invested in or risk losses. On Saturdays and Sundays, he would also shine shoes. At fourteen, he obtained his working papers and found a job at Zimmerman's Grocery Store. In those days, the customer would order what they wanted, and he would bring the items to the counter for them (and restock the shelves). He did not handle the money, the owners of the store did.[92]

---

[92] Stamford Advocate 1/29/1937 p 8, 12/23/1933 p 4, 9/1/1933 p 9.

Another case, not local this time, galvanized the Stamford Italian Community in 1921. Local Stamford Italian Societies held a meeting to protest the conviction of Sacco and Vanzetti with about 200 in attendance. While the Mayor granted permission for the meeting, he advised those in charge that if any law was violated, or if any unpatriotic utterances were made against the government or any of its officers, the meeting would be stopped. A collection of $75 was taken for the defense of the two convicted.[93] Nicola Sacco and Bartolomeo Vanzetti were Italian immigrant anarchists who were controversially accused of murdering a guard and a paymaster during the April 15, 1920 armed robbery of the Slater and Morrill Shoe Company in Braintree, Massachusetts. Seven years later, they were executed in the electric chair at Charlestown State Prison. After a few hours' deliberations on July 14, 1921, the jury convicted Sacco and Vanzetti of first-degree murder and they were sentenced to death by the trial judge. Anti-Italianism, anti-immigrant, and anti-anarchist bias were suspected as having heavily influenced the verdict. A series of appeals followed, funded largely by the private Sacco and Vanzetti Defense Committee. The appeals were based on recanted testimony, conflicting ballistics evidence, a prejudicial pretrial statement by the jury foreman, and a confession by an alleged participant in the robbery. All appeals were denied by trial judge. On August 23, 1977, the 50th anniversary of the executions Massachusetts Governor Michael Dukakis issued a proclamation that Sacco and Vanzetti had been unfairly tried and convicted and that "any disgrace should be forever removed from their names."

In 1924, as the U.S. was working to restrict immigration, local politicians were enabling the discrimination as well. Representative Merritt in a letter to Italian American, Dr. Costanzo writes: "We must guard the quality of American citizenship. Of late years there has been a tremendous increase in the population of insane asylums and homes for the feeble minded. This is not only a tremendous burden on the country, but, worse than that indicates a deterioration of the quality of the population, which endangers the very structure of the government. What I should personally like, if any practical way can be found, would be to make a restriction not based on any particular census, but on a careful investigation of the individual immigrants before they leave their own country for this country. In other words, what we want is limitation on quality rather than quantity. My belief is that any definite restrictive legislation such as is now talked about, would only be temporary and at some time must give way to another system based on fitness." Dr. Costanzo joined with others to protest the enactment of the bill on the grounds

---

[93] Stamford Advocate 11/28/1921.

that it discriminated against Italians, and it appeared that Representative Schuyler Merritt of the U.S. Congress was convinced that it was discriminatory and favored amending the language, (no doubt worried about the impact it would have on his upcoming elections): "we shall attempt to remedy the discrimination as far as possible. I am at present inclined to vote against the entire bill. As I wrote you before, I have so many good friends among the Italians and appreciate so highly the contributions they have made to our national life both in war and peace that I certainly do not want to discriminate against them."[94] By this time, the power of Italians in Stamford, based on their voting block finally was evident.

In the 1930s in Connecticut, the predominant male occupation would have been in the manufacturing and mechanical industries. This would be true for Stamford as well, with laborer being the most numerous occupations. For females, for all of Connecticut, the largest segment would have been for clerical or manufacturing, however, in Stamford Domestic and personal services would have been the predominant occupations. I could not find statistics with respect to Italians only, but In the 1930s a study was undertaken by the Community Chest (which later became the United Way) for this purpose at the request of the Italian Institute (which later became the Italian Center, the organization is discussed in more detail in Chapter 4).

The purpose of the study was to determine the recreational, educational, and cultural needs of the Italians of Stamford. The study simultaneously elaborates on the plight of many Italians impoverished during the Depression and testifies to lingering prejudice against them. The study indicated that school enrollment peaked at the fifth grade, which signified to the study committee that it was a lack of urge for education, exacerbated by economic limitations, which hindered the Italian-American child from taking advantage of the most Americanizing influence available, public education. The report indicates that only a small percentage of the Italians went through high school and achieved some degree of specialized training. In 1930-32, 133 pupils left school, and most of them were over 14 years of age and they left to go to work. Italian children made up 46% of the juvenile delinquency cases in Stamford; mainly for truancy, mischief, and stealing. This compared to 29% of American cases and 25% for "other" cases. The 1930 census showed that Italians made up approximately 22% of the population.

In 1935, the Advocate reported on the success the Big Brothers Club of the Italian Center had on juvenile delinquency in the area. The club began in 1934 and took in 46 boys from Wall St., Pacific St. and vicinity. Included in the

---

[94] Stamford Advocate 2/11/1924, 2/21/1924.

group were a boy who robbed a drunk, one that broke into three liquor stores, and another who performed an autopsy on a dog. Pool room hangouts were wiped out and instead the Big Brothers provided basketball and other entertainment.[95]

The Great Depression disproportionally impacted the Italian community. The study indicates that because so many of the Italian families had such a small margin on which to live, the depression had thrown many of them on public and private relief.

Lucille D'Acunto Limone recounts how her grandparents (Francesco and Lucia Corrente) survived before and during The Depression, by living off the land. Their story is probably typical of many working-class Italians living in Stamford. Both were born in Italy and were married in Pennsylvania. They were "Ritornati" who travelled back and forth until returning to America and settling for good in Stamford in 1923, first living in Waterside, then buying a home on Cerreta Street. Grandpa Francesco found a bargain property that no one wanted because it was near "the dead people." The land was close to St. John's Cemetery in Darien. They had ten children. Lucille describes that grandpa would work when he could as a day laborer (the WPA program was very helpful to Italians at this time who depended so much on the construction industry). Without steady work, the large family lived off of what they could grow in their bountiful garden, and the eggs and meat provided by the chickens they kept. Grandma continued to raise chickens on the property much later in time; Lucille remembers going into the basement and waiting for the eggs being kept warm next to the furnace to hatch. The Depression would affect Grandma Corrente years later, when a grandchild (Robert Vesciglio) who was a caddy, asked her if he could use some of the property to grow grass so that he could practice his golf, she replied "Can you eat it?" Of course, the answer was no that was precious space that could feed her family.

Nancy Lazzaro Fekete recounts that while her grandfather still maintained his job at Norma Hauffman Bearings Corp. on Hamilton Avenue (currently the Americares building) to which he walked each day from Liberty Street (two and a half miles); times were so tough that her mother Nancy had to quit school and go to work at 13 to help support the family. She worked as a seamstress making clothing for upscale department stores. The family even had to take a piano apart once for fuel for the fire to keep warm.

Working as a pre-teen or teenager to assist in supporting the family was not uncommon in the 1920s and 1930s. Joe Gerardi ("West Side unofficial

---

[95] Stamford Advocate 2/14/1935 p 19.

Mayor of Stamford"), was nine when he began delivering newspapers to supplement the family's income. He delivered the Stamford sentinel in the morning and the Advocate in the afternoon. He would get up about 5 am to deliver
to thirty-five to forty customers and get a free breakfast at Tim's Lunch (as
part of a barter for a free newspaper). Doing this he managed to make a few
dollars a week. On weekends, he would make about three dollars by meeting
the trains coming in from New York City, picking up the discarded newspapers, taking them back to to the Stamford News Company to be delivered by
horse and buggy. He started his first business on borrowed money. One day
he saw a "for rent" sign and told the agent he would take it. He then rushed
over to the bank for a few hundred-dollar loan, which he used to buy stock,
put up some temporary shelves, and began his business, during the middle of
the Depression. He opened Gerardi's Italian American Grocery Store of
Stamford in 1936.[96]

Tony Coviello recounts the impact of the Depression on his family. Anthony Coviello, Sr. came to Stamford in 1920, with his father Salvatore. They
were originally from Avellino, Italy. Salvatore was a "ritornati" and moved
back to Italy after six months leaving Antonio behind. Antonio was trained
as a woodworker in Italy, but only found factory work available upon first
coming to the country. This was until he met up with Achille Rustici, a carpenter in Stamford, who took him under his wing. He learned to build
houses. With financial backing from a relative (Costanza Mecca), Antonio
went into business for himself. Costanza's journey and eventual success in
America was not an easy one. She had been born an illegitimate child of a
priest in Italy who found herself in an unhappy marriage, where she had several children that did not survive. She met and fell in love with another man
in Italy and together they decided to escape and start a new life in America.
Costanza found her way to Stamford, and opened a grocery store on West
Main St. This is where she obtained the money to fund Antonio's business.
Antonio was able to build two, two-family homes in Stamford, in addition to
the single-family home he lived in. Unfortunately, when the Depression hit,
he could no longer carry the mortgages on the two-family homes and lost
them. This is a similar story of many Stamford Italians. He was able to retain
the single-family home. On Tony's maternal side, his grandfather (Tomasso
Nardozza) was fortunate to have a job throughout the Depression, and as
such that side of the family fared well. Tomasso and his wife Chiara Salvatore
were also from the same town, Avellino. They came to New York City in
1914. Tony's mother was born in New York City in 1915. Tomasso got a job

[96] *Who's Who Among Americans of Italian Descent in Connecticut*, by Joseph William Carlevale, Carlevale Publishing Co. 1942. P 195.

as a "waterboy" for laborers working on the Pennsylvania Railroad in New York City. During that time, Tomasso learned English while working with many Irish laborers, and for this reason when he spoke, he did so with an Irish brogue. He continued working for the railroad, as a laborer, until he retired; commuting to New York City everyday by walking from his home near the Stamford Hospital to the train station, and back at night.

Rick Morris recounts an interesting twist on the impact of the Depression on the family. Both sets of his grandparents had a role reversal. It was hard for his grandfather and uncle to find work, but his grandmother Maria Maffucci Preziosi and her sister-in-law Rosalia Quaranta Preziosi were able to retain their clothing factory jobs during the 1930s. This carried the family through the Depression, and the men did their share by taking care of the home.

Pasquale Marucco, a grocer who did business under the name Paddy Maruke had to file bankruptcy in 1934 with liabilities of $5,497.23 and assets of $800 as a result of the hard times caused by the Depression.[97]

An oral history compilation by the Works Progress Administration (WPA) includes the anonymous stories of second-generation Italian Americans B.C. and Matilda B. of Stamford, CT. B.C. then in the eighth grade left school at 14 to work. Her first job was in the packing department of the Royal Society silk mill working for 34 hours a week and earing 11 dollars. She wanted to learn how to sew so she got a job at the Stamford Waist Company for eight dollars a week for fifty hours of work. Later as work slowed, she got a job at Murphy's five and ten for $11 a week. Then she went to New York to work at International Tailoring, as a floor girl who would carry out piecework as it was completed and earned eighteen dollars a week. After getting hurt falling down subway steps she came back to Stamford and worked again at the Stamford Waist Company starting at twelve dollars a week. However, two weeks later the National Recovery Act (NRA) was passed, which established minimum wages and she was able to earn fourteen dollars a week, and hours were cut to only 8:00am to 5:00 pm, and no work on Saturday. Two weeks after that the union came in and helped with piecemeal prices. She recounted how she was not allowed to join the union in New York City (it was only for the men).

Matilda B. reports that she was also working since the age of fourteen. She reports that she was a union organizer and based on her stories was tough and outspoken. Her first job in Stamford was at the Individual Laundry, working as a shirt press. She did not have working papers but told the owners that she was sixteen. She went to work at 7:30 in the morning until 6:00 pm, and half a

[97] Stamford Advocate 8/3/1934 p 20.

day on Saturday (fifty-one and a half hours per week) for fourteen dollars. She became a labor organizer and talking on behalf of the other girls approached the boss about a raise. The boss asked the girls who started the strike, and Matilda was fired as a result. She found a job at Anna Costume dress shop. Matilda was a "finisher," someone who sewed buttons and snaps on a dress and turned up the hem by hand for $1.95 a week and working from 8:00 a.m. to 5:00 or 6:00 p.m. After getting in a fight with that boss about that meager pay she quit. She landed a job in Piper and Salerno, a coat shop where she worked from 8:00 a.m. to 5:00 pm and a half day on Saturdays (44 hours) for ten dollars a week, but the shop went bankrupt after six months. From there she got a job at National Pants for three dollars for 58 hours a week. She lasted there a short while until she also got a job at the Murphy's five and ten for fourteen dollars a week (and worked 52 hours per week). She worked there for about two years, and after an argument, where the boss called her a "wop." She quit and went to work at the Stamford Waist Company, working 44 hours a week and getting eleven dollars. She was there nine years at the time of the interview. She started at eleven dollars a week for 44 hours of work. One day a union organizer came and a special meeting was called, at which she asked questions about conditions at the shop including: why they were not allowed to talk at their machines, and why they could not go to the restroom without being followed. The next day the forelady would not give her any work in retaliation. Matilda called the union organizer and things were settled. She stayed at the shop. She recounts stories involving the picket line, including one where the strikers pulled the pants of the foreman down and made him stand in his underwear. According to Matilda he joined the union the next day and everyone forgot about the past and were one big happy family after that.[98]

Mike De Vito born in 1900 to Dominick and Rose De Vito, began selling papers at age eight. He sold papers at the corner of Main and Atlantic Streets. Michael would buy ten Advocates for fifteen cents and sell them for twenty. His mother would provide the seed money. If he didn't sell them all, he would be afraid to go home, so he would have to lay on his best sales pitch: "Please, mister buy my last Advocate." He recalls making his biggest tip ever when two women shopping asked him to watch their horses: "When she came out she handed me a nickel. I felt like a millionaire." At twelve, he began delivering by horse and wagon on Strawberry Hill Ave. School was painful for De Vito, who had a stuttering problem, and no one to assist with the impediment. He began to play hooky, until his mother got a letter from school and told him to either go to school or go to work. At fifteen, he quit school and

---

[98] *From the Old Country, An Oral History of European Migration to America*, Bruce M. Stave, John F. Sutherland and Aldo Alerno, p. 86-88.

got a job as a letter carrier. In those days there were no mailboxes, they had a badge and a whistle. They blew the whistle and waited until the recipient came out to get their mail. In 1930, De Vito met a customer who would have a lasting impact on him. Delivering to the Stamford Wallpaper Company, the foreman of which yelled at him: "Stop that stuttering! I used to be just like you. Now stop!" From that day on, he no longer stuttered. In an interview in 1990, he states: "I am so proud of my nationality. I like to see the progress Italian-Americans have made here, because we were the underdogs when I was growing up."[99]

Joann Napoletano Tipanni notes that her family (Napoletano Brothers Painting Company Owners) lost two family homes: one in Shippan and the other off Oaklawn Ave. in the 1930s because painting and wallpaper work was hard to find during the depression. They rented a home until conditions got better and they were able to build their home on Cross Rd. The Oaklawn property was foreclosed on in 1937.[100]

Frank D. Rich's autobiography recounts that the Rich family was significantly impacted due to the fact they were in construction and that the building industry came to a virtual halt. He relays how due to lack of work his father spent much more time at home during this period, probably to avoid creditors at the office. They made it through on mortgage payments from a Chevrolet showroom he had built. When the Depression hit, the dealer had a tough time making payments on the mortgage, and they negotiated a reduction in payments, which was for the benefit of both of them, as the loan did not go into default, and the Riches were able to survive on the reduced payments.[101]

In 1931, the study indicates that the Family Welfare Society cared for 299 Italian families (50% of the caseload). The Catholic Welfare Bureau had an even higher percentage in its caseload. The Selectman's office did not keep records by ethnicity, but the study surmises that more than 50% of the cases applying for relief in 1932 were Italian families. The study emphasizes that this was due to the fact that most Italians had marginal wages with little opportunity to accumulate, and that the scarcity of jobs forced them to eat into what little savings they had. The study indicates that there was a contrast in homeownership among Italian Americans, which can be found when comparing the more sordid homes around the west branch of the Stamford Harbor and fine prosperous homes in Hubbard Heights. In 1932, there were 2,024 Italian property owners, with approximately $10 million in assessed value.

---

[99] Stamford Advocate 11/21/1990 p 17.
[100] Stamford Advocate 3/20/1937.
[101] *Recollections, Reflections, with assorted Chronicles of Small Beer*, Frank D. Rich Jr.

The study also describes Italian health issues as follows: "Because the Italian comes from a climate very different from that of Stamford, it is felt by many authorities that the process of acclimatization is in a measure responsible for the respiratory illnesses, such as pneumonia, diphtheria, influenza, bronchitis, and tuberculosis, which are most prevalent." The Visiting Nurse Association reported that the T.B. Clinic administered 132 cases (72 patients were impoverished) in 1931 of tuberculosis, and with one exception they were Italian. In the first quarter of 1932, Italians represented 40% of the treatment cases, most of which related to maternity, newborn care, and respiratory illness. The study also indicates that in 1931, the well-baby clinic at Stevens School run by the Public Health Department checked the health of 229 babies weekly and 91 mothers were taught methods of care and feeding, and states "They proved to be very cooperative and interested in learning how to take care of their babies in the "American way." The Department of Public Health records for 1931 on communicable diseases indicated that approximately 36% of the cases were Italian (mostly from Scarlet Fever, Pneumonia, and Infantile Paralysis (there was an epidemic that year).

The study highlights the importance that benevolent societies and political clubs provided to Italians alone in a strange country and that by the 1930s different (non-Italian) fraternal orders such as the Eagles, The Masons, the Odd Fellows, and Red Men admitted Italian members. The Board of Recreation reported that 40% of registration was of Italian Americans, while only 10% of Y.M.C.A. and Y.W.C.A. members were Italian, and Scout troops had an even lower proportion. In 1931, there were 2,423 registered voters (1,785 men and 638 women), with six political clubs (three each for Democrats and Republicans).

The Chamber of Commerce report is informative. It shows that the largest single employer of Italians was Yale & Towne Mfg. Co. (the biggest employer in Stamford) employed about 33% of the Italians (mostly men). The various women's clothing factories together employed about 53% of Italians; mostly women and accounted for 85% of woman's jobs. In fact, in 1930, Jennie Centonze who, as reported earlier fell out of her apartment window to the street at age six was employed at the age of 21 as a machine operator at a dress factory.[102] Italian businesses numbered 393; 22 of which were professional occupations (fairly evenly split among Dentists, Doctors, Druggists, Lawyers, and Nurses). The remaining 371, were various businesses with contractors, tailors, barber shops, grocery stores, and shoe repair accounting for nearly 60% of the total.

---

[102] 1930 U.S. Census.

The report on the cultural contribution of Italians indicates that 60% of members in the Musician Union were Italians, 25% of the high school orchestra was Italian, 40% of the high school band was Italian and 20% of the Stamford Symphony Orchestra was Italian.

The study has good intentions and was commissioned by the Italians themselves. It is obvious that political correctness was not a thought at this time, but it is also clear based on the condescending verbiage that the audience for the study was not fully appreciated. This was likely because of the in-vogue process of "Americanization" of immigrants. This process involved having an immigrant become a person who shares American culture, values, beliefs and customs. Assimilation into America involved learning the language, and adjusting to American culture, values, and customs. The Americanization movement was a nationwide organized effort to bring recent immigrants into the American cultural system. This is a different perspective than the current multiculturalism model. The movement often went beyond education and learning the language to coercive suppression of "foreign" cultural characteristics. The movement has often been criticized as prejudiced against Southern Europeans. This may have been the reason why the Italian Center and United Way eventually parted ways. It appears the leaders described in Chapter 3 bought into the concept of Americanization, but likely did not realize the extent to which the establishment would like to suppress the culture they loved and grew up in. It seemed as if the process was a compromise to achieve their goals of elevating the colony. They fully appreciated the opportunities opened to them in their new country, were grateful for them, and were patriotic toward America. They wanted to demonstrate this to the local population and likely admired a lot of what was considered "American" and wanted to emulate these qualities. They drew the line at certain places though and picked the way forward that worked for them. For the most part, in their recollections, Italian Americans were ultra-patriotic and emphasized their great appreciation for the gifts America bestowed on them. Little emphasis is usually placed on the negative impacts of the Italian-American experience. Perhaps this is due to the emphasis on gratitude for everyday life occurrences that are part of Italian culture that is influenced heavily by religion.

Page 8 of the report reads as follows and speaks for itself:

Italian Characteristics
    In thinking about the characteristics which might be called racial, and that we might find in the Italians of Stamford, it is rather difficult to fix on any set of definite traits as peculiarly Italian. This is in a measure due to the fact that the Italians in Stamford come from various sections and districts

of Italy, each having distinct characteristics and a separate culture. They also have come from every stratum of economic and social life. A man from a family having a distinct heritage of education and economic security in Italy brings that heritage to America and consequently has very little in common with the optimistic unskilled laborer who was a peasant without privileges in his own country. By way of classification, Marino says that you have the emotional type where home conditions were poor; he is pleasure-loving, cooperative but unstable. He employs temptation and persuasion to gain his own ends and consequently goes into small-scale racketeering or politics unless carefully guided in America.

There is also the dogmatic type who were tradesmen or skilled craftsmen in their own country. Serious by nature, domineering and austere, distrustful of any but their own class, and exceedingly sensitive to class feeling — this type of Italian has a most unhappy time adapting himself to American ways.

Then there is the transitional type. They are critical, artistic, loquacious people who subordinate their Italian ways in their effort to express themselves in the American manner. This group finds it much easier to become a part of the community in which they live and they frequently cling to the buoyancy and spontaneity that we think of as being so much a part of the Latin temperament. The professional type as a rule does not come to America, but a few develop out of the transitional type. They are critical, intellectual, resourceful, and have considerable tact and good judgment, and they seldom lose their spontaneity and happy dispositions.

CONTRIBUTION

The Italian of Stamford has in the past contributed his brawn and good spirits to the progress of the town's industrial and social development. Today he has even a greater contribution. His desire to become American, his political interest and thrift have made him a force in the community. He realizes his shortcomings and is genuinely anxious to become an acceptable member of the community. The recommendations of the committee were as follows:

1. As the needs depend on the economic status of the Italians, the first stop would be more and widespread American education, together with vocational counseling.
2. That all foreign-born Italians need to speak and read the English language sufficiently well to be understood and to understand American customs and people.
3. That the use of American institutions such as school libraries, playgrounds, parent-teacher associations, mother's clubs, and health clinics should be encouraged.
4. That the leaders of the Italian colony take more responsibility upon themselves for the Americanization of their less progressive members.

5. That the finer elements of their national culture be preserved and fostered through an art and music center.
6. That the causes of juvenile delinquency be studied by the Italian Colony in the hope that some means may be found to prevent similar cases in the future.

In 1910, the *Guida degli Stati Uniti per l'Immigrante Italiano* was published by the Daughters of the American Revolution (DAR) and written by John Foster Carr. This guide for Italian Immigrants furthered the effort to Americanize Italian immigrants. The guide provided helpful information to immigrants and had good intentions of integrating them into the American society and the national identity as defined by the DAR. Of course, written from the perspective of the relatively homogenous population of the time, bias is inherent. The guides also reveal the DAR's fear of losing American values due to the influx of immigrants, and this fear was echoed by the public, and government officials. The guide was the DAR's solution to this perceived problem. John Carr lectured about Americanization and likely the guide at the Putnam Cottage branch of the DAR. A circular announcing the guide and as reported in the Advocate, states:

> In the past, many of our efforts have been wasted, worthy though they often were. For instance, it is almost useless…to preach in our favorite way American ideals to the immigrant arrival. He knows nothing of our history; at first, he is often incapable of gaining any conception of the origin of our institutions of the idealism that gave them birth and still is working for their perfection. He is not blind to the good or without noble instincts, but he has come to us forced by bitter need for bread….It is a lamentable truth that the things that most impress him here on his first arrival and for long afterwards, are the brutality of our police, our merciless push and drive in a thousand great industrial works, our lack of leisure and inordinate love of money. In political life the things he sees are the corruption and intrigues of politicians.
>
> These passing evils make a permanent impression upon him as long as he remains apart from our life, segregated in his colonies, speaking his native language only, reading his own newspapers. He begins to know something of the heart of our national life when he begins to speak the English language and has stretched out to him the hand of American good fellowship.
>
> And so it follows that the way to make the immigrant, and particularly the Italian, a good American, is not by attempting to drill him in civics, but by opening to him every means of entrance into American life, to make it as easy as possible for him to become an American, and to reach our social and civic standards…

It should be clearly explained to every immigrant that the first necessity for his advancement even in a financial way is to learn English; that for a time, if possible, he should avoid entirely men of his own country until he masters our language and becomes acquainted with our conditions of life…

The guide provided information that would be helpful upon arrival including a few pages of history of immigration to the country; "The United States has always been the land of immigrants. Men of different races have become citizens of this nation and have made it rich and great. America was discovered by the Italian Christopher Columbus, and to another Italian Amerigo Vepsucci it is due its name." There was also a brief explanation of the laws, advice on consulting the Society for Italian Immigrants and employment offices, and information about traveling by rail. The guide provided a list of ways vulnerable immigrants were robbed by thieves pretending to be employment agents, doctors, lawyers, bankers and baggage handlers, and warned to be wary of fees charged for services that should be free. The importance of learning English was impressed, and free public and evening schools, and other means of education were recommended. Dire warnings were provided to protect women from human trafficking. Directions were given for free museums and parks for "wholesome" recreational purposes. Italian immigrants were even encouraged to move into the country to study American farming techniques and purchase land. The guide also detailed laws frequently broken by immigrants out of ignorance, and asks them to study these rules, which include carrying concealed weapons, the sending of threatening letters, gambling, the use of lotteries, insulting the flag, selling unlicensed goods, immoral acts, bigamy, selling votes, cruelty to animals, illegal uses of car tickets, menaces to health and public safety, and killing song birds out of season. The guide also discussed the laws regarding employment of children, hours of labor, injuries while working (and reminds working men to avoid signing papers if they get injured on the job, even if they are given a gift in response for doing so), and the importance of birth, marriage, and death records. The guide contained preconceived notions of Italians, "Do not be against the judges. Helping magistrates in the administration of laws and punishment of the offender and a duty of every honest man," and "The Italians are too ready to resort to violence in quarrels. If this bad habit could be wiped out, the Italians would have been better welcomed immediately in America, since this is precisely what makes them most unpopular with the Americans." It suggested changes in perceived habits: "Throw away all the weapons you have. Keep the honor of the Italian name sacred. Talk in low voices. Try not to do too many spelled gestures, talk and don't get excited in discussions. Take care of your appearance. Be very careful with your personal cleanliness and that of your family. Dress and eat well...Do not abuse drinks. Following these warnings, you will be welcomed back and welcomed by the Americans." The guide also describes those that would be excluded from landing:

> The law of the United States excludes from the landing the foreigners who are idiots, the imbeciles, the weak of mind, the epileptics, the madmen and those who have suffered madness in the five years preceding their arrival. Persons who have suffered two or more attacks of madness at any time prior to arrival, the destitute, those who do not seem able to procure their lives, and those for whom it is fair to assume that they will have to resort to charity for to be able to maintain itself; professional beggars, individuals suffering from tuberculosis, or other contagious diseases, such as those who, although not included in the categories mentioned above, can be judged by the doctor who examines them, mentally or physically deficient, and under such conditions that they can be presumed incapable of living. Polygamists, anarchists, prostitutes, and those guilty of infamous crimes are also excluded from the United States. The wife and minor children of the Italian who took only the first card, if they are found suffering from a contagious disease, have the right to request that their deportation be deferred until it has been ascertained that their illness is incurable. If instead it is proven that the disease of which they are suffering is treatable, they have been allowed to disembark. Individuals of any sex under the age of 16 are not allowed unless they are accompanied by one of the parents.

The book sold for 15 cents in paper and 25 cents in cloth. The Guide was touted locally by branches of DAR and made available at the Ferguson Library and Italian steamship companies made them available. It is somewhat distortive to analyze this in terms of today's standards and although there has been criticism of bias in the Americanization process, a nuanced approach acknowledges that Italians bought into the process and wanted to "better themselves" and wanted to "be Americans." They decided on what they would accept, and what they would reject. For example, Italian American mothers took advantage of Stamford's well-baby clinic and language and citizenship classes. They did not however, embrace "American" recipes. In this regard, the proof in the impact is that much of immigrants' methods and dishes are now "American." Perhaps the method though different than today's approach was a good compromise and though intended to preserve the then current American culture, it eventually evolved into a more democratic melding of the cultures. As Americans chose what they liked from the new array of culture and food, and determining what American meant to them personally.[103] What it means to be "American" is always evolving and never static.

An interview in the WPA oral history with a Stamford "Connecticut Yankee large property owner" Mr. D details his disturbing thoughts about foreigners. Mr. D is decidedly candid, and unapologetic. The prejudices and bigoted thoughts probably reflects what many Stamfordites without familial ties to immigrants, thought about Italians and other ethnic groups: "You know, it's science that's wrecked this country and this city. Fellows iventin' this and inventin' that and other fellows coming from outside to set down here to manufacture. Why, this city and this town's got so many damn industries you can't go anywhere without running into their help. And all foreigners: "Polacks, Wops, Czechs, swedes, and lots I don't know the names of or where they came from. Why, you can walk from the corner of Broad down Atlantic Street to the railroad and hear more double-talk and see more foreign faces than you can in New York. This is a free country and we needed unlimited immigration to develop it. But when the frontier was gone and there wasn't no place to send foreigners out to, we ought to have cut it off clean…. Result was we piled up a jam of non-English-speaking immigrants at our ports of entry along the Atlantic coastline with nothing for them to do but take bread out of American mouths to send back where they came from for Europe to rearm on…..These damn aliens have just about overrun Stamford…What I've got against 'em is that they don't Americanize well. They settle in a section all side by side and carry on as though they were still back where they came from…Take the Italians and the Poles: They're both roman Catholic and mighty well organized, so that if we was to get into a war with either of those countries there's no telling what they'd be able to do in way of undermining…" [104]

Again, the treatment of Italians at that time is a complex issue. Certainly, not all articles were bad. There was an article about Angelo Demarco, an Italian shoeshine ("bootblack") who found a bankbook on Pacific Street and turned the book in. Demarco did well for himself in the town and was well respected according to news accounts and his life truly was an American dream come true. In 1903, an article states: "it is doubtful if any bootblack attracts so much attention as Angelo Demarco, the little Italian lad with whom nearly everyone in town is familiar. He has now saved $600 during his career as a bootblack in Stamford." In October of 1904, an article describes

[103] Stamford Advocate 9/7/1910, 2/19/1914, 5/2/1913, 12/19/1918, 2/1/1911, Notes of Kim Harke Sushon.
[104] *From the Old Country, An Oral History of European Migration to America*, Bruce M. Stave, John F. Sutherland and Aldo Alerno, p. 194-196.

him as a shining example of industry: "Angelo Demarco, the bright faced little Italian bootblack, who has come to be a figure about the streets of Stamford during the past seven or eight years, afforded striking proof of his industry and economy, this week, by purchasing, at a cost of $2,200, a house and lot in School Street. The note-worthy thing about the purchase is the fact that most of the money by which Angelo acquired title to the house and lot was his own saving, and represented nickels and dimes picked up during the eight years he has been polishing boots here. The house is a two-story and attic frame building. It is Angelo's intention to rent the first floor, and to make a home for his parents on the upper floor. Demarco is 18 years old. He is an only son of Michael Demarco, an Italian laborer. The boy was born in Italy and has been in this country about eight years. Since his advent in Stamford, he has plied the shoe-polishing brush, run errands, posed as model for art students, and done various other odd jobs to make money. He is a bright lad, and his sunny disposition and industry have made him many friends." Another article reads: "Angelo is not only the first Stamford bootblack to acquire real estate here, but one of a very few of his age who hold property. It is probably a safe assertion that he is the first Stamford boy to buy property out of his own earnings at that age. Angelo is very modest about his wealth. He seems to have a chance of fulfilling a prophecy made by Rev. Dr. W.J. Long over four years ago, that someday he would be a bloated bondholder." He met and married Madeline Gentile, and they had three sons Michael A., Angelo Carter, and Carter Cardile and three daughters Mary, Concetta, and Louisa. He and his wife were very active in the Emmanuel Church in Stamford and later he became a machinist as Machlett Labs. Some of his descendants still live in Stamford.[105]

In 1898, an article was titled "Italians are all right" because they were voting Republican. In 1906, a trolley jumped the tracks and Stamford residents praised the Italian laborer passengers who did all they could to save the women aboard from injury and to help after the accident.[106] During the depression, the mayor had a committee on unemployment relief, and one of the cases was seeking assistance for an Italian laborer, married with two children, who had been out of work for 4 months, and was three months in arrears in rent and needed fuel, food and clothing.[107] An article in 1919 about the Italian Institute is very complimentary towards Italians (even if a bit condescending): "The Italian people of Stamford number some of the very best citizens of the community. As a

---

[105] Stamford Advocate 11/21/1901, 1/10/1903, 10/11/1904, 10/19/1904, 1/8/1906, 1/13/1960, 4/7/1923, 4/19/1932, 1/19/1934.
[106] Stamford Advocate 2/27/1906.
[107] Stamford Advocate 1/19/1931.

class, they are thrifty, law-abiding citizens, quick to realize the benefits and responsibilities or citizenship or even residence in a land as the United States. Their virtues are so many and their faults so few that real Americans are glad to welcome them to Stamford and to count them among their friends."[108] Some of the Italians (doctors, politicians, etc.) were often featured in social reporting of the advocate (e.g. on vacation, celebrations, etc.).[109] Interactions with other ethnic groups was often cordial.

In 1904, the Advocate requested charitable assistance for the deserving case of Joseph Marucco, who lived at 277 West Main St. At the time Joseph was earning only $1 a day to feed five children (ranging in ages form ten to nine months), and his wife was in the hospital. Two months' rent ($14) was due. This is likely the "Maruke" family described in Chapter 6. This kindness was fruitful, because by the 1920s Joseph was back on his feet and owned his own home and would eventually have eight children, one a Stamford police officer another a boxing champion.[110]

Stamford citizens appreciated and respected Italians' desire for education, and as most Americans liked an underdog. Advocate reporting reflects this in some cases. Vito Giovanni Toglia graduated in 1907, despite obstacles. He was well respected at school and written about in the Advocate: "What can be accomplished by a youth who is in earnest in his desire to obtain an education was well illustrated this week, by Vito G. Toglia, one of the members of the High School graduating class. Toglia was a well-grown boy when he came from his native Italy...When he went to Columbia, for the purpose of taking a preliminary examination, it was found that his chief deficiency was in English idioms. But he not only acquired the language but gained an excellent knowledge of history and English literature. A poor boy, who had to begin in his teens to earn his own living, he entered the Franklin Street school, where he did the work of the eighth and ninth grades in one year. Entering high school, he undertook to do the four years' work in two years, and succeeded so well that he had a good average in the class...A boy of this sort sets an example worthy of commendation. He had ambition, brains and industry. He realized that, in order to achieve success in this country, it is necessary to obtain an education. He wasn't satisfied to drift along. He was a pusher. He saw the prize ahead, and he determined to win it. Handicaps did not deter him, and there was no such word as failure in his vocabulary. That he will make good use of his time in college, and that he will make his mark

---

[108] Stamford Advocate 4/1/1919.
[109] Stamford Advocate 5/16/1913, 5/22/1913.
[110] Stamford Advocate 6/15/1904 p 6.

later, may safely be predicted, in view of his accomplishments thus far." [111]
Vito wrote a piece for the Stamford High School Quarterly in 1907 about a
trip on foot to St. Michael's Cave Church, a sanctuary found within an ancient
natural cave in Monte Sant'Angelo, Italy on May 8th, the Feast of St. Michael.
Vito beautifully describes the natural scenery, the wildlife and domesticated
animals, and the country people encountered on the way. He also describes
the actual church within the cave, and the tale of a man and his mules saved
by St. Michael at the spot. It is obvious Vito is unapologetically proud of his
heritage and decided to share the beauty of his homeland with his classmates.[112]

Vito eventually went on to Harvard from 1908 to 1912. He wrote an
article for the school anniversary report that showed the true character of this
man. He assisted the non-English speaking mother of a young boy obtain
compensation for the death of her child on a construction site. In addition,
he exalts the ideals of truth, justice and fair play. He advocates for small business, and the workers displaced by mechanization. The following are ex-
cerpts:[113]

My first experience after graduation.
    In the summer of 1912, I went to teach at the Camp School, opened
by a philanthropic league, in Valhalla, during the construction of the Catskill
aqueduct. I had been about two months there, when a twelve-year-old boy
was killed on the works, and his mother, unable to make herself understood,
requested my help in ascertaining through whose fault the boy had lost his
life. The proof that it had not been the boy's fault made it possible for her
to get some compensation for her loss from the construction company. But
the feeling of satisfaction for my service in getting the truth did not last
long.
    Some time after that, I was invited to call at the League's office in New
York, to be told, having found it necessary to make some change in the
school program, they were compelled to dispense with my services. As this
was to go into effect two or three weeks later, they offered me two weeks'
vacation with pay. I could not help thinking that the change in the school
program was a mere excuse to hide the truth: the construction company,
which was perhaps contributing to the maintenance of the Camp School,
had made the request to send me away as undesirable, for having helped a
poor woman. Such an action left me wondering whether the League, avow-
edly philanthropic, expressed the teachers to enlighten the workers only on

---

[111] Ibid 6/29/1907 p 4.
[112] *Stamford High School Quarterly Review* 1907, Vol 4, No 4.
[113] Harvard College Class of 1912, Twenty-fifth Anniversary Report (dated June 1937).

their duties as citizens. I saw that it was useless to tell the courteous gentleman that to discharge me with such an excuse was unfair.

After the first experience
In the spring of the following year, I went to teach Italian in a New York secondary school. After obtaining the A.M. degree, I taught Italian at Columbia and at Barnard Colleges, where I remained till 1927. I spent the next two years at Bryn Mawr College as associate (assistant professor) of Italian; and from February 1930 to June 1931 at the College of William and Mary as associate professor of Spanish and Italian.

Life would be a good thing if we could live it according to the ideals of truth, justice and fair-play to our neighbor, and to struggle for them; a struggling life indeed, for without struggle there is no life; but the struggle should be such as fortifies the spirit, and not such as crushes it. But the harm begins when one, having secured for himself a place in the sun, uses his intelligence and his strength and his means to invade that of his neighbors and to suppress them, so that they may not unite and come back to push him away. Such desire has become a true mania, and, as a disease, it is causing incalculable harm, moral and economic, in our country. The maniac ought not to be left free.

I feel that the Government ought to represent the public and take an active part in disputes between capital and labor; and see to it the settlement of them be fair to all the three parties concerned. It ought to take a sympathetic attitude towards the small industries, commerce and crafts; and enact laws to protect them from economic strangulation.

The time saving devices that tend to displace great number of hands ought to be applied gradually in order not to increase the number of the unemployed. And the profit of such devices ought not to go only to the inventor or the owners of them, but be shared with the employees and with the public.

Those of my classmates who have become captains of industry or powerful bankers who control it, may smile at my desire to check the spread of evil in our tormented country; I hold that the true philanthropist is not only the one who gives generously to charitable institutions, but also the one who has kept at work as many men as possible and retributed them adequately; then employers and employees could contribute to maintain the high institutions of learning.

I think that the country ought to have an adequate army, navy and air force to safeguard its interests without the help of any one, and to dissuade the people across the Pacific from dreaming of expansion at our damage.

What I got from the Alma Mater has been a great stimulus in my life and it is still so: I look back at those years and think with gratitude of my teachers, especially of Prof. Grandgent, "Copey," Prof. Gerguson, and of one who was more than a teacher to me – Dr. Bernbalum.

I do not know how Harvard prepares her sons now. I wish the great Universities to lead the public and not to be led by it, but I wish Harvard to be the head of them all forever.

The following Italian Americans were among the first to graduate from Stamford High School, are highlighted in the yearbook: Vito Giovanni Toglia 1907, Joseph DeMino 1913, Charles Sessa 1914, Sanford Francis Palo 1915, Michael Antonio Cantillo 1916, Thomas Lionetti 1916, Walter S. Longo 1916, Elvira Theresa Paganetti 1916, Mary Carlucci 1917, Antoinette Carmela Genovese 1917, Raphael Lionetti 1917, Michael Luciano 1917, and Paul James Rosa 1918. It refreshing to read the words by their classmates describing them, who treat them on par with all students in the school.[114]

Another ally to Italians in Stamford, Sarah Francis Smith, known as the "Mother of Stamford's Adult Education program" was adored by by not only the Italian Colony, but all immigrant groups. She was put in charge of teaching English to immigrants, so that they could pass naturalization tests to become American citizens as part of the "Americanization" program. She was named director of the Stamford adult education program in 1926.

Ms. Smith then organized the Racial Council, to engage and obtain cooperation of the various immigrant communities toward adult education and Americanization. Ms. Smith new that they could open schools and have classes, but they needed buy in from leaders of the various immigrant groups to be allies in promoting the project. The original groups represented in the council were Greek, Hungarian, Russian, Jewish, Polish, Italian, Swedish and African American. Italians were more than willing to participate as it fit into their campaign to elevate the Italian Colony. In 1928, Joseph Carpinella was appointed to the committee. In 1929, Daniel Scalzi and his wife, and sister-in-law Mrs. John Scalzi joined the Racial Counsel. In 1930, the Racial Council sponsored a trip to Washington D.C. Only a few could attend, because of the extreme financial conditions brought about by the Depression. In 1930, Daniel Scalzi spoke about Italian activities in Stamford to the council. He indicated that there were about 12,000 Italians, of which 5,000 were adults, 2,000 were enrolled in elementary school, and 135 in high school. He also spoke about the work of the Italian Welfare League, the Italian Institute, and the Italian Business and Professional Men's Club in assisting in daily problems and promoting assimilation into American life by becoming citizens. He urged support of the Racial Council in promoting friendship among all nationalities, which in turn would make for the contentment and happiness of all members of the community. In 1930, Mrs. Elizabeth Maffucci (wife of

---

[114] *Stamford High School Quarterly Review* 1907 through 1918, Stamford History Center.

Alonzo Maffucci), Guido Pia, Gaetano Coppola also attended meetings. The meetings were held at the various ethnic organizations.

In 1931, Daniel Scalzi was elected president of the council and served as president through 1935. In support of education, he stated: "The evening classes offer not only the chance for learning more English, but the opportunity to meet other people, to enjoy the contacts of people interested in the same objectives, to get a new point of view and to gain courage for meeting the worries of "no job" and "want and distress." Also, in 1931, the council put on an exhibition called "America's Making," where the contributions of the various ethnic groups were displayed. The Italian committee for this exhibition included: Mrs. Elizabeth Maffucci (Alonzo's wife), Mrs. Peter Rosa, Mrs. Ann Caposella, Mrs. Matilda Lanzetto, Mrs. Margaret Sabia, L. Serafino, Dr. A. Sorgi, C. Russo, Guido Pia, and Daniel Scalzi. In 1933, Scalzi as president presided over the adoption of bylaws for the Racial Council. The purposes of the group were listed as: 1. To stimulate interest in the work of the Department of Adult Education for learning English, 2. To spread correct information in regard to the naturalization procedure and immigration matters, 3. Foster friendship among the different racial groups, and 4. To interpret their contribution to America.

In 1933, at a meeting held at the Italian Institute, entertainment included singing of "America" accompanied on the piano by Professor Vincenczo Di Vivo, Joseph Petrone, Miss Greco, and Joseph Congelosi played the accordion, and Carl Martini sang. Dr. Sette spoke briefly about the fact that the fathers and mothers of those prominent in professional life of Stamford in 1933, had given much in hard work, and had made many sacrifices during their struggle of assimilation. Those in charge of the evening included: Mrs. Alonzo Maffucci, Mrs. Peter Rosa, Mrs. Nicholas Cognetta, Mrs. Patsy Chiapetta, Mrs. Vincenzo Santasiero, Mrs. M. Sabia, Mrs. Daniel Scalzi, Mrs. Rose Caposella and Mrs. Joe Genovese. Daniel Scalzi released a statement in 1933 announcing the latest campaign for adult education: "The Racial Council, every individual member, has taken upon itself the fulfillment of its first purpose, its major purpose, the stimulation of enrollment in the Adult Education Classes. It is the duty of every foreign-born citizen to encourage his fellow national newcomer to be engaged. Aspiration to citizenship is their first goal and knowledge of the American language, its laws, its history, the duties of citizenship in the adopted land, can best be acquired in the evening school manned by a very competent staff of teachers. The Council is making an appeal for the biggest enrollment the evening school has ever had. The response will be the measure of gratitude given to the country." In October of 1933, Daniel in a speech to the Stamford Historical Society spoke on the contributions of Italians in Stamford and the work of the Racial Counsel. He referred to Columbus as a man of humble origin who accomplished what he did because he was a dreamer. He pointed out that like Columbus, the Italian immigrant left his home and friends inspired by the hope of better things in the new world. Further, the immigrant's first idea is to conform to the laws of the country; and become a citizen; and many of the immigrants are artisans and skilled workers and have helped in building up Stamford's industry and commerce. Noting that they are grateful to the land of their adoption and loyal to it.

As part of the Tercentenary celebration of Stamford, the Racial Council highlighted the histories of the various groups in Stamford. Obviously not written by an Italian as it is a bit condescending at times, and a little unaware of one of the main audiences of the history (the Italians themselves), the Italian history was as follows: "Sometime after 1890 the Italians began coming to Stamford, taking the unskilled positions. They now form 22 percent of the population or a total of 10,082. It is estimated that about one-half of the foreign-born Italians take out naturalization papers as soon as possible. Of the 10,000 members of the Italian colony, many are in small businesses of their own, these are fruit and vegetable stores, barbershops, shoe repair shops, and small contracting concerns. There is also a small professional group, the members of which act as leaders in the colony. The remaining numbers are employed in the various manufacturing and contracting concerns in Stamford which hire unskilled or semi-skilled labor. One-third of the Italian population is enrolled in either the public or parochial schools of Stamford. Recently, there have been formed Italo-American Girl Scout and Boy Scout troops. The number of Italian voters is 2,423. The Italian of Stamford has in the past contributed his brawn and good spirits to the progress of the town's industrial and social development. Today he has even a greater contribution. He realizes his shortcomings and is genuinely anxious to become an acceptable member of the community. The need for the Italian Institute came into being because of the rapid growth of the Italian population. They became more and more race conscious because they found their customs and mode of living different from those around them. Gradually, they withdrew into their own group."[115]

The majority of Italians lived unassuming lives, working and saving money in hopes that future generations would have a better life. Rick Castigilione describes his maternal grandfather Francesco Bria, a shoemaker who

[115] Stamford Advocate 9/18/1928, 9/26/1928, 1/22/1929, 1/24/1929, 3/12/1930, 11/6/1930, 3/5/1931, 6/4/1931, 9/10/1931, 11/13/1931,12/3/1931, 2/21/1933, 9/22/1933, 10/13/1933, 6/12/1935.

lived on the West Side on Waverly Place where they would all gather for Sunday dinner, as an old sage whose nickname was Solomono. He worked hard, tended a big garden, loved hot peppers he grew and a good glass of homemade wine made from grapes grown and harvested from the trellis in the backyard. Certainly, rings familiar with many readers I am sure. This was in contrast to his grandfather Castiglione, who was a ritornati because he did not enjoy his stay in America.

The road to Americanization for Italians in Stamford was not entirely smooth, but it was better than a life of starvation and no opportunity back in Italy. For many there was no turning back. Instead, they contended with bias among fellow citizens, local press and politicians, violence, at jobs with little opportunity to advance, low wages, dangerous working conditions, and often a life in the slums. The extent to which they were impacted by these obstacles varied among the diverse group. For the most part, their lives were hard; probably the extent to which is incomprehensible to our current sensibilities. However, they pressed on and experienced improvement over time, generation by generation, united in their efforts, to organize politically, rely on the safety net of their community, and demonstrate their worth to the other citizens of Stamford. Despite this difficulty, they were staunch patriots and for the most part upon recollection of their journey, they hardly complained; probably due to the positive disposition and inherent sense of gratitude that is so characteristic of Italians.

CHAPTER 3

Early Community Leaders

A chi vuole, non mancano modi.
(Where there is a will, there is a way.)

For Italians to be successful in their new home they would have to over-come overwhelming odds. Fortunately, there were a few Italians who became community leaders around the turn of the century who recognized impediments for Italians in Stamford, such as not being able to join unions, being relegated to worshiping in the basement of the Catholic Church, under-representation within the government, limited resources, bias, etc. They had the foresight to devise a plan to overcome these impediments and elevate the stature of Italians in Stamford. They came up with a plan to organize, unite, advocate, show that they were patriots for their adopted country, and embark on what I will call a branding strategy to improve the image of Italians, which they executed well. This plan relied on facets of the controversial "American-ization" program that was discussed earlier. As indicated, Italians picked which parts of the program they agreed with. The progress of the Italian Col-ony from their initial circumstances cannot be underestimated. Their success was so great that many Italian Americans living in the city today including me, can be grateful for the opportunities that have been opened for our an-cestors and in turn us.

This chapter will discuss in summary some of the early leaders and the next chapter will discuss some of the organizations they created to meet their goals. It is important to note that in addition to the time necessary to complete their regular jobs, which supported their families, they were extremely active in var-ious organizations and must have had boundless energy. Perhaps this energy just manifested as a necessity to achieve their ambitious goals. Certainly, it was luck that their different inspirations and motivations enabled their paths to cross so that Stamford history could unfold as it did. Some were inspired by religious faith, some by their personal experiences in their new home, others by their paternal instincts and wishes for a better future for their community, and some by the spirit of patriotism inspired by the recent unification of their former homeland.

One can really get a feel for their personalities through their writings. It is important to note these leaders have been highlighted in this chapter, but the work was carried out by contributions from all the members of the Italian Colony, including the laborers and apparel factory workers who persevered dangerous and arduous jobs because they wanted a better life for their families. The unity of all members of the Colony contributed to the great leap forward for Italians.

Shoemaker Pasquale DeCarlo's story is a classic story of best-laid plans. Reverend Pasquale DeCarlo was a Baptist minister who started the first Italian American organization in Stamford (Società di Mutuo Soccorso Fra Tommaso Campenella, a mutual aid society). He was also a founder of the Italo-American Educational Circle (an organization that allowed for educational discourse among Italian Americans). Both organizations were extremely important to Italians in Stamford and very influential in assisting and elevating their lives. These organizations are discussed more in Chapter 4. DeCarlo was born in Calitri, near Naples in 1863. Pasquale's father was a successful merchant, who mentored his son in his business and was proud to hear from friends that, "Pasquale could sell a man a straw hat in the cold weather." He came to America in 1885 (on the SS Britannia) and was married to Maddalene Capossela in the same year. He came to Stamford in 1892. In 1900, records show he rented a home at 4 Myrtle Avenue. At that time, they had five children, Mary A., Angelina, Lucie, Angelo, and Alphonso.[1] They eventually had eight children with only 6 surviving (including Josephine and Alphonsina; it appears that Alphonso died in 1901).[2] De Carlo owned two shoe stores in Stamford (one located at 168 Main Street above Palmer's Market).

Shortly after arriving in Stamford a seminal event occurred that would change the trajectory of Pasquale's and his family's life. He converted from Catholicism to the Baptist faith after meeting a childhood friend (at one time a priest) who prevailed upon him to read the Bible. After this chance meeting, he became divinely inspired to sacrifice any other plans he had for his life to respond to the call from God to become a minister. With this, he turned his attention to improving the lives of fellow Italians, including those in Stamford. He believed by uniting, they could better their lives through education, and mutual support.

He began a school for children in Stamford, hoping this would lead to access to their parents, for he was a Baptist missionary after all. As a missionary, he would have been sent into an area in order to promote the Baptist faith while providing services such as education, literacy, social justice, health care, and economic development to potential parishioners. At the turn of the century, this was classic "Americanization" protocol. Soon after, "Our Mission"

---

[1] 1900 US Census. "They Came by Ship," Mario Toglia, Xlibris Publishing, p 392.
[2] 1910 US Census.

was started. The Baptist Church licensed him as a missionary on September 30, 1895. He was ordained as a Baptist minister on December 7th, 1897 (the first Italian Baptist minister in the State of Connecticut).[3] He established the Associazone Missionaria Battista Italiana in 1899 in Stamford. He later joined the Congregational Church. There is more detail on this in Chapter 5. The reverend then moved on to preach in Detroit. DeCarlo then became an ordained Presbyterian minister and assumed the pastorate of a small mission outpost of the First Italian Presbyterian Church on Taylor Street in Chicago's largest Italian district. By the 1930's he had built the renamed church into the largest Protestant congregation serving Italians in Chicago and became a storied figure among the Italians of Chicago. Members of that church, said of him: "As a man of conviction, sincerity, earnestness and consecration, he is a true friend to little children; he has saved boys from becoming criminals; he has influenced, encouraged, and aided young people to obtain a better education; he has brought peace to many a father and mother through his counsel; and he strives to interpret Christ continuously to all people of all ages." An account of his performing the marriage of a Protestant and Catholic at a time when many thought such a marriage should not occur, appears in a book.[4] Another book describes how the reverend performed the funeral of Chicago mob boss Big Jim Colosimo after the Catholic Church refused to. Colosimo was later succeeded by Al Capone.[5] It appears that he was remarried to Lilla Pearson in 1919 in Chicago. He died and was buried in Skokie, IL in 1947 as a Presbyterian. His contributions to the elevation of the Italian community of Stamford were important, and it is obvious from his life's work and the admiration of his flock that many other Italian communities were made better as well.

THE MARKETING GENIUS

Barber Tony Palo was a man of many talents, who used these talents to elevate the Italian colony. Antonio Palo came from the same area in Italy and was born in Naples, Italy to Mr. and Mrs. Joseph Palo. There are inconsistent birth dates attributed to Mr. Palo depending on the source (either 1865, 1867, 1868, or according to the obituary 1849). He died in Stamford on August 8th, 1935. He was survived by his wife, Katherina (born in Denmark), a daughter Vera Hornez and sons Carelton and Sanford. His son Henry was wounded and declared 100% disabled in World War I. Antonio was a barber for 40

---

[3] Stamford Advocate 12/8/1897, Oak Park Oak Leaves, 8/13/1942 p. 32.
[4] City, Country, Family, Church A Story of St. John Presbyterian Institutional Church, printed in Chicago 1936, Building a Better Community, St. John Presbyterian Institutional Church, Relative Strangers: Italian Protestants in the Catholic World, Frank Cicero, pages 158, 201-203.
[5] *Mr. Capone, The Real and Complete Story of Al Capone*, Robert J. Schoenberg, p. 65.

years in Stamford. He was one of the original incorporators of the Italian Institute, serving as its vice president and president and prominent in other Italian organizations that assisted and elevated the lives of fellow Italians in Stamford. He immigrated to the U.S. in 1884 and came to Stamford in 1887. He operated the Palace Barbershop on Atlantic Street and retired from active business in 1929. He had lost a barbershop when a fire destroyed the Opera House building on Bedford.

Palo was a jack of all trades. There were some articles that he married individuals, as Justice of the Peace.[6] He was a real estate investor.[7] Tony was a court translator. He apparently did very well as he placed a "Wanted Ad" for an employee to take care of horses and to be generally useful about the house and place for his home on 55 Atlantic Street.[8] He also played musical instruments and was in a band.[9]

He was a proponent of barber unions (even for those who worked for him).[10] He was also a member of the Italian-American Political and Benevolent Club. Many of the organizations were present at a meeting at the Woodland Avenue School promoting educational endeavors hosted by Mrs. W.J. Blickensderfer where he gave a speech.[11] However, in 1914 he was suspended for 3 months because of his involvement in starting another political organization in the Third Ward.[12] This was probably the reason that at a meeting to discuss the Fourth of July celebrations that year, Mr. Louis Donatelli (another early leader) stated that if Anthony Palo remained on the committee a number of Italian Social Clubs would stay out of the parade."[13] He was an active member of The William McKinley Italian-American Republican Club and was on the committee for a fundraiser dance that was reported in The Advocate.[14] He even put together a fund for the benefit of a widow (Mrs. Di Barbiere).[15]

He was a Master of Marketing; it can only be imagined how far he could have gone if today's social media was available back then. This skill benefited not only him personally but the whole Italian Colony as well. He was able to influence the portrayal of Italian Americans in a positive light in the Stamford Advocate. For example, in 1903, he managed to get an article in The Advocate

[6] Stamford Advocate 5/25/1903, 11/4/1905.
[7] Stamford Advocate 4/15/1905.
[8] Stamford Advocate 7/6/1906.
[9] Stamford Advocate 12/3/1897.
[10] Stamford Advocate 11/4/1913.
[11] Stamford Advocate 3/25/1913.
[12] Stamford Advocate 8/17/1914.
[13] Stamford Advocate 6/6/1914.
[14] Stamford Advocate 10/31/1916, 9/28/1904.
[15] Stamford Advocate 12/04/1902.

about shaving the Governor of Connecticut, Abiram Chamberlain. "He inspected my shop quite carefully and gave me nice compliments on its appearance." The article goes on to detail that "Palo is quite the politician. He has been at the head of the Italian Republican Club ever since its organization and is supposed to control a considerable number of votes." The article also details that Rev. De Carlo took over the presidency, so Palo's aspirations were turning to the State Board of Barber Commissioner.[16] One article declares, "Friends of Antonio Palo are saying that he would be an excellent candidate for either town or city assessor on the Republican ticket next fall."[17] Although it would be years before Italians would receive support to run for citywide political office, he and others planted the seed that Italians were capable and worthy.

Ever interested in keeping his name in the public, he and his wife were often mentioned in "society" type articles while vacationing or visiting relatives in Norway and on his engagement to his wife.[18] This type of coverage was unusual for an Italian during this time period. There were also articles about illness (he was ill for 3 weeks due to influenza, etc.).[19] He was even mentioned as the peacemaker for the bride's parents when an eloping couple of 16 and 14 got married.[20] One article indicated that he was not related to the Palo on trial.[21] This had to do with a special police officer who accidentally shot a citizen at Woodside Park in 1903.[22] Likely, he did not want his marketing efforts to be sullied by this trial and took preemptive action.

In 1917, he expanded his offerings after selling his business, he began a business where he would go to customers' homes to cut hair, something that was new and all covered in the press. In another article, his barbershop is described as a model barber shop: "There was no new creation in devices and no new point in progress of barbershop, hygiene that he didn't adopt if it is good and there is always an air of cleanliness and fineness about his place that made it a favorite with high class of clientage."[23] Another article declares "Antonio Palo, in the former Opera House block, has introduced another new feature- a machine for scalp and face massage, run by electric power, and said to be wonderfully efficient. Give it a try."[24]

---

[16] Stamford Advocate 3/7/1903.
[17] Stamford Advocate 4/13/1904.
[18] Stamford Advocate 8/14/1903, 4/05/1894.
[19] Stamford Advocate 1/10/1905.
[20] Stamford Advocate 8/20/1903.
[21] Stamford Advocate 7/7/1905.
[22] Stamford Advocate 9/12/1903.
[23] Stamford Advocate 6/1/1917, 12/18/1912, 2/23/1912, 7/1/1897, 9/24/1903, 6/30/1904.
[24] Stamford Advocate 9/27/1905.

An amusing article from the Advocate that kept his name in front of the public was as follows: "Antonio Palo claims to possess the most ambitious hen in town. Yesterday it laid one of the biggest eggs seen in Stamford this season. Mrs. Palo broke it for the purpose of making an omelet and found inside the shell another egg about half the size, and perfectly formed. Mr. Palo thought that possibly Dr. Bigelow of Arcadia might like to see a proof of the extraordinary enterprise of his favorite fowl, and he brought it-the egg, or rather eggs, not the bird –to the office of the Advocate this morning."[25]

There was some bad publicity. He was arrested for an alleged attack on a young woman in his barbershop.[26] Apparently, tensions often ran high at the barbershop because he filed a complaint against Joseph Nardo who slapped him in his shop, but later dropped the charges.[27]

In 1895, he sued another Italian; a former employee, Cafaro, who then opened a grocery store on Canal Street and a barber shop on Pacific Street. Tony Palo had arranged to go into a partnership with Alberto Amendala of New York. Amendala had agreed and was about to pay for a half interest in the business. As he traveled with the funds to Stamford from New York on the steamer Sunny Side, he ran across Tony Cafaro who told Amendala he would be a fool if he paid all that money, because Palo was not doing enough business to make a partnership worth that much money. Upon hearing this, Amendala changed his mind. Palo sued Cafaro for slander.[28]

Mr. Palo's extraordinary promotion skills and desire to elevate his fellow Italians were a great asset to the colony.

THE SECRETARY GENERAL OF STAMFORD

Crescenzo Tamburri was fully dedicated to elevating the Italian colony and a champion for its causes. Crescenzo was born in Settefrati, he came to America in 1885 and then to Stamford in 1895. He was a barber with a shop in the Advocate Building in 1900. He was an officer of many Italian-American Societies, including Società Operaia, Sons of Italy, Società Campanella, Società Vittorio Emanuale, and the Italian Social and Political Club. He lived at 70 Pacific Street.[29] On his death in March of 1915, The *Advocate* reported that his was one of the largest funeral corteges ever seen in Stamford.[30] Mr. Tamburri was very industrious, in addition to his barber duties he offered

---

[25] Stamford Advocate 3/18/20.
[26] Stamford Advocate 3/15/1923.
[27] Stamford Advocate 5/8/1900.
[28] Stamford Advocate 12/5/1895.
[29] Stamford Advocate 2/25/1915.
[30] Stamford Advocate March 1, 1915.

Italian translation services and was a special officer. On August 13, 1900, he was assaulted while trying to break up a disturbance at a party.[31] He also frequently wrote letters or filled out legal papers for Italians.

He was a correspondent for the *Bridgeport "La Tribuana"* and caused a stir in 1907 with his displeasure with the blue laws and how it disproportionately impacted the working class. An article in the Advocate translated his article in English: "We have to go back to the time of the inquisition in Stamford, more than other cities, for the administration in power since last November has decreed that a workingman, after six days of hard labor, has no right on Sunday to drink a glass of beer. Woe to the proprietor of a saloon or the bartender who attempts to give a glass of beer on Sunday to a workingman. Those who give and those who receive are to be prosecuted as delinquents. But if you may drink as much as you want on Monday after 5 a.m. and if you may do the same until midnight of Saturday, why should it be a crime on Sunday? They will say that the law is the law, and it must be respected by all equally, but do the high-class people respect it? They are swimming in whiskey themselves, for there is not a provision of law to stop them. And you know, my country people, who they are, the same people who, at the time of the election were promising you everything in behalf of the working class: but when they got their positions they try to put you in jail, only because you have had the pleasure of tasting a glass of beer on Sunday. And this is not enough. Almost every saloon had music by phonographs. Do you not think it was an outrage to deprive the people of such innocent music? Who did that? The same patres conscripts who have their amusements in the clubs, in spite of the working class, whose guilt consists in fighting for their rights. What do you think of it?" Four months later four members of the staff of the paper were jailed for libel. Not backing down two months later another article by Crescenzo appeared: "Monday, October 7th, is the day of the annual town election. Be careful, because there are people who would like to drag you by the nose, as they have done in the past. I do not belong to any party. I am independent and friendly with all of them. Monday is nearby. Before you go to the ballot box, think of it and see whether the men on the ballot are capable. See if the candidates for office have done their duty, or have tried to better the condition of the working-class... No one of our countrymen should neglect to vote next Monday, and vote for those whom they believe will advance our interests in the town of Stamford." The communication was signed by Crescenzo Tamburri, clever with both razor and pen,

---

[31] Stamford Advocate 9/1/1900.

and a student of local politics.[32] In 1908, he was a proponent of recognizing Columbus Day in Connecticut.[33]

In another article, he offered criticism of the Common Council for planning to spend $200,000 on a public park, when the money could have been spent on other needs of the city including poorly conditioned roads like Pacific, Spruce, Cottage, and Canal Streets (Italian enclave areas): "If you don't want to be struck by telegraph-poles, you must go with a lantern in your hand, and there is always the danger of being stuck in deep mud. But these things the Councilmen do not care for; they want a park, in order to have a cozy place for taking things easy. Why does not the Council do something about the present parks and keep them in good order? Why not provide benches, where the poor mother, with her children, can enjoy the summer and get fresh air?... The new Town Hall, which cost several hundred thousand dollars. Just look at that building and give your opinion. I think it cost too much and does not satisfy the public at all. I had a chat with a prominent politician, and referring to the building, he said the committee was a little bit influenced. By whom? Another politician told me that the Town Hall, at its completion, will entail an expense approximating the startling sum of $500,000. And the worst of it is that the steps are more appropriate to a cellar than a public structure. With Stamford going on this way, we shall never fulfill the duty of a modern city that shall be the pride of its inhabitants."[34]

He passed away on February 24, 1915, and was survived by his second wife, two daughters in Italy, and four children in the U.S., as well as three stepdaughters.[35] In his eulogy, it was noted "Crescenzo Tamburri made the town better because he lived in it; he made these societies better and stronger because he worked in them, and he has left a pleasant memory with all who knew him."[36] His presence in all these beneficial organizations earned him the moniker "Secretary General of the Colony of Stamford."[37] One can tell from what was written about him he was a dependable, pleasant, and respected man who gave so much to and stood up for the Italian community of Stamford. Men of this caliber are a rare commodity.

---

[32] Stamford Advocate 4/5/1907, 8/27/1907, 10/4/1907.
[33] Stamford Advocate 8/28/1908.
[34] Stamford Advocate 2/7/1907 p 2.
[35] Stamford Advocate 2/25/1915.
[36] Stamford Advocate 2/25/1915
[37] "Twenty-Five Years of Progress 1910-1935," The Italian Institute Inc. Stamford, CT.

Vito Pittaro an intelligent, raw, unapologetic, and outspoken advocate for the Italian colony made an enormous impact. Mr. Pittaro was the editor of the first Italian newspaper in Connecticut, author, teacher, banker, and a leader of the Italian community in Stamford having moved there in 1894. He was born in San Fele, Potenza, Italy and studied law at the University of Naples. He came to the U.S. at the age of 26. After residing in New York and Providence for 5 years, he moved to Stamford.[38] He was another founder of the Italian Social Institute (later became the Italian Center) and historian of the Italians in Stamford. He also wrote some poetry, plays and a book (*La Torre di Babele, The Immigration Bond, Nel Paradiso dei Vecchi Membri della Società Operaia,* and *Nel Coma d'un Secolo, Romanzo Storico, Politico e Sociale*).

At one time, he wrote a column in Italian for the Stamford Advocate, called "Della Colonia Italiana (About the Italian Colony); articles that were written in Italian side-by-side with an English translation. The articles noted events by the Italo-American Education Circle, activities of the Società Vittorio Emanuale II, and other happenings in town. Mr. Pittaro was very frank with some of his comments: speaking about Italian language newspapers, he states "and I think they are enough, principally the weekly papers, which most of the time print things which have not a bit of thought for the readers. But every little helps, anyway." Perhaps this is why with Pietro P. Vescio he founded *La Tribuna* in Stamford. In speaking about the Education Circle, he states: "The institution was organized four years ago and had to struggle for its life. Among the members are the most intelligent people of the Italian colony, who through self-denial, defrayed the expenses, but incurred the jealousy of some enemies of the common welfare." In an article criticizing politicians and empty promises to Italians in his "no holds barred" style he writes: "The Italians know that, after the election, the windows are shut, and the protection, the promises, the handshakes, and the "good mornings" are not to be used any more, and they are overlooked as a dog by a cat. And yet we find someone who in his ingenuity, believes that if he is favored in his work, which he can get only if he is skillful and has a pair of strong arms, it is to be preferred to all the politics in the world."[39]

One of his columns is important because it demonstrates the main purpose behind the formation of societies and Italian organizations; that is to elevate the Italian people economically, socially, and intellectually in actuality but also in the minds of the population of Stamford. This was a marketing campaign that was planned, executed by, and for Italians and was ultimately

---

[38] Stamford Advocate 9/17/51.
[39] Stamford Advocate 11/14/1903, 10/1/1903, 10/10/1903.

successful. He offers proof by indicating that Italians in Stamford owned between $125,000 and $150,000 of real estate in 1903, while three- or four-years prior there were few properties owned by Italians (even though the population was relatively the same). He argues for better permanent jobs to improve the city and that the social, cultural, and political organizations and trade unions have done much to improve not only Italians but also the city. Again, he pulls no punches: "I would like to say something about the Board of Trade of this city, but the editors of this paper let me understand they want more facts than criticism, hence I am silent."[40]

In 1902, Mr. Pittaro chaired a meeting to start a branch of the International Labor Union.[41] One object of the union was to increase pay to $2 per day.[42] This was mostly Italians, but this benefited all laborers in Stamford and the surrounding area, and many then and now owe a debt of gratitude to him. Personally, I am thankful because my father was able to join the union when he moved to Stamford.

In Mr. Pittaro's background article, part of the Italian Center's 25th-anniversary publication, he discusses the reasons for starting the Italian Institute (which later became the Italian Center). One reason was to elevate the perception of Italians in the eyes of the Stamford population. He specifically calls out the slur used during that time (beginning in the 1890s) to refer to Italians as "Guinea", which was likely first used because of the dark complexion of many of the Italians who immigrated to America from southern Italy.[43] Guinea is a country in West Africa.

As noted previously, the scope and breadth of discrimination against Italians is undeniable, and it was in this atmosphere of physical violence, overt discriminatory pronouncements by politicians and journalists, that Mr. Pittaro and other Italian-American leaders in Stamford dug deep to focus their energies in a positive manner to elevate Italians in Stamford and combat this bias. Pittaro did so without attempting to sugar coat the facts. Sometimes it is necessary to let others feel uncomfortable in order to get results.

THE COLONY STALWART, MENTOR

Leo Donatelli was an exceptional leader who deservingly commanded respect by his deeds. Mr. Donatelli was born in Roseto Valfortore, Foggia, Italy in 1859, and emigrated from Italy in 1883. He came to Stamford in 1894 to work as a subcontractor to J. K. Ryan (supplying labor) for the New York, New

---

[40] Stamford Advocate 11/7/1903.
[41] Stamford Advocate 6/19/1902.
[42] Stamford Advocate 6/26/1902.
[43] "Twenty-Five Years of Progress 1910-1935," The Italian Institute Inc. Stamford, CT.

Haven, & Hartford Railroad, when the four-track system was installed. He worked in West Virginia prior to this in a similar occupation. Records indicate he lived at 388 Pacific Street. Starting in 1897, he served as the official interpreter in the city and superior court. Politicians who wanted him to exert his influence in the Italian Colony often sought him out.

There were seminal events that occurred in his life, which thrust him into the forefront of the Italian-American community in Stamford. He acquired fame when he and Policeman William Nevins brought about the arrest of Giuseppe Fuda and Nicodema Imposino for the murder of Imposino's wife. Later his work led to the capture and conviction of persons involved with another infamous local crime. It was reported that "with the cooperation of local police, he went to West Virginia where he assumed the guise of a miner, entered the coal mine and in the bowels of the earth, located and caused the arrest of the suspect, Domenico Bove for the murder of his brother-in-law, Giuseppe Bergamo in Noroton." Bove was later imprisoned and served 15 years in prison, after being allowed to plead guilty to manslaughter after his trial began. Mrs. Bergamo, his sister, and Pasquale Marzano, her lover, the others concerned in the murder plot fled to Italy where they were imprisoned. Donatelli was also appointed as a detective.[44] Later in the history of the formation of the Italian Institute, we will see another important life event that propelled him to be regarded by many as the leader of Italians in Stamford.

He was a member of the following organizations: Società Italo-Americana Corte Umberto I., Foresters of America, Italian and Social Political Club (of which he was president), Società Vittorio Emanuele, Società Aviglianese, Società San Manghese, Società Calabrese, Società Pugliese, and the Italian Federation. In 1906, a meeting took place of approximately 150 Italians to nominate, if possible, Leo Donatelli as a councilman of the third ward.[45] This is significant as it appears to be among the first times Italians felt confident enough to even propose an Italian run in local politics. It is not possible to overestimate the respect, and esteem that fellow Italians had for Donatelli, and the extent to which he offered counsel, assistance, and whatever he could to the people of the Italian Colony. In 1910, he spoke at the Universalist Church of Stamford to debate with Bible class Temperance proponents, where he argued for a middle ground between drunkenness and abuse of liquor and total prohibition. He indicated, "Drinking with moderation does no harm. I call whiskey and gin, poison. These liquors as manufactured in this country are far from pure. In

---

[44] Hartford Courant 3/23/1914, *Stamford Advocate* Tercentenary Edition Town of Stamford, CT 1641 – 1941 Supplement of the Stamford Advocate, Saturday, June 7, 1941 p 144, Stamford advocate 3/9/1914, p 1.
[45] Stamford Advocate 8/6/1906.

Europe, where wine and beer are the beverages mostly used, the quality is far better, and the liquors, instead of hurting the system, aid it. I am not here to praise my own business (he was a liquor dealer), but I would not sell to intoxicated people. I would call it a good thing if a law was passed prohibiting treating (because men spend their hard-earned pay on friends, while his wife and children are suffering at home for the necessities of life). I would like to see whiskey and brandy done away with, and I believe that women, especially disreputable women should be barred from saloons." The Bible class by unanimous vote, thanked Donatelli for appearing and presenting his side.[46]

He died in March of 1914 after an operation while being treated for mastitis at 55.[47] His body was sent to North Bergen, NJ where it was cremated and buried. His funeral on March 25th, 1914 was reported on by The Advocate: The pallbearers were Dr. J.J. Costanzo, Dr. A. S. Sorgi, Sergeant William Nevins, Anthony Geronimo, Albert Philips, Joseph Itri, Fredrick Berg and Joseph S. Fairbanks. In his eulogy at Masonic Hall, Albert Philips of the Elks (Stamford Lodge No. 899), said: "Strong, vigorous, self-reliant, and aggressive, he made his own way, buffeted every storm, overcame many obstacles and arrived at a place of power, influence, honor, esteem and respect in the community and the state in which he lived. A good name is rather to be chosen than great riches. It makes secure respectability and credit during life. It ensures the admiration of posterity after death. A man's wife and family, proud of his standing, achievements, and kindly deeds, while he lives can rejoice after his death in the record he has made and the fame he left to shed luster on his name and theirs. Such a name did Leo Donatelli well earn. He was the friend and adviser of the poor, and only time will reveal his benefactions to that class. To the struggling boy who desired an education, his means were largely employed. To the industrious and ambitious young man, he gave a helping hand. And how well do I know. To his countrymen, he was a cherished adviser and leader; to the community and the State an upright and honest fearless, law-abiding, law-enforcing and public-serving citizen…. He was a friend that you could count on at all times, and under all circumstances; he was bold and aggressive in his advocacy of what he conceived to be right, true and loyal to his friends, and to the cause he espoused….To him happiness was the only good, reason the only charity, justice the only worship, humanity the only religion, and love the only peace….I never knew a man for whom I had higher regard. If he had sorrows and troubles, he never allowed them to becloud the lives of others. Wherever he went, he scattered sunshine, and his presence dispelled cares. We ask ourselves, why is it that

---

[46] Stamford Advocate 5/9/1910 p 2.
[47] Hartford Courant 3/23/1914.

this splendid, effective, energetic, conscientious personality, so surcharged with conviction of duty, was so soon cut off. The answer comes back that man's life is not to be counted in years; it is not the days that we live, but rather the work that we do that makes the test of a man's life. It is not an extensive life that counts, but an intensive living, and I am certain that he will bring recognition in his community by a life well spent when measured by what he accomplished."

It was reported that on the day of his funeral, "the procession had at least 1,000 men in line and all over town, Italian folk left their ordinary occupations to pay the last tribute to the man who was, for many years, their recognized leader, socially, politically, and otherwise." Additionally, the flag at Central Park (now Veterans Memorial Park) in Stamford was at half-mast in acknowledgment of his death.[48] Later in Chapter 7, there is an eloquent editorial by a young future leader Attorney Frank Rich that speaks to Donatelli's impact and leadership. Donatelli was a leader in the true sense of the word, and an example not only for his contemporaries but also for leaders today.

IMPASSIONED BY CIRCUMSTANCES

Lesser men would let mistreatment and obstacles prevent them from reaching their potential. Arcangelo Cantore was not one of them. Mr. Cantore, one of the early leaders held many jobs during his time in Stamford. Born in 1877, he was a barber on the East Side (his barbershop was on the corner of Elm and Myrtle Avenue) and lived at 62 Pacific Street, and at the time of his death at 10 Gay Street (a street which no longer exists because it currently lies upon the grounds of the Stamford Mall).[49] He died from a stroke at 44, in the doorway of his home, as he was going out for a walk with his father Deciseo Cantore. He left a wife and four children.[50] He accomplished so much in his short life, who knows how much more could have been accomplished.

He also sold insurance.[51] He was naturalized on September 24, 1901.[52] An incident that occurred early on in his time in Stamford likely influenced and inspired his work in the Italian-American community as a leader. He was fined $5 for slapping Andrew Chute who lived at the same address. Chute indicated in court proceedings that Cantore had issues with him because Chute had made complaints about the Cantore family to the landlord. Cantore indicated the reason for the confrontation was that Chute insulted his

[48] Stamford Advocate 3/25/1914, 3/24/1914 p 6.
[49] Stamford Advocate 1/10/1907,10/21/1907, 5/20/1908, 4/24/1920.
[50] Stamford Advocate 4/24/1920.
[51] Stamford Advocate 11/6/1916.
[52] Connecticut US Naturalization Records

wife many times, making faces, grunting at her, spitting on her, and calling her "guinea." He indicated he confronted Chute about this, and he became angry. Cantore admitted losing his temper and slapping Chute.[53] Of note is that in the article Cantore is described as: "wears his hair pompadour, and altogether is a formidable-looking man when he is excited or angered." The article does not express any opinion on the appearance of Chute. This is clearly an example of the mistreatment of Italians in reporting, based on their ethnicity. It would be highly unlikely for Cantore, his family, and other witnesses to bring up this prejudice and discriminatory treatment in an environment where they were seen as second class if it did not actually occur and where they knew that the testimony of one Anglo-Saxon could outweigh the testimony of many Italian Americans. It is unfortunate as well to be portrayed as he was, by the author of the Advocate article, but it gives insight into what Italians were dealing with during that time period.

Cantore should be admired for not letting this break him and for focusing his energies in a positive direction. Instead, this seminal event thrust Arcangelo, to work on education, obtaining an authority position within Stamford impacting the diversity of power in the city that took into account the Italians' unique point of view, and working to elevate the stature of his fellow Italian Americans. Many others may have or did choose a different direction in response in the face of this unfair system. He worked to become a special police officer by mayoral appointment. The Council first refused to confirm his post and only two days later approved the appointment after some controversy.[54] At that time, some citizens were empowered as police officers to help with policing their communities. Residents of the same ethnic group were employed to interact with their cultural group.

This likely inspired him to engage in politics and he was an honorary president of the Italo-American Progressive Club, vice president of the McKinley Italo-American Republican Club, was on the executive committee of the Citizens League, and a member of the Italian Democratic Club.[55] He was endorsed for grand juror by the Ital-American Political and Benevolent Club in 1910.[56] However, he received the lowest amount of votes (208).[57] He was on the Democratic ticket for Constable in 1914, and then received 1604 votes and ran for sheriff in 1916.[58] He was elected constable finally and

---

[53] Stamford Advocate 10/21/1907.
[54] Stamford Advocate 7/25/1911, 1/4/1911, 1/6/1911, 7/15/1913.
[55] Stamford Advocate 1/23/1904,12/18/19061/15/1909,2/23/1909, 10/2/1916.
[56] Stamford Advocate 7/6/1910, 10/14/1910.
[57] Stamford Advocate 11/9/1910.
[58] Stamford Advocate 9/29/1914,10/14/1914, 10/5/1914, 10/14/1916.

served as constable for several terms before dying of a stroke at 44 in 1920. He was survived by his parents, wife, and four children.[59] His legacy was not only his family but a great deal of contributions to the well-being and stature of all Italian Americans in Stamford all accomplished in a short lifespan.

Cantore's grandson, Michael Cantore, Esq. recounts how his grandfather's early death impacted the family. His uncle, to make money became a bootlegger to pay for his brother's (Michael's father's) schooling. This was only for a short time, and Michael's father had to work hard to pay for the rest of his schooling. This was an example of truancy, in this case, triggered by the loss of a father figure for which the Community Chest study described in Chapter 2 was commissioned to provide solutions.

He also led in elevating his fellow compatriots. Courageously joining in the petition to save the life of Pasquale Esposito (discussed previously in Chapter 2).[60] At a dinner for the Italian Band of Stamford, he gave a speech, which The Advocate reported garnered the most enthusiasm of any other, where he showed the benefits of adopting many American customs. He spoke of the friendship shown Italians by some Americans and called attention to the Esposito case where an American lady saved the young boy's life (so significant coming from him the victim of prejudice not only by native-born citizens but by the courts of his adopted land).[61] He was president of the Campanella Society (described in Chapter 4).[62] He became Sargent of arms for the Sons of Italy in 1915.[63] Quite the life journey from a small town in Italy to cutting hair, to making important contributions in his adopted land. The source of much inspiration to others and a reminder to all that life is fleeting and that we need to make every minute count.

OTHERS ROUNDING OUT THE TEAM

Luckily, for the Stamford Colony, the Team's bench was deep. There were many Italians dedicated to elevating the colony and making Stamford a better place for all. Gennaro Passero was active in the Educational Circle and even performed as an actor in their productions.[64] He was treasurer of the William McKinley Italian Republican Club and served on the committee to bring about the nomination of Leo Donatelli to councilmen of the third

---

[59] Stamford Advocate 4/24/1920.
[60] Stamford Advocate 3/17/1908.
[61] Stamford Advocate 12/10/1909.
[62] Stamford Advocate 12/09/1909.
[63] Stamford Advocate 1/11/1915.
[64] Stamford Advocate 5/2/1901, 2/17/1903.

ward.[65] Another early Italian leader to enter the political stage, later he was nominated as "Grand Juror" for the Republican party in 1907, and again in 1908 when he came in third with 1,993 votes.[66] Gennaro was also director of the Stella D'Italia Brass Band.[67] He was named as a "special police" in 1908 and arrested someone in those duties for disorderly conduct.[68] Mr. Passero was a trustee for the Court Conte di Torino Foresters of America and secretary of the Italian Social Institute.[69] He was implicated by Tony Palo in the disagreement mentioned above about starting another political party in the third ward.[70] He was active in the Sons of Italy and was on the committee to celebrate Columbus in 1917.[71] He participated in the Connecticut Chamber of Commerce exhibit "Own Your Own Home Exposition" whose purpose was to market Stamford and attract New Yorkers to move to Connecticut.[72]

The Benevolent Societies described in the next chapter for the most part had a physician associated with the society. Dr. James J. Costanzo of 15 Broad Street and Dr. A. S. Sorgi of 44 St. John's Place were elected to the office of physician in practically all of the Italian societies. The list included: Tommaso Campanella Mutual Benefit Society, Vittorio Emmanuele II, Society Aviglianese, Loggia Operaia, No. 159 OFFI, Society Pugliese, Society Calabrese, Society Cosentina, Court Conte di Torino, F. of A. No. 178, and the Italian-American Political Club. There is more on Dr. Costanzo later in Chapter 7.[73]

Dr. Sorgi was active in the Italian Center and one of the founders of the Italian Institute. He was supreme delegate for the Order of the Sons of Italy and was a member of the Medical Society of New York, and Vittorio Emmanuale Society of Stamford, and was instrumental in the appeal to save Pasquale Esposito from the death penalty. During World War I, he was the president of the Italian section of the Red Cross. His wife was Anna, and he had four children, Mrs. Marie Kenny, Marjorie Sorgi, John C., and Len Sorgi. He was born in Palermo, Italy. Dr. Sorgi came out with a line of medical products approved by the Patent and Medical Departments at Washington, D.C. that were manufactured in Stamford by the National Chemical Corporation with a laboratory at 140 Greyrock Place. The products were Dr. Sorgi's Health Tonic, for general debility, depression and exhaustion, Man-I-Tu, a hair tonic, which purported

---

[65] Stamford Advocate 5/21/1903, 8/6/1906.
[66] Stamford Advocate 9/30/1907, 10/6/1908, 10/8/1907.
[67] Stamford Advocate 1/10/1908.
[68] Stamford Advocate 12/15/1908, 10/15/1910.
[69] Stamford Advocate 1/17/1914, 2/18/1914.
[70] Stamford Advocate 8/17/1914.
[71] Stamford Advocate 10/12/1917, 10/13/1917, 10/15/1917.
[72] Stamford Advocate 3/10/1925 4/22/1925.
[73] Stamford Advocate 1/8/1914.

to remove dandruff, preserve, and restore the hair, and Rheu-ma-Taint, a liniment that gave relief to sufferers of rheumatism, lumbago and stiffness. However, the corporation was soon dissolved because of troubles of securing ingredients used in the manufacturing of the products.

Unfortunately, toward the end of his life, the State Attorney General of Connecticut, Warren Burroughs served Dr. Sorgi with an order to show cause not to revoke his medical license after 25 years of practicing medicine in the state and despite passing state medical exams. The State contended that the Italian credentials were not proper and that an investigation conducted claimed that the diploma from the College of Palermo was not authentic and in fact belonged to someone else. The investigation started because of an irregularity in the name on the certificate. Dr. Sorgi's first name on the certificate was Antonio, and not Antonius (on the Italian credentials). It was also alleged that Dr. Sorgi practiced medicine under the name Sorgi Triesi in Meriden and Waterbury, and an attempt was made to place evidence into the case that showed a conviction in 1900 of practicing without a license in Brooklyn, NY. This was objected to by Attorney Frank Rich. In repudiation of the testimony on the different name, Dr. Sorgi indicated that Priesi was a relative of his who worked with him, for this reason, the plate outside the door boor both their names, "Sorgi Priesi." Sorgi collapsed in court while under cross-examination. The Dr. replied to a question in the hospital "I will go to court this afternoon, even if I have to be carried in on a stretcher." Unfortunately, Dr. Sorgi died on January 18, 1934, at the age of 63, while in the hospital following his collapse. His attorney F. B. Hickey filed a motion for vindication, in Superior Court claiming the State harassed the physician for ten years on insufficient evidence, stating: "It was one of the most heartrending cases in my experience. To see that old man fighting in court, with a strength that was supernatural in the few days before his death, was enough to move a heart of stone. I know that he would want me to continue this fight to clear his name, not only for the sake of his children but also because his name and lineage were a source of great pride to him."[74]

Joseph DeVito was born on February 12, 1875, in Salerno, Italy. He was an active member of the Italian Institute, in the Republican Club, and Foresters. His occupation was barber starting in 1889 on Pacific Street, and West Main Street, serving as a delegate for Stamford Local No. 5, to the State convention of the Master Barbers Protective Association. He also was an estate administrator. In 1903, he was made temporary chairman of the Italian Democrat Club and stated: "For the past two or three years the Republican Italians

---

[74] Stamford Advocate 5/14/1921, 5/28/1921, 8/6/1921, 10/16/1931, 10/31/1931, 12/23/1931, 6/3/1933, 6/9/1933, 12/5/1033, 12/6/1933, 12/21/1933, 12/22/1933, 12/29/1933, 1/18/1934.

have been saying they had us in the hole. They got me mad and just to show them what we could do, nine other men and I got together and called a meeting to form a club. From what I hear, it seems as if we were going to have most of the Italians with us. People who think that all the naturalized Italians are Republicans make a big mistake. Many of them are socialists, and a big percentage are Democrats." Later the club changed its name to the Thomas Jefferson Democratic Club. He ran for Justice of the Peace. In 1906, he was part of the committee to nominate Lelio Donatelli as councilman of the Third Ward. In 1914, he ran for grand juror.[75]

Mrs. Cecelia Blickensderfer, though not Italian, as discussed previously was a significant help to the Italian-American community in Stamford. From 1840 until World War I, many women, especially elite- and middle-class women, advocated for various reform efforts including the abolition of the death penalty. Her position in society allowed her to become a "public mother." Claiming women's perceived moral superiority, "public mothers" crossed class boundaries, working to provide for those who did not have the means or support to rally for reform on their own.[76]

Rose Russo Caccavello was born on May 29, 1895, in Bovino, Foggia, Italy. She owned and operated the Paradise Grill on Camp Avenue with her husband Frank Caccavello. During the 1920s, under the direction of Sarah Smith, who organized adult education in Stamford, she helped Italian immigrants who came to her home in Springdale to study for their citizenship and organized visits to the White House during the Coolidge administration.[77]

Guiseppe Maffei was born on December 15th, 1878, in Avellino, Italy. He was a barber and owned half of a meat and grocery business at 142 Pacific Street, which he later sold to Ciriaco Loprione (his partner). He was an active member of the Italian Institute, barbers' union, Eagles, and the Italian-American Republican Club. He also took part in theater and the Società Operaia.[78]

Joseph Colucci was born in Bari, Italy on August 16, 1879. He was a city employee providing Italian interpreter services. He was also very active in many organizations including the Italian American Political and Benevolent Club, Società di Mutuo Soccorso Fra Tommaso Campanella. He served during WWI. He lived at 466 Fairfield Ave. In 1910, he ran in the Democratic primary for councilman and was the only Italian name listed in the second ward. He seems

75 Stamford Advocate 1/27/1903, 12/30/1903, 6/27/1904, 10/15/1904, 10/25/1904, 8/6/1906, 2/16/1907, 10/6/1914, 9/19/1916, 10/7/1927, 2/12/1955, 7/12/1957, 7/13/1957.
76 Crumpton, Emily M., "Murder Becomes Her: Media Representations of Murderous Women in America from 1890-1920" (2017). All Graduate Theses and Dissertations. 6634.
77 Stamford Advocate 6/8/1984
78 Stamford Advocate 9/21/1912, 5/13/1922, 5/12/1933, 10/21/1933, 9/4/1936, 6/24/1909.

to have turned around from earlier life where he was in trouble a few times. His story demonstrates to all that mistakes and bad choices do not define us entirely, and that change and evolution are always possible. In 1899, he was arrested at 19 years old for assault on a co-worker at Yale and Towne Works. His story was that walking home the co-worker called him a "guinea" and challenged him to a fight. The co-worker indicated that Colucci called him a "dummy" and threatened to knock a gold front tooth down his throat, at the same time slapping his face. The co-worker's story was corroborated by two witnesses. Colucci originally appealed the case and subsequently changed his mind and paid the fine. Later he was arrested for operating a gambling establishment. The article states "Mr. Colucci is not an anarchist, but anarchists do things very like that, they deliberately and knowingly do things forbidden by the law of the land, something we are all bound to respect, whether we like the law or not." He was also responsible for a good deed in his youth: A commuter leaped off the train in Stamford and fell directly in front of the car wheels on the rear truck. Joseph and a friend at risk to themselves, pulled him out of danger, just before he would have been run over. He later got into a legitimate business and opened up a saloon, and later tailoring. Joseph later became a deputy sheriff, court interpreter, and then a candidate for justice of the peace.[79]

Rosario Martino was born on October 1, 1876, in San Mango Sul Calore, Italy. He worked as a tailor and lived at 52 Stillwater Ave. He was elected grand juror in 1910 and was active in Republican politics. He was a member of the Knights of Columbus, Holy Name Society, St. Theodore Martyr Society (he was one of the original founders), and Società di Mutuo Soccorso Fra Tommaso Campanella. He was instrumental in raising funds for the Italian Institute and was one of its organizers. He was married to Rosina Carpinella. Rosario was a founder and senior trustee of Sacred Heart Church and an officer of the Sacred Heart Holy Name Society. He participated as an actor in theatrical events given by the various societies.[80]

Gaetano Maddaloni was born on January 12, 1874, in Isernia, Italy. He apprenticed with a tailor in Isernia and at the age of eight came to America in 1897. He came to Stamford in 1902 and opened his tailor shop at the corner of Pacific and Main Sts. He opened a men's clothing shop in 1924, and operated G. Maddaloni's Men's Shop on Bedford St. until 1958. He was one of the pioneers of the Italian Colony in Stamford and helped found the Italian Insti-

---

[79] Stamford Advocate 3/20/1940, 7/6/1928, 1/6/1916, 4/29/1899, 3/10/1903, 2/23/1907, 3/10/1903, 8/2/1907, 8/17/1910, 10/11/1910, 3/7/1912, 10/15/1912, 1/6/1916, 7/6/1928.
[80] Stamford Advocate 10/19/1939, 10/20/1939, 7/20/1939, 8/31/1936, 6/29/1936, 1/11/1936, 7/1/1922, 8/30/1920, 4/7/1913, 10/4/1910, 9/28/1910.

tute, Loggia Operaia, Order of the Sons of Italy, and the Italian-American Historical Society. He was treasurer for the Italian-American Educational Circle and signed the petition to save Pasquale Esposito's life.[81]

Pasquale Fortunato was very active in the Italian Institute, and other Italian organizations including the Court Umberto, Foresters, Sons of Italy, Eagles, and signed the petition to save Pasquale Esposito's life.[82]

Theodore Ottaviano was born in February 1873 in San Mango Sul Calore, Italy. While in Stamford, he was a foreman of the Stamford Department of Service. He was a member of San Teodor Martire Society. Theodore also signed the petition to save Pasquale Esposito's life.[83]

M. A. Toglia (sometimes referred to as Michael Antonio Toglia, Miguel Antonio Toglia, or Michele Toglia, depending on the source). Michele also signed the petition to save Pasquale Esposito's life. Michele lived at various addresses in Stamford including, Pacific St. and, 114 West Avenue. Michael worked at for time as Yale and Towne. He immigrated at forty-five from Buenos Aires in 1902 aboard the Coleridge, his occupation was listed at blacksmith. He became a citizen in 1905. It appears Michele would have been related to Vito G. and Gaetano Toglia because he lived at the same address for a time. He eventually relocated to New Rochelle.[84]

Quintino Vetriolo was born in Sala Stellese, a small village several miles from Biella, Italy in 1864. He was an orphan who was reared by the Artino family. At thirteen, he was working in Torino as a bricklayer. In Torino, he received spiritual guidance from the Salesian Fathers under Don Bosco. Saint John Bosco was an Italian Roman Catholic priest and educator, who while visiting prisons, became disturbed to see the number of young boys occupying the cells. He was determined to prevent more boys from suffering the same fate, and so he set up a mission, to educate and serve these young people. Bosco developed a teaching method based on love rather than punishment that consisted of three pillars: reason, religion, and loving-kindness. After a few years in France, Quintino eventually moved to Stamford and lived at 73 Fairfield Avenue. He met Fortunato Meda while working and was introduced to his brother Albino Meda. Fortunato returned to Italy and Quintino became a partner of Albino in his grocery and liquor business. In 1897, Mr. Drago a sales representative introduced Quintino to a woman from New York City, Virginia Cavanna. They were married and had two children Amerigo and Eda. Mr.

---

[81] Stamford Advocate 10/10/1904, 1/31/1912, 6/18/1965, 11/23/1949, 11/10/1948, 4/7/1930.
[82] Stamford Advocate 12/29/1914, 5/2/1964, 5/4/1964.
[83] Stamford Advocate 7/13/1949, 12/11/1933.
[84] Stamford Directories, Alien immigration manifest 4/7/1902, Connecticut U.S. Federal Naturalization Records, 9/28/1905.

Vetriolo was an entrepreneur having many businesses, including a bar, real estate investments, banking, grocery, wine, cigar and tobacco businesses, and imported goods including olive oil. He was also heavily involved with Italian American organizations in Stamford, including the Italian Center, Società di Mutuo Soccorso Vittorio Emanuele III, Società Operaia Italiana di Mutuo Soccorso, Circolo Italiano, the Italian Political Club, and North Italy Mutual Benefit Society. He formed a business partnership with Vito Pittaro that included a steamship ticket brokerage, a real estate and money-exchange. Their relationship later soured, and the partnership was dissolved. He lived in Stamford for about forty years before liquidating all his holdings, retiring at fifty-six, and moving to the San Francisco area after Prohibition closed all the liquor stores. His son Amerigo born November 7, 1900, in Stamford was a Stamford High School and Boston University football star. He worked for the Bank of Italy, an Italian immigrant bank in San Francisco that later became the Bank of America. Amerigo later worked in the wine business in San Francisco.[85]

Virgina Cavanna was born in Racevanna, Italy in 1870. She immigrated to the U.S. in 1877 and lived in New York City, where she worked in a cigar-making factory as a "stripper," stripping the bad spots from tobacco leaves and selling fruit at a family-owned fruit stand, until she was introduced and married Quintino Vetriolo and moved to Stamford. Virginia assisted in running the grocery and liquor store, and steamship business. She counseled immigrants on saving money, acted as an interpreter when they had problems, and even went to Ellis Island to welcome and escort new immigrants. Virginia was the founder of the first woman's society, Adelaide Cairoli.

The biggest members of the team were all the nameless hard-working Italians that do not show up in the pages of the Stamford Advocate but through their concentration on the two pillars of Italian American life: work and family, and the willingness to assimilate propelled the Italian Colony forward. Through this, they were successful in demonstrating their capability as an ethnic group. In Appendix I, there is a list of Italian surnames of Stamford during the period of this history, so that the readers can be aware and take pride in the collective accomplishments of their ancestors. Destiny brought the community's leaders together with the other new Italian immigrants, each from disparate areas of Italy. Each was influenced by their respective life experiences and became united to create a way forward, resulting in a vast array of much-needed support organizations.

---

[85] Stamford Advocate 1/3/1955 p 6, 7/17/2002, p 6, 3/15/1988 p 7, 11/16/1917 p 4, 6/17/1916 p 1, 11/19/1907 p 6.

CHAPTER 4

Italian-American Organizations

"I fratelli uniti tra loro formano un fascio che pùo resistere agli sforzi più robusti. "
"United we stand, divided we fall; Union is strength."

A network of social, political, educational, and mutual benefit organizations were developed for the aid of the Italian community because they were not allowed to join existing organizations. The organizations were not just social, and spontaneous; they were part of the plan to promote the Italian people to the local population, provide much-needed mutual support, and demonstrate strength in numbers. By uniting a community's previously ignored power, these organizations combatted the stifling impact of prejudice. The societies and clubs were also refuges for immigrants who did not speak English and felt unwelcome in America by providing them with comfort and comradery. They provided an outlet for artistic expression and the advancement of education and awareness. Later on, some of these organizations morphed into social clubs as doors began to open to Italians and they could join unions intended for the general population and other organizations with more diverse populations.

Vito Pittaro writes in his history of Italian Americans in Stamford that by the end of the century, the organizations' plans worked and there was recognition by the populous that Italians were fully capable as citizens physically and morally in commercial and industrial development and were here to stay as permanent residents. New families from Italy flowed into the country at the beginning of the new century bringing new vitality to construction, and to industry (mostly at Yale and Towne). Italians cleared and improved neighboring fields that were transformed into gardens and decent and well-maintained residences. He notes that Italians helped Stamford earn the nickname "Beautiful City." This meant that phase 2 of the effort would now be underway. Italians needed to rise to the level of other ethnicities through social and political organizations. Phase 2 started with mutual benefit, educational associations, and political groups created for and by Italians.[1]

"Società di Mutuo Soccorso Fra Tommaso Campenella"
The first Italian organization in Stamford, "Società di Mutuo Soccorso Fra Tommaso Campenella" a mutual aid society was formed in 1894 to create a social backstop for the Italian workforce. It not only provided financial

---

[1] "Twenty-Five Years of Progress 1910-1935," The Italian Institute Inc. Stamford, CT.

assistance in times of need but also nourished the minds of its members. The organization was initially successful in serving as a uniting element for the disparate Italian community. It was located at 18 Pacific Street. The mutual aid society started by a Protestant missionary of the Baptist Church (Rev. Pasquale De Carlo one of the early Italian leaders in Stamford) was basically a self-insurance arrangement for its members. The society is named after one of the most important philosophers of the late Renaissance who was prosecuted by the Roman Inquisition for heresy. Campanella wrote about a utopian society based on an equitable division of labor, communal ownership of wealth, and education available to all. The choice of the philosopher was an obvious anti-Catholic doctrine message by the Baptist who founded the society. Another intent of the organization was to promote the welfare and education of Italian immigrants. The organization sponsored involvement in parades as a way for the immigrants to show their patriotism, pride, and willingness to Americanize themselves.[2] In this way, they could earn the esteem of other groups in the city. This was in part imitating the other immigrant groups that preceded who succeeded by demonstrating the worthiness of the culture and civilization of their homeland.

For example, one of the group's first celebrations (and another means for the Baptists to revel in anti-Catholic sentiment) was the September 20 homage to the "Breccia di Porta Pia," of the Capture of Rome, on September 20, 1870. This was the final event of the long process of Italian unification also known as the Risorgimento, marking both the final defeat of the Papal States under Pope Pius IX and the unification of the Italian peninsula under King Victor Emmanuel II of the House of Savoy. Such a public manifestation did not sit well with Catholics of the city, especially the Irish.[3] Underlying the organization of the society by Baptists was the competition with Catholicism for the hearts and minds of Italians in America. For this purpose, this particular event was chosen to be celebrated. There is more on this competition in Chapter 5.

It also appears that Italians (most likely from the Society) contributed $40 to a fund in October of 1899 to help bring a new factory to town; Rev. De Carlo and Crescenzo Tamburri were organizers.[4] This demonstrated the immigrant community's dedication to their new home and willingness to stay and contribute to the city.

On July 24th, 1894, Pasquale De Carlo, Domenico Noto, Canio Cerreto (Reverend of Bridgeport Italian mission and also from Calitri, Italy), Lelio

---

[2] Stamford Advocate 7/1/1991.
[3] Bridgeport La Tribuna Del Connecticut, 7/13/1907. 4.
[4] Stamford Advocate 10/16/1899.

Donatelli, Pietro Passero, Tornillo Vilantonio, Tony Cafforo and Antonio Cuneo associated themselves into the society. The Society was incorporated under the laws of the State of Connecticut on March 14, 1895. Article 1 of the certificate of incorporation declares, "Since we are children of a free, unified and civilized homeland, we want to establish here in Stamford, Connecticut a mutual aid society called Tommaso Campanella. Article 2 indicates that the purpose is the mutual aid among the members who compose the society, and to promote the instruction and the moral and material well-being of the members. Article 3 indicates the funds from dues can create other resources, such as libraries, consumer cooperatives, and more.

Before the creation of large insurance companies, mutual benefit societies offered risk protection. They usually were organized around residents from the same town in Italy. The Sons of Italy was the first Italian organization to provide such benefits and later served as a model for organizations in Stamford. The regulations stipulated that the participants had to be between 18 and 55 years old, anyone between the ages of 50 and 55 was required to show proof of age before joining, and that the society would only admit men of good conduct, exemplary morality, and robust health. It was required that an applicant be referred by an existing member. For an individual to be accepted, it required two-thirds approval of the members at the meeting. Admission fees were $2 for ages 18 to 25, $3 for ages 25 to 30, $4 for ages 30 through 35, $5, for ages 35 to 40, $7 for ages 40 to 45, and $10 for ages 45 to 55. The regulations provided for four types of members: the founding members, the regular members (those who pay admission fees and the regular monthly dues), the honorary members (were exempt from fees but could not vote), and emeritus members (those who may have been helpful to the society either through funds or services). The monthly fee was $65. Members could be expelled if they feigned illness, committed suicide, devoted themselves to idleness, were scandalous, a drunk, or assaulted or killed individuals. A medical certificate proving illness was required to collect benefits. Sick benefits were $6 a week for 3 months, $3 a week after that, up until 7 months (and through 9 months) $2 per week. For anything after that period, the beneficiary received a lump sum payment of $50. On the death of a member each member was to pay over $1 for funeral expenses, anything left over went to the family. Additionally, upon death, the society paid for two carriages to carry officers of the society to a member's funeral. If a doctor determined that an incurable illness could be improved by repatriation to Italy, the society would pay half of the voyage. Interestingly, a member could be fined for using foul language $2 for the first offense, $3 for the second offense; they could be suspended for 6 months for the third time.

In 1897, the officers were: Leo Donatelli, president; Gaetano Fastiggi, treasurer; and Domenico DeVito, secretary, and meetings were held at Pitt's block at the corner of Main and Pacific Sts. In 1898 and 1899, the officers were: Leo Donatelli, president; Gaetano Fastiggi, secretary; and Crescenzo Tamburri, treasurer; meetings were held at 1 Pacific St. In 1900, the officers were: Leo Donatelli, president; Gaetano Fastiggi, secretary; and Nicola Colucci, treasurer. During that year, the Society along with other organizations that Rev. DeCarlo was involved with (Società Fra Campanella, DeCarlo Mission Adult School, and Circolo Filodrammatico), and two Italian language weeklies (La Liberta and La Luce) requested and received permission to observe the memory of the assassinated King Umberto of Italy:

> PERMISSION is hereby granted to the Italian Colony to have a parade and music to honor the memory of the late King Humbert. The parade to be held at 2 o'clock p.m. on Sunday, August 26th, 1900. Line of march from Pitt's Block, Main Street to Saint John's Catholic Church, Atlantic Street. Dated at City of Stamford, Connecticut, this 22nd Day of August 1900. Homer S. Cummings, Mayor

A memorial service was held at St. John's Church. A band from Port Chester played the music for the march from Pitt's Block at the corner of Main and Pacific Streets. A large picture of the King was carried along with American and Italian flags. Afterward Pittaro, then an editor for "La Luce" gave an address on the late King's life and character.[5]

Not all of the Italian Colony wanted to honor the king. The advocate reported, "No visible exhibition of grief is being displayed among the local Italians over the assassination of King Humbert of Italy…One well-known local son of Italy said today that he deplored the assassination of King Humbert but was not surprised at it. The people of America have no idea of the circumstances of the poorer classes in Italy. They are actually starving, he says, and thinks the country would be much better off were it a republic. He has no sympathy with the anarchists, however, and while there are some socialists in the local colony, he declares there are no anarchists here. Not a few of the local Italians are rejoicing secretly, he says, over the death of the King, but this is only among the more ignorant classes.[6]

In 1901, the officers were: Raffaele Carpinella, president; Nicola Pavia, treasurer; and Joe DeVito, secretary, and meetings were held at 1 Pacific St.

---

[5] "They Came by Ship," by Mario Toglia, Xlibris Publishing. 288, Stamford Advocate 8/20/1900. 3, 8/27/1900. 4.
[6] Stamford Advocate 7/31/1900. 1.

Officers in 1902 and 1903 were Leo Donatelli, president; Nicola Pavia, treasurer; and Bernardo Lupinacci, secretary. In 1904, the officers were: Bernardo Lupinacci, president; Felice Trimboli, treasurer; and Antonio Palo, secretary, and meetings were held at 1 Pacific St. In 1905, the officers were: Domenico Palo, president; Gaetano Maddaloni, treasurer; and Nicola Pavia, secretary and meetings were held at 1 Pacific St. In 1906, the officers were Bernardo Lupinacci, president; Rosario Martino, secretary; and Nicola Pavia, treasurer. In 1907, the officers were: Gaetano Maddaloni, president; Nicola Pavia, treasurer; and Rosario Martino, secretary; and meetings were held at 1 Pacific St. In 1908, the officers were: Gaetano Maddaloni, president; Nicola Pavia, treasurer; and, Crescenzo Tamburri, secretary; and meetings were held at 1 Pacific St. The society had a fundraiser in 1908 featuring entertainment, including a farce with Louis Serafino, and Pietro Jovanna (Govanno), Govanno's four-year-old son sang Italian songs. In 1909, the officers were: Vincenzo Accousti, president; Raffaele Carpinelli, treasurer; and Crescenzo Tamburri, secretary; and meetings were held at 1 Pacific St.

In 1910, the officers were: Arcangelo Cantore, president; Nicola Pavia, treasurer; and Guiseppe DeVito, secretary. In that same year, the society presented a four-act play, "Elenora Di Siviglia" in Italian; the Star of Italy band also gave a concert. This was part of the celebration of the unification of Italy on September 20th. Other societies taking part were Vittorio Emanuele III, Operaia, Court Umberto I, San Manghese, Aviglianese, Caserta, Calabrese, and the Italo American Political Club. Crescenzo Tamburri was the marshal of the parade. In 1911, the officers were: Vincenzo Accousti, president; Guiseppe Colucci, treasurer; and G. Mancusi, secretary; and meetings were held at 1 Pacific St. In 1912, the elected officers were: Raffaele Carpinella, president; Luigi Serafino, vice-president; Crescenzo Tamburri, recording secretary; Pietro Rosa, assistant secretary; Guiseppe Maffei, financial secretary; Joseph Colucci, treasurer; and J. Castanzo, social secretary. In that same year, the Advocate reported on the society's celebration of the birthday of Fra Tommaso Campanella. In 1913, the officers were: Luigi Serafino, president; Felice Trimboli, treasurer; and Crescenzo Tamburri, secretary, and meetings were held at 1 Pacific St. In 1914, the officers were: Luigi Serafino, president; Pietro Govanno, vice-president; Crescenzo Tamburri, corresponding secretary; Guiseppe Martini, financial secretary; Felice Trimboli, treasurer; Dr. James Costanzo, physician; and Gaetano Maddaloni, Raffaele Carpinella and Raffaele Lionetti, trustees. For 1915, the officers were Raffaele Carpinella, president; Guiseppe Colucci, vice-president; Crescenzo Tamburri, corresponding secretary; Guiseppe Carpinella, Rosario Martino, vice secretary; Felice Trimboli, treasurer; Dr. J.J. Costanzo physician; and Raffaele Lionetti,

Tommaso Cantillo and Paolo Viggiano as trustees. For 1916 and 1917, the officers were: Rosario Martino, venerable; Michelle Amaltifano, treasurer; and Felix Trimboli, secretary. In 1918 and 1919, the officers were Giuseppe Milone, venerable; Salvatore Martino, treasurer; and Felix Trimboli, secretary. In 1920, Salvatore Martino was listed as an officer. In 1924, the president was Salvatore Martino at 215 West Main St.[7] From 1930 through 1933, Antonio Parente was listed as an officer.

An insurance company by nature always has controversial claims and arguments about coverage. In 1911, a suit was brought against the society by Mr. Mazzocchi claiming damages of $500 because it was alleged that Vincenzo Accuosta and Arcangelo Cantore (former officers of the society) sought by fraud and subterfuge to nullify claims made against the society. On November 25th, 1910 Mazzocchi claimed sick benefits from the society based on the price of a boat trip to Italy the reimbursement of which was disallowed. The by-laws of the society provided that in case a member was so sick as to require residence in another climate, such passage would be provided. In April 1911, the two indicated that they had the authority of the society to settle the action, but as a condition, they demanded that Mazzocchi sign a letter apologizing for bringing suit. If he did, the benefits would be provided. Mazzocchi wrote and signed the letter. Later that letter became grounds for the expulsion of Mazzocchi from the society. Cantore argued that benefits were allowed a certain amount each week while sick, but the member would have to present a doctor's certificate indicating that the illness was legitimate. Mazzocchi had not provided such proof.[8] Mazzocchi lost the suit.[9]

In Vito Pittaro's history of Italians in Stamford, he indicates, that toward the end of the century, the society began to deviate from its aims by becoming the hand of a few politicians who exerted pressure on newly naturalized citizens for their votes, and religious beliefs (referring to the Catholic/Protestant competition over Italian souls in America) and there was a splintering of the Colony into factions.[10] Although remediating the initial issues that caused discontentment by the promising political and spiritual neutrality eventually the same behavior would resurface due to the roles of various stakeholders. Proselytizing is a requirement of the job for a Baptist minister such as Rev. DeCarlo. Politicians can only stay in power if they are obtaining support from the populous. Because political and religious beliefs are important to our

---

[7] Stamford Advocate 9/10/1910, 9/20/1910, 9/21/1910, 12/11/1911, 1/5/1914, 12/7/1914, 9/9/1912, 10/29/1924, 11/27/1908.
[8] Stamford Advocate 7/25/1911.
[9] Stamford Advocate 11/15/1911.
[10] "Twenty-Five Years of Progress 1910-1935," The Italian Institute Inc. Stamford, CT.

identity and emotionally driven, it was inevitable that this would affect the dynamics of the group. Still, the organization was significant in proving that the unification of the colony could be achieved.

In 1896, many Italians understood that they must be unified in their efforts to realize change. So, they petitioned for an Italian to teach them English at the English as a second language classes sponsored by the city. A petition was presented to the School Committee in 1910 as well requesting a teacher who was conversant in both Italian and English.[11]

Italian Republican Club

The second Italian organization organized in Stamford was a political affiliation organization, the Italian Republican Club. Italians recognized that they would need to show up in numbers to act as a catalyst for change within the community. They also knew that they would need to demonstrate their patriotism in order to project Italians in a better light within the community. Italian Republican Club officers in 1898 were Guiseppe Acunto (president), Pietro Passero (vice president), Guiseppe Sandelli (secretary), Angelo Passero, Carmine Passero and Guiseppe Sandelli (executive committee). This organization was instrumental in demonstrating Italians' voting power and in demonstrating Italians' willingness to Americanize and be a part of the community. Validation of the Americanization through patriotism was noted in an Advocate article titled "Italians are all right."[12] In December, the following officers were chosen: Antonio Palo (president), G. Devito (vice president) Francisco Grimaldi (secretary), and Vincenzo Boccarosso (financial secretary).[13] There was a power struggle within the club in October of 1902 and its elections of local delegates to the state Convention of Italian republicans. Then President Antonio Palo indicated that he was kept in the dark about the convention selection meeting until 3 hours before it convened and as a result, could not inform all the members timely of the meeting. As a result, there were only 25 members at the meeting. At that time, Rev. DeCarlo and Louis Donatelli were named delegates. Afterward, 55 Italians filed applications for citizenship.[14] Another political club formed soon after. In 1919, Chairman Joseph Vitiello sponsored seventeen Italians to become citizens including: Antonio Spatacino, Rocco Scarano, Silvio DeRose, Giovanni Schettino, Luigi Schettino, Giuseppe Corulli, Giovanni Vitti, Nicola Bucciarelli, Tony Bucciarelli, Michele D'Ascenzo, Michele Rainone, Giovanni

---

[11] Stamford Advocate 11/1/1910, 11/2/1910.
[12] Stamford Advocate 10/17/1898.
[13] Stamford Advocate 12/19/1898.
[14] Stamford Advocate 10/2/1902.

Socci, Giuseppe Lapolla, Palmerino Pia, Laviero Tiani, Giuseppe Pasquarelli, and Luigi Lembo.[15]

Italian Political Club

What became known as the Italian Political and Benevolent Club probably started as the Italian Political Club, which was formed by Crescenzo Tamburri in 1898 shortly after the Republican Club was formed. The organization was purposely not affiliated with a specific party. Officers were Gennaro Rosa (president), Leo Donatelli (vice president) C. Tamburri (secretary). In 1899, the club had 104 members who met at Corbo Place, 20 Stillwater Ave. to elect officers. Speeches were given by Gennaro Rosa, Leo Donatelli, Crescenzo Tamburri, George Vitti, V.G. Fastiggi, Jose Maestri, and M. Passaro. Officers elected at the meeting included: Gennaro Rosa, president; Leo Donatelli, vice president; Crescenzo Tamburri, secretary, George Vitti, vice secretary; and Vito Nicola Colucci, treasurer. In 1900, the headquarters was on 12 Black Road, and the elected officers were Donato Corbo, president; Armando Paolino, vice-president; Gennaro Rosa, second vice-president; Crescenzo Tamburri, secretary; Cesidio Vitti, assistant secretary; Michele Pavia, treasurer; and Emilio Carlesimo, Cherubino Socci, Cesare Latte, executive committee.[16] Nancy Lazzaro Fekete, granddaughter of Cesare Latte remembers her grandfather as very politically active, and that once each of his grandchildren became eighteen he would personally walk them down to city hall to register to vote. He considered it a patriotic duty and important to make sure that Italians had representation that was in tune with their needs. In 1909, the club investigated complaints by Italians working for the contractor William McCabe at Halloween Park. In 1910, the officers were: Leo Donatelli, president; Vito Pittaro, vice president; Crescenzo Tamburri, secretary; and Guiseppe Colucci, treasurer. In that year they celebrated Washington's Birthday. The committee in charge included A. Cantore, chairman; Angelo Maffucci, secretary-treasurer; A. Palo, Chas Vuono, Joseph DeVito, and N. Tamburri.

During 1910, Leo Donatelli and other republicans quit the club, offering this explanation: "the Citizens' candidate for mayor stated that I had resigned from the presidency of the club because I could not accomplish my object. I desire to say that his statement was entirely uncalled for and untrue. I did resign from the presidency of the club, but for the following reason: Prior to the town election, I discovered that the club, or at least a portion of it was not an Italian club, but was becoming under the persuasive influence of Dr.

[15] Stamford Advocate 4/9/1919. 12.
[16] Stamford Advocate 12/14/1898, 3/26/1900, 1/16/1899.

Rowell, "Charley Rowell's gang;" and rather than be president of such a club, I did resign…I know as a fact that the Citizens' candidate did a favor for one of the leaders of the so-called club, and he is now using the fact that he has done this leader that favor in order to persuade him and those who he can control to support him for mayor." Speakers discussed unity of the Italian societies, and Anthony Geronimo brought a brass band from the Lyceum to entertain. In 1911, the officers were: Vito Pittaro, president; Antonio Palo, Vice President; Crescenzo Tamburri, Corresponding Secretary; L Demilla, assistant; Angelomaria (Angelo/Alonzo) Maffucci, Treasurer; Joseph Carpinelli, financial secretary; M. Ediano, Censor; August Gargialo, moderator; and V. Accuosti, Nicholas Tamburri, James Rinaldi as trustees. Rocco Sessa, Gerardo Viggiano, and Quentino Vetriolo were council. Felice Trimboli was sanitary inspector.[17] The Stamford directory lists Anthony Geronimo as president in 1911, and 1912. In 1912, at a meeting in Red Men's Hall, the following officers were elected: Leo Donatelli (returning to participate in the club), president; Dr. J. Costanzo, vice president; Crescenzo Tamburri, secretary; G. De Vito, vice-secretary; Angelo Maffucci, treasurer; G. Carpinella financial secretary; Casimiro Tamburri, revisor; R. Lionetti, censore; and F. Trimboli, sanitary inspector. The following were trustees: A. Palo, J. Colucci, and G. Sessa. Counsel were R. Carpinella, A. Pellicci, and R. Sessa.[18] In 1913, the officers were Louis Donatelli, president; Crescenzo Tamburri, secretary; and Alonzo Maffucci, treasurer. In 1914, officers were Louis Donatelli, president; Vito Pittaro, moderator; and Joseph Itri Board of Trustees. In 1915, a certificate of change of name of the Italo-American Political Club to the Italo-American Republican Club was approved by the secretary of state. In addition an amendment to the purpose of the club was filed at the same time and deemed necessary by the appromiate 200 memebers.[19] In 1915, officers were Louis Donatelli, president; Guiseppe Colucci, secretary; and Giovanni Raino, financial secretary.

Italo American Republican Club
    In 1916 and 1917, similar officers as the Italian Political Club are listed in the Stamford directory under the organization Italo American Republican Club: Luigi Donatelli, president; Guiseppe Colucci, treasurer; Giovanni Raina, secretary. The club met at 389 Main St. In 1918/1919, the officers are

---

[17] Stamford Advocate 12/12/1898, 12/28/1998, 10/30/1908, 7/19/1909, 2/21/1910, 2/23/1910, 10/24/1910, 11/7/1910, 11/9/1910, 1/16/1911.
[18] Stamford Advocate 12/16/1912.
[19] Stamford Advocate 12/20/1915.

Alphonso Frasca, president; Luigi Donatelli, treasurer; Giovanni Raina, secretary. In 1920, 1923 through 1931, the Stamford directory lists Vincenzo Piccarero as an officer. In 1924, members included Cesare Malizia, Michele Gentile, Angelo Cioeta, Giuseppe Tamburri, Michele Tamburri, and Alfonso Macari. In 1929, officers included: Joseph L. Carpinella, president; S. B. Esposito, vice president; Ralph Lionetti, Jr., secretary; Peter P. Zezima, treasurer; and John Rose, Louis Caporizzo and Frank Lacerenza, trustees. Charles Vitti was also a member.[20] Eventually, these political clubs would serve as the base for Italians to join not only the political discourse but as a springboard to public service.

Italian Social Club

An organization called the Stamford Italian Social Club was active in 1899, when the group held a dance and social. A dance was also held in March of 1904. A prize was given to Joseph Taglio and Mary Braley for their waltz. In 1921, the Italian Social Institute formed a Girl's Italian Social Club. The officers were Eda Vetriolo, president; L. Tamburri, vice president; I. Rambottino, secretary; L. Cavanna, treasurer and Mary Pavia, Jennie Lacerenza and Mary Lionetti were executive committee members.[21]

Italo-American Educational Circle (Circolo Educativo)

The Italo-American Educational Circle, another important early organization was inaugurated on May 8, 1900 at the Cookes' building at 107 Main Street, next to Town Hall. The organization was started principally through the efforts of Reverend Pasquale De Carlo, Wilmot R. Jones (headmaster of Stamford High School) and Tony Palo. Forty-five Italian residents were present for the first meeting. The circle intended to cover literature, history, psychology, and social questions and was intended to elevate the Italian community through pursuit of education and knowledge. Lectures would alternate weekly between English and Italian.[22] A letter from the committee announcing the endeavor stated: "It is beyond question that one of the greatest adversaries of the human family is ignorance; it is dangerous to society. For this and other reasons we have opened a place of education, where every Italian resident in this city may come...We ask the support of every citizen of Stamford for the success of this institution, where we will try our best to have our people become good citizens." It would also serve to promote the worthiness of Italians as citizens of Stamford. The Advocate reported that "Mr. Jones

---

[20] Stamford Advocate 1/24/1929. 8, 12/4/1924. 6.
[21] Stamford Advocate 2/8/1899. 3, 2/27/1904. 6, 3/4/1904. 6, 1/17/1921. 3.
[22] Stamford Advocate 5/2/1900,. 3, 5/9/1900.

suggested that the Italians be observant and assimilate all that is worthy in their adopted country."

Again, here the religious competition for Italians reared its head: there was some opposition to the Circle voiced by Leo Donatelli, based on the thought that the circle was being promoted by Rev. De Carlo for the purposes of gaining recruits to his Baptist Church. Gennaro Passero also voiced objections to the circle: "The reason I did not take part in the organization is that I do not consider it a society calculated to work harmoniously in the whole Italian Colony, for the reason that it appears by its constitution to be a Republican organization. One of its by-laws reads: "A member, to join this circle, must believe in God. Another says the political affiliation of members is Republicanism. When the organization was first proposed it was given out by those at the head that religion or politics would not enter into it."[23] A committee of five (V. G. Fastiggi, Leo Donatelli, C. Tamburri, A. Cafaro, and C. Sala) was selected to investigate the proposed organization and ensure that it would serve the entire Italian Colony. At the second meeting of the Circle, at 1 Pacific Street Vito Pittaro (as Chairman) reiterated that the principles were objected to by most of the Circle members. As such, Rev. DeCarlo was forced to remove the offending sections of the constitution through a resolution. The resolution passed by 71 ballots to 14 (with one abstention and several members leaving before the vote).[24] In June, the officers were president, Rev. W.J. Lond; secretary, Rev. P. DeCarlo; treasurer, W. Waterbury; and the trustees were Rev. Vail, W.R. Jones, E Willard, G. Grimaldi and A. Palo.

Two hundred and thirty-one persons took advantage of the reading rooms from its opening until June 1, 1900.[25] It seems that members were able to resolve their differences, as the changes to the organization's regulations were worked out so that religion and political affiliation were not conditions for membership, which eventually led to the election on 1/21/1901 of a more diverse group of representative officers. They were Rev. Pasquale De Carlo, director; Leo Donatelli, president; Crescenzo Tamburri, secretary; Albino Meda, treasurer; Vito Pittaro, instructor; Gennaro Passero, librarian; and Quintino Vetriolo and Carmine Passero, trustees. [26] The Circle's first dramatic performance in Stamford was held on May 2, 1901. Mr. Gerardo Metallo entertained with some monologue work. Amateur actors presented the drama "The First of May" the actors were C. Gerardi, M. Caputi, Director G. Passero, L. Tornillo, G. Gerardi, Pierna Antoniazza, A Maffucci and Vito

---

[23] Stamford Advocate 5/11/1900.
[24] Stamford Advocate 5/12/1900, 5/14/1900.
[25] Stamford Advocate 12/1/1900.
[26] Stamford Advocate 11/11/20.

Gaetano Fastiggi. This was followed by a farce with the following cast: A. Gentile, G. Passero, F. Capossela, L. Caposella. The director was V. Pittaro and his assistant was Vito Gaetano Fastiggi. A. Boccarusso played a piano solo as well.[27]

Vito Gaetano Fastiggi immigrated to Stamford in 1890, when he was thirty years old. He became a U.S. citizen on October 20, 1900, in Stamford. Vito worked as a cabinetmaker for St. John's Woodworking Co., and later for Schleicher and Sons, piano manufacturers. In 1902, he moved to New Rochelle, New York. He was a musician, and while in Stamford was involved with the Circolo Educativo and Circolo Filodrammatico. He was also an inventor and held patent number 1,068,637 dated July 29, 1913, for "Improvements in Hot air Apparatus" used in stoves.[28]

In 1903, the Advocate discussed another performance by the Educational Circle. Participants were Mosi Cerreta, Luigi Tornillo, Theodore Furrilli, G. DeCarlo, G. Leone, Canio Capossela, Gennaro Passero, A. D'Egreorio, Luigi Feglinoli. The following officers were elected in 1904: Romolo D'Aloia, president; Giuseppe Laona, secretary; Gaetano Maddaloni, treasurer; and Luigi Figlioli, manager. In 1905, Romolo was able to obtain a piano for entertainments for the group.[29]

The Education Circle also looked out for the welfare of the Italian members. The Advocate reported: "Complaint had been made to the circle that the Italian girls were being discriminated against in Weil & Son's shirtwaist factory in lower Pacific Street. The complaint alleged that the girls were kept in the factory when there was no work for them to do, and that at the most they were not able to make over 25 cents a day." The Circle investigated. Leo Donatelli indicated after the investigation there was no discrimination.[30]

Although not part of the regulations of the group, eventually, the organization reverted to being political and religious, so the Circolo Filodrammatico was founded by mostly Calitrani workers to be free of political and religious influences. The new amateur theatrical group included the following surnames: Fastiggi, Metallo, Tornillo, Maffucci, Rinaldi, Capossela, and DeRosa. The leadership was Gerardo Metallo, chief comic. The group produced "Novantannove Disgrazie di Pulcinella (Ninetynine misfortunes of Pulcinella, a classic character in Neapolitan puppetry), a slapstick farce, and Il biricchino di Parigi (The mischief of Paris), another comedy.[31] Again, the

---

[27] Ibid May 2, 1901.
[28] "They Came by Ship," by Mario Toglia, Xlibris Publishing. 307.
[29] Stamford Advocate 2/17/1903, 10/10/1904, 4/3/1905.
[30] Stamford Advocate 12/1/1900.
[31] "They Came by Ship," Mario Toglia, Xlibris Publishing. 296.

organization was important in that it showed unifying the Italian Colony was possible.

The Settefratese revived their own Circolo Educativo founded by Michael Tamburri in the 1920s. In 1925, the Society's rooms were on West Main St. and Michael Tamburri was president. Other active members were Anthony Tamburri, Councilmen Joseph Carpinella, and Alfonso Macari. That year one of the speakers was the editor of the Italian-American newspaper, *Il Progresso*. Another program in 1926, was presented about the Settefratese judge, Pasquale Venturini.[32]

Società di Mutuo Soccorso Vittorio Emanuele III

Società di Mutuo Soccorso Vittorio Emanuele III was incorporated under the laws of Connecticut on April 30, 1901, and was another mutual self-insurance group. An ad in the Stamford Advocate by Crescenzo Tamburri announced the formation.[33] It was located at 152 Pacific Street. The original subscribers were Crescenzo Tamburri (secretary), Felice Trimboli, Gaetano Ferrara, Antonio Terenzio, Cesare Latte, Vito Pittaro (president), and Carmine Passero. Carlo Rosso was treasurer. The articles of incorporation indicate that the purpose of the corporation was "To aid, help and assist members of the Society in cases of sickness, death, and other distress, and to elevate their civil, moral and social standing, and to disseminate general knowledge among them.

The list of founders was as follows:

Crescenzo Tamburri	Francesco Luongo
Alvise Ruserick	Gaetano Ferrara
Antonio Terenzio	Michelangelo Pastore
Antonio Pellicci	Arrigo Arrigoni
Cesare Latte	Antonio De Matteo
Carmine Passero	Michele Abbatemarco
Giuseppe Passero	Michele D' Amato fu Giovanni
Charles Passero	Francesco Sisto
Aneslmo Pagliarulo	Giuseppe Cristiani
Francesco Passero	Pietro Micile
Angelo Saltarelli	Andrea Martinelli
Giovanni Patricelli	Leonardo Piacenza
Michele Patricelli	Michele D'Amato
Antonio Patricelli	Giovanni. D'Amato
Antonio Cianculli	Felice Trimboli

---

[32] Stamford Advocate 6/8/1925. 1.
[33] Stamford Advocate 4/22/1901. 1.

Lorenzo Vento
Donato Corbo
Michele Bonomo
Vincenzo Margotta
Luigi Russo
Francesco Tortora
Canio Lorusso
Benedetto Pensiero
Luigi Cilfoni
Natale Candido
Michele Caporino
Tomaso Adesso
Raffaele Borio

Raffaele Persecchini
Michele Vaccaro
Gennaro Frate
Carlo Rosso
Nicola Colabella
Carmine Graziano
Vito Pittaro
Gabriele Mallozzi
Michelangelo De Marco
Giuseppe Rossi
Nicola Astone

The articles of incorporation indicate that it was obligatory to celebrate annually the anniversary of the assumption of the thrown by Victor Emmanuele II (August 3, 1900). Additionally, you could not become president of the society if you were also president of another mutual benefit society. An applicant to the society needed to be sponsored by an existing member and must have been accepted by a majority of votes of the members. It was prohibited for members to discuss what occurred at meetings. Members were not eligible to receive health benefits until after one year of membership. No benefits would be paid for alcohol abuse-related illness, fights, attempts on their own life, or voluntary mutilation of one's body. All sickness benefits had to have a doctor's certificate. Health benefits were $6 per week for the first 3 months, and then $3 weekly after that. After 6 months, the member was not entitled to any subsidy for another 6 months but was allowed visits with the prescribed doctor and received a 50% reduction of the monthly fee and other fees. When a member died, each member contributed $1 to a funeral fund. The Society paid $75 for funeral expenses. The Society provided a carriage for four delegates from the Society to attend the funeral. The regulations provided for three types of members, Ordinary (those that pay entrance and monthly dues), Honorary, and Emeritus.

In 1901, the officers were: Vito Pittaro, president; Crescenzo Tamburri, secretary; and Carlo Rossi, treasurer. Meetings were held at Italian Circle Hall, Pitts Block. In 1902, the officers were: Vito Pittaro, president; Crescenzo Tamburri, secretary; and Francesco Tortora, treasurer. In 1903 and 1904, the officers were: Vito Pittaro, president; Crescenzo Tamburri, secretary; and Felice Trimboli, treasurer. In 1905, the officers were: Vincenzo Cianculli, president; G. Itri, secretary; and J. Teotora, treasurer. In 1906, the officers were Crescenzo Tamburri, president; S. DeCorleto, secretary; Felice Trimboli, treasurer. In 1907 and 1908, the officers were: Vito Pittaro, president; Crescenzo Tamburri, secretary; and Felice Trimboli, treasurer. In 1909, the officers were: Vincenzo Cianculli, president; Crescenzo Tamburri, secretary; and Felice Trimboli, treasurer. In 1910, the officers were: Vincenzo Cianculli, president; Crescenzo Tamburri, secretary; and Giovanni D'Amato, treasurer. In 1911, the officers were: Vincenzo Cianculli, president; Crescenzo Tamburri, secretary; and Felice Trimboli, treasurer. In 1912 through 1914, the officers were: Gennaro Frate (one of the first Italian settlers in Darien), president; Crescenzo Tamburri, secretary; and Felice Trimboli, treasurer. In 1915, the officers were: Luigi Serafino, president; Alberto Petrosini, secretary; and Felice Trimboli, treasurer. In 1916, the officers were: Felice Trimboli, president, and Alberto Petrosini, secretary. In 1917, the officers were: Felice Trimboli, president, and Charles Passero, secretary. In 1918/1919, the officers were: Vito Pittaro, president, and Alberto Petrosini, secretary. In 1920, Alberto Petrosini was listed as an officer. From 1923 through 1928, Giuseppe Divasti was listed as an officer.

The organization lasted for about three decades. In addition to the self-insurance, the organization was intended to elevate the Italians in the community, through the social and political affirmation of the Italian people in the eyes of others, by severing the bias of the local American press with the facts, to alleviate the intolerance, and discrimination against the working class, and to spread awareness of the rights and duties of citizenship.

Celebrations of the American Independence, advocated by the Vittorio Emanuele III Society with public demonstrations at Woodside Park, allowed for interaction with all the town authorities, and demonstration of the willingness of Italians to be part of the community. The occasions were successful with notable individuals flocking to congratulate and fraternize with the Italians on the day most dear to the American people. According to Pittaro, with these social and patriotic 4th of July celebrations, the Vittorio Emanuele III Society from 1903 to 1907 was able to maintain the high moral reputation of the whole Colony. The Picnic of 1907 was successful in garnering prestige and allowing for fraternization with other groups through activities such as baseball, musical concerts by the then-famous Attanasio Band, motorcycle races, orchestra music, dancing, artistic balloons, and brilliant fireworks by Emilio Carlesimo (who was a carpenter/contractor in Stamford for forty years). The solidarity of the Italian colony in its social and civil displays helped win over the general population. The society celebrated its annual Fourth of July picnic in 1910 at Woodside Park. The celebration included horse races, baseball, and a greased pole (no one was able to reach the top and claim the $10 prize). Fireworks were the main attraction at night. The ninth annual picnic was held in 1911, with a parade, and events including a concert, baseball, horse races, foot races, sack races, a greased pole contest, dancing, and fireworks. The officers and committees included: Charles Passero, president; Vincenzo Ciancuilli, president of the society; Crescenzo Tamburri, secretary; and Daniele Scalzi, treasurer.[34]

Successful in its aims and in recruiting members, the Society bought a plot of land on the corner of West Avenue and Ferris Avenue for the purpose of erecting a building. This later turned into a conflict between banking partners Quentino Vetriolo and Vito Pittaro. Vetriolo was a businessman first, and despite being active in Italian societies foreclosed on the mortgage for the property in 1910. The building was sold at auction and purchased by Mr. Vetriolo for more than the mortgage. Mr. Vetriolo actually took out an advertisement in the Advocate that read: "Quintino Vetriolo of 157-159 Canal St., desires to inform the public that he is not in any way connected, either for business or any other reason with V. Pittaro of this city, therefore is not responsible for anything that said Pittaro may do."

In 1912, the elected officers were: Gennaro Frate, president; John Scalzi, vice president; Crescenzo Tamburri, corresponding secretary; Mario Terenzio, assistant secretary; Daniel Scalzi, financial secretary; and Felice Trimboli, treasurer. Also in 1912, the society sent a cable to the King of Italy in sympathy, after he escaped an assassin's bullet. The society also had a Fourth of July picnic in 1913. It included horse races, wrestling, bicycle races, and fireworks. Gennaro Frate was president of the society. Vincenzo Accuosti was chairman of the picnic committee. The president in 1924 was Giuseppe Di Vasta, 235 Greenwich Ave.[35]

Girolamo Savonarola Benefit Society of Stamford

The Girolamo Savonarola Benefit Society of Stamford was active in 1903. Elected officers in that year were: Rev. P. DeCarlo, president; P. Codella, vice president; M. Jovanna, secretary; Benedetto Mallozzi, treasurer; and trustees G. Centonze, Nicola Collini, C. Scoca.[36] Girolamo Savonarola was an Italian Christian preacher, reformer, and martyr, renowned for his clash with tyrannical rulers and corrupt clergy. After the overthrow of the Medici in 1494, Savonarola was the sole leader of Florence, setting up a democratic republic.

---

[34] Stamford Advocate 7/3/1911, 10/23/1934. 8.
[35] Stamford Advocate, 3/15/1907, 3/27/1907, 1/3/1908 p1, 4/28/1910. 5, 5/11/1910, 7/5/1910, 3/15/1912, 4/11/1913, 5/10/1913, 5/13/1913, 7/2/1913, 10/29/1924.
[36] Stamford Advocate 4/15/1903. 6.

William McKinley Italian Republican Club

In 1903, officers of the William McKinley Italian Republican Club included Leo Donatelli, President; Gennaro Rosa, Vice President; Vito Pittaro, secretary; and Gennaro Passero, treasurer. The council included Vito Nicolo Colucci, Raffaele Carpinelli, Carmine Passero, Anseimo Pagliarulo, Vincenzo Moavero, Gaetano Clapes, Gaetano Maddalani.[37] This seems to be a split off from the original Republican Club as some of the players were involved with the 1902 ruckus between Palo, De Carlo and Donatelli. In 1903, Republican Party leaders worked to get the two groups to unite in agreement, heal divisions, and present a united front and were able to reinvigorate the membership. In 1904, officers included: Gennaro Rosa, president; A. Cantore, vice-president; Gennaro Passero, treasurer; V. Pittaro, corresponding secretary; C. Tamburri, recording secretary; Cesare Latte, Giuseppe Pompa, Giuseppe Terenzio, council; and Elia Pia, sergeant-at-arms. In 1917 officers included: G. Passaro, president; Tony Palo, vice president; O. Cavaliero, secretary; Felice Trimboli, cashier; and J. Racaniello and G. Russo board of examiners.[38]

Italo-American Progressive Club

The Italo-American Progressive Club was organized in December 1904. It held its meetings in the barbershop of Romolo D'Aloia (the first elected Italian) on Main Street. The group grew out of the Educational Circle and was working to provide a large library for the members to use. The Club seems to be related to the Italo-American Young Men's Republican Club, which provided fencing lessons (in both American and Italian methods) with expert Capt. Philip Andrower in 1905. Officers in that year were: Alonzo (Angelomaria) Maffucci, president; Daniel R. Scalzi, vice president; Paul Chiapetta, secretary; and Louis Capossella, treasurer. Officers elected in 1906 for the Young Men's Progressive Club were: Angelo Maffucci, president; Michele Clapes, vice president; Paul Chiapetta, financial secretary; Gaetano Toglia, corresponding secretary; Louis Capossela, treasurer; Fred Cavaliere, sergeant-at-arms; and Samuele DeMarco, assistant sergeant-at-arms. Officers elected in 1907 were: Alonzo Maffucci, president; Vito Luongo, vice president; Gaetano Toglia, corresponding secretary; Pasquale Chiapetta, financial secretary; Fred Cavaliere, treasurer; Samuele DeMarco, sergeant-at-arms; and Frank Passaro, manager of hall. The club put on theatrical productions, including a play entitled "Lo Schiavo Di San Domingo" in 1907. Entertainment in 1908 included the singing of Albert Iovanna, a three-year-old, followed by a farce given by Louis Serafino, Giovanni Ciriaco and Joseph Caposella, and

---

[37] Stamford Advocate 5/21/1903, 1/2/1912.
[38] Stamford Advocate 12/12/1903, 1/23/1904. 6, 8/17/1903. 1, 1/29/1917.

dancing and music. In 1911, Vito Pittaro was president, but was suspended for three months because against club rules, he held "public office" as an evening schoolteacher. Anthony Geronimo took over as president.[39]

Dante-Shakespeare Society

On July 9, 1904, a certificate of organization was filed at the Town Clerk's office for the Dante Shakespeare Society. The organization seems to be a Baptist mission society that aimed to Americanize Italians (more on this in Chapter 4). The objectives listed were: to establish a college where young people may obtain physical, moral, and intellectual education; and to found a home for homeless Italian children. The subscribers were Aristide W. Giampietro, Gaetano Carado, Romolo D'Alvia, Nicola Colline, and Vincent Pecoraro. By-laws were approved and the following officers were elected in 1904: Rev. Aristide W. Giampetro, president; Gaetano Corrado, secretary; N.H. Sherwood, treasurer. Contributions of $375 were collected. In August, a meeting was held among the Italian colony where Corado (a lawyer) spoke of the necessity of educating the young Italians of Stamford, "to bring them in line with American ideals and life." At the same meeting Rev. Giampetro declared it to be "the duty of his countrymen to educate themselves, and thus become worthy of America." Romolo D'Aloia an agent for the Bridgeport journal, "Il Sola" was active in Stamford for a time and dedicated himself to Italian causes. In June of 1904, he circulated a petition to Governor Murphy of New Jersey for the pardon of Anna Valentina, who was convicted of murder and was scheduled for punishment by death. Mrs. Blickensderfer who assisted in the Esposito case also assisted here. Valentina was eventually pardoned. D'Aloia ran for grand juror in 1904 and won.[40]

Società Operaia Italiana di Mutuo Soccorso

Società Operaia Italiana di Mutuo Soccorso di Stamford was organized on March 13, 1905, with the intent of expanding upon and countering the two societies previously formed: Tommaso Campanella (with religious affiliations) and Vittorio Emmanuel (with political affiliations). The aim was to amalgamate the total of the Italian population into one organization, to demonstrate affiliation with the members' new country, America, and to promote a spirit of free religious and political choice while attempting to avoid regional splintering of the Italian community. Article 2 of the incorporation

---

[39] Stamford Advocate 3/10/1905,4/8/1905, 8/1/1905,1/15/1906, 1/4/1907, 10/13/1908, 11/28/1908, 1/7/1914. 3, 3/25/1911. 6, 3/23/1911.
[40] Stamford Advocate 7/9/1904, 7/11/1904, 8/8/1904, 8/12/1904, 2/21/1903, 6/24/1904, 9/23/1904, 10/04/1904.

document indicates that the purpose of the formation was: "To aid, help, and assist the members of Society in case of sickness, death, and other distress, and to elevate their civil, moral and social standing; and to disseminate general knowledge among them." The subscribers of incorporation were: Arcangelo Cantore, Michele Caputo, Vincenzo Moavero, Gaetano Maddaloni, Evasio A. Meda. The list of society founders was as follows:

Maddaloni, Gaetano	Vetriolo, Quintino
Grimaldi, Achille	Figlioli, Luigi
Izzi, Eduardo,	Passero, Gennaro
Fedele, Antonio	Gervasio, Antonio
Racaniello, Giuseppe	Moavero, Vincenzo
Racaniello, Ambrogio	Petrilli, Salvatore
Cantore, Archangelo	Pastore, Michalangelo
Caputo, Michele	Campanile, Raffaele
Ferrara, Raffaele	Gufliano, Pietro
Arduino, Arturo	Palmieri, Gerardo
Angelici, Luigi	Leone, Giuseppe
Pittaro, Vito	Tamburri, Crescenzo
Meda, Albino	De Rosa, Carlo
Restaino, Canio	Sansone, Pasquale
Cardone, Raffaele	Carlesimo, Benedetto
Rinaldi, Vincenzo	Meda, Alfonso
Cianciulli, Vincenzo	Beliatore, Ermenegildo
Trimboli, Felice	Gesso, Gioacchino
Petrilli, Antonio	Lombardo, Giuseppe
Lione, Gerardo	Prunotto, Giuseppe
Ferrando, Carlo	Fulvo, Battista
Esposito, Eduardo	Ucciferri, Giovanni
Arduino, Pietro	

Article 4 of the regulations indicates that the society is independent as to politics and religion. Admission was open to all Stamford Italian Americans of "good character", who worked in the arts or a trade. Applications for membership needed to be signed by two existing members. To be admitted into the society under Article 13, the member must: be of good physical condition, with no chronic diseases, have good moral character, must obtain a "yes" vote from 75 percent of the members present for voting, and between 18 and 50 years of age. The initial admission fees were $1 for ages 18 to 25, $2 for ages 26 to 35, $5 for ages 36 to 45 and $7 for ages 46 to 50. Monthly dues were $1, twenty-five percent of which went to a mortuary fund. The society would pay no more than $136.50 for each disease. After a year in the society, the beneficiary was entitled to $7 per week in sick benefits for the first 13 weeks and $3.50 a week after that. In addition, there were grants of up to $20 for special diseases of the eyes, ears, nose or throat and special surgeries.

The Society met on the second Sunday of each month at 487 Main St. The initial officers were president, Gennaro Passaro; secretary, Crescenzo Tamburri; and treasurer, Felice Trimboli. The organization was issued a certificate of incorporation as a non-stock association on March 24, 1905. In 1906, the officers were: Arcangelo Cantore, president; Crescenzo Tamburri, secretary; Felice Trimboli, treasurer. In 1907, the officers were: Gennaro Passaro, president; Crescenzo Tamburri, secretary; and Felice Trimboli, treasurer. Meetings were held at Pitt's Block. In 1908, the officers were: Arcangelo Cantore, president; Crescenzo Tamburri, secretary; and G. Leone, treasurer. 1909, the officers were: Gennaro Passaro, president; Luigi Serafino, secretary; and G. Leone, treasurer. 1910, the officers were: Vito Pittaro, president; Luigi Serafino, secretary; and G. Leone, treasurer. At its most active stage, it had 190 members. In 1910, they held their second annual banquet at Mechanics Hall with Mayor Rowell attending. [41] In 1911, the officers were: Pasquale Sansone, president; Vito Pittaro, secretary; and Felice Trimboli, treasurer. 1912, the officers were: Gaetano Maddaloni, president; Luigi Serafino, secretary; and Felice Trimboli, treasurer. In 1914, (as part of the Sons of Italy) the officers elected were as follows: Luigi Serafino, venerable; Carlo Caputo, assistant venerable; Gaetano Maddaloni, ex-venerable; Archangelo Cantore, orator; Alberto Petrosino, secretary of archives; Raffaele Cardone, secretary of finances; Felice Trimboli, treasurer; Vincenzo Moavero, Ciraco Fabrizio and Michele Caputo, trustees; Luigi Cerreta, first ceremoniere, Antonio Sabia, second ceremoniere, Luigi Metallo, first sentinel; Carmine Bassone, second sentinel and Dr. James J. Costanzo, physician.[42] At one time offices were at 18 Pacific Street. In 1915, the officers were Luigi Serafino, venerable; Carlo Caputo, assistant venerable; Gaetano Maddaloni, ex-venerable; Archangelo Cantore, orator; Alberto Petrosino, secretary of archives; Raffaele Cardone, secretary of finances; Felice Trimboli, treasurer; Vincenzo Moavero, Ciriaco Fabrizio, and Michele Caputo, trustees; Luigi Cerreta, first ceremoniere, Antonio Sabia, second ceremoniere; Luigi Metallo, first sentinel; Carmine Bassano, second sentinel; and Dr. James J. Costanzo, physician.[43] In 1916, (under the Sons of Italy) the officers were: Vincenzo Cianculli, venerable; and Alberto Petrosino, secretary. Meetings were held at

---

[41] Stamford Advocate 1/3/1911, 11/28/1913.
[42] Stamford Advocate 1/15/1912, 12/23/1914.
[43] Stamford Advocate 12/23/1914. 6.

12 Pacific St. In 1917 through 1919, the officers were: Giuseppe Maffei, venerable; and Nicola Cognetta, secretary. In 1920 and 1923 through 1924, Antonio Conetta was listed as an officer. The president in 1924 was Alberico Parrella, 242 Pacific Street. From 1925 through 1933, Amerigo Perella was listed as an officer. From 1936 through 1938, Fred Contarano is listed as an officer. In 1939 and 1940, Vito Pittaro is listed as an officer.

In addition to the benefits the society provided, often (which was the case of most of the organizations) there were social activities with entertainment. In 1912, at a meeting Dominico Mancini and Raphael de Culto sang a few songs, and Antonio De Angelis played guitar and mandolin. Many of the organizations became consolidated under the Sons of Italy. In 1963, only 8 members remained when they voted to dissolve the organization. These members were Anthony Fiore of 50 Victory Street (president), Rocco Sessa of 33 Taylor Street (treasurer), Ciriaco Iovanna of 25 Taylor Street, Domenico LoBuglio, Tuttle Street, Luigi Pellegrino, 305 W. Main Street, Francesco De Costanzo, 25 Durant Street, Vincenzo Lobozzo, 41 Hale Street and Vincenzo Zabatta 295 Cove Road.[44]

Building Laborers' Union

Cesare Latte was president of the Building Laborers' Union (Unione Del Lavoratore) in 1906, and union members participated in the Labor Day parade in Stamford accompanied by the Cappellieri Band of Port Chester. The headquarters was listed as 68 Liberty St.[45] Nancy Lazzaro Fekete remembers her grandfather, Cesare Latte, as a strong union man and active in the Democratic Party. Cesare was a stonemason who built the house they lived in at 13 Liberty Street and was very talented with people and personal relationships. This skill benefited him in organizing workers for union purposes and voters for political purposes. In 1909 Giuseppe Pompa is listed as an officer of the union.[46]

Italian Social Institute/Italian Center

Most of the following is directly from the history as compiled by Mr. Pittaro and is in his usual frank, no holds barred fashion. The Italian Institute actually was born out of an attempt to form a federation of state societies in 1908 for the benefit of Italians living in the U.S. sponsored by the Italian government. This event brought about the solidarity of the united societies

---

[44] Stamford Advocate 12/18/1963.
[45] Bridgeport La Tribuna Del Connecticut 9/15/1906 p. 2, 10/20/1906, Budget Report of the State Board of Finance (CT) 1910, Connecticut Bureau of Labor Statistics 1909, 1912.
[46] Stamford Advocate 10/29/1924, 3/9/1909. 3.

of Stamford to improve the lives of Italian immigrants and showed they could move beyond political, religious, and regional differences. In that year, a circular was issued from the Colonial Institute in Rome, through the Italian Consulate in New York requesting the organization of local colonial committees of America to build in Rome a permanent representation for foreign expatriates and discuss the pressing problems of interest to the Italian communities abroad. Six Stamford associations signed up to help form a local committee, and four of these organizations with twelve delegates went to New Haven to commence organization. The first meeting of delegates resulted in much enthusiasm among the attendees. They elected officers that would move forward with the united committee. The elected officials included representatives from the major cities in Connecticut: Doctor Vincenzo D'Elia of New Haven, President; Gaetano Cuccaro, of Bridgeport, Vice President; and Vito Pittaro of Stamford, Secretary.

A second meeting took place in Bridgeport at 62 Cannon Street on June 21, 1908. The Stamford Association's delegation composed of 18 members was complete and ready to move forward and attended the event. However, only three of the New Haven societies and four of the Bridgeport societies showed up. The other state delegations were absent, which meant a certain defeat in moving the committee forward because a quorum was not present. In his history, Pittaro notes that it became even more futile as the delegates of the New Haven and Bridgeport companies began to quibble about the petty expenses of stationery and printing, which amounted to a few dollars per association. Pittaro also notes there was much friction and jealousy regarding the appointment of the Connecticut representative in Rome. The president of the fledgling federation Doctor D'Elia, was about to declare the meeting closed and the project of a Committee abandoned, due to the small number of delegates who attended, when Mr. Lelio Donatelli, delegate of the Society Tommaso Campanella of Stamford, stood up and denounced the procedure and decorum of the state associations' delegates both present and absent, and in a noble gesture asked the Stamford associations to agree to organize their own local committee, and at their own expense. Pittaro noted that the delegates of Bridgeport and of New Haven were "humiliated as they deserved to be" and that they "ran away like rabbits." With this act, Mr. Donatelli garnered much respect among the group and solidified his role as the leader of the Stamford Italian community.

The united Stamford committee moved ahead by themselves, and drew up a memorandum, illustrated and printed in their own words. Their document had a very wide distribution both in Italy and in the United States, including at the Federal Department of Labor, which requested several copies because of the interest it aroused. The "Herald Italian," a New York news-paper, and the "Messenger" of Rome made favorable comments about it. The agreed-upon areas to work on were: 1. Military service for Italians living abroad. 2. Application of inheritance laws. 3. Labor protection and workers' savings. 4. Teaching of the Italian language. However, in reality, it was noted that the passage of time combined with the acquisition of American citizen-ship and the newly united Italian government reforms, would by themselves take care of the first three items of concern to most expatriates: leaving only the teaching of the Italian language in public schools. This attempt at ad-dressing expatriates' needs outside of Italy became sidelined by the Italian government because of the Italo-Turkish war of 1911-12, and then by World War I, and as such the committee never went far.

However, this new stage of demonstrated social solidarity by the local Stamford organizations then inspired the local leaders to join together to im-prove the Italian American community in Stamford as a united front, rather than through the fragmented groups that had developed. This resulted in the proposal to have "an Italian house" as a social and cultural training ground for Italian immigrants, and for its future generation of Italo-Americans.[47] This eventually led to the formation of the Italian Social Institute (and then later the Italian Center).

The Advocate attested to the success of the association and its aim for a united Italian community:

> A federation of all the Italian societies in this city, with a view to im-proving the intellectual, social and moral status of the Italian colony, is now being perfected. Among other things there is a plan for the erection of a building containing a hall in which to hold meetings of the societies and for other purposes. As practically every man of Italian birth in this town be-longs to one or another of the various fraternal and benevolent associations composed of people of that nationality, the new federation will be a strong organization, and capable of accomplishing a great amount of good. All of the societies were represented by their presidents at a meeting (the second of the sort) held Tuesday evening in C. Tamburri's place of business in the Advocate building. The scope of the federation was agreed upon, and var-ious plans for its operations will be submitted to the affiliated societies at once. Among them are the scheme for a building already referred to, and the encouragement of the musical school and Italian brass band under the leadership of Prof. Pumpo of 290 Pacific Street. V. Pittaro of the Society Vittorio Emanuele was elected general president of the federation, and Crescenzo was elected general secretary. Meetings are to be held on the first

---

[47] "Twenty Five Years of Progress 1910-1935," The Italian Institute Inc. Stamford, CT

Tuesday of each month. As explained by President Pittaro, the object of the federation is to unite the Italian residents of Stamford in an association through which, more readily than by the separate efforts of societies or individuals, it will be possible to carry out plans for the betterment of the Italian population, and to assist each other by moral and, if necessary, financial support; to encourage sociability and generally to elevate the standard of life, by encouraging sobriety, and honesty, teaching newcomers how best to use the privilege of American citizenship. Whether the federation will take any active part in politics will be determined later. There is no doubt, however, that the Italian colony would be ready at any time to those candidates for local offices, whom they believe would mostly advance what they conceive to the best interest of the city.

One of the things at which the federation will aim is to overcome the prejudice against the nationality which exists in some quarters. It is not considered fair that, because a small percentage of the Italian-born people get into the police courts, often through ignorance, the whole colony should suffer in reputation. It has been found that some people have a prejudice against everyone who has not fully mastered the English language. As a matter of fact, a large number of the Italians who came here have a fair education. Many of them have shown that at the night schools, which they attended in order to get help in mastering the English language. They are highly appreciative of the public schools, and of the opportunities afforded their children by free educational facilities. A good many of the Italians are now to be found in the mechanical trades, and there are trade unions whose membership is almost wholly Italian.[48]

The Colony's work at elevating their stature in the community was working, as even reporting was favorable to Italians.

Although ultimately not successful because of a lack of support from the Italian government, it was the success in uniting Stamford societies for this federation that lead to the idea in 1909 to create and incorporate the Italian Institute in Stamford in order to consolidate the Italian groups and make them a more powerful block. It was their ambition to attain a closer harmony and better cooperation among the various Italian societies and other related organizations by means of this centralizing agency.[49]

Pittaro explains the details of the formation:

In 1909, the initiating council decided to form a regular corporation with subscriptions of $25 for each share. The committee hired the lawyer Louis

---

[48] Stamford Advocate 8/9/1907.
[49] "Twenty-Five Years of Progress 1910-1935," The Italian Institute Inc. Stamford, CT.

Curtis to draw up the organization's statutes, regulations and Deed of Incorporation conforming to the laws of Connecticut. The "cash" subscriptions were received by several associations and individuals, and as soon as the $1,000 capital was reached, incorporation of the Italian Social Institute was completed on December 8th of that year. The first officers were the following: Lelio Donatelli, president; Antonio Palo, vice president; Vito Pittaro, secretary; Angelo (Alonzo) Maffucci, treasurer; councilors: Gennaro Passaro, Vincenzo Accuosti, Arcangelo Cantore, Vincenzo Cianciulli and Vito Sabia. Their management began in the month of January 1910.

In 1911, the Stamford Advocate reported the following officers: Antonio Palo, president; Angelo Maffucci, treasurer; Vito Pittaro, secretary; and Directors Antonio Palo, Angelo Maffucci, Vito Pittaro, Gennaro Passaro, Vito Sabia, Arcangelo Cantore, Vincenzo Cianciulli, and Vincenzo Accuosti.[50] They had no regular meeting place but rented halls in Stamford. They desired a home of their own.

The rest of the history is translated from Italian. In Pittaro's dramatic style and words, he writes: "it was hard work to keep the institute moving forward, there was a lot of work and many sacrifices made, dealing with personal ambitions, and the bad faith on the part of some that may have discouraged some; but the administrations that succeeded one another until 1918, albeit with slow progress, were able to keep the corporation steady for eight long years, contenting themselves with payments and subscriptions of even 25 dollars a week." Pittaro writes that the patient collections by Messrs. Paolo Nardozza, Vito Sabia, and Pasquale Fortunato deserve to be remembered. In this period from 1910 to 1918, in which the colony was attempting to erect the Italian Social Institute, the march of the successive events absorbed the time and resources of private individuals, groups and organizations in different ways and away from the goal of a united Italian organization. These events included the need to erect an Italian Catholic church in the greater center of the West Side, the absorption of many fragmented organizations into the Sons of Italy, the many natural disasters that needed to be funded through the Red Cross, and the obligations of world war for both the United States and the homeland. With the constant progression of such events, year after year the attention towards the building of the institute was waning. Still, the administrations pushed on for their stated noble aims:

a) to promote the Italian organizations, legally recognized by the state of Connecticut, to federate for mutual well-being and civil improvement, while remaining administratively autonomous.

---

[50] Stamford Advocate 2/14/1911.

b) to terminate, when requested, any dispute that might arise between organizations, and to settle any disagreement between members and associations with judgments informed in justice and in accordance with the statute of the company in dispute.

c) to contribute as far as possible to defend the Italian nationality in these United States; when its prestige is crippled or its morality is unjustly offended, without however failing in complying with the common laws that govern the adopted homeland.

d) to cooperate with the Italian and American authorities for the protection of abandoned Italian children and those compatriots who, deprived of means, or unable to work, intend to repatriate or be placed in some shelter.

e) to inculcate the Italians residing in this city and neighboring villages to belong to some social security association if they want, with a greater probability of obtaining all those benefits in which this federation will be able to take an interest.

f) to refrain from any religious and political propaganda while reserving the right to defend the interests of Italians when they are collectively threatened by political and religious measures.

g) to facilitate the teaching of the English language in adults as much as possible, encouraging them mainly to attend evening schools, and encouraging them with annual awards in the name of the Italian Social Federation.

d) to help, through colonial meetings and other expedients, the Italian social institute, live up to its complete function of general Italian culture.

From 1910 to 1918, the Italian colony about twelve thousand strong between emigrants and their descendants continued their efforts to realize their dream of an Italian house that would encourage the unity and brotherhood of the Italian community and make their mark in all aspects of Stamford's civil, cultural and educational spheres. The greatest affirmation of Italian and non-foreign-born residents' social solidarity occurred at the outbreak of World War I, when Italy joined with America and other allies. Another event that helped amalgamate the community was the merger of the local Stamford mutual aid societies with the Sons of Italy. During that time, the Italian community was even able to show their patriotism for their adopted land, by raising funds for the Red Cross, at an event that featured the Italian General E. Gulielmotti, which raised the patriotic fervor in the city to new heights.

At this point, they had no regular meeting place but instead rented various halls in Stamford. In 1910, the Advocate reported on the ambitions of the united societies to erect a building to house them all under a three-story structure. The basement would be a gymnasium, with shower-baths and possibly a bowling alley. The first floor would have a fully equipped banquet room, with a kitchen in the rear. One of the floors would have a hall for entertainment of various sports, and a stage. On the other floor would be lodge rooms and committee rooms. Reporting complimented the Italians: "The plans for the new building affords another proof of the enterprise and industry of a class of men who supply no small share of Stamford's activities, and who are constantly adapting themselves to conditions in this country, and encouraging their children to make the best of their opportunities for education and advancement in a free land."[51] Slowly, but surely the marketing campaign was working in Italians favor.

Pittaro's narrative continues: A desire for the house was not enough, action was needed. Unfortunately, the first attempt for a permanent home was unsuccessful because once neighbors found out that a contract that had been drawn for the purchase of property on Greyrock Place, north of Main Street involved the Italian community complaints were made to the seller who then backed out. The owner offered a tract of land for the same price fronting 50 feet in Greyrock Place, south of Main Street. After careful consideration of the situation, it was deemed advisable to accept the proposal. The land was not built upon but instead sold later once the hopes of a "Casa Italiana" were realized. Finally, the opportunity arose in July 1918, when Giuseppe Boccuzzi, gardener of the Scofield house on South Street reported to the Campanella Society that its owner was in the process of selling his property. Vito Pittaro, secretary of the Italian Institute at the time visited the property and was ready to recommend the purchase to the Board of Directors. In August 1918, the board made a resolution, "Considering that the furnishing of the house is of the utmost importance for the immediate use that the Institute will be able to make, be it resolved: To give full powers to its officers, namely President, Treasurer and Secretary to devise all means so that said property was bought by the Institute for the price of $15,000." The contract was signed with a $1,000 deposit but funds up to $7,500 were required to be paid in cash by October of 2018. The officers worked hard to raise the money, but only about $2,000 had been collected by mid-September. In order to avoid losing the deposit if the money was not paid by October 1, appeals were sent out:

Stamford, Conn., September 11, 1918.
Countrymen:
    The great patriotism shown on many occasions by the Italians of Stamford in this world conflagration for the right of the law, justice, and democracy of the oppressed peoples, will be recorded in the glorious pages of our

---

[51] Stamford Advocate 2/18/1910, 2/19/1910.

Colonial History. Hundreds of our bold youth sacrifice and will sacrifice their lives on the battlefield, while thousands of us have a sacred duty to use all our material and moral energies to inspire them to victory and protect them today as in the post-war period. Our colony may very well be proud of what he has done and intends to do in all useful and patriotic demonstrations, starting with the Red Cross and ending with the Liberty Bonds without neglecting for a single minute the cooperation of Propaganda for our homeland of origin as for this one of adoption. But never has it felt like today, the need to have an Italian house, and since the opportunity arises and is presented very favorably, the Italian Social Institute, after ten years of work, struggle, ill-founded critique, and a thousand other difficulties, will be with the first of next month of October a done deal. For this purpose, all Italians, men, and women, are asked to attend a mass meeting which will be held next Sunday, the 15th at 2 p.m., at the Lyceum Theater, Atlantic Street. The report will also be given in said mass meeting from the money collected and sent for the refugees of Friuli through the Pro Patria Committee, and appropriate measures will be taken to commemorate the anniversary of October 12, legally honoring the great figure of Christopher Columbus.

Countrymen:
We are united and above any personal tantrum, let us firmly and resolutely aim to plant a sword in the heart of Prussianism and the Bicipid Eagle, and the flag of stripes and stars alongside our Tricolore on the Italian Social Institute.

Pittaro notes, this circular produced the greatest enthusiasm in the Colony but did not translate into more money for the purchase of the house. There were just 15 days left until the October payment due date and enthusiasm was not enough; they needed cash, for the goal had not been reached. Without this cash, 10 years of slow, hard work would be for naught, and a deposit of $1,000 would be lost (about $19,000 worth today). This is when fate intervened and Mr. David Granelli became a "saint" providing a mortgage loan, which added $3,000 to the building fund, this left only $2,000 to be raised. Mr. Scofield allowed for a second mortgage payable the following year.

Unfortunately, that was not the last of the setbacks, they were paying in Liberty Bonds, and upon learning this, Mr. Scofield was quoting the bonds at 96.50 percent. After many requests, Mr. Scofield finally relented. Mr. Granelli, even agreed to waive the first six interest payments on the loan. All things worth having are worth the effort, and finally, the Italians had their home. There were three floors in the building, with three rooms on the first floor, two halls and two rooms on the second floor, and three bedrooms on the third floor. There were two rooms for art and crafts school. Columbus Hall was used for theaters, social gatherings, conferences, patriotic events, mass meetings, and gymnastic exercises. The basement was used as "bowling alleys."

In the last three months of 1918, the house was cleaned up, inventory of the furniture was taken, preparation of heaters and putting everything in place for the opening to make it ready for the new administration. The plenary meeting took place in February 1918 at which the election of the new Board of Directors took place. The old Scofield house then became the center of the Italian Colony, where social gatherings and various society and lodge meetings took place. Former Secretary Pittaro declared "The mission of this last Board of Directors is finished, the house is yours, manage it as you know best, and you can. I leave you my best wishes in the full success to which it is destined." The new administration was elected as follows:

Officers:	Directors:
Luigi Serafino, President	Michele Genovese
Quintino Vetriolo, Vice President	Giuseppe Mancusi
Joseph Vuono, Treasurer:	Giuseppe Carpinelli
Antonio Conetta, Secretary	William Humble
	Felice Trimboli

Pittaro's history reads: "The new administration, after the purchase of the Italian House, assumed a new responsibility, that of being able to maintain it and make it socially and economically useful, honoring the Italian community with all its activities, respecting the laws of the country and perpetuating the Italian community's principles, inculcating in the souls of our children the feeling of devotion, and of admiration and pride for the homeland of origin."

In 1919, the following were elected as directors: Giuseppe Vuono, Quintino Vetriolo, Luigi Serafino, Michele Genovese, Giuseppe Mancuso, Antonio Conetta, Giuseppe Carpinella, Guglielmo Umile and Felice Trimboli.[52]

In 1920, the Italian Institute held a carnival at its 76 South Street address to rave reviews: "The carnival exceeds all others in attractiveness of layout. Not in a long time has a carnival been staged here wherein layout of booths and ground has been so architecturally correct and so really attractive. The illumination of the ground is particularly attractive...There is an atmosphere of newness and of neatness about everything that pleases the visitor." Spaghetti and chicken dinners were featured, and guests could eat indoors or outdoors. There was a dance pavilion as well. Officers were Louis Serafino, president; Quintino

---

[52] Stamford Advocate 2/6/1919. 6.

Vetriolo, vice president; Antonio Conetta, secretary; and Joseph Vuono, treasurer. Other active members included: Joseph Mancuso, Joseph Carpinella, Thomas Tella, Michele Genovese, Vito Sabia, Frank Rich, Mr. Ignazio, Michael Genovese and Thomas Tella.[53]

It soon became evident that this building was inadequate, as it was not adapted for wedding celebrations, dramatic presentations, or other activities requiring a large hall. The association acquired in April 1921 from Charles W. Pickett, land on Guernsey Street to the rear of the South Street property. Upon this land, the Guernsey Street Hall was erected and its doors opened on February 7, 1925. That important event was celebrated with a three-day program that included an open house, patriotic speeches, entertainments and a grand ball.[54]

An Italian language school for children aged ten and over was established. The teaching was entrusted to Mr. Michele Amalfitano who was the Director of the school and to Prof. Giuseppe Ventura, who was replaced by Mr. Alfonso Frasca (1920) who held the school until July 1921. In the school year 1922 a qualified teacher was hired, Professor Fulvia Giannini La Porta, which had a fairly large class for those times (more than one hundred pupils,). She was replaced in 1923 by Alberico Parrella, Lieutenant in the Italian Army.

At the end of 1923, due to lack of funds the Italian School was suspended. There was a desire to build a hall that could be used for entertainment, dances, performances, and "Mass meetings," "Columbus Hall." The administration of the institute was composed of the President, Lawyer Frank Rich, the Vice President, Mr. Tommaso Tella, the Secretary, Mr. Paolo Nardozza, the Treasurer Mr. Ignazio Lupo, and Committee Members Messrs. Gaetano Maddaloni, Vito A Salvatore, Luigi Serafino, Antonio Rambottini. Giuseppe Maffei Pietro Rosa and E. Zezima, agreed to sign the construction contract for the building of "Columbus Hall," based on the design and specifications of the architect Frank Urso, with Vuono Construction Co. for the sum of $ 59,000.

The suspension of the Italian language due to lack of funds was disappointing. It was for this fact that the Italo American Business and Professional Men's Club "and the Directors of the Institute, assisted by Dr. J. J. Costanzo, did their utmost to obtain that in the "High School" Italian was placed among the compulsory teaching subjects, on the same level as French and Spanish. The campaign was a success and Professor Raul Este Palmieri who was already teaching French was also commissioned to teach Italian.

[53] Stamford Advocate 8/10/1920. 1.
[54] Stamford Advocate Tercentenary Edition Town of Stamford, CT 1641 – 1941 Supplement of the Stamford Advocate , Saturday, June 7, 1941 p. 160.

Columbus Hall was dedicated on February 7, 1925. Throughout this period, the Italian Social Institute had carried on as a stock corporation, membership to which was obtained through purchase of a share of stock. The leadership decided to change the status of the organization to a non-stock corporation. Officers in 1929 included: Peter Rosa, president; Vito S. Salvatore, vice president; Alphonso Frasca, financial secretary; F. Cantanaro, recording secretary; and Alonzo Maffucci, treasurer.[55] Mayor Keating, attended the dedication and expressed the people of Stamford's pleasure with the efforts of the Italian citizens to adopt the customs of America and to become good citizens. "The city of Stamford is proud of the work of her Italian citizens who have made a substantial addition to the public buildings of our city. Your people are an industrious, hard-working group. Some 25 years ago, you started to come to Stamford with stout arms and healthy bodies. You have been saving and this building is one tangible result of your efforts. You have always been prompt in meeting your obligations and are a real asset to the city." Reverend Father Kelly also spoke at the dedication: "This shows what can be done by a united people with proper leaders. Several years ago you were linked together by the Italian societies. Neighborly love has been characteristic of you during these years. It has helped you to greater power. You have been loyal law-abiding citizens, and I hope you will be. You have always been ready to do what you have been called upon for Stamford. By your love and loyalty you will be able to do still more for Stamford."[56] On September 4, 1931 the incorporation papers were filed as a non-stock association with the following stated purposes: 1) To conduct, maintain and manage a center where the history, culture, customs and laws of the United States of America may be taught any and all persons of Italian decent residing in the town of Stamford, CT, 2) To render necessary aid and other relief to the poor and needy, and to administer and dispense funds entrusted to it for such purposes, and 3) To conduct and provide educational, recreational, athletic and social facilities for the spiritual improvement and physical development of young people, as well as for grown men and women.[57] Joseph J. Vuono was the first president; W.W. Graves, Vice president; Frank Rich, secretary; and Alonzo Maffucci, treasurer. Other Charter members included Dorothy Heroy, Frank D. Rich, Harry T. Hart and Rose-Claire Sichel.

The Italian Institute applied twice to be a member agency of the Community Chest in 1931. Once refused because it was more of a social club, then because it was determined that the needs were not defined sufficiently.

---

[55] Stamford Advocate 3/15/1929 p8.
[56] Ibid 2/9/1925. 1.
[57] Stamford Advocate Tercentenary Edition Town of Stamford, CT 1641 – 1941 Supplement of the Stamford Advocate , Saturday, June 7, 1941 p. 160.

After the comprehensive report of the works and needs was completed, the Italian Institute was admitted.[58] This report is described in Chapter 2. The association with the Community Chest was ended shortly thereafter.

In 1933, the institute set up a school for children and adults, having as a teacher, Mr. F. Franchina. Joseph Vuono was president of the Italian Center in 1933, other officers were: William W. Graves, vice president; Alonzo Maffucci, treasurer; Attorney Frank Rich, secretary. Finally, in 1934 Widow Andrea Cappabianca, reconstituted and maintained the "Andrea Cappabianca" school for an entire year, which had been attended by over 400 alumni was under the competent direction of the teacher Professor Fulvia Giannini La Porta. In 1934, the organization provided vocational courses to the unemployed, including classes in clay modeling, charcoal drawing, water coloring, architectural modeling, elementary electricity and chemistry.[59] Drives for new members were successful in 1935 under the leadership of Joseph Carpinella. In 1936, Frank Rich was president of the Italian Center. In 1937 six pupils were awarded trips to Italy for their excellence in Italian language studies: Margherita Rosa, Nicolina Morelli, John Nastasi, Edmondo Seraffino, Emanuele Benvenuto, and John Ponziani.[60]

Pittaro also exclaims that the ideals and hopes of Evasio A, Meda, promoter and advocate of an Italian Catholic Church in the Colony of Stamford, "allowed the return for Italians to the religion of our ancient fathers from which emigrants were extirpated from by the dominant religion of Protestantism."[61]

There were two groups in the Italian Center: The Italian American Historical Society and the Spinoza club.

Spinoza Club (part of Italian Center)

Arnold N. Maddaloni founded the Spinoza Club in 1932 to commemorate the 300th anniversary of the birth of philosopher Benedict de Spinoza. Spinoza was one of the foremost promoters of 17th-century Rationalism and one of the early and seminal thinkers of the Enlightenment and modern biblical criticism, he is considered one of the most important philosophers of the early modern period. The group studied philosophers, and psychology. Members in 1933 included: Maurice Epifanio, Ralph Treglia, and Joseph Iannazzi. In 1935, members included: Ludivico Claps, president; Joseph Iannazzi, vice president; Victor Succi, secretary; and Alfred Marini, treasurer.

---

[58] Stamford Advocate Tercentenary Edition Town of Stamford, CT 1641 – 1941 Supplement of the Stamford Advocate , Saturday, June 7, 1941 p. 163.
[59] Stamford Advocate, 1/26/1934.
[60] Stamford Advocate 4/5/1935, 5/9/1935, 5/29/1937. 11.
[61] "Twenty-Five Years of Progress 1910-1935," The Italian Institute Inc. Stamford, CT.

The discussion group was active for 20 years and later became known as the Italian Center Group Forum.[62]

Italian American Historical Society (part of Italian Center)

The Italian American Historical Society was an organization devoted to keeping records of the activities of the Italian American community in Stamford and was organized in 1942. The recorded history went back to 1884. The original members: Ignazio Lupo, president, Peter Consenti, vice president, Vito Pittaro, secretary-archivist, Pasquale Chiappetta, vice-secretary, Joseph A. Tozzoli, treasurer, Louis Serafino, Gaetano Maddaloni, Joseph Itri, Peter Vescio, Vito A. Salvatore, Ciriaco Iovanna, Peter Rosa, Rafaele Chianelli, Nicola Cognetta, Gennaro Passaro, Prof. Giuseppe Ventura, Frank Aiello, Thomas Treglia, Frank Arduino, Nunziato Tamburri, Thomas Tella, Bruno Amato, Raffaele Campanile, Michele Abate. Tragically, it is not evident where these records have been placed.[63]

Società Foresters of America (Corte Umberto II No. 165)

In 1905, Joseph Itri was a member of No. 56 Order of Foresters and began an Italian branch of the organization. The Advocate indicated: "The society will accept as members only English speaking and cultured Italians of the city."[64] The organization was a mutual benefit society and was located at 251 Pacific Street. In 1907 and 1908, the officers were Pasquale Fortunato, Chief Ranger; Giacamo Sarno, financial secretary; Giovanni D'Amato, treasurer. They met at the Knights of Pythias Hall. In 1909, the officers included: A. Taddeo, chief ranger; Louis Robustelli, sub-chief ranger; G. D'Amato, treasurer; G. DeVito, financial secretary; D. Viggiano, senior woodward; T. Tregra, junior woodward; G. Russo, senior beadle; Vito Tortora, junior beadle; D. DeVito, lecturer; D. Dasaro trustee; and Dr. John F. Harrison, physician. In 1910, the officers were: James Sarno, Chief ranger; Joseph Itri, sub-chief ranger; John DeMott, treasurer; Joseph DeVito, financial secretary; V. Pecoraro, recording secretary; Dr. A. Preziosi, court physician; C. Russo, senior woodward; Gia Russo, junior woodward, G. Valenti, senior beadle, M. Cicale, junior beadle, P. Ferraro, lecturer and trustees F. Demino, J. Tambrosio, and V. Tortora. In 1911, the group sponsored an excursion to Coney Island, the committee included the following: James Sarno, chairman; Ignazio Lupo, Joseph LiVolsi, Luigi Robustelli, A. Machio, James Melillo, Antonio Sansone, and John Russo. In 1913, the officers were: Joseph Itri, chief ranger; M. De Vito, secretary; P.

---

62 Stamford Advocate 2/4/1999. 4, 5/22/1933. 8, 6/20/1933. 8, 2/28/1935. 13.
63 Stamford Advocate 11/23/1949. 5.
64 Stamford Advocate 5/19/1905.

Fortunato, recording secretary; G.B. Russo, senior woodward; F. Macchio, junior woodward; P. Stabile, senior beatle; N. Spera, junior beatle and; G. Failacci, lecturer. In 1914, the officers were Joseph Itri, Chief Ranger; V. Ursane, subchief ranger; P. Lamberti, treasurer; J. De Vito, financial secretary; J. B. Russo, senior woodward; A Contaliti, junior woodward; M. Pacelli, senior beadle; S. Tisani, junior beadle; M. Passero, lecturer, and J.F. Harrison, physician. The trustees were P. Ferraro, A. Spagnoli, L. Robustelli, F. Macchio and G. Civale. In 1915, the elected officers were: Joseph Itri, president; Dominic Manchino, vice-president; Louis Donatelli, treasurer; Joseph DeVito, financial secretary and Pasquale Fortunato, recording secretary. In 1916, the officers elected were: Pirin Diana, Chief Ranger; Joseph Itri, sub-chief ranger; John Raina, financial secretary; P. Robustelli, treasurer; B. Fortunato, corresponding secretary; B. Stabile, senior woodward; D. Lacchio, junior woodward; and A. Alphonizio, senior beadle; D. Sansone, junior bettle; P. Lombardi and A. Cicale, trustee; A. Passero, lecturer; and Dr. William Scofield, physician. The Court Umberto No. 165 and Court Conte di Torino, No. 178, foresters gave a ball in 1916. The committee in charge included: V. Pecoraro, chairman; Joseph Sementino, secretary; P. Stabile, treasurer; A. Contaldi, A. Iannazi, V. Ingenito, G.R. Russo, J. d'Amato, G. Loffredo, S. Troncone, A. Burriciello, Joseph Carpinella, R. Celotto and F. Macchia.[65] In 1917, the officers were: Pirin Diana, Chief Ranger; sub-chief ranger, Joseph Itri; P. Fortunato, recording secretary; C. Sexerrenimo, junior woodward; S. Macchio, senior woodward; and D. Mancini, lecturer. Giuseppe Epifanio born in Italy on June 4, 1871, and living in Stamford starting in 1900 was a member. In 1918/1919 the officers were for Corte Umberto 1, #165: Joseph Itri, Chief ranger; Giovanni Riana, financial secretary; and Joseph Devito, treasurer, and for Corte Conte di Torino, #178: Carmine Passaro, chief ranger; Vincenzo Picoraro, financial secretary; and Vincenzo DiPrete, treasurer. In 1920 and 1923 through 1929, Vincenzo DiPrete is listed as officer of Corte Conte di Torino, and in 1923 through 1929, John Raina is listed as officer of Corte Umberto. . In 1924 the president of Court Conte di Torino, No. 178 was Vincenzo Pecorara, 25 Myrtle Ave. and of Corte Umberto I. No 165, was John Raina.[66] Mr. Itri's membership in the society was likely instrumental in getting him on the ballot (the first Italian elected as constable). In 1930, the listed officer for Corte Conte was Vincenzo DiPreta, and for Corte Umberto Bruno Amato. In 1931 and 1932, the listed officer for Corte Conte was Vincenzo DiPreta, and for Corte Umberto Joseph DeVito. In 1933 and 1934, Joseph DeVito is again listed as officer for Corte Umberto.

---

[65] Stamford Advocate 1/4/1910, 6/13/1911. 6, 11/27/1916, 12/29/1908. 6.
[66] Stamford Advocate 12/12/1916,6/26/1917,5/11/1915, 12/29/1914, 1/13/1914, 12/23/1913, 7/15/1913, 11/15/1930, 10/29/1924, 12/21/1905. 3, 6/21/1906, 11/20/1906.

There was also a different Forrester Benevolent Society set up by Italians, Court Benevolence F. Mazzini, No. 8500 A.O.F. In 1905, the elected officers were Chief Ranger Vincent Pecoraro; sub-chief ranger Frank Basco; treasurer, Baldassaro Paulucci; secretary, Michael Iovanni, sub-secretary, P. Daddona; senior woodward P. Pimpinella; junior woodward, M. Russo; senior beadle, M. Di Napoli; junior beadle I. Giannattasio, and trustees L. DeAngelis, S. Pannoni, M. DiNapoli, and auditors P. Pimpinella, S. Pannoni and L. Giannattosio. Meetings were held at 162 Atlantic. In 1906, elected officers were: Chief Ranger Vincent Pecoraro; sub-chief ranger, J. Baine; treasurer Baldassaro, Paolucci; secretary Michael Iovanna; sub-secretary Pasquale Pimpanella; senior woodward M. Russo; junior woodward, P. Terlizzi; senior beadle M. DiNapoli; junior beadle C. Montanaro; trustees M. DiNapoli, R. Sesso, T. Cantillo; auditors P. Iovanna, P. Terlizzi, P. Daddona. In the same year, the organization sponsored a concert and ball that was attended by non-Italians as well. Before the ball there was a parade in town. The entertainment for the evening included comic recitations by Miss M. Christle, clarinet solo by Professor E. Pompo, a mandolin and guitar duet by Antonio DeAngelis and Salvatore Pannone, a buck and wing dance by Professor Olson and selections by the "Famous Stamford Quartette."

Italian Workingmen's Benefit Society
    The Italian Workingmen's Benefit Society was active in 1905. In that year they elected Dr. Gennano as the society's physician. Officers were elected in May 1905.[67]

Società Aviglianese di Mutuo Soccorso
    Founded with 75 members and incorporated with the State of Connecticut on August 18, 1905, this organization appears to be the first regional (Italians and their descendants from Avigliano, Italy) mutual aid society. The articles of incorporation indicate that the purposes of the organization were to aid each of its members and at the same time promote their instruction and their moral and mutual good, and to furnish such financial and other aid to its members in case of sickness, accident, death, or other adversity. Other purposes are to foster the retention and continuance among members of their ties as countrymen and the brotherhood which has made traditional the solidarity of the people from Avigliano; to promote respect and obey the laws and institutions governing this country; to honor the great name of Italy. The articles also indicate that

---

[67] Stamford Advocate 4/8/1905. 6, 4/10/1905.

the organization will not be affiliated with any church or other religious organ-ization, or with any political party, nor candidate of a political party. They also specifically state that no person shall be ineligible for membership on account of his religious or political beliefs. The admission fees established according to age, were as follows: from 18 to 25 years of age $1.00, from 26 to 30 years of age $2.00, from 31 to 35 years of age $3.00, from 36 to 40 years of age $4.00, from 41 to 46 years of age $6.00, and from 46 to 50 years of age $10.00. Monthly dues were $1.50. To be admitted an applicant had to be recommended by an existing member and had to pass a medical examination. Upon admission members had to swear an oath: "I hereby swear to be faithful to the Aviglianese society, to respect its laws and to cooperate in every way possible in its growth for the purpose of honoring-through its greater social prestige-the Italian name in this country." Sickness benefits were a weekly payment of $7.00 for the first three months, and then $3.50 afterwards up to six months, and then $2.50 a week, up until one year (the maximum payout being $201.50. Death benefits were $150.00 for the member and $50 for a spouse's death. Voting on motions were made by a secret vote, with half the number of the members present at the meeting plus one vote deciding the motion. The by-laws were revised in 1935 by a committee that included: Carlo De Bartolomeo, Francesco S. La-Bella, Frank Lacerenza, Vito Zaccagnino, Salvatore Telesca, Vito Romano, and Guiseppe De Bartolomeo. The founders of the organization included the fol-lowing names:

Gennaro Rosa (president)
Vito Vaccaro (vice president)
Vito Colucci (treasurer)
Pietro Galasso (corresponding
   secretary)
Leonardo Piacenza (finance
   secretary)
Leonardo Bochicchio (curator)
Vincenzo Claps (curator)
Pietro Mancusi (adviser)
Antonio Genovese (adviser)
Gaetano Claps (adviser)
Paolo Viggiano (adviser)
Vito Romano 1 (adviser)
Vito Romano 2 (adviser)
Egido Colucci (adviser)
Luigi Piacenza (promoter)
Canio Lorusso
Donato Nardozza

Donato Corbo
Nicola Lovallo
Francesco Lovallo
Donato Ferrara
Angelo Lorusso
Giacomo Sabia
Giovan Battista Sabia
Leonardo Genovese
Angelo Lacerenza
Domenico Lacerenza
Donato Telesca
Giuseppe Colucci
Paolo Colucci
Giovanni Tolla
Francesco Verrastro
Leonardo D'Andrea
Rocco Genovese
Vito Summa
Andrea Galasso

Francesco Luongo
Berardino Grosso
Vincenzo Genovese
Francesco Martinelli
Domenico Sabia
Frauletto Colucci
Vito Donato Coviello di
  D. Antonio
Vito Palladino
Francesco Masi
Domenico Guglielmi
Michele Piacenza di Luigi
Michele Genovese
Vincenzo Sabia
Michele Vaccaro
Andrea Martinelli
Francesco Telesca
Vincenzo Telesca
Tommaso Vaccaro
Domenico Telesca

Vito Donato Sabia
Pietro Colucci
Gerardo Viggiano
Paolo Nardozza
Donato Nardozza (2)
Giuseppe Gerari
Martinelli Giacomo
Corbo Giovan Battista
Tortora Giuseppe
Bochicchio Pietro
Romano Vito Di' Giuseppe
Mancusi Canio
Sabia Vito Fu Donato
Colucci Vincenzo
Vaccaro Francesco
Vaccaro Donato
Genovese Rocco (2)
Rinaldi Vincenzo
Rinaldi Giuseppe
Luongo Vito

The regional societies grew as a result of the influx of immigrants from specific towns and were meant to provide a ready-made social network of paesani, comfort to new immigrants, and easier integration into American life. It grew to 225 members by 1929.[68] In 1906, the elected officers were Gennaro Rosa, president: Vito Vaccaro (who owned a beer bottling operation), vice president; Pietro Calasso, corresponding secretary; Leonardo Piacenza, financial secretary; Luigi Piacenza, treasurer and the society christened its flags and paraded on Labor Day in celebration. Some of the 75 founding members included: Vito Colucci, Vincenzo Colucci, Pietro Colucci, Donato Ferrara, Andrea Galasso, Pietro Galasso, Domenico Lacerenza, Angelo Lorusso, Canio Mancusi, Francesco Martinelli, Luigi Piacenza, Michele Piacenza, Guiseppe Rinaldi, Vito Romano the first, Vito Romano, the second, Gennaro Romano, Vito Summa, Domenico Telesco, Francesco Verastro, Palo Nardozza, Donato Nardozza and Michele Vaccaro. Their first annual picnic started in 1908, which was celebrated at Woodside Park on Labor Day. Frank Labella of the society built a triumphal arch for the occasion in front of Corbo Hall on Stillwater. The annual picnics were grand affairs usually starting with a parade in the morning and winding up with fireworks in the evenings. The society held an annual dance as well. During the day there were music, dancing, and games,

---

[68] "Twenty-Five Years of Progress 1910-1935," The Italian Institute Inc. Stamford, CT.

and horse races. The society held its third annual picnic at Woodside Park in 1910. It started with a parade that included the "Star of Italy Band", the Campanella, Vittorio Emanuele III, Court Umberto, F. of A., Caserta, Calabrese, Cosentena, and Aviglianese societies, and Norwalk and Port Chester bands. The Italian Political and Italian-American Progressive clubs were also included. Events included a 15-mile bicycle race, baseball, horse races, dancing, and fireworks. The Labor Day festivities in 1911 included greased pig and greased pole competitions.[69] In 1910, the officers were G. Mancusi, president; M. Claps, vice president; P. Nardozza, secretary; S. Labella, treasurer; and V. Accousti, president of the society. In 1911, elected officers were as follows: Vincenzo Accuosti, president; Salvatore Labella, vice-president; Paolo Nardozza, recording secretary; Leonardo Accuorsi, financial secretary; Michele Vaccaro, treasurer. In 1912, the officers were Vincenzo Accousti, president; Tony Salvatore, secretary; and Joseph Mancusi, treasurer. In 1912, the society celebrated Labor Day and its fifth annual picnic at Woodside Park. It began with a parade, including the Colonial Band, and 400 participants marching. They played a game where the participant was blindfolded and would then attempt to break jars with presents in them. Fireworks capped off the event which was planned by the following committee members: Vincent Accuosti, president; Paul Nardozza, secretary; Vito Orsino, treasurer; and Guiseppe Giuseppe Mancusi, president of the Aviglianese Society. In 1914, the officers were Vito A. Salvatore, president; Michael Claps, vice president; Paul Vardazzo, secretary; Joseph Mancuso, financial secretary; Leonardo Accursi, Vito Orsino, and Pietro Galasso, trustees; and Dr. A. S. Sorgi, physician. In 1915, the Aviglianese Society officers included: Vito Salvatore, president; Vincenzo Picoraro, financial secretary; and Joseph Carpinelli, treasurer. The following were elected officers in 1915, M. A. Genovese, president; Joseph Mancusi, vice president; Paul Nardozzi, secretary; and Vito Sabia, treasurer. In 1916 through 1919, the officers were Vito Biase, president; Andrea Rosa, treasurer; and Serverio Labella, secretary. The society met at 202 Stillwater Ave. In 1920, the president was Vito Salvatore. In 1923 through 1930, and 1932 Vito Romano is listed as an officer in the Stamford directory. In 1924, the president was Paul Nardozza, 38 Finney Lane.

In 1926, the society held a banquet in honor of Professor Elio Gianturco, a native of Avigliano, Italy who was in the U.S. on a six-month scholarship awarded for excellence in Italian literature and music. He was giving lectures at Columbia University on Italian literature and modern music. The officers in 1935 were Vito J. Coviello, president; Guiseppe DeBartolomeo, vice president; Carlo DeBartolomeo, corresponding secretary; Vito Zaccagnino, treasurer;

[69] Stamford Advocate 12/11/1911, 9/1/1906, 9/4/1906, 9/3/1908, 9/5/1908, 9/2/1909, 9/8/1914, 12/10/1938, 4/13/1915, 4/19/1984, 9/5/1911, 11/20/1939, 9/3/1912, 1/14/1997.

Vito Orsino, federation secretary; and Giuseppe Santarsiero, auditor. The society celebrated its 35th anniversary in November of 1939, just after the outbreak of World War II, the keynote speaker spoke about the young Aviglianese: "Now we are at the beginning of another 35 years in our history. Ahead of us lies the future; and, for our young people, in particular, the future is filled with much uncertainty. Like the early Aviglianese, many years ago, these young people are experiencing a sense of confusion in a work torn asunder by hatred and strife. Unless they can turn to us who are older, with a sure knowledge that they will find in us understanding and comradeship, and a sense of strength that comes from the spirit of unity and mutual helpfulness, these young people of the second and third generations of our people, may not be able to face the stress of present-day conditions. They must have something to which to anchor themselves. And what stronger anchorage can we give to them than to remind them of the traditions of our Aviglianese people?"[70]

Società Italiana di M.S.S. Teodoro Martire, fra I Cittadini di S. Mango Sul Calore

The society was incorporated on June 28, 1906, and was for Italians and their descendants from San Mango Sul Calore, Italy. The articles stated that the objects of the society are to aid, help, and assist the members of the society in case of sickness, death, or other distress, to elevate their civil, moral, and social standing, and to disseminate general knowledge among them.[71] The society offered a health insurance policy to new immigrants and helped them get settled in Stamford. The founders of the society are listed as follows:

Giovanni Boccuzzi di Angelo	Giovanni Faugno di Francesco
Nicola Catino fu Pasquale	Sabato Giannitti
Raffaele Carpinella	Gaetano Coppola
Angelo Lionetti di Antonio	Nunziante Giannitti
Teodoro Catino di Michele	Raffaele Lionetti di Michelangelo
Angelo Lionetti di Giovanni	Giovanni Melchionno
Giovanni Lionetti	Raffaele Maria
Guiseppe Coppola	Teodoro Maria
Guiseppe Uva	Orazio Di Nardo
Pasquale Bocuzzi di Angelo	Guiseppe Borea
Angelo Giannitti di Teodoro	Giovanni Marena
Raffaele Boccuzzi	Ferdinando Uva
Guiseppe Faugno	Giovanni Comforti

---

[70] Stamford Advocate 4/16/1928, 10/29/1924, 9/3/1910, 9/6/1910, 9/5/1911, 9/3/1912, 11/20/1939, 12/22/1914. 6.
[71] Stamford Advocate 7/16/1906

Raffaele Lionetti
Guiseppe Marena
Raffaele Martino
Rosario Martino
Salvatore Martino
Enrico Giannitti
Saverio Coppola
Raffaele Uva di Nicola
Raffaele Faugno
Nicola Martino
Francesco Lionetti
Giovanni Potito
Carmine Melchionno
Guiseppe Boccuzzi
Catello Coppola
Valentino Coppola
Raffaele Coppola di Teodoro
Guiseppe Carpinella
Michalangelo De Marco
Raffaele Coppola di Giovanni
Raffaele Boera
Pasquale Catino
Carmine Boccuzzi
Teodoro Uva
Angelo Giannitti di Biagio
Giovanni Pierni
Generoso Tosone
Domenico Martino
Gaetano Follo
Sabato Boccuzzi
Generoso Moccia
Sabino Caruso
Francesco Faugno
Michele Carpinella di Raffaele
Guiseppe Lionetti
Venanzio Martino
Teodoro Ottaviano
Salvatore D'Elia
Antonio Potito

Raffaele Lionetti fu Teodoro
Teodoro Boccuzzi
Sabino Ottaviano
Domenico Prizio
Teodore Lionetti
Teodoro Catino di Carmine
Angelo De Marco
Domenicantonio Lionetti
Raffaele D'Elia
Raffaele Coppola di Teodoro
Angelo Raffaele Coppola
Carmine Lionetti
Giovanni Faugno di Carmine
Ciraco Catino
Vito Borea
Leonardo Borea
Domenico Milone
Guiseppe Catino
Nicola Catino di Teodoro
Giovanni Mottola
Pietro Giannitti
Pasquale Boccuzzi di Angelo
Sabato Coppola
Gaetano Conforti
Giovanni Uva
Michele Pierni
Giuseppe Sibilia
Michele Vozzella
Vincenzo Coppola
Teodoro Catino di Nicola
Nunziante Coppola
Domenico Magliano
Raffaele Uva di Pasquale
Pasquale Ottaviano
Giovanni Boccuzzi di Nicola
Angelo Ottaviano
Michele Ottaviano
Lorenzo Ottaviano
Raffaele Di Nardo

In 1910, they celebrated their fourth annual picnic at Woodside Park with a street parade, and games competitions, including bicycle and trotting races, baseball, dancing, and fireworks. The elected officials in 1911, were as follows: Rosario Martino, president; Giovanni Comforti, vice-president; Salvatore Martino, recording secretary; Giovanni Vozzella financial secretary; Giovanni Boccuzzi, treasurer; and J. Costanzo, doctor. In 1924, the president was Theodore Ottaviano at 126 Spruce St.[72] The Society still exists to this day, currently, the annual benefits provide $30 a day for 20 days in case of sickness and $100 toward hospital bills. In 1927, a solemn mass was held in honor of the patron saint of San Mango, Saint Teodoro. A band and parade through the Italian section and the center of town was held in the afternoon, and a solemn vesper at 7:30 pm was held at Sacred Heart Church. The streets of Schuyler Avenue and Stillwater Avenue were illuminated during two days of festivities. Salvatore Martino, president, Raffaele Coppola, secretary, and Sinibaldo Coppola, treasurer were the committee in charge.[73] A separate social club was formed on January 5th, 1950, in part because the society was forced to exclude people older than 45 from its health insurance policy.[74] The incorporators listed for the San Manghese Social Club of Stamford were Theodore Coppola, Bonifacio Moccia, Anthony Borea, and Ralph Boccuzzi. The social club owns the property at 107 West Avenue, where the San Manghese annual feast was held. Many Stamford Italians have fond memories of growing up and attending the feast with carnival rides, Italian food and candy, and entertainments all under the festive lighting erected each year for the occasion. The current president Teodoro Melchionno laments that unfortunately, the cost of running the feast has become prohibitive; instead the social club runs an annual picnic and mass for San Teodore. He also indicates that, like many other Italian social clubs it has been hard to attract younger generations to join.

Stone Mason's Union

The Stone Mason's Union No. 23 was located in Stamford and had Italian presidents or secretaries listed for the organization. In 1906, Paul Rosa was listed as the secretary. In that same year, Paul Rosa was arrested for an assault after an argument with Daniel Moriarty at a Black Road Saloon. The two got into a heated discussion about religion. In Chapter 5, the religious animosity between the Italians and the Irish is discussed. The argument led to blows and a stab wound to Moriarty's shoulder. This may be why in 1908, the president was G. Ferretti. Societies often had regulations regarding criminal records. In 1909, Paolo Rotante was listed as an officer of the union.[75]

---

[72] Stamford Advocate 5/28/1910, 12/11/1911, 10/29/1924.
[73] Stamford Advocate 8/25/1927. 3, 8/26/1927. 1 and 2.
[74] Stamford Advocate 4/1/2001.
[75] Stamford Advocate 3/9/1909. 3.

In 1911 and 1914, the secretary was Enrico D'Aprile. In 1911, the organization posted in the Stamford Advocate calling attention to contractors that on April 1, wages would increase from $3.50 to $4 per man per day, and asked for contractors who were agreeable to contact the union. In 1906, the union received bad press as it was reported that a man was beaten, and half killed in Stamford because he refused to join the union. As early as 1892, the Bricklayers' and Plasterers' Union seemed to be in conflict with the stone mason's Union, and seemed to distance themselves and perhaps try to undercut the organization, "Several members of the Bricklayers' and Plasterers' Union informed a representative of this paper last night that unfair inferences injurious to their organization had been drawn from an article printed last week, in which it was stated that work on certain buildings in town had been suspended because of some difficulty caused by the failure to employ union workmen...The members of the Bricklayers' and Plasterers' Union. Includes all except two or three of the men employed at that trade in Stamford...We are working under the second annual agreement between employers and employees, made and signed on January last. There is not now, nor has there been, the slightest friction between us and the bosses. I know nothing about the affairs of the stonemasons' union. We are willing to work upon any job our bosses contract to do." I do not find Italian names related to the Bricklayers' and Plasterers" Union, as such one can assume this was a rivalry related to ethnicity (e.g. Italians were not allowed or were recipients of bias in that union so they started their own).[76] That is until 1911 when Andrew Cerreta was initiated into Local No. 8 of the Bricklayers' and Plasterers' Union of Stamford. Andrew was born in Calitri on August 30, 1890, the son of Vincenzo Cerreta, who came from a long line of stonemasons. In 1901, he accompanied his father to the United States on the "Nord America." Eventually, he settled in Stamford with his father. He was a newspaper boy, and shoeshine boy, worked at Yale and Towne, the old Leather Shop, the Wire Shop, and other jobs before apprenticing as a mason. He later partnered with Phil Capporizio to form a masonry business, "Capporizio & Cerreta."[77]

Società di Mutuo Soccorso, Provincia di Caserta
Mr. Tommaso Treglia initiated and organized the society on November 22, 1908, and incorporated the society under the laws of Connecticut on February 22, 1909, for Italians and their descendants from the province of Caserta, Italy, under the name Società di Mutuo Soccorso di Minturno e Provincia di

---

[76] Stamford Advocate 1/7/1914. 3, 3/29/1911. 2, 2/14/1911. 5, 1/10/1908. 1, 3/1/1906. 4, 6/1/1892. 1, 3/27/1906. 3, 9/19/1906. 1.
[77] "Celebrating the Heritage," by Mario Toglia, Xlibris Publishing. 337.

Caserta. The organization was well received for three years, however some members felt that not enough consideration was being given to the members that were not from Minturno. A new incorporation was filed under the name Society Provincia di Caserta. At a special meeting in 1913, the society voted a special thanks to the society Dr. J. Nemoitin for his tireless energy and consideration, and to increase his fee by 50 cents per member.[78] The society under its president Alphonse Frasca, petitioned their congressman to vote against the Burnett bill. The congressman responded "I shall surely oppose the Burnett bill as long as it contains the section requiring that immigrants shall be submitted to a literacy test. Whether a man can read or write, in my opinion, is not a test of his honesty and intention to be a good loyal American if he is given the chance." A local plea for protest by Italians against the bill, written by Pirin Diana was carried in the Advocate in Italian and English translation. Mr. Diana argues that the result would be a great reduction in immigration and argues that legislation is against their own interest. That it not only would negatively affect its citizen's faith in government but also would hinder economic growth. Without the engine of cheap labor of immigrants, industrial and agricultural development would recede and in turn, wealth and prosperity in the United States would be negatively impacted. After the veto of the bill, Mr. Diana is quoted as saying: "It casts a glory on the closing days of President Taft's administration." Mrs. Blickensderfer, friend to the Italians was quoted as saying: "The uneducated Italian does not worry me as much as some others. He is a worker and thrifty. The pick and shovel men are not as a rule criminals. Someone must do the laborers' work. Educated men cannot and will not do it. We must have laborers. At Essex Market of twenty-one vagrancy cases not one was an Italian. Some of these absolutely illiterate foreigners have hearts of gold. They respond splendidly to any demonstration of real sympathy and friendship. A bill is needed to shut out those of diseased mind or body; it is they who commit the crimes and cause the trouble."[79]

The society held a meeting in 1917 for members who had been included in the national war draft, to discuss questions they had and what provisions could be made for dependents of these men.[80] The society took umbrage with Dr. Sorgi based on his remarks about the Italian Community not supporting the Red Cross enough. This resulted in a resolution being sent to the Italian delegate of the Red Cross in New York demanding Dr. Sorgi's removal as head of the district office of the Red Cross. Officers elected in 1940 were: Antonio

---

[78] Stamford Advocate 2/4/1913.
[79] Stamford Advocate 2/7/1914, 1/3/1913, 2/15/1913.
[80] Stamford Advocate 8/24/1917.

Lazzaro, president; Antonio Verrico, vice president; Eugenio Mallozzi, corresponding secretary; Tommaso Adipietis, financial secretary; Evangelista Gentile, treasurer; Albert Perella and James Rizzi, trustees; Vincenzo Vigliotti, Domenico Pagliaro and Agostino Bruno, health officers; Giovanni Cortese, hall officer; Antonio Sorgente, representative to the board of directors of the Italian Institute. They celebrated the 40th anniversary of the society in 1949, members there to celebrate included: N. Tamburri, Dr. Jacob Nemoitin, F. LaRocca, J. Santagato, C. Sessa, and T. Treglia. The Forty-first anniversary was observed at their clubrooms at 69 Greenwich Avenue, forty members attended including, Joseph Fiorelli, Thomas A. Dipietro, Thomas Teriglio, Attorney Charles Sessa, Frank LaRocca, and Dr. Nemoiten.[81]

Società Calabrese

The Calabrese Society was organized on April 3, 1910, for Italians and their descendants from the province of Calabria, Italy. The purposes of the society were social, benevolent, and patriotic. The president was James D'Amico, and the treasurer was Charles D. Vuono. Honorary life members in 1910 included Anthony Geronimo, John H. Shipway, Dr. Charles E. Rowell, Hon. F.J. Tupper, William Ziegler, Joseph H. Moll, Hon. Charles D. Lockwood, William F. Waterbury, Joseph G. Houghton, John J. Looney, Thomas J. Pritchard, Robert Whittaker, Albert Phillips, and Dr. Sorgi. On Sunday, September 11, 1910, there was a benefit performance to raise money for the society at the Lyceum Theater. The five act play "La Virginia" was presented in Italian. Also on that day, the two flags of the society were christened. The sponsors for the American flag were Dr. C.E. Rowell, and Mrs. F.T. Towne. The sponsors for the Italian flag were Leo Donatelli and Mary Vuono. There were roughly 120 members in 1910. Elected officers for 1911 were V. D'Amico, president; N. Cognetta, vice-president; L. Berlingo, treasurer; D. Valentino, secretary; G. Gaetano, vice secretary; F. Medici, financial secretary; trustees, P. Consentino, A. Colombano, P. Medici, and M. Toscano; and Dr. A. Sorgi, physician. The society presented the play "Tosca" with the following performers: P. Cosentino, R. Bernardini, N. Pascale, D. Valentino, N. Cognetta, F. Cognetta, D. Posca, G.B. Micelotti, S. Lazoppino. After the performance there was dancing. The committee in charge included Messrs. Amalfitono, Cosentino Pascale, Valentino, Cognetta, Posca, Michelotti, and Lazoppino.[82]

---

[81] Stamford Advocate 12/16/1918.
[82] Stamford Advocate 9/1/1910, 9/8/1910, 9/12/1910, 12/28/1910, 2/23/1911.

Società Mutuo Soccorso di Pugliese

The Articles of Association for the Società Mutuo Soccorso di Pugliese were filed in December 1910. The purpose of the organization was to help, aid, and render assistance to the members of the society in cases of sickness, death, or other distress, elevate their civil, moral, and social standing and disseminate general knowledge among them. The subscribers were Nicola Collini, Leonardo Demino, Propsero Gianvito, Nicola Pavia, and Allesandro Melfi.[83]

Società Cosentina

A Società Cosentina Gaetano Argento is listed on 32 Liberty Street. In 1910 the elected officers were: Joe Berlingo, president; E. Belmonte, vice president; S. Cofone, secretary; F. Belmonte, vice secretary; A. Bruno, treasurer; T. Belmonte financial secretary; trustees, E. Berlingo, F. Cofone, F. Marzullo; and Dr. A. Sorgi as physician. This organization was in Greenwich at one time with Umile Imbrogno as president. The organization was sued by Louis Sementini in 1914. Sementini claimed $100 in damages claiming the society did not live up to its agreement to pay sick benefits and also illegally expelled him from membership and from the office of secretary. Drs. Sorgi and Costanzo testified as to Louis' illness. Sementini won the case.[84]

Società Aurora

The society composed of the natives of the Province of Salerno was organized at the Alhambra Theater (owned by Anthony Geronimo). The founders were Messrs. Sansone, D. Mancini, D'Amico, Rev. Barone, A. Petrosino, C. Passaro, G. Passaro, M.D. Amato and G. Carlino. The flags of the society were dedicated on October 20, 1912. The president in 1912 was Pasquale Sansone. In 1924, Frank Morro, was president, and the organization was located at 52 Pacific Street. In 1936, the Aurora Mutual Benefit Society officers were Anthony Gervasio, president; Rosario Ganino, vice president; Joseph Lionetti, corresponding secretary; Joseph DeVito; financial secretary; Sabatino Sgritta, treasurer; Guiseppe Presutto, Bruno Ganino and Anthony Sansone; trustees.[85]

North Italian Social Club

The North Italian Social Club was organized in 1912. Anthony Geronimo was president in 1932 and 1933. In 1933, officers included: Bruno Ro-

---

[83] Stamford Advocate 12/9/1910. 6.
[84] Stamford Advocate 12/28/1910, 5/8/1964, 1/20/1914. 8, 2/15/1914. 9.
[85] Stamford Advocate 10/21/1912, 10/19/1912, 10/29/1924, 1/22/1940, 7/11/1949, 12/29/1936. 2.

botti, vice president; David Granelli, corresponding secretary; Buff Prelli, sergeant at arms; John Draghi, financial secretary. The society had a dance in 1933; some of the proceeds from the event were donated to the Red Barrel fund (described later in Chapter 7). Other members during that year included: Bonfiglio Preli, Angelo Boldrighini, G. Valentini, Attilio Fontana and A. Serra. The club also had a women's auxiliary; the officers of which in 1933 included Josephine Mascarello, chairman; Mrs. Eugene Nosenzo, vice chairman; Miss Elbina Sabini, corresponding secretary; Miss Isabelle Capri, financial secretary; Lydia Raiteri, treasurer, and Mrs. Bruno Robotti, Mrs. Stephen Raiteri and Mrs. A. Benevelli, were trustees. In 1936, officers were: J Mazzoli, president; L. Bacco, vice president; A. Fornaciari, corresponding secretary; F. Benevelli, financial secretary; F. Sapelli, treasurer; E. Nosenzo, H. Bracchi, C. Guasco, board of trustees; B. Robotti, A. Sanscione, F. Diotalevi, A. Sarra, A Bacco, board of governors; M. Rondano, F. Boccadoro, A. Boldrighini, P. Cavanna, L. Bacco, house committee, B. Robotti, P. Cavanna, L. Ferrero, application committee, and A. Foligno, sergeant at arms. The organization was involved with the formation of a bocce league in 1940.[86]

Ladies Lodge A. Cairoli of the Order of the Sons of Italy
This was the first Italian women's society in Stamford. It's officers in 1913 were Mrs. Virginia (Cavanna) Vetriolo (who was founder and first president of the organization), venerable; Mrs. L. Mascarella, assistant venerable; Mrs. C. De Vito, secretary; Mrs. M. D'Addone, financial secretary; Mrs. L. Maffucci (likely, Elizabeth, Alonzo's wife as he sometimes went by the name Lonnie), treasurer; Mrs. M. Maddaloni, orator; Mrs. M. Ediano, Mrs. M. Sessa and Mrs. R. Pavia trustees; Mrs. Carmela Scalzi and Mrs. J. Rossi masters of ceremonies; Mrs. N. Capossela and Mrs. J. Pavia sentinels. In 1915, (as part of the Daughters of Italy), officers included: Virginia Vetriolo, venerable; Margaret Pannone, treasurer, Maria L. Maffucci, secretary. The president in 1924 was Clara Mecca, 211 West Avenue.[87]

Carmella Scalzi (of the Scalzi Paint store family see Chapter 8) is remembered by her granddaughter Patricia Scalzi as the most affable woman she knew. Patricia remembers huge dinners at her grandparents' house on Ralsey Road (which was very close to her family's house) with extended family. She remembers Carmela rolling out ravioli and using dandelion greens. Patricia also remembers excursions with her grandmother on the bus to the Westside to meet with family and friends. Her grandmother's presence remains with her

---

[86] Stamford Advocate 10/29/1937. 22, 9/20/1932. 8, 2/16/1933. 8, 2/27/1933. 8, 3/17/1933. 8, 12/4/1933. 8, 3/11/1936. 5, 8/6/1940. 14.
[87] Stamford Advocate 11/10/1913, 10/29/1924, 4/17/1914.

even though she has passed, as she thinks about her every day. This exemplifies what many Stamford Italian Americans feel about their grandparents who worked hard, sometimes serving on society committees and still finding time to make memories with family. For many Italians, time spent with Nonna remains a comforting feeling that remains with them long after Nonna is gone.

In 1916, the officers were: Virginia Vetriolo, venerable; Margaret Pannone, treasurer; and Maria L. Maffucci, secretary. In 1917, officers included: Anna DeRosa, venerable; Margaret Pannone, treasurer; and Maria Farenga, secretary. In 1918, officers included: Anna DeRosa, venerable; Maria Cesareo, financial treasurer; Maria Farenga, corresponding secretary; and Caterina Costanzo, treasurer. In 1920, Maria Adelaide Chiatappa, is listed as an officer in the Stamford directory. In 1923, Mrs. Anna DeRosa is listed as an officer. In 1924, Mary Chiapetta DeRosa is listed as an officer. In 1926 through 1934, and 1936 through 1940 Clair Mecca is listed as an officer.

Aviglianese Political Club

The club elected new officers in 1915: M. A. Genovese, president; Joseph Mancusi, vice president; Paul Nardozzi, secretary; and Vito Sabia, treasurer. Vito Sabia was employed by the city of Stamford and was involved with founding of the Italian Center.[88]

North Italy Mutual Benefit Society

The North Italy Mutual Benefit Society was formed in 1913 to encourage the social, civic, and moral welfare of its members and to help each other in case of sickness or need. The incorporators were: Quintino Vetriolo, Agostino Cavanni, Councilman Antonio Geronimo, Antonio Maggi, and Anton Rambottini. The society participated in the 275th Anniversary parade of the founding of Stamford in 1916 and was active at least into the 1940s. One of the members Paul Bacco was a contractor who constructed sewers for the city in the Shippan area in the 1920s and 1930s and built 10 of the Merritt Highway bridges: including the Lapham Avenue Bridge (Route 165), Guinea Road Bridge, Long Ridge Road/Route 104, Wire Mill Road Bridge, Frenchtown Road Bridge, Rippowam River Bridge, Easton Road/Route 136 Bridge, West Rocks Road Bridge, Newtown Turnpike Bridge, and Metro-North Railroad Bridge. The presence of these artistic and unique bridges is one of the reasons that the Merritt Parkway is listed on the National Register of Historic Places. The work was funded by the Franklin Delano Roosevelt Works Progress administration and provided many jobs for local laborers who had been

---

[88] Stamford Advocate 4/13/1915, 7/14/1927.

suffering through the Great Depression. Bacco was born May 9, 1884, to Luigi and Paolina Bacco in Alessandria, Italy, and lived at 172 Fifth Street in Stamford.[89]

Committee of Italian Red Cross
In 1912, at the Lyceum Theater various societies gave entertainment for the benefit of the Red Cross Society in the Turko-Italian War. About $400 was collected. The committee in charge of the event was comprised of Leo Donatelli, Dominick Crasandi, Angelo Cappabianco, Luigi Serafino, Leo Acuosto, and Vincenzo Trimboli. The united Italian societies at Woodside Park held the first grand festival for the benefit of the Red Cross on September 6, 1915. The affair raised $1,000. It started with a parade that included over a thousand men in the morning and concluded with fireworks in the evening. The Colonial Band led the way and Q. Vetriolo was grand marshal. A 10-mile Bicycle race took place at the park and was won by John Feretta and moving pictures were shown during the afternoon. The committee in Stamford had the following officers in 1917: Dr. A. S. Sorgi, president, Louis Donatelli, treasurer, and Vito Pittaro, secretary. In 1936, the committee arranged for the Italian Consul General to speak at the home of Joseph Gerli on Weed Avenue. The members of the committee included Vito Pittaro, president; Zanetto Cappabianco, treasurer; Pasquale Chiapetta, secretary; Cav. Pietro Rosa, Tenente Benedetto Corbo, Tenente Alberigo Parrella, Dr. Lindo De Francesco, Attorney Charles Sessa, Pietro Cosentino, among others. [90]

Caserta Benefit Society
The Caserta Benefit Society founding member was Thomas Treglia (who was also president of the Operaia Society, charter member of the Italian Institute board of directors, and member of the Minturnese Club and Italian Center).[91] A flag dedication ceremony was held in September of 1916. At this event, Mayor Treat told the Italians assembled that their love of their flag, and the spirit of patriotism which they had always manifested, were admirable characteristics of the Italian people. He congratulated them for their love of country, and for the strides they had made in America, where he said, they are rapidly becoming a part of the life of the nation. Alphonso Frasco was president of the society. Domenico Melillo, the orator of the group delivered

[89] Carl Lobozza's Journey ThroughTime. 38" Stamford Advocate 2/21/1941, 1/25/1940, 3/31/1938, 1/14/1921, 10/27/1913, 5/1/1916, 8/16/1927, 9/21/1927, 7/14/1928, 7/12/1929, 1/3/1931, 2/17/1931, 7/11/1931, 5/11/1932.
[90] Stamford Advocate 2/12/1912, 11/15/1917, 9/7/1915, page 1, 3/27/1936.
[91] Stamford Advocate 9/12/1962, 5/24/1956.

an address. The committee arranging the ceremony were: Antonio Conetta, secretary; Salvatore Conetta, treasurer; Vincenzo Pecoraro, chairman; Achille Vitti and Alphonso Frasca. Antonio Lazzaro was president of the society, honorary member of the Paganini and Saint Cecilia Musical and Dramatic Club, financial secretary of the Local 449 and corresponding secretary and president of the Minturnese Social Club. In 1917, the society held a meeting to explain the World War I draft to members and to indicate that they would provide benefits for dependents. Another benefit was held in July of 1926 at the hunting lodge of Nunziato Tamburri in North Stamford. One hundred members attended. Committee members were Thomas Treglia, Antonio Perella, Clemente De Lucia, Ralph Treglia, G. Cortese, A. Pagliaro, P. De Carlo, A. Vigilotti and P. Sabatiello. Frank LaRocca was a past president as well. In 1924, Enrico Parente was president and the organization was located at 14 Alden St. The clubrooms were at 69 Greenwich Ave. in 1941.[92]

The Sons of Italy

The society celebrated Columbus Day in 1917. The committee in charge included Domenico Mancini, chairman; E. Giannitti, treasurer; P. Rosa, secretary; L. Serafino; N. Cognetta, G. Passero, N. Pace, G. Carpinella. There was a parade in the evening at 7:45, with a mass meeting later on in the high school assembly hall. Dr. J.J. Costanzo presided, and Judge Charles D. Lockwood was a speaker. The band paraded about the city in the morning.[93] Sons of Italy 1918 officers were: Rosario Giamo, grand deputy; Giuseppe Maffiucci, ex-venerable; Gaetano Maddalani, Venerable; Dominica Ferranga, assistant venerable; Angelo Cesareo, recording secretary; Fortunato Caputo, financial secretary; and Vito Pittaro, Ignaccio Lupo, Alberto Petrosino, Arcangelo Centare, Carlo Caputo, trustees; Pietro Rosa, lecturer; Luigi Altomari, inside sentinel; Michael Giordano, outside sentinel; Guiseppe Martone, warden; and Giovanni Ferretti.[94] Many of the separate organizations that had organized early on consolidated into and affiliated themselves with the Sons of Italy.

La Società Mutuo Soccorso fra Settefratesi "Capitano Alessandro Venturini" di Stamford

The society was formed on April 15, 1916, and incorporated under the laws of Connecticut on April 25th, 1916. It is named after a Settefratese who was killed in the First World War. The purposes of which were the following: To enable the members of said corporation to aid and assist one another

---

[92] Stamford Advocate 9/25/1916, 8/24/1917, 10/29/1924, 7/19/1926, 4/25/1975, 7/8/1941.
[93] Stamford Advocate 10/12/1917.
[94] Stamford Advocate 6/26/1918.

when in need; and to aid and succor the families, widows, and orphans of the members, when in want and to practice benevolence towards all.

A list of the founding members are as follows:

Buzzeo Pasquale	Terenzio Giuseppe
Buzzeo Marino	Terenzio Vincente di Ant.
Colarossi Michele	Tamburri Giuseppe fu
Carella Luigi	Crescenzo.
Carella Antonio	Tamburri Sabato
Conetta Donato	Tiani Serafino
Conetta Onesto	Vitti Achille
Conetta Michele	Vitti Nunziato
Conetta Silvestro ·	Vitti Giuseppe
Conetta Antonio	Vitti Nazzareno
Conetta Domenico	Vitti Antonio di Gius.
Capocci Giusto	Vitti Raffaele fu Michele
Di Preta Vincenzo	Vitti Raffaele fu Loreto
Di Preta Nicola	Ioli Domenico
Di Preta Giuseppe	Latte Alfredo
Del Pianto Antonio	Latte Cesare
Frattaroli Michele	Loppittoli Ernesto
Frattaroli Luigi	Macari Michele
Frattaroli Nicola	Mancini Antonino
Farina Pasquale	Pompa Luigi
Farina Luigi	Pellicci Antonio fu Fr.
Gentile Francesco	Perella Antonio
Gentile Antonio	Pompa Antonio
Pia Orazio	Vitti Domenico
Pia Michele	Vitti Gerardo
Pia Vincenzo	Vitti Battista
Pia Guido	Ventre Giuseppe
Pia Antonio	Vagnone Marco
Pia Gerardo	Zezima Ermenegildo
Palomba Domenico	Zezima Vincenzo
Socci Rossini	Zezima Pietro
Socci Gerardo	Zezima Mario
Socci Tommaso	Zacarola Francesco
Socci Giuseppe	

In order to be entered into the lodge, the following requirements had to be met one had to be Italian or a descendant of an Italian father, or born in Italy, have good morals and a sound body, demonstrate that you were sustaining yourself with a job and be honest. In addition, the applicant had to be 18 and older, but not older than 50, show that the applicant had no chronic diseases, and had not been convicted of serious crimes. An applicant must have his form signed by themselves and an existing member and accompanied by a $1 fee. If the applicant was illiterate and could not sign, they would make the sign of the cross witnessed by two people.

The entrance fee into the society ranged from $2 to $12 depending on the age of the applicant. Afterward, the monthly fee was $1.25. The benefits included financial assistance in the event of illness, medical assistance, and medications (including operations and special illnesses), and funeral and mortuary expenses. In case of sickness, the assistance was $10 per week for 3 months, $5 for the next three months, and $3 a month after that. After receiving a full year's assistance, a doctor's note was required to receive additional benefits. The incorporators were Achille B. Vitti, Orazio Pia, and Guiseppe Terenzio. In 1917, there was a dedication of the flags (Italian and American) of the society at Red Men's Hall. Homer S. Cummings and Mrs. W.J. Blickensderfer were sponsors for the American Flag and Dr. Antonio Fanoni and Miss Louise Tamburri for the Italian flag. The committee in charge of the event included: E. Zezima, S. Conetta, A. Conetta, P. Zezima, V. DiPreta, and A. Vitti. In 1925, the Society had a dinner in honor of Dr. De Prete of New York City at the Davenport Hotel in Stamford. Alphonso Macari, president of the society opened the night and introduced Joseph Tamburri of High Street as the Toastmaster. In the Doctor's speech, he urged the continuation of the work to Americanize the Italians in Stamford. Additionally, an appeal was made for contributions to a fund to build a school in Settefrati. The society marked its 50th anniversary in ceremonies at the Italian Center in 1966; in attendance were Achille Vitti and Guido Pia, two of the original members.

One winter day in 1931 a few Settefratese were standing and shivering on a street corner trying to forget the cold until one of them came up with the idea that they should start a social club. They rented a garage for this purpose, building a fire in the middle of it. They each chipped in a gallon of wine, and played cards for the wine, losers paying up. With this money, they rented a better place. The Settefratese Social Club was formed, and it held meetings at its clubrooms on Anthony Street. Later those who could afford chipped in money and when they were able, they bought a property on Virgil Street. In 1933, the officers were Achille Vitti, chairman; Emilio Terenzio, secretary; William A. Tamburri, Louis Zezima, Charles Vitti, Joseph Carella, and Cesare Latte were on the advisory board. From 1936 through 1940, Emelio Terenzio is listed as an officer. In 1938, the society held its annual outing at Geriak's Farm. The Colonial Band gave a concert. The committee in charge of the event included the following members: Achille Vitti, Raffaele Vitti, Pasquale Buzzeo, Antonia Buzzeo, Vincenzo Pia, Joseph Pia, Anthony Buzzeo, Joseph Carella, Antonio Carella, Anthony Di Pianto, Aruzio Malizzio, Francesco Gentile, Emilio Terenzio, Gerry Zezima, John Presto, Rosino Socci.[95] The advisory board was Achille Vitti, chairman; Emilio Terenzio, secretary; William A. Tamburri, Louis Zezima, Charles Vitti, Joseph Carella and Cesare Latte. Emilio Terenzio was born in Settefrati in 1894, and was a veteran of WWI, serving in the Italian army.[96] In 1939, the annual benefit dance was held at Columbus Hall, the committee in charge included A. Vitti, L. Zezima, T. Pia, A. Buzzeo, R. Buzzeo, R. Vitti, A. Vitti, G. Pia, E. Terenzio, M. Frattaroli, V. DePrete, P. Buzzeo and M. Zezima. In 1936, the Settefratese woman formed their own social club, which organized trips for members and family.[97]

There is a reference to another society "Anserici Alberico" in Stamford for the Settefratese. This is the oldest Settefratese organization in the U.S., founded in 1891. The organization is named after Alberico Anserici, a monk who lived in Settefrati and wrote about visions he had as a child while in a coma. It is believed that Dante was inspired by these writings when he created the Divine Comedy. Members paid $2 a month, and in return received free medical attention, $14 per week for the first 12 weeks of illness, and $10 a week for the remaining weeks up to 40 weeks. They also received $400 upon the death of the member and $100 upon a member's wife's death for funeral expenses. The organization was primarily for New York residents, but for a year before the founding of La Società Mutuo Soccorso fra Settefratesi "Capitano Alessandro Venturini" di Stamford there was a branch in Stamford. This branch became part of the "Capitano Alessandro Venturini" di Stamford in 1916.[98]

First and Third Ward Republican Club

A "ward" is an optional division of a city or town for administrative and representative purposes, especially for purposes of an election. These districts were created for the purpose of providing more direct representation. Stamford was divided into six wards. Italians seemed to be most concentrated in

[95] Stamford Advocate 8/25/1938. 8.
[96] Stamford Advocate 4/27/1916, 4/19/1966, 3/23/1925, 4/16/1917, 10/24/1933, 11/9/1965, 11/3/1970, 7/22/1961, 11/30/1985. 5, 10/24/1933. 8, 11/19/1970, Gravinese Mutual aid Society 75th anniversary booklet, March 30, 1996.
[97] Stamford Advocate 2/8/1939. 8, Gazzetta Settefratese Vol 1, June 1947.
[98] *Una Nuova E Piu Grande Settefrati Sul Suolo D'America*, Mario Vitti, 62, Gazzetta Settefratese Vol 1, June 1947.

the first, second, and third wards in the early 1900s. See Appendix J for a map and description of the streets making up the wards. The "West Side" overlaps the First and Third Wards. In 1926, members included Louis Vaccaro, C. Sabia, C. Vitti, J. Preziosi and W. Zezima. In the same year, the following officers were elected for the club: Joseph Carpinella, president; S.B. Esposito, vice president; Ralph Lionetti, Jr., secretary; and Peter Zezima, treasurer. The Board of Directors were Joseph T. Prezioso, Anthony D. Sabia and Joseph T. Tamburri.[99] In 1928 and 1929 the officers were: Carpinella, president; S.B. Esposito, vice president; Ralph Lionetti Jr. secretary; Peter Zezima, treasurer, L. Caporizzo, J. Rosa and F. Lacerenza; trustees, C. Galasso, sergeant-at-arms.[100] The First and Third Ward Republican Club officers in 1930 were J. Carpinella, president; Charles Sessa, vice president; William A. Sabia, treasurer; Ralph Lionetti, Jr., secretary; and Christine Uva, sergeant-at-arms. Leonard Mancusi, Aurelio Rich, and Frank Lacerenza were trustees. William Viggiano, Charles Vitti, Anthony Sabia, Joseph Santasiero, Dr. Frank Sproviero, and Paul Pavia were elected to the advisory board. Carpinella was elected president for the seventh time in 1930. Other officers were Nicholas Colucci, vice president; Ralph Lionetti, Jr. secretary; Frank Frattaroli, treasurer; Christine Uva, sergeant-at-arms; and Ralph Ienner, Louis Sisto and Nicholas Caruso, trustees. The same officers were in place in 1932 and 1933. Other active members of the club in 1933 included A. Rich, Louis L. Caporizzo, Joseph Rinaldi, Anthony Frattaroli, Peter Caruso, Salvatore Rosa, John Carlo, Angelo Rinaldi, William Ienner, Frank Grassi, William Sabia, Carmine Montanaro, Louis Vaccaro, John Catino, James Caruso and William Caporizzo.[101] In 1932, Michael J. Frattaroli ("Pop") was endorsed to run as the Republican nominee as constable. He garnered 999 votes in the primary, not enough to win. In 1933, the club announced it was changing its name to the First Stamford Italian American Republican Club. The I.A.R.C. president Dr. Frank J. Sproviero was not happy with this, as he believed his organization had the right to the name and engaged legal action. Carpinelli moved forward and announced they would take members from all over the city and set up a membership committee consisting of: Harry Fedele, Vito Colucci, Charles Vitti, Tony Trolla, V.A. Sabia, A. Summa, T. Stefano, A. Dinecola, L. Cerretta, T. Lovallo, A. Zinicola. A. Circitano, C. Rosa, C. Montanaro, F. Gentile, R. Ienner, C. Zerillo, I. Zerillo, L. Caporizzo, J. Tamburri, J. Laureno. Other members of the club included: Philip Maffei, Joseph Iannazzi, Salvatore Cianculli, Louie De Luc, Vincent Pecorara, and Charles Passero. In

[99] Stamford Advocate 3/10/1926, 7/6/1926, 3/13/1929, 2/1/1926.
[100] Stamford Advocate 3/14/1928.
[101] Stamford Advocate 3/14/1931, 3/9/1932, 3/17/1933, 8/3/1933.

1934, the organization held a New Year's party where Alfred Socci and Mary Calitri entertained. In 1935, active members included: Anthony Fedele, Patrick J. Moruke, Charles Vitti, Joseph L. Carpinelli, Frank Grassi, Dominick Frattaroli, Canio Ienner, Louis Caporizzo, Raffaele Ienner, Patrick Caporizzo, Leo Spignesi, Dominick Sabia, Anthony Rich, Nicholas Tarzia, Thomas Pompa, Angelo Rinaldi and Michael Gasbarro. In 1937, elected officers included: Joseph L. Carpinella, president; Charles Vitti, vice president; Ralph Lionetti, Jr., secretary; Frank Frattaroli, treasurer; J. Michael Cantore, Angelo Rinaldi, and Anthony Pompa, trustees; Dominick Frattaroli, Anthony Fedele, Leo Spignesi, Joseph Rinaldi and Harry Fedele, house committee. In 1938, elected officers included: Joseph L. Carpinella, president; Charles Vitti, vice president; Ralph Lionetti, Jr., secretary; Frank Frattaroli, treasurer; Michael Lionetti, sergeant at arms; William Sabia, Aurelio Rich and Angelo Rinaldi, trustees; Dominick Frattaroli, Harry Fedele, Leo Spignesi, Joseph Rinaldi and Anthony Fedele; house committee; Anthony Fedele, William Grasso and John Laureno, membership committee. The club celebrated their sixteenth annual outing in 1939. Members of the committee included: Councilman William Sabia, Frank Grassi, Paddy Moruke, Ralph Lionetti, Charles Vitti, Leo Spignesi, Charles D'Andrea, Patrick Caporizzo, Anthony Rich, A. Rich, Ray Ienner, c. Ienner, M. Frattaroli, Frank Frattaroli, D. Frattaroli, a. Fedele, Carlo Galasso, William Tamburri, Vito Sabato, Angelo Rinaldi, Nicholas Tarzia and Joseph Rich.[102] In 1936 through 1940, Ralph Lionetti is listed as an officer in the Stamford directory.

Society of Saint Vito Martire and Marie S.S. Del Carmine, Inc.
The first public celebration of St. Vito occurred in 1920. The neighborhood of Stillwater Ave. and Finney Lane was the epicenter of the gathering. Two west side streets that were populated by Italians. Stillwater Avenue was also known as "The Black Road" because the road was the location of several coal stables in the late 19th century, whose wares stained the road black. The celebration was opened with the firing of several salutes, shortly after followed by the Sons of Italy band playing selections near the image of Saint Vito and then parading through the streets of the city. At night, fireworks by Mase de Luscio and Domenico Manquiri went off while Italian delicacies were sold in the streets. The next day was followed by a high mass and parade through the city. The committee in charge of the celebration included Leonardo Accursi, president; Cesare Latte, vice president; Vito Biance, secretary;

---

[102] Stamford Advocate 9/13/1933, 9/20/1933, 12/13/1933, 12/8/1933. 8, 9/16/1932, 9/13/1932, 1/4/1934, 12, 3/15/1937, 6/19/1935, 3/10/1938, 7/22/1939.

Luigi Piacenza, treasurer. Others included in the committee included: Domenico Mancusi, Antonio Conetta, Severio Labella, Pasquale Summa, Pietro Mancusi, Vito Luongo, Canio Galasso, Leonardo Altieri, Angelo Vito Lovalo, Berardino Lovalo, Leonardo Piacenza, Francesco Bochicchio, Vito Suarne, Vito Summa, Jr., Giuseppe Summa, Tommaso Genovese, Donato Sileo, Francesco Lacerenza, Gerardo Gerardi, Salvatore Pace, Giambattista Lovallo, Salvatore Tolla, Canio Summa, Vincenzo Colucci, Bernardo Lupinacci, Vito Santarsiero, Domenico Garaffa, Giuseppe Carpinelli, Vito Colucci, Michele Claps, Bartolomeo Gerardi, Vito Vaccaro, Antonio Di Muro, Vito Nardozza, Francesco Longo, Salvatore Coviello, and Francesco Pironti. These men likely included those that initiated the request to build an Italian national church, Sacred Heart. The event was so successful it continued year after year and engendered pride among Italians in the city, as the clergy of St. John's sanctioned and supported the festival, including the statute being carried in procession through the streets as was the custom in Italy. The significance of this sponsorship cannot be emphasized enough, as this practice was previously used to look down upon the Italians by other Catholics. It was a great source of pride and spark for Italians to unite. Severio Labella constructed a small chapel to house the statue during the festival. In 1921, the second year of the celebration, the Sons of Italy Band played, led by Maestro Tozzoli and paraded through the streets of the west side. Vito Biase was president and Francesco Lacerenza secretary of the committee putting on the event. In the third year of the festival, a carnival was held to raise funds for the building of Sacred Heart Church. Eventually, the festival was moved to the Sacred Heart Church grounds. In 1935, Michael Vaccaro, president of the St. Vito Martyr Society was found not guilty of violating a city ordinance in setting off aerial bomb fireworks, explaining that he had ordered noiseless fireworks, and the manufacturer of the fireworks indicated that the wrong fireworks were shipped and paid a $25 fine. Society of Saint Vito Martire and Marie S.S. Del Carmine, Inc. were separate societies and merged in 1943.[103]

Novelli Dramatic Association

In 1921, Guiseppe Ventura, Augusto Pietrosino, Raffaele Chianelli, Frank Arduino, and Attilio Del Monaco filed incorporation papers for the Novelli Dramatic Association. The purpose of the organization was to be a school for the theatric arts concentrating on historical dramas.[104]

---

[103] Stamford Advocate 11/27/1943, 6/21/1920, 6/17/1921, 6/19/1922, 6/21/1926, 6/16/1930, 6/19/1936, 8/30/2001. 33.
[104] Stamford Advocate 3/5/1921. 3.

Italian Social Club

In 1920, 1924, and 1926 Peter Rosa is listed as officer of the Italian Social Club in the Stamford directory. In 1933, 1937 and 1939, the name Northern Italian Social Club appears in the Stamford directory. In 1940, Joe Mazzoli is listed officer of the social club. In 1934, 1936, 1937 through 1939, the directory lists Albert Sessa as officer of the Italian Social Institute with meeting place at 76 South St. In 1938 and 1939, Joe Mazzoli is listed as an officer. In 1940, Joseph Capone is listed as officer.

Stamford Master Barbers' Protective Association

In 1926, the Stamford Master Barbers' Protective Association elected the following officers: Carlo De Bartolomeo, president; Louis Robustelli, vice-president; Joseph DeVito, recording secretary; and Emilio Greco treasurer. Louis Colucci, Frank Lasandra and Vito Tortora were elected to the Board of Trustees.[105]

Italian American Democratic Club/ First-Third Ward Italian American Democratic Club/ West Side Italian American Democratic Club/ Wilson Democratic Club/Stamford Italian American Association/I.A. Political Association

The First-Third Ward Italian American Democratic Club was organized in 1929 and had clubrooms at 50 Spruce St. and 124 New Spruce St. In 1932, a new slate of officers was elected. Samuel Coppola was president, succeeding Alfonso Vacca. Joseph Robertucci was vice president, Mariano Pimpinella, financial secretary; Nicholas L. Cerulli, corresponding secretary; Jerry Esposito, treasurer; Frank Franzi, house manager; Board of trustees, R. Gannis, chairman; Amerigo Giancola, Vincent Vinci, Michael Macri and Frank Salvatore. In 1936, Joseph Robertucci was reelected president of the club and was named chairman for three consecutive terms. Other officers elected were Anthony Romano, vice chairman, Jerry Esposito, treasurer; Alfonse Vacca, corresponding secretary; Nicola Rizzi; financial secretary; Leonard Meloni, steward; Thomas Tarrantino, sergeant-at-arms. In 1931, the Wilson Democratic Club formed with the following officers: Rocco Muscatello (World War I veteran), president; Vito Longo, vice president; Charles S. Telesco, Secretary; and Alfonso Cantalini, treasurer.

Rocco Muscatello was also the president of the Fraternal Order of Eagles in 1914 (the only Italian officer listed in that organization). There were other

---

[105] Stamford Advocate 7/20/1926.

Italians that were part of the fraternity and in 1911 the following Italians participated as members of the second-place degree team (the team participated in ritualistic ceremonies): Joseph DeMarco, Angelo Cavillo, Fred Cavalier, Rocco Muscatello, and Charles Passaro. Anthony Geronimo also participated in the club in 1915. Mr. Muscatello represented the club at a convention in Spokane in 1915. Rocco was a candidate for assessor in 1928. He served as garbage inspector for the city, and foreman of the construction and maintenance crew. In 1931, Domenico Martella nominated Mr. Muscatello (who was chairman of the club for six years) as honorary president of the Italian-Democratic Club for life. He was unanimously elected. At this same meeting, the club voiced its disapproval that Alphonse Vacca who had been promised a position with the town had not actually been given employment. Acknowledging that the party was making empty promises to the Italian electorate, they "pledged themselves for a loftier aim than "cheap speculation" to obtain jobs, naming respect for their race as their purpose." At that meeting the following delegates to the state convention were elected: Domenico Martella, George S. Matto, Frank Coperino, Michele Pastore, and Anthony Rubino. Unfortunately, Muscatello committed suicide by gas inhalation at 52 at his home on 41 Iroquois Rd. after suffering for many years with chronic arthritis. Also in 1931, Frank Coperino was elected chairman of the Italian American Democratic Club when various members of the club felt the leaders of the club were not working to obtain recognition for Italian Americans from the directors of the Democratic Party. Other officers elected were George DiMateo, assistant chairman; D. Privato, secretary, and Edward Paolino, treasurer.[106]

In 1932, the club endorsed Vice President Vito D. Longo for constable. In 1933, the Wilson Democratic Club held its annual spaghetti dinner. The Wilson Democratic Club officers in 1933 were Vito Longo, president; Bruno Robotti, vice president; Philip Franchini, secretary; Orlando Cantalini, assistant secretary; Frank Cessario, sergeant-at-arms; and trustees were Rocco DeCarlo, Vincent Ursone, and Fiore Cavalier. In the same year, they passed a resolution favoring the repeal of the Eighteenth Amendment. The club held an outing in August 1933, with dancing music provided by the Stamford Marine Band led by Professor Pasquale Zaffino. Entertainment also included Bocci games. Members involved with planning the event included: Patsy Sullo, Patrick Arruzza, Charles Morsa, Emilio Lupinacci, Tony DeLuca, Patsy Pezzimente, S. Perrone, Frank Greco, Michael Macri, Joe Caruso, Tony Ottanio and T. Pistinninzi. In 1936, Archibald Volante was listed as an officer.

---

[106] Stamford Advocate 7/3/1911, 7/19/1915, 12/5/1924, 9/22/1928, 8/13/1931, 8/27/1932, 1/11/1939, 12/30/1939, 9/19/1962, 8/5/1931.

In 1935, Joseph Sementini was elected chairman of the executive committee of the Italian-American Political Association (succeeding resigning Nicholas Cerulli). Attilo Cordillo was elected treasurer, and Leonardo Mellasie, house manager. In 1936, the elected officers were: Alfred A. Volante, president; Vincent Ursone, vice president; Domenic D'Agostino, secretary; Ralph Tartaglione, assistant secretary; Earnest Raffaele, financial secretary; Alfonso Cantalini, treasurer; Frank DiMassi, sergeant-at-arms. The clubrooms were at 49 Pacific St. In 1939, the officers were: Albert Latte, chairman; Amedio Corrente, vice chairman; Frank Genovese, corresponding secretary; Salvatore Raffaele, treasurer; Frank Tarantino, Stefano Pompone, and Amedio Paolin, trustees. In 1940, Albert Latte was listed as an officer of the Wilson Democratic Club. In order to unify the Democrats, in 1934 the Stamford Federation of Italian American Democratic clubs was formed. Four clubs representing every ward agreed to forget factional differences and political animosities to abide by the axiom "In union there is strength." The clubs joining were: the Italian American Democratic Club, the West Side Italian American Democratic Club, the Wilson Democratic Club, and the First and Third Ward Italian American Democratic Club. Assistant prosecuting attorney Frank J. DiSessa was elected president of the federation; Patsy Sulla, first vice president; Joseph Mastrich, second vice president; Dr. Dominic A. Zaccardo, secretary; Joseph Robertucci, treasurer; Patrick Arruzzo, financial secretary; Ignazio Lupo, and Dr. Zaccardo, publicity agents. DiSessa was assistant attorney general of the State of Connecticut starting in 1935, began practice in Stamford in 1931, and was prosecuting attorney of Stamford City Court from 1933 to 1935.[107] In 1934, the Italian groups allied with the Pulaski, Colored, Irish, and Slovak Democratic groups and had an outing at which Alfred Volante was the chairman. In 1936, the First-Third Ward Italian American Democratic Club elected the following officers: Alphonse Vacca, president; Jerry Esposito, vice president; Anthony Romano, treasurer; Dave Moruke, secretary and publicity agent; Salvatore Torlenzo, financial secretary, and Anthony Esposito, sergeant-at-arms. The board directors were Joseph Robertucci, Arnold Vacca, Charles Russo, John Larrocco and Louis Presutto. Leonard Vallero is also listed as an officer with the organization. The Club held free naturalization classes in 1937 twice a week under the direction of Alfonse Vacca, David J. Marrucco and Joseph Robertucci. The first student to secure his naturalization rights under the direction of the instructors was Gerardo Salvatore of Fairfield Ave.

---

[107] *Who's Who Among Americans of Italian Descent in Connecticut*, Joseph William Carlevale, Carlevale Publishing Co. 1942, 159.

In 1932 and 1936, the West Side Italian American Democratic Club also held naturalization classes at 120 Stillwater Ave. In 1933, Florence Lupinacci, and Mary Loglisci were in the woman's auxiliary, and other members of the club included: Patsy Sullo, chairman; Patsy Arruzza, treasurer; Frank Greco, Stanley Perrone, Michael Macri, Louis DeLuca, Emillio Lupinacci, Thomas Pestininizi, Marino Dink. During the Depression, the club held fundraisers for the poor of Stamford, including a play "La Figlia D'un Corso" in 1934 under the direction of Joseph Ventura. In 1935, elected officers included: Patsy Arruzza, president; Patrick Arruzza, vice president; Michael Inzitari, secretary, and Frank Palumbo, treasurer. In 1936, Patsy Sullo was elected president of the West Side Italian American Democratic Club, and band practices under the direction of Patsy Zaffino were held. Other members of the West Side Italian American Democratic Club in 1937 included: Frank Grecco, N. Tiscia, Marino Dink, John Indondi, Ralph Yorfino, Anthony Poccia, Patsy Arruzza, Jr., John Grecco, Michael Macri, Frank Palumbo, Patrick Arruzza, and Patsy Pizzimenti.[108] The Stamford directory lists Arnold Vacca as an officer in 1940.

Second and Fourth Ward Italian-American Republican Club

In 1933, Attorney P. Lawrence Epifanio was reappointed as delegate of the second and fourth ward Italian-American Republican Club (which seems to be a different club than First and Third Ward Club). In 1933, it appears to have changed its name to the Italian-American Republican Club, Frank Spoviero was chairman. In 1936, its president was Salvatore Catino. Salvatore was born in Stamford on January 24, 1901, to Theodore and Grazie Vozzella Catino. He was described as the most dynamic political figure of the Depression years in the city. Catino managed the Stamford and Greenwich Transit companies. He was instrumental in getting Charles E. Moore elected mayor of Stamford in 1938; and served under Moore as chairman of the Board of Public Safety and the public works commissioner. Daniel Scalzi was the chairman of the executive committee and was also president of the Racial Council, an organization of men and women of foreign heritage who sought to avail

---

[108] Stamford Advocate 1/31/1936, 9/19/1930, 9/30/1930, 1/30/1931, 8/20/1931, 1/25/1932, 8/8/1932, 11/27/1933, 1/18/1934, 7/12/1934, 10/19/1934, 11/28/1934, 12/7/1934, 10/9/1936, 10/22/1937, 11/10/1937, 10/17/1931, 9/14/1932, 1/10/1933, 6/13/1933, 1/10/1936, 1/12/1939, 6/21/1940, 10/21/1940, 8/3/1935 p8, 6/17/1935. 8, 6/21/1935. 2, 3/6/1937. 8, 5/1/1937. 16, 5/18/1983. 10, 8/12/1933., 7/19/1932., 6/27/1932., 8/3/1932, 4/8/1933, 8/15/1933, 11/20/1934, 6/15/1935, 6/27/1936.

themselves of the privileges and advantages of Americanism. He assisted many to obtain citizenship.[109]

Società Gravinese di Mutuo Soccorso

The society began on April 11, 1921, by Pietro Casareale, Domenico Martinelli, and Vincenzo Mercadante and is still active today. The society was incorporated to promote a spirit of fraternity and goodwill among its members (Italians and their descendants from Gravina, Italy) and to provide a means for mutual aid and protection. The society assists members in case of sickness, and beneficiaries in the event of a parent's death. The society provides tuition assistance as well. Its members must be 18 years or older and are former residents of Gravina di Puglia, Italy, or direct descendants of such members. Also eligible are the husbands of women born in Gravina di Puglia. The Society's first act of mutual aid was in 1921 when Nicola Terlizzi, drowned in Stamford after only being in America for six months. The Stamford directory for 1940 lists the Gravinese Social Club at 181 West Main St. Pietro Casareale was born in Gravina on June 2, 1877, and operated a grocery store in Stamford. Dominick Martinelli was born in Gravina on August 26, 1891, the son of Michael and Theresa Musso Martinelli. He was an employee of Yale and Towne and a U.S. Army veteran of WWI. The three raised money for a proper burial for Terlizzi. Vincenzo Mercadante was a barber with a shop at the corner of Cove Spring Road and Long Ridge Road. Giovanni Sacco, born in Gravina, Puglia, Bari, Italy on February 25, 1876, son of Antonio and Teresa Tullia Sacco was a founding member. Mr. Sacco was a shoemaker. Frank P. Vetti was treasurer for most of the time from its founding until his death in 1965. He was assistant superintendent of the County Courthouse in Stamford. During the period of the history of this book, the presidents of the society were: Pietro Casareale, Frank Lasalandra, Michael Angelastro, Raffaele Loglisci, Carmine Santore, Frank Vetti, and Anthony J. Sacco.[110] The Society is active to this day. The current president Anthony Ferraro expressed his pride and interest in celebrating Gravinese culture (its food, the connection to the mother country, including their local celebrations and history) in the present and preserving it for future generations. At a recent dinner dance held once COVID restrictions were lifted, he felt gratification and fulfillment witnessing his son carrying on the tradition of parading the patron saint of Gravina into the ballroom, just as many of his ancestors have done. This connection to their past is very powerful and comforting for many Italians in Stamford.

---

[109] Stamford Advocate 2/24/1936, 1/6/1933, 5/1/1933, 9/4/1936, 2/23/1988.
[110] Stamford Advocate 2/10/1961.

Minturnese Social Circle

The Minturnese were part of the Caserta Society, but in 1927, Mussolini redistricted the town from the Caserta region to Lazio. Since they were no longer part of Caserta they broke off into their own society. Minturnese Social Circle (Circolo Sociale Minturnese) had its first meeting on January 9th, 1939 and was organized on Sunday, May 14th, 1939. At the first meeting was chaired by Pasquale Massone as temporary president and Adamo Camerota as secretary. The first meeting was held at 76 South Street (The Italian Center). It was estimated that about 1,000 persons who were born in Minturno or whose ancestors came from that city resided in Stamford at the time. Elections were held on February 12, 1939, and the elected officers were Mariano Pimpinella, president; Pasquale Massone, vice president; Pasquale LoPiano, recording secretary; David Marucco, financial secretary; Ernest Mallozzi, treasurer; Francesco Pensiero, sergeant-at-arms; Antonio Rizzo, clubroom custodian; and the Board of Directors consisted of Antonio Romano, Nicola Rizzi, Filippo Pensiero, clubroom officers were Antonio Esposito, Antonio Pensiero. The organization was to provide recreational interests for young people.[111] In April 1939, the club headquarters were rented for $30 a month at 237 West Main Street. In July of 1939, a woman's Auxiliary was formed and expenditures of $10 were approved to celebrate this event. In September, the "Party Committee" was founded. This committee organized recreational activities and eventually a collection of funds to purchase the headquarters. The first dinner dance was held in December of 1939 and raised $206.12. In June of 1940, a softball team was started. The first bocce courts were built in July of 1940 for $6. In September of 1940, Francesco Corrente donated the first bocce set and Nicola Rizzi was hired as a bartender at $8 per week. Frank LaRocca was the past president and one of the founders. Contrary to other Italian regional social clubs in Stamford today, the Minturnese Club is actually very active and well attended by members.

Italian Institute Welfare Association

An Italian Institute Welfare Association was organized in 1929, with the following temporary officers: Louis Serafino, president; Alphonso Frasca, treasurer; and F. Cantarano, secretary. The association worked with the Family Welfare Association. The intent was to provide welfare work among Italian American residents of Stamford. Alphonso Frasca worked as a sewer improvement inspector for the city, and Yale and Towne.[112]

---

[111] Stamford Advocate 5/16/1939, 8/10/1948, 7/23/1930.
[112] Stamford Advocate 11/25/1929.

Columbus Ramblers of Stamford

In 1931 through 1933, the Stamford directory lists Peter Latte as secretary of the organization. Meetings were held at 3 Liberty St.

Italian Professional & Business Men's Club

Italians formed a club called the "Italian Professional & Business Men's Club." Attorney Charles Sessa and Attorney P.L. Epifanio were presidents. In 1933 the elected officers were: Dr. Peter J. Somma, president; Attorney Frank J. DiSessa, vice-president; Dr. Alfred Sette, secretary; Charles Tarantino, treasurer; and Vincent Santaserio, sergeant-at-arms. The officers stressed the need for its members to take an active interest in the civic, commercial, social and moral welfare of the community and to promote good government and good citizenship. Directors in 1933 were Peter Rosa, Alonzo Maffucci, Joseph Genovese, Daniel Scalzi, Anthony Sabia and Rocco Genovese.[113] Joseph Genovese born in Santa Margherita di Belice, Agrigento, Italy in 1886 was a clothing manufacturer with offices at 101 Main St.[114]

Italian American Democratic League

Domenico Martella was born in Italy in 1880 and lived in Stamford for 24 years (starting in 1924). He was a member of the Italian American democratic Club in 1931 and gave a speech at a fundraiser honoring Senator Guglielmo Marconi on the invention of wireless telegraphy, noting that it had saved thousands of lives at sea and linked the world together. At a meeting of that club in 1933 it was decided to form a new organization, the Italian American Democratic League to better express the desires of Italian Americans. Martelli was asked to work on the new organization. He was elected temporary president, and John Conte temporary secretary at its first meeting in July of 1933. There was opposition to this group from Carmine Preziosi, who wrote a letter to the editor regarding Martella, and Frank Macchio who did the same. In 1934, the following officers were elected: Domenico Martella, president; John Bregialio, vice president; Judith Robertino, secretary; Patsy Masone, assistant secretary; Anthony Sansone, treasurer; Nick Cavalieri, financial secretary. Martella ran for Grand Juror in 1936 and lost. The group associated itself with Major Alfred N. Phillips, Jr. Judith Robertino was born in Bari, Italy in 1914 and immigrated at the age of two. She would later become Controller for Technomic Publications. In 1936, active members included: Gus Belmont, Louis de Francesco, Cesidio Zezima, Nicola Cavaliere, Anthony Tufaro, Antonio Sansone, Charles Sabia,

---

[113] Stamford Advocate 2/18/1930, 1/17/1933.
[114] *Who's Who Among Americans of Italian Descent in Connecticut*, Joseph William Carlevale, Carlevale Publishing Co. 1942, 411.

Michael Biondino, Carlo Morsa, Silvio Guarniere, Sandrino Roscillo, Samuel Rogiero, Mrs. Patsy Masone and Mrs. Louis Gabriele. In 1937, Charles J. Morsa was trustee. Frank Macchio was president. Other members included Anthony Uva, Michael Clapes and Nicholas Cerulli. The Italian American Democratic League opened up clubrooms in 1938 on Stillwater Ave. and Callahan St. Nicholas Cerulli was elected president, Vincent Vitti, vice president; Anthony Lupinacci, treasurer; Louis De Luca, secretary; Vito Coco, sergeant-at-arms; Charles Morsa, Anthony Vitti, Adamo Cammarato, Philip Penserio and John J. Mercede trustees.[115]

Italian War Veterans Association

In 1932 through 1934, and 1936, the Stamford directory lists Primo Eusibio as officer of the Italian War Veterans Association. In 1937 and 1938, Benedetto Corbo is listed as officer. Mr. Corbo president of the association served as a lieutenant in the Italian army. He was active in the Italian Center's school. In 1936, the group sponsored the first showing in the U.S. of a movie depicting the building of roads and bridges in Ethiopia by the Italian army at the Palace Theater. An Italian Legion Auxiliary was initiated in 1935. Marietta Cognetta was president. Other officers included: Lydia Bonaparte, B. Pendleton, Madeline Chiapetta, first vice president; Angelina Coppola, second vice president; Judith Robertino, secretary; Minnie Mascia, assistant secretary; Mrs. A. Carnicelli, treasurer; Josephine Moscarello, historian; Mrs. M. Cantavero, chaplain; and Mrs. M. Serafino, Mrs. L. Chapinelli, Mrs. R. Guariro, Mrs. A. Sabatini and Mrs. I. Telesco, executive board members.[116]

Italian American Democratic League

The Italian American Democratic League was initiated in October of 1933, and had club rooms at 481 Main St. In 1934, Lorenzo Gambino was a member. There was a Fairfield County Italian American League active in 1932, Joseph Carpinelli was a member.[117]

---

[115] Stamford Advocate 8/12/1937, 2/4/1938, 6/16/1948, 11/14/1938, 10/3/1936, 8/27/1936, 3/9/1936, 5/28/1935, 5/21/1935, 12/28/1934, 7/10/1934, 6/5/1934, 5/15/1934, 3/17/1934. 6, 7/24/1933, 6/23/1933, 12/14/1931, 11/15/1988, 4/16/1937, 9/5/1936.
[116] Stamford Advocate 6/5/1936, 12/3/1930, 3/31/1938, 3/29/1938, 10/27/1936, 6/2/1936, 1/10/1935.
[117] Stamford Advocate 1/11/1932, 12/1/1933, 5/12/1934, 9/23/1934, 2/19/1935, 5/4/1938, 12/8/1938.

Italian American Citizen Club of Springdale

The Italian American Citizen Club of Springdale was organized in July of 1934 with clubrooms at Ryan St. The organization seems to have been a political club affiliated with the Democratic Party. The officers of the club were Louis D'Ademo, president; James Totare, vice president; Michael De Angelis, corresponding secretary; Nicholas Volpi, financial secretary; Michael Volpi, treasurer; Nick Carlino, John Cappiello, and Carlo Buccino, trustees; Patsy Herlizzo, Carlo Strade, Frank Corrente, Cristofolo Risolo, and Charles Marsiglia, directors; and Antonio Rodo sergeant at arms. In 1936, the meeting place was 44 Ceretta St. In 1937, the president of the club was Michael DeAngelis, and a house committee to plan future events was named and included: Nicholas Volpe, chairman; Luigi D'Ademo, Antonio Roda, Francesco Corrente, Peter C. Sileo, Carl J. Ferrara and John B. Melfi. A women's auxiliary was formed in May of 1937 with the following officers: Mrs. Peter C. Sileo, president; Mrs. Nicholas Volpe, vice president; Mrs. Henry Pinto, secretary; and Mrs. Michael DeAngelis, treasurer. Other members of the auxiliary included Mrs. Olivia Strate, Mrs. Luigi D'Ademo, Mrs. Carmen Ferrara, Mrs. James Ippoliti, Mrs. Sinibold DePompa, Mrs. Dominick Vesciglio, Mrs. John Conti, Mrs. Frank Corrente and Mrs. Sam Ippolito. In 1938, Peter C. Sileo succeeded Michael DeAngelis as president. Other officers elected were: Sinibold DePompa, vice chairman; Samuel Guarino, finance secretary; Nicholas Volpe, treasurer; Carl J. Ferrara, corresponding secretary; and Carl Strate, Frank Corrente and William Pinto as trustees.[118]

Lodge Lega Arena Dasa

Lodge Lega Arena Dasa formed in 1936 as a mutual benefit society. The lodge retained a doctor (also a member) for the members of the lodge. They were also entitled to flowers at funerals, widows' benefits, and hospital expenses.[119]

Siciliana Mutual Benefit Society, Inc. Stamford

An article of association was filed for Siciliana Mutual Benefit Society, Inc. Stamford in December of 1937. Emanuele Parrino was a member.[120]

---

[118] Stamford Advocate 7/23/1934, 3/8/1937, 5/26/1937, 7/5/1938, 12/12/1938, 12/19/1938, 2/26/1941.
[119] The Arinese, an Italian American Community in Stamford, Connecticut Louis Gesualdi, 2000 John D. Calandra Italian Institute.
[120] Stamford Advocate 12/23/1937. 17, 11/20/1944.

Columbus Republican Club

The Columbus Republican Club was formed in 1939 and was located at Peter Zezima's, (the president) home at 226 West Main St. The membership committee members were Achille Vitti, and Nicholas Colucci. Members of the ways and means committee were Luis Zezima, chairman; Dr. Frank Spoviero, Anthony Lacerenza, Salvatore Zezima, Dominick Romaniello, Michael Stolfi, and Anthony Zezima.[121]

Nurney Club

The Nurney Club seems to be a social club started in the 1930s. A club permit to sell alcohol was applied for by Peter Terenzio in 1935, and by Henry P. Vacca in 1936, and Giovanni Vitti in 1937 and 1938. Florindo Conetta is listed as an officer in 1936 through 1940 in the Stamford directory.[122]

Paragon Association

The Paragon Association appears to be a social club related to politics, which was not exclusively Italian, but had many Italian members. In 1935, the staged boxing bouts to raise money for a Christmas basket fund. Members included Charles J. Morsa, Charles Tallo, William Mancusi, Thomas Caporizzo, Al Vacca, and Leonard Vallano. In 1936, Eugene Sessa was elected chairman at the club rooms at 183 West Main St. at the same meeting it was reported that 133 new voters were registered. Russel Gaudio is listed as an officer in 1938 through 1940.[123]

First Italian and American Women's Democratic Club

In 1935, Mildred J. Coppola was president of the First Italian and American Women's Democratic Club. In that year the group presented the play "La Colpa Vendica la colpa" (a sin vindicates a sin). The lead roles were performed by Marion A. Ventura and Nicola Cognetta.[124]

Catholic Women's Council

The women of Sacred Heart Church formed a council. In 1939, they were active in raising money with a spaghetti supper. The committee included: Mrs. Fredrick M. Lione, chairman; Mrs. Robert J. Lessard, cochairman; and members, Mrs James Costanzo, Mrs. E. Gaynor Brennan, Mrs.Frank Rich, Mrs. Frank Andrea, Mrs. Ralph Cerreta, Mrs. S. Benjamin

---

[121] Stamford Advocate 6/3/1939. 8.
[122] Stamford Advocate 9/5/1935, 18, 10/23/1936, 10/10/1937, 10/17/1937, 10/10/1938.
[123] Stamford Advocate 10/31/1935, 2/21/1936, 4/16/1937. 8, 12/19/1951, 7/1/1940.
[124] Stamford Advocate 2/26/1935.

Esposito, Mrs. Peter Rosa, Mrs. Paul Pavia, Mrs. Joseph Giancola, Mrs. Frank Gaipa, Mrs. Anthony Marrucco, Mrs. Rocco Genovese, Mrs. Anthony Sabia, Mrs. Patrick Maruke, Mrs. John Scalzi, Mrs. Charles Lopriore, Mrs. Pasquale Chiappetta, Mrs. Anthony Moraio, and Mrs. Louis Robustelli. In 1940, the following names are among the committees: Mrs. Vincent Giampietro, Mrs. Julia Conetta, Mrs. Peter Rosa, Mrs. Paul Pavia, Mrs. Nicholas Martinelli, Mrs. Gaipa, Mrs. Ennia Grannetti, Mrs. William Telesco, Mrs. Dominick Scutti, Mrs. William Sabia, Mrs. M. Prelli, Mrs. Frederick Leone, Mrs. Lucian Robustelli, Mrs. Anthony De Vito, Mrs. Anthony Marucco, Mrs. Joseph Rustici, Mrs. Rocco Da Dinaro, Mrs. C. De Vita, Mrs. Rose Scinto, Miss F. Carlucci, Miss Antonetta Monti, Miss Angela Claps and Miss Rose Scinto from Sacred Heart Church; Mrs. William Vuono, and Mrs. Frank Rich, from St. Mary's Church; Mrs. Ralph Costanzo, and Mrs. Anthony Sabia from St. John's Church, and Mrs. Henry Costanzo from St. Cecilia's Church.[125] Mrs. Dominick Roina is listed as an officer of the Stamford Council of Catholic Women in 1939 and 1940.

Augusto Fornaciari Post No. 10, Italian American World War Veterans of the United States

Augusto Fornaciari was a Stamford resident who died in World War I (See Chapter 7). In 1941, Joseph Farenga, another WWI veteran was elected president of the group. Other officers were Henry Costanzo, senior vice commander; William Vaccagnino, junior vice commander, Dr. D. Zaccardo, Chaplin; Frank Barrella; officer of the day; Joseph Palo, rehabilitation officer, Ernest Mallozzi, historian, Joseph Gatti, quartermaster, Anthony Sabia, judge advocate; Anthony Caputo, sergeant at arms. The trustees were Canio Ferrara, Joseph Colucci, and Leonard Piacenza. The adjutant was Carlo J. DeBartolomeo.[126]

The following organizations are listed as Italian societies in 1924: Società Alta Wolia, A. Colombana, president 29 Garden St.; Società Giovinese, Michael Gira, 255 West Main St; Union of Labor, Guiseppe Carella, president, 27 Finney Lane. In 1906, Nicola Pellicciari is listed for the Piano and Organ Workers Union No. 40 in Stamford. In 1909, Salvatore Agritta is listed as officer and the meetings were held at 101 Pacific St.[127] Dr. A. Sorgi is listed as president of the Society Mazzini. Theodore Ottaviano was president of the Labor Union No. 101 in 1908.[128] The Stamford directory lists the Italian American Citizen's

---

[125] Stamford Advocate 10/9/1939. 8, 3/29/1940.
[126] Stamford Advocate 10/24/1941, 4/17/1946.
[127] Stamford Advocate 3/9/1909. 3.
[128] Stamford Advocate 10/29/1924, 3/27/1906, 1/10/1908.

Club in 1938 through 1940. The Italian legionnaires is also listed as an organization in 1936 through 1940, with Emilio Terenzio as an officer in 1939 and 1940. The Waterside Republican Club is listed in 1936 with P. Lopiano as officer.[i] Stephen Franco is listed as officer of the Loyal Order of Moose in 1940. Frank Magda is listed as officer of the Woodmen of the World in 1933.

The wide variety and number of Italian American organizations result from the diversity of the Italians themselves. In the early years of immigration, there were more organizations that included all regional groups, as the population grew there were more organizations that pertained to specific towns or regions (because there were more Italians from these towns or regions). Additionally, political organizations started out as general clubs, but then morphed into clubs specifically for a party and then into parties by the ward of its members. There were attempts to unite all groups under one block, but this was only temporarily successful and could not work because of the different religious, political, and occupations of the diverse group. As time progressed, Italians were more incorporated into the general mainstream population. As a result, separate organizations became less necessary and the organizations morphed into solely social organizations.

Before this occurred, the Italian community through their own efforts (having been excluded from existing organizations) was able to harness the power of unity to their benefit in terms of representation in government, self-security, and worker's rights. The Italian organizations were a welcome respite for new immigrants providing socialization opportunities that would not have been available due to language barriers and the general unwelcoming atmosphere of other citizens existing during these times. These organizations would also provide a means of passing on Italian culture and traditions to future generations. Religious practice was one of these traditions. Dignity in and acceptance of Italian religious expression would also test the Italian community in Stamford.

---

[i] Stamford Advocate 4/8/1936.

CHAPTER 5

Religion

Chi la dura la vince.
(Good things come to those that wait.)

R eligion is an important aspect of Italian culture. There is diversity of religions among Italians. As a result of unique aspects of Italians' practice of
religion, religiosity became more complex in America. True religious freedom
was not experienced in the early immigrant experience because of their unique
practices. Religious choice was not entirely new to Italians, but the ratio of
Catholics to other religions of the populous certainly was a change for Italians
who immigrated to Stamford. This difference was partially a result of how religious practices developed in the state. Of all the colonies, only Maryland (established by a Catholic) granted religious freedoms. The First Amendment,
which establishes the separation of church and state was adopted on December
15, 1791. This Amendment only prohibited the federal government from in-
terfering in a person's religious beliefs. Before 1818, Connecticut was a theocracy, where membership in the Congregational Church had at one point been
required for those voting for or participating in public office. Connecticut's
1818 Constitution disestablished the Congregational Church and provided for
a limited form of religious toleration in its Article 7:

> It being the duty of all men to worship the Supreme Being, the great Creator
> and Preserver of the Universe, and their right to render that worship, in the
> mode most consistent with the dictates of their consciences; no person shall
> by law compelled to join or support, nor be classed with, or associated to,
> any congregation, church or religious association.... And each and every so-
> ciety or denomination of Christians in the state, shall have and enjoy the
> same and equal powers, rights and privileges; and shall have power and au-
> thority to support and maintain the ministers or teachers of their respective
> denominations, and to build and repair houses for public worship....
>
> (Janis, 486)

At one time the law made the State Church the lawful congregation and sub-
jected all persons who neglected attendance there on "the Lord's Day" to a fine
of twenty shillings. It also forbade "separate companies in private houses," and
inflicted a fine of ten pounds, with "corporal punishment by whipping, not
exceeding thirty stripes for each offense," on every "person, not being a lawful
minister," who shall presume to profane the holy sacraments by administering
or making a show of administering them. Enforcement depended on the town.

162

Some towns were more lenient than others. In many places, nothing could prevent the seizure of property of non-conformists who refused to pay the clerical tax, and often they were temporarily imprisoned.

This did not prevent the first Baptist Church in Stamford from being established in 1773. Because there were fewer Catholics in the state, it was not until 1849 that construction began on a modest house of worship for Catholics in Stamford once their numbers reached 100 parishioners (mostly Irish). This began regular Catholic services in Stamford. It was not until the late 1800s that Italians arrived and began to practice religion in Stamford. They soon began to understand that religious life was different in America. There was more choice here (there was a choice in Italy too, but here Catholicism was not the dominant religion). Religious practices were very different from those in Italy. Protestant and Catholic hierarchies were vying for their souls, even if the ethnic majority Irish parishioners were not happy to congregate with them. In many interviews, the animosity between the two groups was not discussed initially, but once pressed on relations, most interviewees agreed that the Irish were not a friend of the Italians for the most part and were often abusive. Religious practice was geared to their Americanization but was achieved by separating them from worship with non-Italians. For Catholics at St. John's in Stamford, this meant that Italians were to worship in the basement of the church, and for Baptists, a separate house of worship.

The 1881-1882 Boyd's Directory of Fairfield County lists Reverend Antonio A. Arrighi's home at 29 Myrtle Avenue. Arrighi was born in Florence, Italy in 1835 and served as a drummer boy in Garabaldi's army. He was wounded and captured during the Siege of Rome in 1849 and was sent by the Pope to Civitta Vecchia, where he was an Italian galley slave who endured years of torture. He remained a prisoner for two years, receiving seventeen lashes across his back upon release. Arrighi came to America in 1855. He fought in the Civil War, for Company F of the 1st Iowa Infantry. Mustered in on May 14th, 1861, and mustered out on August 20th, 1861, serving at the battle of Wilson's Creek, Missouri. He completed his education at Ohio Wesleyan University and Dickinson College. In 1869 he graduated from the Boston Theological Seminary. Soon after graduating he returned to Italy and founded the Methodist church in Italy. In 1875, Arrighi was the first man of the Protestant faith ever ordained in Rome. In the early days of his ministry, he was mobbed by Roman Catholics, and his church was sacked. In 1881 he founded the first Italian mission in America at the Five Points, NY. His autobiography is *Story of Antonio, The Galley-Slave; A Romance of Real Life*. Other than lectures in Stamford, there is not much written about Arrighi's mission in Stamford, he may have just maintained a home in Stamford temporarily while traveling, giving lectures, and collecting funds that would be used for his evangelism efforts in Italy.[2]

Rev. Pasquale DeCarlo (one of the early leaders previously discussed) of the Italian Baptist Church began mission work in 1893. He came from Calitri, a town known for Protestantism. However, his emigration preceded the time of Baptist awakening in the town described below (Barone, 101). He first began with an evening school at home, where he taught young and old Italians to read and write and gave them religious instruction. A few weeks later, he started Sunday school. Mr. DeCarlo had a number of prominent church people of Stamford assisting him with meetings held twice on Sundays and once during the week. He translated the hymns into Italian. An article indicates, "The sweet though uncultured voices of the singers blend harmoniously and on the listening ear. Italians are lovers of music and those that attend the mission are no exception. They generally have voices of high register and take the upper notes with ease musically, though never have been trained.[4] This became very popular so he approached the Baptist Church to obtain a larger place to continue the mission. This is when "Our Mission" was opened up on Pacific Street.[5] The Reverend stated that at about the same time The Roman Catholic Church had an Italian-speaking priest stationed in Stamford. The priest tried to dissuade Italians from taking the reverend's lessons. He continued his work nonetheless and gained a steady following. Reverend DeCarlo presided over the congregation in various outreach ministries and under different names: West Stamford Mission, Our Mission, and First Italian Baptist Church.

In fact, this was not just a Stamford phenomenon. There was a competition among the Christian denominations. The Catholic Church feared a loss of the faithful in favor of protestant churches nationwide and The Catholic Church moved to organize associations and parishes for Italians abroad (Piccoli, *passim*). American Christians both Protestant and Catholic found the religious manners of Italians appalling. Both agreed that Italian immigrants were largely ignorant of Christian doctrine, prone to idolatry and superstitious sentimentality. However, Italians were highly religious, just in different ways. They relied on a tradition of localized and communal religion that was not so dependent on clergy and church. Most were anti-clerical, based on how they had been treated by both the government and the church in Italy.

---

[2] Stamford Advocate 9/25/1912, 5/21/1880, The Yankee Volunteer A Virtual Archive of Civil War Likenesses, collected by Dave Morin, International Students at Dickinson College Snapshots II profiles compiled and presented by Timothy Sidore,
[4] Stamford Advocate 11/8/1897.
[5] Stamford Advocate 1/23/1899.

The Protestants were first to focus on the religious potential among the Italians. They saw the needs of the immigrants and tried to fill them. By improving their lives and socializing them to Protestantism, they expected Italians to be responsive to the "correct faith." To reach them, Protestants began providing social services, settlement houses, recreational activities and inducements of food, toys and candy to entice them to church and Sunday school. Their motto became "Americanization through evangelization." Eventually, Catholics copied the Protestant methods. They created national parishes, allowed Italians to use the upstairs, (not just the basements) to worship and imported orders of nuns and priests from Italy. With time, the Catholics won the battle for Italians in America and in Stamford (Mercandate, *passim*).

The mission was then moved to a building on Richmond Hill Avenue. The reverend was a convert himself. He lamented that it was harder to get Italian women to convert. Rev. Pasquale DeCarlo was advertising in the local paper preaching to Italians around the 1890s: "Italian Church, corner Greenwich Avenue and Mission Street…. Sunday school 10 am, preaching 7:45 pm: Prayer-meeting Thursday evening at 7:45."[8]

An article in The Advocate in 1894 describes a Christmas Festival sponsored by a new Baptist mission on Pacific Street. Over 100 children of various nationalities and colors, many of them Italians, gathered in a room over Kenefe's blacksmith shop. Miss M. Lavignetta of the Bleeker Street Methodist Mission (New York) spoke in Italian to them. Each of the children received candy, a little wooden dish of cake, and a toy furnished by the Baptist Church and more fortunate children, respectively. Distribution of free soup also began and was to continue twice a week with local butchers contributing the meat and school children the vegetables.[9] Italians also provided charity where they could. In 1898, an article in the Advocate describes how DeCarlo collected money among the Italians for the benefit of an orphanage. The total collection was $15, and the article indicates that the sum represents a great deal from men who work hard for small wages.[10]

Reverend DeCarlo performed a wedding ceremony of Italians Benedeto Mallozzi and Concerto Capossella on January 16th, 1899.[11] He married Carmio Capossella and Maria Lacadamo on June 24th, 1899, but they wanted to make sure they had proof if they decided to return to live in Italy and went

---

[8] Stamford Advocate 7/30/1898.
[9] Stamford Advocate 1/5/1894.
[10] Stamford Advocate 6/27/1898.
[11] Stamford Advocate 1/16/1899.

to the town clerk to obtain it.[12] Another marriage took place in December, Vito Antonio Tornillo and Catherine Schiaffino, with a reception at Franklin Hall. Also in that month, Rev. DeCarlo married a cabinetmaker, Micheli Abati aged 25 to Vincenza Cerrecti at the groom's home on Cedar Street. The bride was only 18 so consent from a Selectman was required (her parents lived in Italy). The couple was married in New York the day before but they wanted a religious ceremony as well. It was an intimate affair with about 20 people present.[13]

It appeared that the congregation was growing; however, in 1903 a change occurred. In 1903, Rev. De Carlo decided to leave the pastorate to join the Congregationalists. A week later, the members of the Italian Baptist Church voted with only one dissenting vote to leave the Baptist denomination and to organize a Congregational Church. An entire congregation switching religions is unlikely a common occurrence and would seem to demonstrate that the reverend was a charismatic minister and well-liked by parishioners. The reason given for the change was that the requirement of immersion in the Baptist denomination was an obstacle to the growth of the church.[14] First accounts indicate that it was an amicable split. The West Stamford Sabbath-School Mission Society agreed to move forward with building the church and elected the following officers: Reverend DeCarlo, president, Salvator Russo, secretary, Benedetto Pensiero treasurer, Nicolas Colline, Scivator Spravoire, Benedetto Mallozzi, trustees. In June of 1903, Rev. DeCarlo welcomed ten new members to the church, bringing the total to 27.[15] However, later it appeared that this was controversial, as F.H. Divine published a letter in The Advocate discrediting DeCarlo and indicating he was discharged.[16] DeCarlo had already accepted a job in Hartford with the Congregational Church. In fact, the Hartford Courant reports that DeCarlo had to explain himself before beginning work for the Hartford Congregational Italian mission since he previously served a Baptist Church (Barone, 88). A power/money struggle ensued. Rev. Alfio Manutilla, M.A. was made temporary minister in charge of the First Italian Baptist Church of Stamford. Italian services were to be resumed at the old mission rooms on Pacific Street until the National Home Society and Baptist State Convention could erect a permanent location.[18] Rev. Aristide Giampetro was ordained to the ministry and installed as pastor of the Italian Congregational Church in

---

[12] Stamford Advocate 9/22/1899.
[13] Stamford Advocate 12/12/1899, 12/8/1899.
[14] Stamford Advocate 4/9/1903.
[15] Stamford Advocate 4/25/1903, 6/6/1903, Waterbury Evening Democrat, 4/7/1903.
[16] Stamford Advocate 4/9/1903.
[18] Stamford Advocate 6/6/1903.

March of 1904.[19] Giampetro then received a letter from the Congregational Missionary Society of Connecticut that indicated his services were no longer needed. The Stamford Church then voted to become an independent Church and continue Giampetro as its pastor.[20] In 1905, the Society voted to return to the Baptist fold, they were allowed back, once of course they retitled the Church and property to the Baptist convention.[21] Various ministers succeeded Reverend DeCarlo: Aristide W. Giampietro (1904-1906), Vincenzo di Domenica (1907-1908)[22], and then Alfredo Barone (1909-1911). The last mention of the Italian Baptist congregation occurs in the 1911 Stamford Directory. The church building on the corner of Richmond Hill Avenue and Mission Street was taken over in 1910 by an African American AME congregation, called Bethel AME. The building still stands today (See Appendix F for the location and religious walking tour) (Barone, 64).

Rev. Alfredo Barone began his religious work under the title "Alpha and Omega; Italian Independent Baptist Missionary Work in the United States." He held Sunday meetings in the houses of residents that were in sympathy with the movement. Pastor Barone made general appeals for aid, financial and other, to carry forward the work. J. Wilbor Richardson took out an ad revoking his endorsement of Rev. Barone: "To the public: Notice is hereby given that on a certain date in 1909, the undersigned gave to Rev. Alfred Barone a certain letter of recommendation and endorsement, as he was then in the employ of the National and State Baptist Mission Boards, conducting Italian mission work in Stamford. Such connection having been discontinued, and Rev. Mr. Barone having ceased to be an employee of the regular Baptist denomination, I wish to cancel and withdraw said endorsement and recommendation." The Advocate reported that Mr. Barone, continued to spread the pamphlets which contained the endorsement, in his efforts to get money for the needy. Mr. Barone said "he was engaged in a missionary work, not for any church, but for all churches that follow the leading of Christ.... My work leads me through Connecticut, Massachusetts, New York, and New Jersey. I spend a couple of months in each state, going from door to door, soliciting subscriptions in my plan by having each person contribute two cents each month toward the fund.... I feed and clothe the poor. I help all people who ask for help.... I am willing to work from 6 in the morning until 11 at night, as I have been doing, because I know I am helping the suffering people.... I am not connected with any church or any society, have no board

---

[19] Stamford Advocate 5/28/1904, 7/28/1904.
[20] Stamford Advocate 12/23/1904.
[21] Stamford Advocate 2/14/1905, 2/17/1905.
[22] Stamford Advocate 9/19/1905.

of directors, no trustees, no officers, and in fact am a whole missionary board myself."

Rev. Barone was no stranger to opposition during his theological career. He was born in Oliveto-Citra-Dogana, Salerno on May 25, 1869, and resided in Calitri from 1882 to 1899. Alfredo started in a Catholic seminary. He rejected Catholicism and converted to the Baptist faith. After conversion, his aristocratic parents disowned him. He began his evangelization efforts in Calitri and the surrounding areas during the 1890s. Calitri had become a center of spiritual awakening and questioning in the late nineteenth century. It appears that Protestantism took hold there. Many of the members of the Baptist church in Stamford were Calitrani. In Italy, he was stoned, imprisoned, and an attempt was made to burn him at the stake. In an account from "Beyond Memory" a young Italian boy, Francesco Sannella describes the scene as Alfredo (as a Baptist Missionary) approached the town of San Sassio, the boy cried out "Protestante" (Protestant). The street became crowded. The antagonisms born of their traditions, combined with actual terror, transformed these peace-loving townspeople into a mob. A shower of stones fell about Alfredo. Francesco later, in the U.S. working in a shoe factory, to help support his family, stood on the edge of a crowd as Rev. Barone spoke and threw stones as he did in San Sassio, only to have his heart touched by the Spirit of God. He converted to the Baptist faith. In the same book it also states that Barone "l'evangelista di Calitri" (the evangelist of Calitri) after preaching in nearby Trevico, was arrested and spent nine days in jail. Barone left for America in 1899 because many Calitrani had immigrated, support for the church in Italy had stopped or changed hands, and his brother Giovanni immigrated to head a mission in Waterbury, CT. After about a decade of service in the northeast, breaking with the formal Baptist Church (as noted in the public notice referred to above), he formed his own missionary society (Barone, *passim*). In April of 1912, Rev. Barone contracted for the building of a building on Rose Park Ave. for the Alpha and Omega Society.[25] Barone died in 1950 and is buried in Woodland Cemetery alongside his wife Rosina. The head stone is inscribed solely with Barone, with an Italian crest above and a blank book balanced above the crest. Within the crest are the initials A and O, for Alpha and Omega Assembly, the name of the religious society he formed in 1910 after leaving the Baptist Church (Barone, 96-98). William DeMartino is listed in the Stamford directory, as Scoutmaster for the Boy Scout troop associated with the Baptist Church in 1928 and 1930.

---

[25] Research by Richard Morris on First Italian Baptist Church, located at Stamford History Center, Stamford Advocate 1/15/19103, 1/22/1910, 1/29/1910, 2/5/1910, 9/19/1911, 12/5/1911, 12/12/1911, 4/25/1912.

The Methodist Church under the direction of Rev. C.H. Priddy, pastor (the same pastor who pushed the temperance movement in Stamford, see Chapter 8) and Rev. E.R. Lewis, assistant pastor, also courted the Italians. In 1912, the church started an Italian Sunday school for Italian children under fourteen years of age, and unaffiliated with another church. The purpose of the school was not only religious training, but also to teach citizenship. Patriotic songs and drills were used.[27]

A competition among the churches for the hearts and minds of Italians began. In the "Twenty Five Years of Progress 1910-1935," The Italian Institute Inc. Stamford, CT, the San Manghese society refers to the conflict between Catholics and Protestants: "In cooperation with the numerous Aviglianese Italians for erection of the Italian Church, for scouting out and raising the Christian spirit in the Roman Catholic apostolic faith, depressed and misled by infiltration of Protestant ideas."[28]

The arrival of the Italians took the Irish aback as they began to settle along Pacific Street and in the West Side. Especially in terms of religious practices, where they were referred to as "Image worshippers, superstitious, given to emotionalism." A letter in The Advocate branded them, "Not true Christians."[29] In fact, Italians were not allowed to worship upstairs at St. John's the Catholic Church built by Irish parishioners. They were relegated to the basement for their services. Elaine Vacca Kanelias, granddaughter of Vincenzo Vacca, recounts personal family oral history that tells the story of how her Uncle Tripoli "John" Vacca attempted to join the upstairs mass at St. John's as a child, and got an ear full from Monsignor Coleman, who told him that Italians had to go downstairs for mass.

On May 8th, 1887, The Stamford branch (St. Augustine Council No 41) of St. John's Catholic Church was initiated, and one of the first members was Joseph Triacca, who emigrated from Germany (but likely had Italian lineage based on his last name) (Bolanowski, 80). The Church was built by and was a majority Irish congregation. During the mid-90s, the character and composition of the Catholic community in Stamford began to incorporate Catholics from places other than Ireland; Catholics from Italy and Poland began to grow in numbers(Bolanowski, 89). The first Italian name to appear in their records was Maria Crucia Laurio, baptized July 3, 1887 and the first Italian name appearing in the marriage registry was Donato D'Elia and Carmela Polisano, married on April 13, 1888. A mission exclusively for Italians was given at St. John's in August of 1895. A large number of Italians attended

---

[27] Stamford Advocate 11/30/1912, 12/14/1912.
[28] "Twenty Five Years of Progress 1910-1935," The Italian Institute Inc. Stamford, CT.
[29] Stamford Advocate 6/30/1991.

both the special 5:30 am mass and the 7:30pm rosary and benediction.[32] It is interesting to note that the event was not even mentioned in the Connecticut Catholic newspaper though the paper continued to report throughout 1895 about events in Ireland (Bolanowski, 90).

The Advocate reports a mission given at St. John's Church in Stamford for Italians: "The Italian language will be used and every effort will be made to reach Italian Catholics. The Italian population in Stamford is so large that it is found a difficult problem to minister to them. A service is held for them every Sunday in the basement of St. John's Church. As there is no Italian priest there, the work of the church has been somewhat handicapped. It is believed there is a field here for an Italian mission, and good results are looked forward to."[34]

By 1902, the church was forced to confront the change in demographics of the flock; forty percent of the congregation was Italian. Even with these numbers, it would still be three years before an Italian priest was assigned to St. John's (Bolanowski, 112). On August 15th, 1903 (Feast of the Assumption) the Italians were offered a special morning mass. The celebrant was Father Pasquale Monzelli, (from New Rochelle) who preached the sermon in Italian. After mass, the Italian congregation continued the celebration with a parade to Woodside Park (now Scalzi Park) followed by entertainment (Bolanowski, 118). The Stamford Advocate describes it as follows: "It is observed as a Holy Day by Roman Catholics generally, but the Italians always celebrate it in an elaborate manner. Before the mass, the Societies Campanella and Vittorio Emanuele, headed by the Barsagliere band of New York had a parade. In it was an open carriage in which contained ex-Mayors Tupper and Cummings. When the mass was over about noon, there was a celebration outside the church with firecrackers. The parade again formed, and after going through the principal streets, proceeded to Woodside Park...there will be a display of fireworks."[37] Stamford Italians did not give up their customs despite what non-Italians thought.

In 1904, the Polish community broke off from St. John's and formed their own church. The Italian constituency of the congregation also chose to go off on their own from the dominant Irish population. In May 1904, Father Philipe Montesante from Palermo, Italy held a mission for Italians in the lower chapel of St. John's where the Poles had worshipped previously. He also celebrated Mass in the area of Greenwich near the Stamford border referred to as "Dumpling Pond" (Bolanowski, 121) Other missionaries who

---

[32] Stamford Advocate 8/22/1895; Sacred Heart Church Golden Jubilee booklet 1973.
[34] Stamford Advocate 5/12/1900.
[37] Stamford Advocate 8/15/1903.

came to Stamford to administer to Italians were Fathers Peter Lotti, Oreste Alussi, and James Anovazzi. In 1905, Father Antonio Rizzo, who was born in Italy but ordained in the United States became assistant pastor. Over the next 5 years, the population of the parish would grow thirty percent (with the majority being Italian).[39] Father Rizzo arranged for a weekly mass at 8:30 am just for Italians, which began in April.[40] In his February of 1905 sermon, the advocate reported Father Rizzo showed much promise as a preacher with much force and eloquence when he urged a general unity of Christian denominations with the Catholic Church as being the only effective way of combating agnosticism and socialism. In July of 1907, Rev. Rizzo urged parishioners not to be discontented by lack of wealth and that they could be happy though poor. The sermon was a plea to people to be contented with their lot in the world, and while striving to better it in every legitimate way, not to be envious of another man's superior fortune or attainments. He declared that worldly riches were not the most desirable possessions. He said that after all, the distribution of these worldly riches was regulated by the Almighty power and to revolt and complain against any seeming unequal distribution was in fact a revolt and a complaint against this Divine Power.[41]

In true Italian-American flare on May 1, 1905, the day of the wedding of Joseph Bruno of Mt. Vernon to Christina Nanize of the Dumpling Pond district at St. John's all tradition was broken when they rode from the bride's home to church in automobiles; the bride and groom in a big Cadillac touring car. Prior to then it was well established for the bride and groom to arrive at church in a horse-drawn carriage. The Advocate even noted that this was a first for Stamford.[42] Later in the year, a weeklong mission catering to the Italians began on November 19 (Bolanoski, 124). Another was held the following year from November 5th to the 12th, with the press indicating it was well attended. At Christmas, a special mass for the Italians was held in the lower chapel (Bolanoski, 127).

The year 1913 brought clearly into focus the fact that St. John's parish was no longer a predominantly Irish parish. At the end of the year, there were an equal number of English-speaking communicants as there were of Italian descent. There were 220 baptisms of Italian babies compared to 120 from the Irish community (Bolanoski, 146). However, it was not until November 15, 1920 that Italians met for the purpose of forming an Italian parish. A building lot 440 feet by 150 feet on Schuyler Avenue had been purchased for

[39] Stamford Advocate 8/15/1903, 122
[40] Stamford Advocate 8/15/1903, 123, Sacred Heart Church Golden Jubilee booklet 1973.
[41] Stamford Advocate 2/6/1905, 7/22/1907.
[42] Stamford Advocate 5/1/1905.

this purpose. The news account reported that there were 2,000 Italian Catholics in Stamford at that time. The previous annual report of St. John's however, listed the number at double that (Bolanoski, 175).

In 1913, the Italian men's society of St. John's elected the following officers: Peter Iovanna, president; Joseph Maffei, vice president; Desiderio Gianicello, financial secretary; Carmine Passero, recording secretary; Rev. N.P. Coleman, chaplain. There were fifty-six members. Frank Servio LaBella was one of those member/founders of the church.[47] President Pietro Iovanna had written a letter to the Bishop of Hartford requesting permission to form an Italian parish in Stamford. It was almost a year after the formation of the Society of the Sacred Heart of Jesus was founded that an answer to his letter was received. In his letter of January 10, 1914, the Bishop's secretary, Reverend William H. Flynn, answered: "The Bishop, first of all, needs information as to the number of Italians who attend Mass and receive the Sacraments, because these are the only ones in whom there can be entrusted the building of a church and then supporting it. If they contribute with generosity, then he can take into consideration their petition; otherwise, for the time being, it would be useless to even think about this."[48]

Father Kelley was appointed Assistant Pastor at St. John's Church and was put in charge of the Italian speaking people of the parish. After administering to the spiritual needs of his Italian parishioners, a committee of 72 men was formed for the purpose of erecting a church of their own in June of 1920. The committee and Father Kelley requested that the Pastor of St. John's Church obtain the approval of Bishop John J. Nilan of Hartford to take steps towards the formation of the Church of Sacred Heart.[49]

In the meantime, Father Kelley obtained a certificate from the State of Connecticut dated November 20, 1920, thus establishing the "Sacred Heart Church Corporation, Stamford". On November 30, 1920, the property on Schuyler Avenue, owned by Henry K. McHarg and Schuyler Merritt, was purchased by the Sacred Heart Church Corporation for the sum of $8,000 with a down payment of $1,000 and a promissory note of $7,000. An article in the advocate reads: "If it be assumed that the people of that nationality prefer a place of worship of their own, they are sufficiently numerous and prosperous to provide it. At the same time, too much encouragement cannot be given to Italians and to other alien-born people to become accustomed as soon as possible to the English language."[50]

---

[47] Stamford Advocate 8/5/1955.
[48] Sacred Heart Jubilee, Stamford Advocate 3/26/1913.
[49] Sacred Heart Jubilee, Stamford Advocate 9/25/1920.
[50] Sacred Heart Jubilee; Stamford advocate 11/20/1920.

Tony Coviello tells of the admiration many Italians felt for their beloved Father Kelly, for his leadership of the Italian community in the church, and for taking up the cause of an Italian parish and doing so in their language. This esteem for an Irishman was no small feat when understanding two personal interactions the family had encountered with the Irish in America. The first encounter relates to Tony's father, who was a devout Catholic for his entire life. One day, as a boy going to mass at St. John's he became disillusioned with the church when he witnessed an elderly Italian woman being prevented from sitting in the pew at St. John's Church because she did not have money to place in the offering box attached to the pew. From that day, he stopped going to church until that is, Sacred Heart Church was built. The second encounter, which was much more tragic did not occur in Stamford but certainly impacted the family's views. The incident happened to his maternal side of the family the Nardozzas. Tony's great-grandfather Nardozza came to New York City and worked sweeping out an Irish saloon. At that time, Italians were taking some of the jobs away from the Irish and there was bad blood between the groups. Two thugs were beating up his great-grandfather when his great-grandmother heard the commotion and came out and confronted the assailants. They threw her to the ground, and at the time she was pregnant. This caused her to lose the child. Additionally, his great-grandfather's brother came to assist and chased the attackers. One of the thugs, drew a gun and shot him to death, and then blamed the shooting on Nardozza, who was taken to jail and stayed there over Christmas until the truth came out. Eventually, the widow lost her mind and was institutionalized, and two of her daughters disappeared at this time and were never heard from again. Despite the Nardozza family's experience, the leadership and kindness of Father Kelly were enough to mitigate the mistrust of the Irish for this family.

In 1921, the Italian community of St. John's came out in force on Saturday and Sunday June 18 and 19 to celebrate the feast of Saint Vito, the Patron Saint of Avigliano who was a Sicilian martyred in 303 by Romans when he was just 13 years old. There was a procession of the Saint Vito statue on Saturday. The Sons of Italy band played. On Sunday, a solemn high mass was held in the basement chapel. This event was so successful and created so much Italian pride that a church committee was formed so that they could finally have a place of worship where they could hear the word of God spoken in their native tongue and could participate in age-old celebrations and observances practiced in their ancestral towns. The committee of 72 men went forth every Sunday afternoon to the homes of Italians, to ask for donations to pay for the newly acquired Church property and for the Church that was yet to be built. Each family and working person gave as generously as their means allowed. The land acquired was fully paid for before the church was built on it (Rinaldi, *passim*).

On February 9, 1923, Bishop John J. Nilan designated Sacred Heart Church as a parish and appointed Reverend John, J. Kelley as its pastor. Beginning February 18, 1923, all parish services were being held, on their appointed days and hours, in the basement of St. John's Church in the name of Sacred Heart Church until whatever time the new church would be built. In March of 1923, Reverend Father Kelly took over as principal of St. John's School. The Italian Colony conducted many fundraisers for the building fund of Sacred Heart. In 1923, they held a carnival on Schuyler Ave.[52]

Finally, work on the new Sacred Heart Church was about to begin in 1923. The design called for a seating capacity of 800 persons and would cost about $60,000. In September of 1923, bids were sent out to different contractors and the contract for building Sacred Heart Church was awarded to F.D. Rich and Company. The cornerstone was laid on November 18, 1923 by the Most Reverend John G. Murray, Auxiliary Bishop of Hartford (Bolanowski, 180). A cornerstone collection that day totaled $1,660. On that day Reverend Father Silipagni of the Church of Our Lady of Loreto, New York spoke and appealed to them to uphold their traditions, and to be proud of the realization of their long-felt desire for a local church of their own. Bishop Murray stated: "What you have already done in your parish has been an inspiration to this entire diocese." The Sons of Italy Band played.[54] A building fund fundraiser was held at the Elks Lodge in February of 1924. Ralph Lionetti was general chairman of the event and was assisted by Peter Rosa, secretary of the executive committee, and Rocco Genovese, treasurer.[55] The Church of the Sacred Heart was completed and dedicated on Sunday, May 11, 1924 at 10:30 AM by Most Reverend John J. Nilan, Bishop of Hartford.[56] Italians were finally allowed to have a church all their own, and observe masses in the regular chapel (not the basement) and in their own language. God had not abandoned them. Sacred Heart Church is still to this day, labeled an "Italian National Parish." Churches were labeled after a specific ethnic community, to ensure that priests who could speak that language would be present in the parish. Mass is still celebrated in Italian at the church.

In his autobiography, F. D. Rich recounts that his father had some trouble while building the church. It turns out that due to a design flaw, there was an issue with plaster flaking off the ceiling of the new church. Parishioners

---

[52] Sacred Heart Jubilee; Stamford Advocate 3/23/1923, 5/11/1923.
[54] Stamford Advocate 11/19/1923.
[55] Stamford Advocate 2/23/1924.
[56] Sacred Heart Jubilee booklet, 1973

dressed in their Sunday best became annoyed as white plaster particles drifted down on them. This was eventually corrected (PAGE #).

The Holy Name Society, the Rosary Altar Society, and the Children of Mary church groups worked to raise funds for the liquidation of the parish debt incurred to build the church. Amazingly, in the midst of the Great Depression, the parish debt of $75,000 was paid by 1931 (Rinaldi, *passim*).

The 1905 Stamford directory lists the First Italian Congregational Church. Reverend Vincenzo di Domenica was the pastor in charge. Meetings were held at Richmond Hill Avenue and Mission Street.

I found reference to two Italians who were a member of the Jehovah's Witnesses. Canio Cestone was born in 1886 in Calitri, Italy. He lived in Stamford for approximately 70 years, and was an employee of the Electric Specialty Corporation and a landscaper. Canio and his wife Julia Lupinacci Cestone attended Jehovah's Witness Bible instructional seminars. In 1980, Canio partook in the annual Jehovah's Witness memorial celebration for the sixty-fifth year. Charles D. Tarantino was a member of the Christian Science Church (Toglia 2013, 356).[59]

The Italian-American community is diverse and there were different faiths represented by the group. Early Italian religious practice placed them in a "no mans" area. It was true that they were sought-after parishioners by the echelons of the religious denominations, but in practice, they were shunned by fellow congregants once they joined the various churches. The language barrier exacerbated this separation. Worship split by ethnicity became the answer. In the end, the Catholic faith won in terms of the number of Italian Americans as parishioners. Through separate worship, Italians also won, because they were able to continue the practices they grew up with.

---

[59] See also: Stamford advocate 10/1/1990, 9/30/199o, 3/29/1980, 5/1/1975, 4/17/1974, 4/30/1975, 1/6/1954.

CHAPTER 6

Arts, Sports, and Culture

La vita è breve e l'arte è lunga.
(Life is short, Art lasts)

The artistic tradition is deeply rooted in Italians. Art, architecture, and music are all an important part of Italian culture. Italian artists have created some of the world's most famous art. As of 2022, Italy has 58 designated cultural and natural landmarks, more than any other country in the world, making up about 5% of the UNESCO list of World Heritage Sites. The 2021 Best Countries rankings placed Italy as the number one country in the world for cultural influence. The country has achieved this while amounting to about .78% of the world population, and .059% of the earth's surface. Italy may not be considered a world military superpower, but because of its affinity for arts and culture, they certainly are the world's cultural and lifestyle superpower.

Italian immigrants brought this sense of art and culture with them when they came to Stamford. It was intertwined with all they did; if there was a parade, important meeting, or celebration, it included a band. Their education always included some form of art. Even with a full-time job, they expressed themselves after hours with some form of art. Art was always part of their life. Often, they were self-taught. They were proud of their art and culture and wanted to use it to demonstrate to others that they and their culture were worthy of admiration and as a result they were worthy citizens. Italians in Stamford in the early 1900s, would have benefited from the fame of Enrico Caruso, who hit number two on the American pop charts with I Pagliacci- Vesti La Guibba (On with the Play) in May of 1904, and then number 1 in August of 1907. Later on in the 1920s, they would have benefited from the popularity of the Italian actor Rudolph Valentino. Americans throughout the country were recognizing and accepting the cultural contributions Italians could make to America.

Early on Italians' musical talent was displayed in Stamford. As reported by the Advocate in 1881, a street performance by an Italian band entertained a crowd.[1] Vincent DeVivo (called "maestro") was a piano teacher and toured the theaters in the USA in 1890. In 1897, Marino Passero and T. Madonno, mandolin players performed at the Stamford Wheels Club Sociable; notable because they were performing at a non-Italian sponsored event[2] A Brass

---

[1] Stamford Advocate 5/13/1881.
[2] Stamford Advocate 12/17/1897.

Band formed in 1907; the first Italian band in Stamford. The Band Stella D'Italia (Stars of Italy) was given a rave review in the Stamford Advocate. Prof. Pumpo was the band leader, and Paul Chiapetta was the assistant. The program included "The Star Spangle Banner," "La Favorita," "Mezzanotte," "Non t'amo piu," and "Allegri Beviamo." In 1908, the director was Gennaro Passero. It was later renamed the Sons of Italy music band and came under the directorship of Giuseppe Antonio Tozzoli, a shoemaker from Calitri. Giuseppe Antonio Tozzoli came to Stamford in 1903. He was a self-taught musician. Tozzoli led the band for more than 20 years. He formed a music school, and many of his students became professional musicians.[3] Bands were very popular at parades and events and many of the members were Italian. The Colonial Band offered its services to welcome back the troops from WWI in 1917. Alphonso Frasca, manager of the band, in an Advocate editorial states: "to furnish music on that occasion free of charge. We are animated in this by a sentiment of love and veneration for the free institution of America, and hope that this welcome home to the boys will engender a strong feeling of patriotic fervor in defense of not alone our liberty, but our rights as well."[4] In 1921, the following officers were elected for the Colonial Band: C. Vacca, leader; A. Zaffino, assistant leader; P. Pia, secretary and treasurer; and J.L. LiVolsi, business manager.[5]

The Italian Institute sponsored an Accordion Club under the direction of Patrick Tartell. Club members included Joseph Petrone, Ronnie Grecco, Joseph Congelose, Anthony Mancini, Gabriel Scalise, and Salvatore Forlenzi.[6]

In 1934, the Marranzini Concert Band gave a free outdoor concert sponsored by local officials and organizations. The event also featured Italian folk dances. G. Marranzini was born in Italy and composed his first composition at the age of nine.[7]

Jerry (Gaetano) Esposito formed his Colonial Band in 1936. He played the drum and conducted the band at concerts. Before 1936, he played trombone for Carlo Vacca's marching band and with the Sons of Italy Band. Mr. Esposito's real job was as a garment worker, his first job in Stamford when he emigrated from Minturno at the age of 15 in 1905. After moving away for a time, he returned and resumed the garment worker job until 1968 when he

---

[3] Stamford Advocate 11/22/1907. See also, Richard Morris and Mario Toglia (DATE?).
[4] Stamford Advocate 3/12/1917.
[5] Stamford Advocate 4/18/1921.
[6] Stamford Advocate 3/8/1933.
[7] Ibi Stamford Advocate d 6/28/1934.

retired at 78. He got his musical training from a barber, Tony Daddona who had a shop at the corner of West Main Street and Stillwater Avenue.[8]

There was a West Stamford Band, of which Michele Vallario was a member. Mr. Vallario was also an officer of the First and Third Ward Italian American Democratic Club in 1936.[9]

Charles D. Tarantino was in the real estate and insurance business and had offices at 1 Bank St. Charles began as a clerk, but later resigned to open a studio for instruction of the mandolin, where he had at least fifteen students. He was a talented musician, also performing as the piano player at the Lyceum Theater. He performed as part of the De Para Trio. He also performed with his wife Gertrude playing the mandolin, and she the piano. Mrs. Tarantino also performed recitations.[10]

Stamford resident, E.G. Tarantino wrote the words alongside T.A. Metz's music to "We'll Come Back," a patriotic song that was popular nationally in 1917.[11] It is unclear, but likely that E.G. is actually Gertrude E. Tarantino (Charles' wife). The words are:

> We're going across the ocean, to fight for Uncle Sam;
> We're going to fight to a finish and win as quick as we can.
> With hearts full of love and souls aflame
> We're going to fight for our good name.
> So, mothers, sisters, sweethearts too,
> You must be brave; we're fighting for you.
> Chorus
> We'll come back. Yes, we'll come back.
> Now don't you fear for us, my dear;
> Don't you sigh nor shed a tear.
> We'll come back: we will all come back.
> Just you think of us, write to us, knit for us. We'll come back.
> When the war is over and we are home once more.
> Then there'll be days filled with sunshine
> Of peace and good cheer as before;
> There'll be a hot time; you wait and see.
> For we're going over for victory.
> So loved ones all and sweethearts true,
> You must be brave; we are fighting for you.

[8] Stamford Advocate 7/28/1975, 1/10/1908.
[9] Stamford Advocate 5/4/1914.
[10] Stamford Advocate 11/2/1916, 12/14/1911, 12/11/1911, 11/2/1911, 1/24/1921.
[11] Stamford Advocate 11/3/1917.

Vincent Botticelli a barber on 918 Hope St. was also a talented musician. He was a member of the Stamford Symphony Orchestra (playing the violin) and was the director of the Springdale Symphony Orchestra. He also played the mandolin. He was a descendant of the famous artist Botticelli. Born on December 15, 1901 in Bovino, Italy, he emigrated from Italy at 19 and attended the Damrosch School in New York, graduated from the Julliard School of Music in New York City, and taught at the New York Conservatory of Music. He spoke at a Flag Day ceremony in 1939.[12]

Drama was also important to them. In 1901, as part of a benefit for the Educational Circle Stamford had its first Italian dramatic performance. The performance included monologue work by Mr. Metallo, a drama called "The First of May," which was followed by a farce and then by music.[13]

Minstrel shows were very popular in Stamford, especially among Italians. The Aliia Club presented many performances in the city. They were organized as a welfare agency for the Italian Colony in 1925. The officers included: Henry Costanzo, president; Peter P. Vescio, vice president;, Michael J. DeVito, recording secretary; Anthony Montagnino, financial secretary; Joseph Palo, treasurer; and board of directors: Felix Varese, Michael Maddaloni, Nicholas Colucci, Sylvester Paganetti, and Patrick D. Tartell. In 1925, they gave a charity ball to raise funds for needy children, the committee arranging the affair included Patsy Maruke, chairman; Patsy Tartell, Peter Vescio, Mario Gardella, and Matthew Scinto. The club was under the direction of Anthony V. Corbo. The officers of the club included: Fredrick M. Lione, president; Michael J. DeVito, vice-president; Adolph Salveto, treasurer; Matthew Scinto, financial secretary; and Dr. D. A. Zaccardo, recording secretary. In 1927, over a thousand were in attendance to see the acts, which included: Patrick D. Tartell on accordion, dancing by Eddie Mack, Amelia and Don Julian, and Fannie Itri, magic by J. Metallo. A children's dance revue included: A. Sarni, F. Francesconi, R. DeVito, Viginia Lee, Tootsie Vaccaro, Rita Maffucci, Helen Vaccaro, K. Arcidancono, and L. Goglia. Comedy was provided by Ralph Martino, Joe Lombardi, and Paul Pavia. The Scalzi-Haggerty Brunswick orchestra played. Other music was provided by Anthony Palo, Anthony Palermo, Charles Rich, Samuel Geneovese, Felix Varese, Betty Zaccardo, J. Palermo, Joseph Lombardi and Phillip Mancini.[14]

The Santa Cecilia Paganini Music and Dramatic Club was organized in 1931 by Aniello Preziosi and performed at the Italian Center and various other venues in Stamford and surrounding towns. In 1935, they celebrated the third

---

[12] Stamford Advocate 3/7/1992, 6/13/1939, 3/11/1939, 5/16/1930, 5/25/1925, 4/29/1925.
[13] Stamford Advocate 5/2/1901.
[14] Stamford Advocate 4/21/1927, 11/4/1925, 1/6/1926.

full year of their formation with a glee club concert that included the following: "Italian Street Song," "Venetian Love Song," "Serenade Rimpianto," song by Anna Rizzi and accompanied on the piano by Slyvis Preziosi; "Torna A Sorrento," sung by Clara Iovanna, and accompanied by Linda Sessa, "Sylvia," sung by Anthony Ragonesi, accompanied by Mrs. Frank Spoviero, "Parlez moi D'Amore," a duet sung by Mrs. Sproviero and Frank Telesco. The string ensemble, Frank Prenciotti, violinist and Thomas Preziosi, guitar and Antionette Giampietro played piano. The program concluded with folk dances. In that same year, the following officers were elected: Rosario Ganino, president; Frances Pisatelli, vice president; Grace Forte, secretary; Linda Sessa, treasurer; Frank Princiotti, concert master; Michael Lasalandra (played violin), publicity agent. The fifth annual concert was given in 1936 and the members who participated included Anna Rizzi, Marie Sproviero, Clara Iovanna, Marie Preziosi, Josephine Mascarella, Ida Telesco, Linda Sessa, Grace forte, Anthony Ragones, Peter Vescio, Anthony Sorgente, Mario Cardillo and Daniel Telesco. In 1938, the group presented "The Ungrateful Son." The cast included Pasquale Massone, Annita Pezzi, Antonio Sorgente, Frances Valenti, Mrs. Alonzo Maffucci, Vincenzo Lobbozzi, Michele Tangi, Filippo Anzeloni, Antonietta Lazzaro, Elisabetta Lioneti, and Antonio Lazzaro. Anna Rizzi sang selections from Italian operas, Frances Valenti sang popular Italian songs. Vincenzo Lobbozzi entertained in the farce "Death of the Baroness." The group presented the play "Malacarne" written by Stefano Interdonato for the benefit of sick members of the Minturnese Club in 1940. In the cast were Rachael Aiello, Olga Biagione, Frank Aiello, Giuseppe Vartuli, Pasquale Arruzza, Antoinetta Lazzaro, Enrico Fabrizio and Pasquale Massone. Anna Rizzi, Raffaele Bochetta, and Enrico Fabrizio sang. Tex Slim and his Western Mountaineers sang popular cowboy songs with Sadie Natale, and were accompanied by Frances Pisitelli, Celeste Labbadia, Frank Nicolais, and Mario Uelazza. The orchestra playing between acts consisted of Samuel Robertino, Frances Piscitelli, Viola Laztocy, Salvatore Preziosi (Aniello's brother), Aniello Preziosi, Marian Maffucci, Gaetano Preziosi, and Silvia Preziosi (Aniello's sister). The officers of the group in 1940 were: Pasquale Massone president; Carlo Bivona, vice president; Frank Cardillo, treasurer; Pasquale Arruzza, representative and speaker.[15] Aniello also founded the Preziosi School of Music. He was born in Calitri, Italy on February 21, 1889 and came to America in 1903. He worked for Yale and Towne for twenty-two years and then at Pitney Bowes. Upon his retirement, he returned to teaching music. He was a veteran of WW I (Toglia 2013, 355).[16]

---

[15] Stamford Advocate 4/5/1940, 4/9/1940, 1/4/1940, 2/25/1938, 10/11/1935, 2/15/1935, 12/4/1935, 8/30/1938, 6/4/1936.
[16] See also: Stamford Advocate 2/24/1932.

Pasquale "Patsy" Zaffino made a significant contribution to the musical life of Stamford. He was born in Italy and was a bandleader in the Italian Army. Patsy was a music teacher for many years in Stamford. He also led the Stamford Marine Band. As part of the "New Deal" in the 1930s the Federal Emergency Relief Administration (FERA) was formed. FERA was a grant-making agency authorized to distribute federal aid to the states for relief. In November of 1934, FERA funds were used in Stamford to form a municipal band. The idea was that so many were unable to pay for entertainment, and so many musicians were unemployed that forming the band would serve two purposes. It was established under one of the "white collar" projects of FERA. The band provided free concerts in public buildings during the winter and in parks in the summer. He led the WPA band of Stamford (Stamford's Federal Band) from 1936 until his death at 46 in 1940. Frank W. LiVolsi was WPA band supervisor under Mr. Zaffino. For the six months ended June 30, 1939, the band gave 40 concerts, with attendance of over twenty thousand (including public school assemblies). The City of Stamford sponsored the band for performances in city parks during the summer. In a letter to the editor by Sal Toscano, Mr Zaffino's direction is lauded: "much credit should go to that young leader. Patsy Zaffino, who rehearses the 33 members with real capacity. Maestro Zaffino gives to the band a delightful cooperation to make every musical effect more expressive and precise."[17]

Other music teachers listed in the 1925 directory were: Louis Caputo, 133 Myrtle Ave., Edward Ferucci, 37 Henry St. Louis Giancola (also a policeman), 95 Liberty St., William Tamburri, 35 First St., and Joseph Ventura, 79 Worth.

The 1935 Stamford directory lists the following music teachers: Linda Cappabianca, 48 Strawberry Hill, Edward C. Ferrucci, 373 Elm St., Ralph A. Festo, 60 Highview, Julius F. Friese, 434 Main St., Pasquale Melfi, 18 Frank St., Neil D. Prezioso, 87 Richmond Ave., Frank Princiotti, 54 Henry St., Annette Tamburri, 32 Oak St., and Pasquale Zaffino, 20 Parker Ave. The same directory also lists Sabatino Monaco under mosaic work.

Gerardo Metallo immigrated to the U.S. in 1900, on the "First Bismarck" and listed his profession as sculptor, at 15 years old. He went to live with his brother Angelo in Stamford. In addition to performing dramatic work for the Italian Circle, he was a self-taught magician.[18] He was born in Italy on September 21, 1884, and resided in Stamford for 47 years. He was a painter and a member of the Society of American Magicians. When it came time for him

---

[17] Stamford Advocate 8/30/1940, 8/7/1940, 8/1/1939, 8/9/1938, 6/20/1936, 4/29/1935, 2/13/1935, 1/14/1935, 11/8/1934, 9/20/1932, 7/19/1932, 8/21/1930.
[18] Yonkers Tribune 10/27/2014

to marry, he returned to Calitri to find a wife. He returned to America with his fiancée, Rosa Maria Margotta (Rosina) in 1909. The occupation listed on the return ship manifest was juggler. Gerardo and Rosina were married, moved to Providence, Rhode Island and had Vincent and daughter Mary. It was in performing on stage that Gerardo found his true avocation: show business. When World War I broke out, he volunteered for the Italian army as an interpreter. He brought his family back to Calitri where his third child Josephine was born. The war ended in May 1919, and Gerardo traveled throughout Italy to entertain the Allied troops. He started with Barnum Circus as "Met Ako" the Chinese illusionist. In 1920, he joined a circus called the "Miss Dixxies." By that time, he was performing magic tricks and a mentalism act, with help from his daughter Mary. He ran a "black art" show for many years. Black art magic is the use of a stage fitted with a black velvet curtain background, using assistants and other props that are hidden by black shrouds. Careful lighting helps keep the secret a mystery to the audience. He was the originator of many large illusions. Other magicians have noted that his levitation technique was so good due to his uniqueness and great skill and knack of originality. He originated a famous trick among magicians, the "blooming rose bush trick." The trick involves a plant that grows in front of your eyes, and blooms flowers as well. The Metallo family returned to Stamford in 1921 and lived at 28 Ann St. He was a painter by profession and church art restorer, and worked in various houses of worship in the area. His oldest child Vincent became a magician in his own right. Mary died at the age of seventeen. Unfortunately, Gerardo committed suicide at the age of 63 with a .32 caliber revolver. He had been in ill health for two years prior. After his death, his son Vincent organized the Stamford Gerry Metallo Ring no. 97 International Brotherhood of Magicians, Inc. in his father's honor.[19]

The earliest record of Italians in a parade that I could find is in 1898. The parade began at Central Park (now Veterans Memorial Park), proceeded down Atlantic St., to Henry St., to Pacific St., to Manhattan St., to Pacific St., to Main St., to Elm St., to Hawthorn St., to Main St., to West Park Place, to River St. to Main St., to Atlantic St.to Broad St. to Summer St. to Woodside Park (Scalzi). The committee in charge of the event were: G. Acunto, president; A. Meda, Treasurer; and C. Tamburri, secretary. The grand marshall was F. Limangelli, with V. Russo and G. Lione as aides.[20]

In 1907, the Società Italiana Di M.S.S. Teodoro Martire, fra I Cittadedini di S. Mango Sul Calore had a ceremony to christen the new flag of the society as part of Memorial Day celebrations. They had a parade in the morning and

---

[19] Stamford Advocate 5/5/1948; Lance Rich.
[20] Stamford Advocate 9/19/1898.

then a picnic at Woodside Park (Scalzi). There were field and track events, baseball, motorcycle and footraces and of course, music (including selections from Operas). The festivities were capped off at the end of the night with fireworks. It was intentional that the Italian Colony show not only their patriotism for their new country, but also demonstrate what culture they themselves brought to the table.[21]

Later in July, Italian organizations showed their patriotism again by participating in the Fourth of July celebrations. Of course, the Italians had to demonstrate the worthiness of their culture as well; the observance was combined with celebrating the centenary of Garibaldi. It was estimated that there were 1500 Italian men in the parade, demonstrating there was a new big player in town. The route started at the corner of Main and Pacific Street under the direction of Marshals Dr. A. Sorgi and Q. Vetriolo. The parade route was through Main Street to Stillwater Avenue, to Spruce, to West Main, to Main to South, to State to Pacific to St. John's Park to Main to Park Row to Atlantic, to Broad to Washington Avenue to Woodside Park. The societies involved included: Società Fra Tommaso Campenella, Stone Mason Union No 23, Hodcarriers Union No 101, Italo-American Progressive Club, Stamford Italian Band, Società Operaia Italiana, Foresters of America, Società Aviglianese, Società San Manghese. Local politician Mr. Kenealy gave a speech stating: "It goes to show the marked improvement your people have made since they first came to Stamford a few years ago. It shows evidence of prosperity; it shows evidence of thrift; it shows evidence of industry. You are making your way in this country as fast as any people who ever came here." The Italian Colony marketing apparatus was working! The ice that had formed between the Italians and the other locals was melting.[22]

In September of 1907, the Italian Colony celebrated the birthday of a united Italy, under the auspices of the G. Mazzini Political Benevolent Society to show off their culture. Representative Rowell elected with the backing of the Italian Colony (as gratitude for assistance during the Esposito case) gave a very complimentary speech on Italy and Italians in America.[23]

In 1908, the Stamford Italian Colony invited Champion Italian Marathon runner Dorando to present him with an award and demonstrate to the locals how admirable Italian athletic skills were. The medal was gold and contained the coat-of-arms of Connecticut, the Italian and American flags, and an eagle. It was inscribed, "To Dorando Pietri, from the Italian colony of Stamford,

---

[21] Stamford Advocate 5/29/1907 and 5/31/1907.
[22] Stamford Advocate 7/5/1907.
[23] Stamford Advocate 9/19/1907, 9/21/1907.

Connecticut."[24] In October of 1909, there was a celebration of Columbus Day. Leonardo Matteo was the grand marshal. There were floats, one of which was a reproduction of the caravel Santa Maria. There were seven carriages in the procession, in the first, Mayor Tupper and Leo Donatelli. In the second were Antonio Geronimo and Antonio Palo. Speeches were given at Realty Hall about Columbus and other famous Italians. Garibaldi and Mazzini were lauded during the speeches. "They fought for the poor and oppressed; they fought to free Italy and give her national life. They fought for all those who were suffering from poverty and misery and they fought not to find but to make a new world." The united societies celebrated Columbus Day in 1910. The marshall of the parade was V. D'Amico, and D. Maffucci and C. Passero aided. The route of the procession included Main, Pacific, State, Atlantic, and Spruce Streets on the way to Woodside Park. At the park, there was a band concert, horseracing, dancing, and fireworks. The following arranged for the parade: A. Palo, president, G. Sarne, first vice president; C. Tamburri, second vice president and secretary; L. Serafino, assistant secretary; F. Trimboli, treasurer[25]

Among the patriotic celebrations of this period, in addition to the Columbus Day observance was the Sixth Centenary of Dante. The celebrations were under the auspices of the Italian Colony societies gathered under the leadership of Mr. Domenico Mancini. As part of the celebration, a bust of the great Italian poet was presented at Stamford High School. All the city and school authorities and the associations attended, and the well-known journalist Agostino De Biase of New York was the official speaker.[26] Domenico Mancini was born in Eboli, Salerno, Italy in 1876. He settled in Stamford in 1903. In 1925 he began a business as an agent for manufacturers and importers of linens (Carlevale, 241).

The Pia family had talented musicians. Elia Pia was the porter for the Advocate Building. He would perform at the annual Advocate clam bake for employees. Elia led the Colonial Band in 1911. His son Orazio was a tenor in the chorus of operas put on by St. John's and in the choir of the church. Orazio was the only Italian in the ensemble, and the only other Italian in the choir was Mario Terenzio.[28]

Italians brought the tradition of Carnivale with them to Stamford. Young Italians wore masks and costumes on Shrove Tuesday. On the west side, they

[24] Stamford Advocate 12/19/1908.
[25] Stamford Advocate 8/27/1910, 10/13/1909, 10/11/1910.
[26] "Twenty Five Years of Progress 1910-1935," The Italian Institute Inc. Stamford, CT.
[28] Stamford Advocate 2/20/1914, 2/15/1912, 10/12/1911, 8/21/1911, 8/29/1910, 6/24/1907, 1/4/1907, 12/10/1906, 4/11/1917.

would go house to house to celebrate the last day before the Lenten season. One party led to trouble when the organizing brothers (the Iannuzzi brothers) got into a fight. Brothers Peter and John were locked up and had to pay a fine of $10.[29]

Domenico Melillo, known as "professore" was an artist in Stamford, but would not sell his paintings. He made money by writing letters in Italian for those in the area that could not write in Italian and wanted to keep in touch with family in Italy. He did barter with the paintings and Dr. Nemoitin had a few of his paintings. Elaine Vacca Kanelias indicates that family lore is that he wrote speeches for Firello LaGuardia and had an exhibit at a museum in New York. In March of 1911, the professor gave a lecture in Italian at Middletown, Connecticut entitled "L'Italia e America."[30]

In 1933, a high school Italian club sponsored a carnival of Italian literature that included awards for three participants. The works discussed included Poems by Dante, the art of Michelangelo, and the achievements of Garabaldi, Mazzini, Il Conte di Cavour, Cellini, and others. Participants included: Benny DeSalvo, Thomas Kenny, Gertrude Mellilo, Joe Sacco, Adeline Dessa, Giovanna Morelli, Everett Mastrich, Margaret Fabrizio, Angelino Coppola, Louis De Panfilis, Lawrence Ieva, Sally DeMartino, Ray Laureno, Mary Pezzi, Mary Simonetti, Antonette Carlucci, Antonio Santarsiero, Joe Goodfriend, Alfred Marino, Gerald Grocco, Tony Cardone, Pat Sabia, Rocco Cassone, Carmella Randl, Helen Vagedes, A. Telesco, Frances Gerardi, Charles Franchina, Jerry Macari, Carmine Russo, Susie and Teresa Evaristo.[31]

Mary Vuono was an important Italian American business leader and promoter of the arts. She was born Maria Miceli in Potenza, Italy on March 23, 1882, and moved to Brooklyn the following year. At age 19, she married Charles D. Vuono, co-founder, and president of the Vuono Construction Co., which built the Old Stamford Town Hall.[32] She opened the Strand Theater in 1915, resulting in a great business and more importantly, profits that were so good that she bought the building. She built a new Strand, and even greater profits allowed her to purchase the building next door. Soon, however, there was a downturn in business at the Strand. This did not deter Mary Miceli Vuono; she succeeded in obtaining a mortgage of $100,000 from the Stamford National Bank, based on her business reputation. She turned business around, and by 1924, she commissioned an architect to design an opulent vaudeville and motion picture house seating 2,000. She hired Thomas

---

[29] Stamford Advocate 2/9/1910, 2/28/1911.
[30] Stamford Advocate 3/11/1911.
[31] Stamford Advocate 5/18/1933.
[32] Stamford Advocate 11/11/1978.

Lamb (a famous theater architect) to design the Palace Theater, the design of which replicated the Rivoli Theater and was dedicated on June 2, 1927.[33] Lamb was a prominent designer of the 1920s and 30s who had designed more than 300 theaters throughout the country. He was the first to visualize movie theaters as "palaces" instead of "vaudeville houses."[34]

The inaugural program featured "The Star Spangled Banner," Overture ("Il Guarney") played by the Palace Orchestra (whose musical director was Mary's son William), Janosky & Company in a variety of acrobatic sensations, Bert Rome and Henry Dunn in "Harmony as you like it," Ed Janis and Girls in "Keep stepping," a song and dance revue, Dave Kramer and Jack Boyle, Barney Rapp and his Palm Beach Orchestra and on the screen "Rookies" a silent comedy starring Karl Dane and George Arthur with Marceline Day. All this was included for the price of 50 to 75 cents depending on seating. In a remembrance in the Stamford Advocate, the Palace is described as "reeking of elegance, from the wide marble staircase, crystal chandeliers, marble lobby floors, and air conditioning, to the plumed hat of the uniformed doorman right to the military-style uniform of the ushers." Some movies actually had their first run in Stamford before going on to New York City.[35] Harry Blackstone performed magic, the Three Stooges performed their signature slapstick routines, and Red Skelton his comedic routines live on the stage there. The theaters provided temporary relief during the depression, as for less than a dollar, one could go to the movies. During the 1930s the Palace actually stopped all movies in progress to transmit the radio show "Amos n' Andy" through the sound system. It was Mary's idea to keep business up as people started to stay home to listen to the program. Mary offered three acts of vaudeville, a short subject, the Paramount News and a feature movie, all for the price of a movie ticket.[36] The Palace is listed on the National Register of Historic Places.[37]

Mary was described by her grandson as "a pioneer," "a pistol," and a "real character." He goes on to say, "Generous, feisty, astute, outspoken, independent and indomitable and was a typical housewife with six kids when in 1915 at age 33, she decided to go into the theater business.[38] The Palace was opened to block out competition from the major chains.[39] The theater was converted to a motion picture house soon after. In 1931, during the

[33] Stamford Advocate 11/2/2003, 6/27/2002.
[34] Stamford Advocate 8/4/1999.
[35] Stamford Advocate 5/22/1983.
[36] Stamford Advocate 10/16/2002.
[37] Stamford Advocate 8/4/1999.
[38] Stamford Advocate 5/28/1995.
[39] Stamford Advocate 10/4/2003.

depths of the Depression, she leased the Palace and Strand as well as two theaters to Paramount Publix, but the chain went bankrupt and Vuono took the theaters back. In 1936, a year after her husband died, she leased them again, only to regain control 10 years later.[40]

In 1927, she attempted to halt the Town of Stamford from erecting a new high school on Strawberry Hill on the grounds that it was restricted zoning as a residential area, and she requested $35,000 in damages. Mary Vuono sold her estate on Strawberry Hill Avenue (where the Fountain Terrace condominiums are today), and moved into an apartment above the theater. The Strand fell victim to Stamford Urban renewal program in 1966.[41] She fought this and obtained a temporary injunction to demolish. She argued that the theater property was not in the renewal quadrant, and therefore, not needed for renewal, and that the theater was neither unsanitary nor substandard. She indicated that others, including F.D. Rich, the renewal sponsor would profit at her expense. She asked for $250,000 in damages.[42] She lived in the apartment at the theater until she died in 1978 at the age of 96. It is said that people often see her ghost in the theater.[43] She was active in the Italian Center and served as head of the women's committee for membership.[44]

Robert Serafino, born November 26, 1914 in Stamford was the son of Luigi and Donata Maria Mecca Serafino. He earned a bachelor's degree from New York University, a six-year certificate from Fairfield University, and served in World War II. After the war, he was a political analyst at the U.S. embassy in Rome. He was a teacher in Stamford, the first foreign language consultant for the state department of education, assistant director of the National Defense Education Language Institute, chairman of the foreign language department at the Educational Testing Service in Princeton, NJ, and the foreign language supervisor of New Haven Public School System. He was an active member of the Modern Language Association, COLT, and UNICO.[45]

In one case art led to violence in Stamford. A dance exhibition was given at Red Men's Hall, where Dan Mecca of New York and his wife came to put on a tango exhibition (which they did often in Stamford). A quarrel started about the partition of the proceeds of the night between Mecca and Antonio Romano. Romano was stabbed by Mecca. Romano was cut in the chest below the lungs, two or three wounds in his thigh, and a number of wounds in

40 Stamford Advocate 5/28/1995.
41 Stamford Advocate 9/20/1966.
42 Stamford Advocate 8/10/1966.
43 Stamford Advocate 10/4/2003
44 Stamford Advocate 4/12/1939, 3/29/1938.
45 Stamford Advocate 9/11/2003.

the groin. The Advocate reported: "Mecca had the reputation here among people who knew him of being a member of the so-called Monkey Gang of New York. In appearance, manner and language he resembles the popular conception of the so-called New York gangster." Mecca confessed to stabbing Romano because he had made insulting proposals to the woman who danced with Mecca. Mecca saw Romano make a movement toward his hip pocket and fearing Romano had a pistol, he stabbed him.[46]

Twin brothers Archie D. and Alfred A. Volante born in Atina, Italy had a dancing school. Alfred was a WWI veteran and inspector, and city parks commissioner for the city. Archie also a WWI veteran was a mechanic for the city.[47]

Brothers Natale (Natalino) born on March 12, 1895 and Salvatore Napoletano born on November 10, 1903, immigrated to the U.S. from Isernia, Italy in 1921 with their other brothers and settled in New York City. The two brothers did not like city life and decided to move to Stamford shortly thereafter, and started the Napoletano Brothers painting and wallpaper hanging business. They married sisters Jennie and Mary Giancola. They were well respected worked in many well-to-do homes in the Fairfield County area, and gained customers mostly by word of mouth. Both were members of Painters Union 192 of Stamford. Natale had gone to art school in Italy and was a veteran of World War I in Italy. Natale painted a night sky with a star motif on the ceiling of the former Laddin's Terrace in Stamford. He also did murals in homes, and paintings as well. Natale's daughter Joann Dipanni recounts that they were inseparable, and would take a walk to smoke a cigarette every morning after breakfast and before going to work. She also remembers that her uncle enjoyed tending to his garden. According to Joann, her father never went back to Isernia, and regarded the United States as the best country in the world for all it brought him.[48] This sentiment is very common among Italian immigrants; they are fierce patriots of the U.S. and demonstrate immense gratitude to the country.

Enrico Blosio born on September 6, 1898, came to the U.S. in 1923 from Marcianise (Caserta) Italy. His brother, Francesco had planned to make the trip but became ill, so Enrico took his place. He was the only one from the family to eventually immigrate to the U.S. Enrico was a veteran of World War I. He served for Italy in Austria and received injuries there. He was engaging the enemy from inside a building when he was shot in the shoulder. He continued to hold his position when the enemy first fired mustard gas into the building

[46] Stamford Advocate 2/17/1914, 3/2/1914.
[47] Stamford Advocate 1/23/1965, 2/27/1965, 3/18/1920, 8/18/1916, 5/3/1916.
[48] Stamford Advocate 5/2/1966, 10/7/1970.

and later bombed the building, which collapsed around Mr. Blosio. Unable to locate him, he was declared dead and his family was notified that he had died in combat. The French were the first to introduce tear gas in August of 1914. However, it was the Germans who developed chemical weapons further. Mustard gas, introduced by the Germans in 1917, blistered the skin, eyes, and lungs and killed thousands. Enrico was a survivor, he was eventually found and after a year of rehabilitation in Austria, he was able to return to Marcianise to his family's surprise. He received the honorary title of cavalier for his service. Unfortunately, the woman he was engaged to married someone else in the meantime; thinking he was dead. The injuries he suffered on the battlefield would stick with him his entire life, and in fact, while living in Stamford, he often found himself sick and had to be hospitalized.

Not able to find work in Stamford, because of the depression he worked in a factory in Jamestown, NY, 6 days a week for $22 per week. After saving enough money, he returned to Italy for a few months and then departed for Stamford again. He found work this time as a house painter, doing decorative designs on walls, ceilings, and facades. This was his profession in Italy. He worked most often with the Napoletano Brothers. His son, Emmanuale (Manny) emphasized that his father was not just a painter but an artist. He used his craft to create wood grain, marble, brick, or stone effects. He painted several church interiors in Stamford, among them St. Johns, and St. Clemens. He made several trips back and forth to Italy. On one trip, he married Assunta Lasco. In 1924, the United States Congress passed the Johnson-Reed Act, revising American immigration laws around individuals' "national origins." The act set quotas, a specific number of visas available each year for each country. These laws were biased against Italians. At the beginning of the Great Depression in 1930, President Herbert Hoover issued instructions banning immigrants "likely to become a public charge." Immigration fell dramatically as a result. Though Franklin D. Roosevelt liberalized the instruction, many Americans continued to oppose immigration on economic grounds (that immigrants would "steal" jobs). Immigrants, therefore, had to find an American sponsor who had the financial resources to guarantee they would not become a burden on the state. Often the sponsors were family that had immigrated earlier. Paesanos from the same town in Italy were also often sponsors. The Blosio's did not have family in Stamford, but fortunately, the Limone family accepted the responsibility of being their sponsor. In 1932, he convinced Assunta to come to Stamford, as by then he had become a citizen. She joined him with their two daughters, Antonette, and Nina, and their son, 6-month-old Emmanuel.

Enrico's number came up in the draft for World War II, but he was able to get a dispensation. He lamented that this was the only lottery he ever won. Working on the American Cyanimide building in Stamford as a painter, he was injured after falling from the roof. Luckily, for Enrico he landed in a pile of sand that was being used in construction. He was given last rights and the family was told that it was likely he would die. Again, Enrico, ever the survivor, had other plans. Other Marcianese families helped the family while Enrico recuperated. Mr. Blosio was a member of the painter's union. Due to the unpredictability of his employment; (he only got paid when he had jobs), Enrico never bought property but rented instead and did so for his entire life. In his spare time, he arranged drama and musical entertainment. He played the mandolin and was self-taught. With Michele Accinni, Enrico wrote the lyrics to a song (in a Neapolitan dialect, "Turmiento E stu Core," "Tormented is this Heart." The song is about a love for someone that is far away. The music was by Antonio Delli Paoli.

Manny describes his father, similar to many Italian fathers at that time, as a man a few words and not overly affectionate, in terms of hugging and kissing. When Manny went to war, his father did not kiss him goodbye but shook his hand. Enrico like many men demonstrated his love in other ways. Manny recalls, growing up he did not know it, but they were poor. He wanted to buy some skates to play hockey on the Mill River near Richmond Hill with all the other kids. His father forbade it because he was afraid that Manny might fall through the ice. Manny had his mind set, and when the opportunity arose (there was a thrift shop with used skates that were the wrong size and had no shoe laces), he saved his money and purchased them. Skating on the ice, he heard his name called and knew instantly he was in trouble. His father told him to come home and asked where he got the skates. Manny told him the story, and the next day his father told him to come with him, without explanation, and he bought him new ice skates. A memory of the love his father had for him (as good as any kiss or hug) that he carries to this day. I am sure many Italians can relate to Mr. Blosio's story for they too had fathers who did not speak often but when they did, it was important and impactful. They also can relate to the struggles that their fathers endured either through war or through facing bias without giving up and always looking to improve the lives of their children and engendering that feeling of hope for a better future through tenacity and hard work.

Another artist, painting contractor was Louis Sementini, born in Naples Italy. He started in 1910 as a meat purveyor. He eventually moved into painting contracting with his sons Joseph and Frank. In 1915, he won the contract to paint Hart School for $1,500. However, the painters' labor union would not allow all three to work on the school, as they were not members of the union. Union membership was required by resolution of the town council. The union did allow two of them to work as labor bosses. Joseph Vallario was a painter.[49]

Edith Arcano, born in Stamford to Francis and Rose Celosi Arcano was a teacher of modern dance. After teaching at Arthur Murray Studio in Stamford, she opened her own studio, Edith Arcano Studio of Modern Dancing at 24 Park Row. Vincent Geronimo (known as Jimmie Delaney) was an instructor of dancing, piano, harmonica, baton, singing, and impersonation. He was born in Calitri, in 1908. He came to Stamford in 1916. Geronimo won the tap dancing New England States Championship in 1935. His studio was at 6 Stephen St (Carlevale, 196).

Italians made their mark in sports as well. Being a member of a Team with other ethnic backgrounds helped Italians become accepted by other Stamford citizens.

Michael Antonio Cantillo graduated from Stamford High School in 1917. His nickname was "Injun" and was one of the greatest centers on the football team and played basketball as well. It was reported in the Advocate, "he was one the greatest athletes Stamford ever had, never playing on a losing team except in one game." In 1913, he played center on the Stamford High School football team, which won the state championship. He was a World War I Army veteran and had worked at Conde Nast Publications.[51]

Michael Luciano graduated from Stamford High School in 1917. Small in stature, he was dubbed "shorty" in the high school yearbook, and is described as having "a pair of big brown eyes, which are the envy of more than one girl." He was the star of the 1917 football team, and played basketball, a candidate for the baseball nine and a member of the school military company. He was one of the first to sign up for the Navy in 1917 and was on a submarine, the U.S.S. Harvard with forces in England.[52]

Paul James Rosa graduated from Stamford High School in 1918. He was halfback and captain of the 1917 football team, and during the three-year span in which he played the football team lost only one game. In 1915, Stamford won seven games while scoring 124 points to the opponents' 34. His ambition was to become a clerk or stenographer, and he ended up working for Southern New England Telephone Company for 41 years.[53]

Tommy Alfano a native of New York City moved to Stamford after serving with the American Expeditionary Forces (AEF) in France in World War

---

[49] Stamford Advocate 12/30/1910 p 7, 10/10/1935 p 8, 2/16/1915 p 1, 4/2/1942 p 8,
[51] Stamford Advocate 7/21/1962, 7/30/1962, 6/3/1964.
[52] Stamford Advocate 5/1/1917, 7/15/1918, 2/21/1919.
[53] Stamford Advocate 7/30/1962, 7/21/1962, 7/9/1962.

I. He first played with the Old Sound Beach All Stars in the 1920s for five years. It had one of the best semi-professional records in Connecticut and went undefeated in 1923. In 1929, Alfano's two run, home run broke the eight to eight tie and won the game in the ninth for the Stamford Pros who came from behind to win the city baseball championship. Later he played for the Stamford All Stars of the New York-Connecticut League coached by Felix LiVolsi. This team played against the professionals from the Pittsfield Eastern League training in Stamford. Tommy finished his playing days as third baseman for the Holy Name A.C. in the Twilight League. Later Alfano became an umpire and instructor. He worked in the Board of Recreation City Senior Leagues and semi-pro games, and was highly rated as one of the best plate umpires. He and his wife Wilhelmina were also active in the Italian American Republican Club.[54]

In the 1920s, a basketball team called the Columbia Ramblers with members Moruke and Abbazia thrilled local crowds with their play.[55] The Marrucco ("Moruke") family had a few sports heroes in it. Giuseppe (Joseph) Marrucco came from Sante Maria Infante, Italy in the late 1800s and got a job as a laborer and sent for his young bride Maria Carmella "Carmina" Coppola. He then got a job at Yale and Towne and purchased a home at 36 Rose Park Ave. They had five boys and three girls (Lucien, Tony, Paddy, Eddie, Dave, Olympia, Fanny, and Grace). After school, the older boys would go down by the railroad tracks and behind stores in downtown Stamford to pick up discarded pieces of coal to bring home for cooking and heat. Olympia married Ernest Mallozzi who owned Mallozzi's Market, first located on Rose Park Ave., then on West Main St. Lucien the oldest was born in 1894, and joined the Stamford Police Department and served for many years until his retirement. Tony was born in Stamford on February 27, 1899. He attended Merrill Business College and the RCA School for Sound Motion Pictures. Tony played baseball with many of the local teams: as an outfielder with the Aberdeen A.C. in 1913 and 1914 with Jimmy Giblin's Boys Club (which were the County Champs), winning 16 straight games. He played with the Spelke Team in 1915. He joined the "All Stamfords," in 1916, and continued through the 1920 season. On July 4, 1918 with Frank Woodward of the St. Louis Cardinals pitching and Chief Myers of the New York Giants catching, the Penn Red Caps were defeated 9 to 1. His top game was in 1929, when the Sing Sing Prison team was defeated, stopping their 16-game win streak. Moruke had a perfect day at bat. He also played basketball with Co. G in

---

[54] Stamford Advocate 1/24/1961, 11/16/1938, 6/26/1934, 5/21/1934, 3/24/1934, 7/5/1929, 5/26/1922, 5/22/1922.
[55] Stamford Advocate 3/12/1928 p 14, 2/27/1928 p 14.

1918 and later with the Stamford Big Five. He with "Beef" Carlson comprised the best forwards combination in the county. In 1921, with the Sound Beach team (which won the County Championship) he had an errorless season. After retiring from active play, he coached the Sacred Heart Big Five, the Yale and Towne girls' teams, as well as promoted and booked games throughout the East. He was also the manager for his brother Eddie Mack. Tony served two years as a member of the Board of Education, City Housing Authority, seven years as a member of the Hubbard Heights Golf Club Commission, and as chairman of the same for two years. In 1950, he was president of the independent Baseball League and later vice-president of the Twilight League. He was the founder of the Stamford Old Timers and a scout for the Boston Red Sox and the Philadelphia Phillies. He was a projectionist for the Stamford Theater for 47 years and lived at 38 Ursula Place.

Eddie "Mack" was a professional boxer and held the title of New England Bantam Boxing Champion. He was also the swimming coach at the Stamford Yacht Club and coached two Olympic swimmers, Janet Bradenburg, and Gloria Callen. He started the Stamford Boxing Club in 1919. Paddy was born on the West Side, on October 17th, 1903. He was a former professional sportsman and became a deputy sheriff of Fairfield County. He was also a booking agent handling Yale University football hero Albie Boot, "Big Jim" Weaver, Ken Strong, and the Original Celtics. In booking the Celtics in 1929-1930, they failed to pay the required fee, so "The Sheriff" booked them into Westport and had a Deputy Sheriff attach their guarantee of $550. His booking agency booked the Chicago Bears and Brooklyn Dodgers. He coached the "All Stars Girls" basketball team. He served on the Republican Town Committee and was a member of the Italian Center, Holy Name Society of Sacred Heart Church, and Richmond Park Republican Club. Paddy hated to evict people, and simply would not serve eviction notices during the holiday season, and everybody knew it. In a letter to the editor after Paddy's death, the writer states: "The people in the west side of Stamford could come to Paddy for legal aid, advice and even financial help, and did so without hesitation. They were his dependable bank of friends and votes which formed one of the bases of his political position, and people to whom he gave help when they were helpless often became quite successful and never forgot Paddy's kindness."

David, the youngest Maruke, wrote a column for "La Tribuna." He also was a candidate for justice of the peace and was secretary and vice president of the First and Third Ward Italian-American Club. He enjoyed cartooning, and in later years taught cartooning to children at the Yerwood Center.[56]

John A. Scalzi, Jr. born March 22, 1907, to John A. Scalzi, Sr. and Carmella Genovese, was one of Stamford's all-time star athletes. In the Stamford High School class of 1927, John earned more letters, in football, basketball, and baseball, than any other student in the history of the school. At Georgetown University, he was captain of the varsity football team and an honor student, graduating in 1931. The 5-7, 170 lb. Scalzi competed and excelled as a quarterback, punter, and kick returner. A ninety-five-yard kickoff return against West Virginia and Michigan State brought Scalzi national recognition, while Scalzi would also deal with the coverage of a 2-0 loss to NYU at Yankee Stadium when it was determined that Scalzi stepped on the goal line for a punt, leading to a safety and then defeat. John was awarded the Joseph A. Wilner Trophy as Georgetown's most valuable player by vote of the student body. He also played baseball and basketball there. His ability attracted major league scouts who signed him for a cash bonus with the Boston Braves in 1931. Bonuses were rare during the Depression. Unfortunately, he retired after an arm injury in 1933. Mr. Scalzi played with the Brooklyn Dodgers professional football team. He later served on the Park Commission and Scalzi Park was named in his honor after his tragic death in a car accident.[57]

The West Side Athletic Club filed articles of association with the secretary of state on July 15, 1926. The subscribers were Louis DeLuca, William V. Mancusi, Leo J. Possidento, Tony Delupica, Alfred A. Ferretto and Thomas A. Ferretti. The club put on amateur boxing matches, and baseball games. They won several city championships (1926, 1929, and 1931). In 1931, William Galasso was listed as an officer in the Stamford directory. The Clubrooms were at 160 Stillwater Avenue. Active committee members in 1932 included Frank Accurso, Dominick Lombardo, Louis DeLuca, William Mancusi, Joseph Gerardi, Tony Docimo, Nicholas Accousta, and Leondard Mancusi. Officers in 1934 were Michael Lione president (also voted captain of the baseball team); John Lionetti, vice president; William Golasso, recording secretary; Peter Accousta treasurer; Louis DeLuca, William Mancusi, and Frank Lupinacci, board of trustees; and Nick Tarzia sergeant-of-arms.[58]

---

[56] Stamford Advocate 3/4/1987, 1/29/1995, 1/28/1995, 2/25/1987, 11/30/1977, 8/9/1972, 7/31/1972, 1/7/1972, 8/27/1940.

[57] Stamford Advocate 9/17/1962, Tribute to John A. Scalzi, Jr, Moe Magliola, Sports Editor Stamford Advocate, hoyabasketball.com.

[58] Stamford Advocate 7/16/1926, 1/14/1927, 5/22/1930, 10/9/1931, 10/22/1931, 3/23/1932, 4/17/1934.

Sheriff Pete Accousta was an important part of the Stamford Baseball scene. He started his career on the West Side in the 1930s as a manager and coach, where his brother Nick was a well-known baseball figure. He was very prominent in the Stamford Twilight League and Little League Baseball.[59]

Michael F (Mickey) Lione was a policeman (starting in 1939) and star football player at Georgetown, where he later was an assistant coach in the early 1930s. He also played semi-professional baseball and professional football but was most famous in Stamford as a Coach. Mr. Lione died at 45 in 1954. At Stamford High Mickey, was chosen for All-State honors in football three times. He was captain of the 1929 State championship High school team. In 1951, Mr. Lione co-coached the Stamford All-Stars of the local Little League who won the world championship of Little League at Williamsport.[60]

Cleeko Marchetti won many golf tournaments in the 1930s including a pro-amateur event.[61]

The Stamford Old Timers Association honors past local sports figures from Stamford. The following is a list of local Italian American sports figures honored by the organization. Patrick E. Lione, born in Stamford in 1897, was a veteran of WWI, serving in the infantry, and worked for Vuono Construction. Patrick was a semi-pro baseball player and boxed under the name Paddy Lyons. Angelo Pace was born in Italy. Angelo was one of the best lightweights in New England during the 1920s. He was Connecticut lightweight champion and Junior Welterweight Champion of Connecticut. His brothers, Willie Lenny, and Sally also fought, and they all became known as the "Fighting Angelo Brothers." He defeated the world's lightweight champion, Sammy Mandell in a non-title fight. He was also excellent at track and field and swimming. Mr. Pace was a special police officer, and active in the Italian American Republican Club. Fredrick M. Lione, Sr. was born in Stamford in 1901. He played on the Stamford Pro basketball team. Alfred W. ("Red") Abbazia was born in Stamford in 1904. He played semi-pro basketball and later was a local coach. He also competed in national bowling tournaments. John R. Franchina was born in Stamford in 1904. John was an umpire in the semi-pro baseball league. He played guard on a strong Stamford traveling football team in the 1920s and 1930s. He was named a special constable in 1933. Frank LiVolsi played football professionally. He was a president and secretary of the Stamford Board of Education, Board of Representatives, and State Representative in 1937. Aurelio Rich, born in 1905 was among the founders of the Twilight League. Aurelio played semi-pro baseball. Mr. Rich

---

[59] Stamford Advocate 5/21/1963, 5/18/1963, 12/3/1941.
[60] Stamford Advocate 6/8/1954.
[61] Stamford Advocate 7/21/1936, 10/21/1936, 10/27/1937, 5/10/1938.

was appointed official boxing and wrestling timekeeper by the governor of Connecticut. He was active in Republican politics and was president of the Richmond Park Republican Club. Joseph A. Caporizzo was born in 1907 in Stamford. He was appointed plumbing inspector for the city in 1938. He managed the boxer Angelo Uva, and had his sports reports published by the advocate, earning him the moniker "Stamford's baseball authority and historian." Louis A. Montagnino was born in Stamford in 1910. He managed the Stamford Gas and Electric team in the state industrial league in the 1930s when they won three state titles. Louis worked for the company for 41 years. He played and managed semi-pro baseball. He received baseball contracts from the Yankees in 1930, Minneapolis Millers in 1933, Brooklyn and Pittsburg in 1935. However, they were not enough for him to consider a career in baseball, so he decided to remain and play in the area. Born in 1907, Frank J. Chicatell won the "Athletic Prize" all-around student in his senior year of high school. He played football on the 1926 state championship Stamford High football team. Frank received the Matthew H. Kennedy Athletic Award when he graduated in 1928. He had 6.6 seconds in the 50-yard dash and 13 seconds in the 100-yard dash records at the Stamford YMCA. He was a supervisor for the Board of Recreation, and later a special police officer. Edward V. Bella born in Stamford in 1906, was a member of the 1926 state football champion team. He received a baseball tryout with the Cincinnati Reds in 1931 and was sent to play at Chattanooga, TN where he developed arm trouble. In the fall of 1931, he played football with the Stapelton Staten Island Club of the NFL. Ed coached the Connecticut Nutmeg girls' softball team that dominated the sport during 1938 and 1939. He was a veteran of WWII. Frank N. Benevelli born in 1914 was involved with the management of various sports leagues in the city. Tony Mammone born in 1914, was known as Stamford's "Mr. Golf." He directed tournaments at Stamford's municipal golf courses and created and nurtured various golf leagues and tournaments. He was named caddy master and assistant to pro-Dave Stewart. He caddied for such celebrities as Babe Ruth, Bobby Jones, Ky Laffoon, Norton Smith, and National Open Champion Tony Manero. Mammone and professional Stewart performed a dangerous act. Mammone held the ball in his mouth, fingertips, chin, forehead, toes, and on the back of his head, while Stewart hit drives of over 200 yards. Andy Robustelli, born in 1926 was a professional football player with the NFL for 14 years. It is believed that he is the only player in the NFL to play in every conceivable game in both leagues, including the championship games, Pro-bowl games, and sudden-death games. Charles "Annunziato" Manley was a professional boxer in the 1920s. He owned and operated the Charles Manley Co., a carpentry business in Stamford. His brother Sammy "Manley" Annunziato wanted to fight in the Olympics, but in the Hartford tryouts, it was determined that he was one pound overweight. He was a member of the Elks starting in 1941. Lore is that the brothers fought under the name "Manley" so that their parents would not recognize them in press accounts of the bouts. Many Italian American fighters adopted Americanized names because of discrimination, and sometimes due to difficulty for others to pronounce their names. John A. Laureno ("Sharkey") was born in 1912. He played outstanding baseball, football, and basketball at Stamford High. He worked for the Stamford Board of Education in 1936 and later had an officiating and coaching career. Canio Edward Ienner was born in 1903, and managed a few baseball teams in Stamford. Canio was active in the Richmond Park Republican Club. Alfred P. Annunziato born 1915, was contracted to play minor league baseball in the Texas Triple A league. Alfred was inducted into the minor league's Hall of Fame in 2003. Thomas S. LiVolsi won the Dr. Frank H. Barnes athletic prize for outstanding achievement in 1928. He was a semi-pro lineman. Thomas worked for the Advocate and owned the LiVolsi Liquor Shop. Some other honorees include Frank DeVito, born in Stamford in 1908, John Catino born in Stamford in 1904, William A. Caporizzo born in 1911, Edward J. Livolsi born in in Stamford in 1907, and Paul Viola born 1913 in Stamford. Joseph Zezima was born in Stamford in 1915. He was the son of banker Louis Zezima. He played semi-professional baseball. Later he became captain of the Stamford Fire Department and was involved with performing at Knights of Columbus minstrel shows.[62] Dominick M. (Bozo) Fabrizio born in 1913, played on the 1929 State Championship football team. Clarence J. Fedeli was born in 1925 was a coach, and umpire locally. Jack "John" Pia was born in 1912 in Settefrati, Italy. He attended Stamford High School in 1928, but dropped out of school during the depression. He was the owner of Jack Pia & Son fruit and vegetable market. Fred Robertucci born in 1923, later joined the police department and was coached police athletic league teams in Stamford. Bill LiVolsi played on the Stamford High football team from 1937 through 1940, and on the baseball team from 1938 through 1940. In 1940, he lead the team in total yards, once running a kickoff back 85 yards for a touchdown in the state Championship, and another time 105 yards (no touchdown). He played shortstop and in 1939 led the team in batting. Homer Foglio was born in New York City in 1914. He played with various Stamford

---

[62] Stamford Advocate 7/19/1979, 2/21/1936, 11/16/1938, 12/9/1970, 5/27/1987, 4/1/1995, 6/28/1972, 11/15/1997, 10/24/1987, 5/8/1933, 1/27/1971, 2/18/2004, 1/7/2000, 1/22/1995, 1/23/1975, 1/20/1972, 1/28/1991, 12/27/1977, 7/19/1980, 7/28/1987, 9/30/1983, 2/4/1967.

teams and later signed with the Panama City Baseball Club, an affiliate of the old St. Louis Browns. In 1938, he rented out the Yale and Towne ground floor and opened a boxing gym and became one of New England's biggest and best known fight trainer and managers.[63] Rocco Macchio was born in 1911. In 1929 and 1930 Rocco played hardball with the championship winning Lone stars. In 1931 he joined the army. William "Sonny" Parese was born in 1921. He was captain of the 1938 Stamford High team and the leading batter with a .434 average. Sonny played professional baseball with the Moultre Club in the Georgia Florida League. Michael G. Salvatore was born in 1909 in New York City. He graduated in 1929 from J.M. Wright Technical School and was a carpenter. He was a member of the Italian American Republican club and played on several local teams. Michael A. "Puggy" Vitti was born in 1918. He carried his first golf bag at the age of eight. Puggy was head pro at Hubbard Heights. He was a "Class A" member of the PGA for 52 years. Frank J. Robotti was born in 1913. He was a wholesale meat seller and served two terms as a member of the Stamford police commission. He played semi-pro ball.

The relationship of grandparents to grandchildren is a special one in Italian family and culture. In many cases, grandparents provide significant assistance in raising the next generation of the family, either through contributions of time and experience, emotional support and even financial support. It is very common for grandparents to live with their children in an extended family. Such was the case for Nancy Lazzaro Fekete, who grew up living upstairs in the house her grandfather built. Her grandparents, Cesare Latte and Cornelia Orsola Colarossi were an integral part of her life. She remembers her grandfather walking her back and forth from school every day and once a week stopping at Abbazia's pharmacy for an ice cream. She recounts that although they were poor monetarily, they were rich because they were blessed with many friends and family. Their house on the corner of Liberty Street and West Main was the house where everyone would stop by. It occurs to her that integration into society was not entirely easy for Italians, and the simple act of getting together to share a conversation and food was a comfort to many as it was hard to make friends in a new country. It helped engender optimism among them. Saturday afternoons would always certainly bring friends that would come and enjoy her grandmother's pasta as they sat underneath the grapevines. The vines would provide the grapes for homemade wine (another Italian cultural staple), and friends and family would enjoy peaches or oranges soaked in the wine when they stopped by. Cornelia would

---

[63] Stamford Advocate 7/30/1990, 10/14/1991.

make vinegar from the wine when it went too long, nothing was wasted. There was an extra lot by the house on Liberty Street where plenty of vegetables would be grown including tomatoes, cucumbers, and peppers to name a few. She remembers with fondness tending to the garden with the entire family after school each day, using a wagon to carry the water that nourished the plants. As with many Italians, the holidays were special with plenty of food, fish on Christmas Eve (stuffed calamari, fried smelts, snails to name a few), and pizza every New Years with homemade tomato sauce (gravy) that was jarred each year. Food is an important part of Italian-American culture but is not covered in this history.

The above are just some of the examples of how Italians incorporated their love of art into their work and hobbies. This integration of art and excellence in sports propelled the stature of Italians in the eyes of other groups in Stamford. It broke down barriers between Italians and others and was instrumental in humanizing and engendering empathy for them, and then acceptance. It would take some time for Italians to be recognized at national levels but naturally, they did rise to this level. For example, some famous Italian residents of Stamford include:

Dave Abbruzzese – Pearl Jam's drummer.
Michael Dante – major league player, actor
Tony Dipreta – cartoonist, Joe Palooka
Jimmy Ienner – music producer
Carol Iovanna – newscaster for Fox
John "Sharkey" Laureno – athletics organizer
Mickela Mallozzi – host and executive producer of travel PBS series.
Ezio Pinza – opera singer
Dave Puzzuoli – NFL football player
Dave Racaniello – major league player
Andy Robustelli – NFL player; member Pro Football Hall of Fame
John Anthony Scalzi – was a major league baseball player
John J. Scalzi – war honor recipient
Dan Sileo – NFL player; broadcaster
Bobby Valentine – major league player; manager

CHAPTER 7

Politics/Military

Ogni muro è una porta.
(For every obstacle in life, there is always a way over it)

Italians in Stamford knew they had to engage politicians to help combat prejudice against them. They knew that their message would be more impactful if there were more of them participating in the political process and offering a diverse representation of the citizenry. This was one tool in their kit to elevate the Italian community. Progress was slow but steady. The colony was patient; starting with backing candidates that supported policies that affected the Italian Colony favorably, and eventually, as time went on they began to win elected positions themselves. Albeit the early elected positions were lower-level ones, with persistence they would move up the power hierarchy (though to achieve the highest levels in Stamford it would take time periods after the era of the history covered here).

Domenico Palo (brother of early leader Antonio Palo) was the first Italian appointed special policeman in 1898. In 1900, he made an arrest of a quarreling couple, who cursed at him. In the court, the woman told the court, she did not know Palo was an officer; but mistook him for an ordinary "Dago" as the street was full of them. He died in 1908 at forty-three. One hundred and thirty members of the Società Campanella attended and acted as escort for his funeral.[1]

In gratitude for the assistance provided by Mrs. Blinckensderfer in the case of Pasquale Esposito, the Stamford societies threw their support to a candidate that she backed, George P. Rowell. The candidate's platform was to secure the abolition of capital punishment. This was noted in a letter to the editor penned by Dr. A. T. Sorgi in which he states: "Certainly the Italian people of Stamford will appreciate Mrs. Blickensderfer's desire because they know she was the only faithful assistant of theirs to help us prevent Esposito's execution for a crime of which we believed, and still do believe, he was innocent."[2] It would take much longer to accomplish this, the death penalty was not ended in Connecticut until 2012.

Italians demonstrated their appreciation of Mrs. Blickensderfer and politicians took note and participated in a gathering at her home in 1912 where she hosted the Società Calabrese (of which she was an honorary member).

---

[1] Stamford Advocate 11/16/1898, 12/18/1900, 1/7/1908, 1/8/1908.
[2] Stamford Advocate 10/13/1908.

About 200 persons, representing every Italian society in town, gathered at the Blickensderfer home on 138 Grove Street. Town officials attending included Town Clerk, Treasurer, Town Physician and School Physician. The Società Calabrese gathered on Pacific Street and headed by the Italian Band and men bearing red lights and torches made their way to the home of the Blickensderfers. In Mrs. Blickensderfer's speech to the crowd she said, "The Italian must look out for his self-respect. Careful grooming of this virtue would help him in every walk of life, because he would place himself on a level with those with whom he was associated, even though they be not of his nationality, and would tend to lessen the turning toward crime and wrong doing."[3]

The Stamford societies continued to hold onto to the connection to the mother country. An article in the Advocate relaying the desire by the Società Campanella to sponsor a memorial mass in honor of the late King of Italy, who had been assassinated by an Italian-American anarchist, exhibits this.[4]

As more Italians immigrated to Stamford, the existing governing order was on alert to the perceived impact that could result on a shift in the balance of power. In 1910, the Advocate reported on new voter registration activity that was increasing among Jewish and Italian clubs in the city. The reporter commented that if it turned out that they voted together as a unit as had been speculated, they could swing elections. Mr. Spelke of the Jewish club, who had run as a candidate for councilman in the second ward, denied that they would be voting as a block. In July of the same year, the Advocate reported that an Italian club announced its intention to enter the field of politics and endorse an Italian for nomination. It was also reported that the Jewish club would as well. The article goes on to state: "If the first thought of a naturalized citizen is that he must do all in his power to secure the election of men of his race or nationality to public office, he is drifting away from the right conception of citizenship. The main test for office should be fitness to perform its duties. If the candidate is able to do the work and to do it well, and if he is a man of integrity, it matters little whether he was born in Italy, or in Illinois…, or whether he worships in the church or in the synagogue…. To vote for a man simply because he is an Italian, or a Swede, or a Pole, would be clannish and bigoted. To hold any prejudice against a man because of his race or nationality would be equally narrow."[5] Of course, the degree to which you buy into and agree with these arguments depends upon how your particular point of view is informed by your experience and how the needs of your race and nationality are being met. Italians would have to prove that an Italian was fit to perform these duties.

---

[3] Stamford Advocate 7/9/1912.
[4] Stamford Advocate 8/6/1900.
[5] Stamford Advocate 1/11/1910, 7/9/1910.

Italians were able to show their patriotism for their new country and appreciation for being accepted as fully capable citizens after President Harrison's declaration of Columbus Day as a holiday. Stamford Italians celebrated Columbus Day in fine style in 1911 with a two-hour parade. The Advocate reads: "The celebration of Columbus Day by the united Italian societies of Stamford proved conclusively that the day is fast becoming one of the most prominent of the holidays. Not only did the Italian people turn out for the celebration, but also persons of nearly every nation. In the parade there were nine societies, all of Stamford, four bands and drum corps, about five hundred members who walked two by two in the line of march; about fifteen wagons and barouches, and a number of floats. The societies represented were: Society Campanella, Operaia, Vittorio Emanuele III, Foresters of America, Court Umberto I, Italian Benevolent and Political Club, Italo-American and Progressive Club, Aviglianese, Manghese and Calabrese." After the parade, a play "Girl of the Golden West" was put on at Realty Hall, with dancing later in the evening. In 1916, celebrations were under the auspices of the united Sons of Italy societies and included a ball with the P. Chiapetta six-piece orchestra, the Sons of Italy and Colonial bands, a parade with 700 participants. Following the marchers was a decorated float, depicting Columbus's discovery of America and the progress of Italians in America. Michael Pierrenzo impersonated Christopher Columbus and Mary Mongousi Queen Isabella. Later on Benedetta Pumpo of St. John's Place, a 13-year-old lectured on Columbus and the significance of Columbus Day. Q. Vetriolo was grand marshal. Proceeds of the event were donated to the Italian Red Cross." In 1924, Italian residents of Stamford presented the city a bronze bust of Christopher Columbus, designed by Phillip Lagano, a Stamford youth. The presentation speech was given by Dr. Antonio Sorgi. At that time, Columbus Day was a legal holiday in Connecticut. Mayor Alfred N. Phillips, Jr. accepted the bust and read his speech in Italian, expressing his deep appreciation of the gift and commending the Italian race for their ready assimilation of American customs and their love for their country of adoption. Columbus Day was celebrated in 1925 at Halloween Park (now Cummings Park) with "one of the best displays of fireworks set off in Stamford in years." In 1926, the parade was eliminated due to complaints by merchants about customer access to businesses, and instead, a band concert on Town Hall Plaza took place and fireworks were displayed at Halloween Park.[6] In 1937, a three-day program celebrated Columbus Day, with concerts, speeches on the contributions of Italians to America beginning at the Revolutionary War, sporting events, and a dinner dance.[7]

[6] Stamford Advocate 10/12/1911, 10/9/1924, 10/11/1924, 10/13/1925, 10/8/1926, 10/13/1926, 10/12/1916.
[7] Stamford Advocate 10/11/1937.

In 1912, the Democratic candidate for mayor, John J. Looney, courted the Italian vote. He promised that if elected they could enter the selectman's office at any time without a feeling that he considered himself on a higher plane than they. Another Democrat, Mr. Hanrahan said the Italians in Stamford deserve credit for the progress they had made, and that the Democratic Party would be fair to the Italians. Mr. Leary spoke about the assessment of property, advocating for a system that would be progressive, imposing less on the poor man and more on the rich man's property.[8]

Italians were able to demonstrate their abilities and commitment to the city by contributing to business organizations. A Board of Trade was reorganized in Stamford in 1912 under the slogan "I believe in Stamford" and included the following Italian Americans: Leopold Barzaghi, (Vita Criscenzio) V.C. Corbo, Joseph Colucci, A. D'Alessandro, Leo Donatelli, August Garfiula, A, Geronimo, the Genovese Brothers, Canio Lavello, E. Mazza, M. Mostrach, Alonzo Maffucci, G. Passaro, Gennaro and Romano Rosa, Charles Rosso, Vincenzo Sabia & Bros, G. Sabia, Michele Toscano, Quintino Vetriolo, and Vuono Construction Co.[9]

The Italian Colony continued to show their patriotism and appreciation of their new home, by participating in the Founders Day celebrations in 1914. An Italian, Joseph Itri was part of the program committee.[10]

Romolo D'Aloia, a barber on Main Street was elected as grand juror in 1904 and was part of the Italian Democratic Club. Mr. D'Aloia appears to be the first elected Italian in Stamford. He along with Vito Pittaro were representing the Italo-American Directory Co., which was preparing a "general guide" for Italians. Romolo was also president of the Italo-American Young Men's Club in 1905. Romolo sold his barbershop at 442 Main St. to E. Expositis in 1905 and moved to White Plains.[11]

Anthony Geronimo (son of John Geronimo and one of the first families to settle in Stamford) became one of the first Italian political figures in Stamford. He was married to Lottie Zella, who was Jewish. He started as a movie and vaudeville theater proprietor and was the first to take up moving pictures and vaudeville in Stamford.[12] In 1913, he announced plans to build a theatrical theater on Bank Street, so that he would have the Alhambra (Vaudeville Theater), the Lyceum as a moving picture house and the new building as a "first-

---

8 Stamford Advocate 10/2/1912.
9 Stamford Advocate 10/17/1912, 10/2/1912.
10 Stamford Advocate 8/27/1914.
11 Stamford Advocate 10/11/1904, 10/04/1904, 11/21/1904, 3/17/1905, 6/7/1905, 7/18/1905.
12 Stamford Advocate 5/22/1931, 12/30/1916, 10/28/1914.

class theater."[13] Not only the planned theatrical entertainment itself was dramatic, but also backstage happenings were as well. During the middle of a show at the theater, an actress died after appearing on stage at the Alhambra. In a sketch she told the two other cast members on stage she would pay their board bills, she left the stage, walked behind the scenes and fell into the arms of the stage manager and died.[14] He also had a film company that released "A Romance of Stamford," for which Stamford was the backdrop and the cast was all Stamford residents.

Politics was also a part of his life. Geronimo was elected to the Board of Assessors in 1908.[15] Running up to the election during the nominations, Geronimo indicated he wanted to withdraw in favor of Dr. Van Vleet, but the convention emphatically told him he was their choice and he yielded to persuasion.[16] Geronimo caused a stir at a meeting at the Italian political club in 1910 by favoring one candidate over another, but in his candid style, he was forthright in telling the candidate why. They actually shook hands and the other candidate indicated he admired his frankness.[17] He was a newly elected councilman in 1912.[18] Ever the showman, his advertising for the councilman election of the Third Ward in 1914 included a full-grown Russian bear, wearing stage clothing riding around in his car with a placard reading "Vote for Anthony Geronimo for Councilman, he's a bear."[19] He was on the Board of Health committee in 1914 and was elected president of the Connecticut State Democratic league in 1916.[20] In 1922, he announced his candidacy for mayor, but was not elected mayor. This is still a significant milestone for Italian Americans in Stamford, as it was the first time they dared to reach this level.[21]

The Great Depression took a toll on Stamford and especially Italians. As Selectman, (the first Italian American Selectman of Stamford) Geronimo responded and arranged for donations for the needy in 1932, where he distributed Christmas baskets containing a Christmas dinner and some foods to carry the families through the following week. He also collected donations of clothing, groceries, and coal.[22] Selectmen Geronimo devised a way to supply

---

[13] Stamford Advocate 1/22/1913.
[14] Stamford Advocate 12/26/1912.
[15] Stamford Advocate 11/4/1908.
[16] Stamford Advocate 10/24/1908.
[17] Stamford Advocate 10/7/1910.
[18] Stamford Advocate 12/31/1912.
[19] Stamford Advocate 11/3/1914.
[20] Stamford Advocate 7/18/1914,10/24/1916.
[21] Stamford Advocate 10/11/1956.
[22] Stamford Advocate 12/20/1932, Stamford Advocate Tercentenary Edition Town of Stamford, CT 1641 – 1941. Supplement of the Stamford Advocate, Saturday, June 7, 1941 p. 12.

food to many Stamford families whose wage earners had been jobless for months on end. Shoppers who could afford it were urged to buy extra food when making their own purchases and would drop them in a red barrel set up in grocery stores, the barrels became known as "Geronimo's red barrels."[23] Anthony Geronimo declared himself out of politics on October 19th, 1932 after the democratic Committee endorsed Maj. Alfred N. Phillips Jr. for Mayor instead of Geronimo. He refused to throw his support behind the chosen candidate.[24] Phillips did go on to win the Mayoral race. Geronimo left Stamford after selling his theater business and went to Florida where he was engaged in real estate for a considerable amount of time. He returned to Stamford after the collapse of the real estate market in Florida and lived at the family home on West North Street.[25] He was elected to the board of directors of the Italian Center in 1932.[26] In 1934. Geronimo joined a new party the "Fusion Ticket," and in a rally declared: "If you've got any independence in your blood, let's show them we can put it over."[27] He died after an illness in November of 1934.[28] He had remarried after his first wife died and he is buried at St. Patrick's cemetery in Meriden.[29]

Joseph Itri was born in Isernia, Italy on March 19, 1880. He was a barber by trade, with a shop located at 251 Pacific Street, which was sold to Pasquale Stabile when his constable duties took up more time. He was treasurer of the Italian Institute. He was also an early Italian American political figure in Stamford. In 1903, Pittaro advocates for Itri to be a special policeman. In 1906, he was nominated as a delegate to the Senatorial convention. He spent $1.50 on his campaign for Constable in 1907. He also ran as Grand Juror in 1907. As a Democrat, he was successfully elected constable in 1908, the Advocate report reads: For the first time Stamford has an Italian constable and in Joseph Itri it is confidently expected there will be found a man who will fully justify the confidence that has been placed in him." He received 1,407 votes. In 1910, he received 1,351 votes. Itri was named a special police officer by the mayor. He also served as an interpreter for courts and police. He was a member of the Court Umberto, Foresters.[30]

---

23 Stamford Advocate 4/7/1979.

24 Stamford Advocate 10/19/1922.

25 Stamford Advocate 11/30/1934.

26 Stamford Advocate 2/1/1933.

27 Stamford Advocate 9/29/1934.

28 Stamford Advocate 11/30/1934.

29 Stamford Advocate 11/30/1934.

30 Stamford Advocate 4/25/1952,4/20/1927 11/2/1921, 4/1/1919, 1/2/1917, 4/27/1915, 2/8/1911, 2/8/1911, 10/4/1910, 7/6/1910, 3/19/1910,10/6/1908, 9/28/1908, 9/26/1908,

In 1912, Francesco (Frank) Gagliardi a barber was a candidate for justice of the Peace for the Democratic Party.[31]

Professor Giuseppe Ventura was born in Pizza, Calabria, Italy. In 1915, he came to Stamford and became active in the affairs of the community and was a member of the Italian Center. He believed in the Democratic Party as a party of the people that could do most in helping the Italian American people and often gave political speeches at events. He was one of the founders of the "Italian American Protective Association" out of Port Chester that worked to help Italians facing injustice, and to bring the Italian culture to the people. He participated in theatrical presentation and was a music teacher by profession, having graduated from the Conservatory of Music in Naples.[32]

Stamford Italians made their impact upon Stamford through early public health policy. Dr. J.J. Costanzo, M.D. was born in May 20, 1884 in New Haven, the son of Luigi and Maria Costanzo. He was married to Katherine J. D'Elia, and had two sons, Louis P. and Victor P. Costanzo. He was the first Italian American City Health Officer in 1919 and had a distinguished career in the city of Stamford in which he utilized pragmatism in application of health rules and looked out for the rights of ordinary citizens.[33] He would eventually become City Health Commissioner in 1954 and retired in 1968 at 79. He was a pioneer in the field of public health education and his career has striking resemblances to that of recent National Health Director, Dr. Anthony Fauci. Before other cities had established effective public health facilities, Dr. Costanzo had initiated measures here in Stamford. As health director, he initiated sanitary sewerage and an expanded sewer system for Stamford, was one of the pioneers in the inoculation of the Salk vaccine, performed tests on children in Stamford to determine the effectiveness of the vaccine, saw Stamford through the Spanish Flu epidemic, and made great strides in the control of diphtheria, typhoid, and scarlet fever. He also was an early proponent of clean air. He graduated from Yale University, the University of Illinois medical school, and came to Stamford in 1910 to practice obstetrics. In 1931, he studied ophthalmology at Columbia University and set up practice as an eye specialist. He was one of the first commissioners on the Board of Public Safety and was a member of the Board of Finance for 12 years. He served for a short time as police surgeon,

---

8/15/1908, 8/13/1908, 10/14/1907, 10/8/1907, 10/2/1907, 7/29/1907, 7/17/1907, 9/1/1906, 8/30/1906, 8/27/1906, 10/5/1905, 8/15/1905, 10/24/1903.

[31] Stamford Advocate 10/14/1912.

[32] Stamford Advocate 12/12/1933, 1/30/1934, 8/29/1994, 2/18/1919, 10/28/1930, 12/14/1931, 1/14/1959.

[33] Stamford Advocate 4/1/1919.

and during World War II sat on the Stamford Draft Board. He was an active member of the Italian Center for over 30 years.[34]

In 1911, after a near collision with another car on a bad road in New Haven, he was arrested on breach of peace and reckless driving of an automobile, but was discharged by the judge. Deputy Sheriff Uhl, who made the arrest said he attempted to remonstrate with the doctor, and the physician "sassed" him back. The judge remembered the road himself and said he could hardly blame the doctor.[35] He lived or had offices at the following addresses: 24 Willow St., 15 Broad Street, River Street, 65 South Street, 38 Urban Street, and 368 Atlantic Street.[36] As a member of the health board, he gave criticism of milk inspection enforcement, because it appeared only small merchants were being ticketed and the larger businesses with violations were not. The Milk Inspector protested with an editorial in the newspaper, and the newspaper found fault with the system of reporting rather than the inspector. He advocated on the part of small businesses by highlighting the costs for these businesses to keep up with the new milk regulation laws and expressing the inequity of these laws but was overruled by other board members who indicated that "the law was the law and they had to uphold it, and the legislature could change it if it were wrong." He also, urged the cleanup of Mill Pond because he felt it was causing malaria cases in Stamford. He actually got malaria himself.[37] In 1914, the Board of Health enacted a privacy law, where they noted that lists of contagious diseases and people afflicted with them would not be publically listed, and only provided to the commission. This had come to a head because Yale & Towne Lock Company (the largest employer in Stamford at the time), was able to view the posted list and wanted additionally to be informed of people on the list that worked for the company. Dr. Costanzo was weary of this thinking the information would be used to discharge the employees. The motion was carried anyway. He was placed on the "Pollution of Streams" committee. Dr. Costanzo argued to oblige every milk-dealer to install a pasteurization plant and was part of the committee recommending milk distribution for babies. Dealers protested against enforcement of milk ordinances. However, the pasteurization law seemed to work in 1917, as the milk tested had far less bacteria. Dr. Costanzo in retort to complaints about the higher price for milk (as a result of the

[34] Stamford Advocate 10/16/1972, 10/19/1972, 3/4/1968, 3/19/1968,3/29/1967, 1/8/1913, 6/23/1913, 7/19/1913, 8/16/1913, 2/7/1914, 2/2/1917, 2/9/1917, 3/25/1954, 4/13/1954, 5/28/1954, 6/9/1954, 5/14/1955, 7/8/1955, 8/2/1955, 3/22/1966, 3/29/1966.
[35] Stamford Advocate 5/10/1911.
[36] Stamford Advocate 6/9/1913, 10/17/1914.
[37] Stamford Advocate 9/6/1913, 9/8/1913, 9/13/1913, 10/4/1913, 5/8/1914, 7/10/1914, 5/4/1917.

new rules) said those people should consider the expense of possible funerals because of impure milk.[38]

In 1916, Joseph Fallace, one month and 21 days old died and Dr. Costanzo diagnosed him with polio (called infantile paralysis at the time). He lived in a six-family frame tenement house, which was quarantined. The father was allowed to leave the house so he could work after taking a prescribed bath and other precautions. The Police Department then began a house-to-house canvass to ascertain the sanitary condition of premises in the city. The Board of Health adopted a resolution to request $1,000 for the costs of precautionary steps to guard Stamford against polio, which was epidemic in New York at the time. The steps included registration with the Health Officer of all children under the age of 15, who came from jurisdictions where the disease was prevalent, and keeping them under observation for a week; systematic inspection of tenement houses and other sections for suspected cases; inspection of every yard in the city to see that the sanitary ordnances regarding manure and garbage were being observed and that all premises are kept in sanitary condition. During this time there were some cases occurring in the city and more precautions were taken. An order prohibiting children under 16 years of age from attending performances in theaters, and clergymen were asked to discontinue Sunday school classes. All children from New York had to bring a certificate showing that they were free from symptoms of the disease, and that they were not in an infected district for a period of 30 days. There were of course arguments about these precautions.[39]

Dr. Costanzo was elected City Health Officer in 1918. He outlined his policy on the prevention of disease in Stamford to the Health Board in June to applause: "I aim to accomplish a great deal by the search for and supervision of infected persons, and the control of the infected discharge. Prompt, intelligent disinfection of all excretes, isolation of the infected person, and the search for and supervision of mild, early convalescent, and unrecognized carriers are matters that shall require attention …. how to avoid disease should be taught to our citizens, and I believe our public school system can accomplish it. Medicine must furnish the subject; let the public school system do the teaching." He made sure to educate parents about not sending their children to school when they were sick. He held this office until January of 1923.[40]

---

[38] Stamford Advocate 1/17/1914, 7/18/1914, 4/16/1915, 10/8/1915, 5/11/1917, 9/7/1917, 12/7/1917.
[39] Stamford Advocate 7/10/1916, 7/19/1916, 7/25/1916, 7/26/1916, 8/2/1916.
[40] Stamford Advocate 5/14/1918, 6/7/1918, 8/29/1918, 1/2/1923.

The year 1918 also brought about concern over the Spanish/Russian Flu. The doctor advised on precautions and mitigating infection, which are reminiscent of statements made by health officials over a hundred years later during the COVID epidemic. Dr. Costanzo asked the police to strictly enforce the spitting ordinance, he also asked the railroad to add additional cars on lines at rush hour to prevent crowding, and all doctors were asked to report all cases. He issued a bulletin that read: "Epidemic Influenza is a highly contagious disease in the early stages. It is spread directly from person to person by contact with secretion from nose and throat, use of towels, cups, and other object contaminated with the secretions. Patients, for their own good, and for the protection of others, should remain in bed during febrile stage, and stay at home for a few days after. Indiscriminate visiting of influenza patients is one direct cause tending to spread the disease. Guard against use of a common drinking cup, roller towels, soda water glasses, pipes, toys and other articles recently mouthed. There is no cause for alarm if the above precautions are heeded." By October, due to prevalence of the flu (184 cases of influenza, and 135 cases of grip) an order was issued excluding children living in affected areas from school (Liberty Street, Finney Lane, Virgil Street and Stillwater Avenue; i.e. West Side Italian American sections) and a resolution to prohibit meetings in assembly halls of public schools. Dr. Costanzo issued advice on protocol during the Stamford Liberty Day Parade: "Everybody should dress warmly, don't crowd. Keep a reasonable distance from your neighbor…if you feel the need to expectorate, do these things in your handkerchief…In general, people should remember that the best way to avoid the disease is to get plenty of fresh air and sunshine, to refrain from visiting people ill with colds or grip, to keep the mouth and teeth clean, to dress warm, to avoid exposure to sudden changes and to avoid worry, fear, and fatigue. It is important that you stay at home on the first indication of a cold…" Later resolutions were adopted prohibiting sessions of public and private schools, church services, theatrical performances, and other public gatherings. Barbers were ordered to wear gauze masks while shaving people or cutting hair. By the 18th of October, reported cases climbed to 843 cases and an order was given to prohibit the visiting of sick people in the hospital. The Red Cross was providing meals to families stricken and prostrated by the flu. Auxiliary hospitals were opened to handle the flu patients and immunizations were obtained. There were objections to restrictions, including church services, and placarding infected houses. However, the doctor was adamant that all mass meetings be prohibited, and that placarding would only create fear and apprehension. He also answered criticism about how restrictions were ordered: "Much is said about the saloons being open and the churches closed. It may be that the Board of Health was more concerned for the welfare of people who patronized the churches. Anyway, we ordered saloonkeepers to prevent people from loitering in their places, to take precautions to sterilize glasses used in their places, to remove chairs and tables. I must say that the saloonkeepers have shown a willingness to comply with our orders without complaint or cavil. If the epidemic becomes worse, I shall recommend that the saloons be closed too." Thirty-three-year-old, Mrs. Lucia Masone of 241 West Main St., thirty-two-year-old Rosaria Docima of 193 Stillwater Ave. and forty-three year old Vincenza Melfi of 2 Hazel St. died in November of 1918. Rosaria and Vincenza left behind two and three children, respectively. Augustina Rosa of 30 Virgil St., wife of Marco Rosa died at 28 of influenza in October of 1918. Sadie, one-year-old daughter of Mr. and Mrs. Peter Catino of 75 Canal St. died in October as well. As did laborer Domenico Media (thirty-seven years old) leaving behind a widow and two children, Mary, Buccheri, wife of Sebestiano of 116 Pacific St., and thirty-five-year-old Calem Bamassia wife of James Bamassia, of Camp Ave., who also left behind two children. Others dying included five-year-old Francesco DeLuca of 75 Canal St., twenty-three-year-old Angelina Bocchicchia of 68 Liberty St., Mary Abbetemarco of 468 Spruce St., twenty-eight-year-old Carmine Bassano, and twenty-eight-year-old Giuseppe Baroni of 194 Stillwater Ave. By November, there were 172 deaths from grip, influenza, and pneumonia within two months and the epidemic was considered over.[41]

In 1919, Dr. Costanzo advocated for a full-time Health Officer that would inspect food and milk, improvement of ventilation in the city's theaters, and recommended that a committee be formed by the common council to improve faulty housing conditions in the city. He urged the installation of storm sewers and extension of the house sewer service to more streets. In addition, a free treatment clinic for persons suffering from venereal diseases was opened with the help of funds from the state. He also criticized changes in garbage collection and asked that beaches be made fit for bathing. He even enlisted the help of Anthony Geronimo to use his theaters in a video education campaign on communicable diseases. A regulated slaughterhouse for meats was proposed as well.[42]

In 1926, Dr. Costanzo was appointed a member of the City finance Board by Mayor Keating. He was also made a member of the Public Safety Board. He resigned from that board in 1931 because business connections required his

---

[41] Stamford Advocate 9/21/1918, 10/7/1918, 10/9/1918, 10/12/1918, 10/13/1918, 10/15/1918, 10/16/1918, 10/18/1918, 10/19/1918, 10/22/1918, 10/24/1918, 10/29/1918, 10/29/1918, 10/30/1918, 11/9/1918, 3/3/1920, 1/18/1921, 12/23/1922, 1/1/1918, 10/25/1918, 10/21/1918.
[42] Stamford Advocate 1/3/1919, 5/29/1919, 6/10/1919, 6/19/1919.

absence from the city. He later rejoined and became chairman of the Board of Finance. He was also elected Honorary Grand Master of the Sons of Italy in 1931.[43]

In 1916, more Italian Americans were gaining office. Judge Joseph De Vito ran for the Republican nomination for constable, and Alonzo Maffucci ran for the Republican nomination for second selectman.[44] In 1913, he was an officer in the Rippowam Lodge #24 I.O.O.F. of the Odd Fellows (Noble Grand), and was the only Italian listed as an officer. He is also listed as esteemed lecturing knight with the Elks in 1917 through 1919 (again the only Italian officer in the club). Alonzo was an ex-president of the Italian Institute, treasurer of the Italian Institute Board of Directors, and the Stamford Real Estate Board. He had a real estate business and made a lot of sales to other Calitrani living in Stamford on the west side. He was elected twice to the Board of Assessors in 1918 and 1928. He also served on the Board of Tax Review from 1933 to 1940, acting as its chairman for six years (Toglia 2007, 307).

Councilman Charles D. Vuono was a member of the common council in 1916 and served on the street committee from 1914 to 1916. He carried out a commendable street improvement plan. He was born in Acri, Italy on June 16, 1879. Mr. Vuono entered the contracting business in Stamford in 1904, incorporating the Vuono Construction Co., two years later with his brother Joseph J. Joseph was born in Brooklyn in 1885 and was president of the board of governors of the Italian Center and vice president of the Italian Institute. Joseph was secretary and treasurer of the Vuono Construction Company. The company built Stevens, Wall St., Rogers and Franklin schools, the First Congregational Church, The Strand, Palace and Stamford Theaters. Joseph was a candidate for the Common Council in 1932.[46]

Joseph L. Carpinella was born in New York City December 13, 1888, the son of Mr. and Mrs. Raffaela Martino Carpinella, who were born in San Mango Sul Calore, Italy. The Stamford Advocate reported on their Golden Wedding Anniversary in 1928.[47] His father Raffaele was president of the Society Campenella.[48] Known as the "The Big Man" from the West Side, he lived in Stamford for 80 years. He served in WWI. He was an active leader in Republican politics on the city, county and state levels. He served nine terms

---

[43] Stamford Advocate 8/10/1926, 8/11/1926, 9/10/1926, 10/14/1931.
[44] Stamford Advocate 9/19/1916, 3/4/1950, 10/8/1918.
[46] Stamford Advocate 10/23/1917, 10/9/1917, 5/13/1917, 9/14/1915, 10/28/1912, 11/6/1912, 3/19/1915, 4/7/1917, 6/14/1917, 10/23/1912, 10/23/1936, 10/4/1933, Stamford Advocate Tercentenary Edition Town of Stamford, CT 1641 – 1941. Supplement of the Stamford Advocate, Saturday, June 7, 1941, 156.
[47] Stamford Advocate 1/28/1928.
[48] Stamford Advocate 12/11/1911.

under the Common Council government in Stamford. During that time, he served on the Council's police and fire commission. He was county organizer for the Fairfield County League. He was president of the Richmond Park Republican Club.[49] There is a city park, "Carpinella Park" at Hoyt Street and Strawberry Hill Ave. dedicated to him. He resided at 52 Stillwater Avenue.

His career in politics began on June 5, 1917, as a volunteer interpreter for purposes of voter registration day. It appears that there was a large push ordered by President Wilson to sign up more voters[50] In 1918, it appears he requested an exemption from the draft because of dependent parents but was denied.[51] He left for basic training at Fort Slocum, NY in August of 1918.[52] He was elected council member in 1920. In 1921 and 1923, he was on the Fourth of July celebration committee in charge of badges. Italians used these days of celebration to show their commitment and pride in being a part of the U.S.[53] In 1921, he was on the "Walks" Committee. Other committee work dealt with property tax abatements, and road works."[54] In 1926, he was again elected as president of the Italian Republican Club and served on several committees.[55] He was also on the Fire Committee and in 1926, he helped collect donated swimsuits for children, so they could enjoy the wading pools and street showers.[56] He ran in the Republican primary for Selectman in 1926 but came in second.[57] In 1927, it appeared that there was some partisanship on the town committee. The Republicans were in the minority, and voiced displeasure with being left out of discussions on proposals and then being given short time to vote on them. Joseph Carpinella was vocal about this.[58] In his fourth term, Councilman Carpinella was appointed industrial investigator by the state Labor Department, the appointment was to last from July 1, 1928, through July, 1931. For some unexplained reason he was dropped from the appointment after six or eight months of service but was reinstated in 1929 for a two-year appointment[59] In 1928, another Italian, William A. Tamburri ran for the Republican nomination as a councilman in opposition

[49] Stamford Advocate 12/20/1969, 11/2/1928.
[50] Stamford Advocate 5/26/1917.
[51] Stamford Advocate 2/19/1918.
[52] Stamford Advocate 8/2/1918.
[53] Stamford Advocate 6/14/1921, 5/19/1923. Stamford Advocate Tercentenary Edition Town of Stamford, CT 1641 – 1941. Supplement of the Stamford Advocate, Saturday, June 7, 1941.
[54] Stamford Advocate 6/28/1921, 3/28/1922, 7/11/1922, 7/6/1926, 1/3/1927.
[55] Stamford Advocate 3/10/1926, 6/24/1927, 3/14/1928, 6/18/1929, 9/6/1929.
[56] Stamford Advocate 7/28/1926.
[57] Stamford Advocate 9/14/1926, 9/18/1926, 11/1/1926.
[58] Stamford Advocate 9/13/1927.
[59] Stamford Advocate 5/19/1928, 6/25/1929 6/16/1931, 7/1/1931.

to Carpinella. Carpinella won the nomination and later the election with 2,463 votes.[60] In 1930, he was gifted a diamond ring by colleagues at a testimonial dinner.[61] In 1930, Carpinella and other council members met to give the mayor power to appoint the committee to look into the claim that unemployment in the city was causing a reduction in the quantity of milk being purchased for babies. The mayor was worried about loss of health to city children.[62] The councilmen upon hearing that Mr. and Mrs. William De Carlo and their eight children were put out of their home at 107 Diaz Street, found alternative housing and steady work for the husband with Frank Palmer, a local contractor.[63]

In 1930, there was a Democratic sweep at the elections but Carpinella held on in the Third Ward, thanks to the women's vote.[64] In 1931, when a countywide Italian American Republican group was formed, Carpinella was elected its leader.[65] In 1931, there was a proposed charter revision to the Stamford government that would have taken powers away from the council in favor of the mayor. The Italian American organizations, both democratic and Republican, organized against this.[66] In November 1931, he was appointed another county appointment, "County Sealer of Weights and Measures." He lost the position in 1935.[67] In 1932, it looked as if William Sabia was interested in running for Councilman in the Third ward, and feelers were sent out anonymously through the local political reporters (in the political chat section of the paper), that at first suggested Carpinella would not run, and then disclosing Sabia was interested. Turns out Joe was not ready to go, he was reelected with 2,600 votes.[68] He was a proponent of the repeal of the dry laws in 1933.[69] Carpinella filed for the nomination of State Senator for Stamford but withdrew his nomination in the name of party unity in 1942. He announced running again though in 1943.[70]

James Bonomo, brother of Joseph Bonomo (WW I veteran) ran for "Board of Relief" under the democratic ticket in 1920, but lost to the Republi-

---

[60] Stamford Advocate 10/4/1928, 10/11/1928.
[61] Stamford Advocate 1/16/1930.
[62] Stamford Advocate 7/29/1930.
[63] Stamford Advocate 8/13/1930.
[64] Stamford Advocate 11/5/1930.
[65] Stamford Advocate 9/21/1931, 1/15/1932.
[66] Stamford Advocate 10/23/1931, 10/26/1931.
[67] Stamford Advocate 11/14/1931, 7/6/1935.
[68] Stamford Advocate 7/21/1932, 9/15/1932, 11/8/1932, 11/9/1932.
[69] Stamford Advocate 6/15/1933.
[70] Stamford Advocate 10/8/1942, 8/2/1943.

can candidate. James was involved with the Fraternal Order of Eagles and appeared as an officer (the only Italian for many years). He was secretary in 1914, vice president in 1916 and president in 1917. Other Italians in the organization included Joseph DiMarco, Fred Cavilier, Vito Lonzo, and Louis Gagma. The Bonomos brothers were charged with keeping a gambling house in 1926.[71]

In 1926, at a meeting of the Lincoln Republican Club, Dr. Sorgi announced his return to politics after a 10 year absence and that a mass meeting would be held at which Gen. Giuseppe Garibaldi and Congressman Fiorello La Guardia of New York would speak on behalf of the Lincoln club and in defense of Town Counsel Frank Rich.[72]

Lawrence Epifanio ran as a council member for the Third ward in 1928 and received 7,906 votes to be elected. He was president of the Italian Professional & Business Men's Club. He was later appointed prosecuting attorney in Stamford and then as Stamford City Court judge. He was born in Stamford on December 26, 1902, the son of Joseph and Philomena Epifanio and died on February 23, 1985 at the age of 82. He served as president of the Stamford Bar Association from 1959-60 and was admitted to practice before the Supreme Court of the United States. He was one of the founders of the Italian Center.[73]

Attorney Frank Rich (not to be confused with the construction contractor Frank D. Rich) was one of the first Italian Americans to graduate from Stamford High School. A 1908 Stamford advocate article describes him: "Frank Rich winner of the prize for athletics, got a sort of ovation. He pitched for the school baseball team and played on the basketball and football teams. He is in the incoming senior class. Rich is of Italian extraction." He was captain of the baseball team, and excelled at academics as well, winning the second prize in an essay contest for his submission "Has the Policy of the United States in Relation to Cuba Been Justified?" Other articles describe him as "Rich is an Italian boy, who is completing the full High School course in three years...The High School is justly proud of the boy," "But, inasmuch as it is only a story about a boy who has accomplished things in the face of difficulties, and who is likely to make his mark in the world, that part of it can be left to the imagination," "When he arrived here, he could not speak a word of the English language...He intends to study engineering and, unless lack of funds prevent, he undoubtedly will become a successful engineer.

[71] Stamford Advocate 4/17/1914, 2/19/1915, 10/19/1916, 6/23/1917, 9/18/1920, 10/5/1920, 1/6/1926.
[72] Stamford Advocate 8/20/1926.
[73] Stamford Advocate 10/29/1928, 11/5/1928, 11/7/1928, 6/2/1943, 3/15/1947, 3/28/1947, 2/24/1985, 2/25/1985.

Folks who know the young chap-he is 18 years old- and appreciate his many good qualities feel that it would be a shame if a lack of money were to deprive him of a course of university study."

Rich was born on November 29, 1890 in Castelfranco, Italy, to Michael and Marie Rich who worked as a foreman for a contractor. They lived at 51 Cottage Street. Rich obtained a scholarship to go to Dartmouth College to study engineering, he went there for two years and then transferred to Sheffield Scientific School at Yale. He was involved with the questioning of his amateur athlete status when he received a $5 award for being the best athlete. Rich was highly regarded in the town and his return from college and college exploits were often covered in the news. Rich went on to law school at Yale and was a member of the editorial staff of the Yale Law School. He wrote an eloquent tribute to Lelio Donatelli upon his death that was published in the Advocate: "the community as a whole has lost a most unselfish and useful member. The humble artisan of Campania, the vine-grower of Apulia, the rugged peasant of Calabria, the orange grower of Sicily, as they left the shores of their native land and arrived here, friendless and unknown, found in him a counselor and a guide, a help in time of need, a comforter in time of sorrow…Much is heard, these days concerning the problem of assimilation, raised by the recent large influx of migration. Theories of all sorts are current—those who wish to shut the gates and admit no one, those who wish to make learning of some sort the test of admissibility, and, finally, those who wish to establish certain physical measurements as the earmarks of the desirability of the prospective American citizen. If we analyze Mr. Donatelli's life work, and study at some length his activities in this city, it will dawn upon us that he has grappled with the problem and really pointed out the true solution: the improvement of the economic conditions of the immigrant…Mr. Donatelli's work was not confined merely to the economic help of his fellow-countrymen. He was always striving to inculcate upon them the civic ideals of this country, and thus impart that necessary knowledge to fit them to bear the burdens and duties of citizenship. The newcomers who knew but little of the history of the nation, and nothing of the machinery which turns the wheels of government, found in Mr. Donatelli an ever patient and helpful instructor. Thus, he gradually helped to mold the immigrant into a citizen and by fitting him, he laid the foundation for a better second generation." Rich passed the bar in 1916 opened an office and was married to Alice Foley in 1917. He served with the 102nd Infantry of the 26th Division in World War I and was one of the two Stamford men sent to mobilization camp upon being drafted. In 1924, he replaced Charles D. Vuono as a member of the Republican Town Committee and by 1925 was Town Counsel for Stamford.

Later he was named as a member of the Park Commission and served from 1926-1928. He also served as a member of the City Board of Finance for six years, retiring from office in 1934. Rich ran for the republican nomination for State Representative in 1938 against Vincent Giampietro and the winner Rev. George V. Hamilton. He was a president of the Italian Center in 1935. He passed away at 60 on February 19, 1951.[74]

Joseph J. Tedesco was born in Torrington and came to Stamford as a child, where his father had a fruit and vegetable market. In 1932, he was a delegate to the state convention for the Democrats. Joseph was a candidate for the Board of Education in 1932 and one on the Democratic ticket with 7,183 votes. This was after a recount was requested, where initially it was reported that the Republican challenger won. There was a mistake in taking the figures from a Third Ward machine. As a result he won by four votes. Part of his platform for running the school system was that he would give preference to local teachers when hiring. He was quoted as saying, "I am happy to have been elected and pledge my efforts to work for the best interests of the pupil, teacher and taxpayer." Mr. Tedesco was elected vice chairman in 1933. Joseph was reelected in 1934 and was chairman of the Buildings and Grounds Committee. Joseph was manager of the Stamford Motor Sales Co. at 64 Summer St., which sold Hupmobile, Marmon and Dort automobiles in the 20s. He was in business at that address with Joseph J. Vuono and Albert E. Mitchell. In 1935, he incorporated his own automobile sales business Joseph J. Tedesco Inc.[75]

Joseph Matrich was born in Telese, Benavento Italy on September 22, 1886. He was the proprietor of Stamford Storm Windows. He ran as a Democratic candidate for constable in 1912 and was known as "Joe Barry." He was a constable in 1914 and was appointed an investigator for the Department of Justice in 1934. Joseph later became a banker and helped form the Italian Loan Association. He was also chairman of the Italian American Democratic Club. Matrich later was elected councilman as a Democrat in 1926 and served on the fire and street committees. Serving on these committees he took no guff, an article quotes him as saying: "Maybe Mr. Langley needs more time to consult his superiors to determine what his action will be. Any intelligent man could make up his mind on a little lousy appropriation of

[74] Stamford Advocate 6/26/1908, 3/6/1909, 5/4/1909, 5/8/1909, 6/5/1909, 6/25/1909, 7/1/1909, 7/2/1909, 2/10/1910, 6/22/1911, 6/14/1913, 6/20/1916, 6/30/1916, 9/19/1917, 3/17/1924, 10/7/1925, 1/3/1928, 10/7/1938, 10/12/1938, 2/20/1951.
[75] Stamford Advocate 8/27/1932, 9/6/1934, 8/22/1934, 10/11/1933, 9/5/1932, 9/4/1932, 9/3/1932, 8/28/1932, 8/16/1932, 3/10/1920, 3/20/1920, 1/27/1937, 1/25/1937, 5/14/1935, 10/2/1934.

$4,000 in five minutes. The Democrat members of the council are not political tools and do not have to consult any superiors. We consult the people and play no politics. In the future if the Republicans want to play politics, they'll get what they're looking for and get it damn strong." He received 1,954 votes to be elected as member of the common council in 1930. At a stormy meeting of the Italian-American Democratic Club in 1931 members expressed dissatisfaction with Mastrich for not producing recognition from party leaders for Italians doing so much for the party and a changing of the guard was voted for. Mastrich then withdrew from the councilman ticket in 1932 in the name of party unity. Instead, Michael A. Genovese ran. Michael A. Genovese had run as town treasurer on the Democratic ticket in 1928. In 1934, Mastrich got a Department of Justice job, as an investigator, but turned in his credentials later in the year.[76]

Joseph A. Penachio started off as a special police officer in 1923. From 1925 to 1938, he was a constable. During that time Penachio rescued a mother and her two children from a burning house in Springdale, prevented an inebriated husband from shooting his wife and two children in North Stamford, and saved a seven-year-old boy from drowning in Springdale. Mario Frattaroli was a policeman in the 1930s.[77]

William A. Sabia was elected in 1934 as councilman and again in 1936, and 1938. Peter Daddona was also elected councilman in 1938 and 1940. The 1936 Democrat congressional delegates from Stamford included the following Italian names: Rocco DeCarlo, Lawrence J. DeMott, Frank Greco, Domenica Martella, Mrs. Susan A. Petro, Pasquale Sullo, Miss Marion A. Ventura, and Dominic A. Zaccardo. Democratic nominations for councilmen included Peter E. Daddona, and Patsy Sullo. Democrat Board of Finance nominations included Michael A. Genovese, Board of Education included Dominic A. Zaccardo, Grand jurors included Domenico Martella, State Representatives included Frank W. LiVolsi, justice of the peace included Marino Passato, James P. Romanzo, for constables Nicholas L. Cerulli, Emiddio Iacuzio, and Town and City Committee from the wards included James P. Romanzo, Mae Ambruso, Helen Campanile, Edward Ballo, Alfonzo Cantalini, Rocky DeCarlo, Angelina Fabrizio, Florence Pittaro, John Muha, Bruno Robotti, Ralph Tartaglione, Agnes Costello Goggin, Patrick Arruzza, Gaetano Esposito, Joseph Robertucci, Frances Lupinacci, Michael Claps,

---

[76] Stamford Advocate 4/9/1934; Stamford Advocate 10/10/1912, 7/27/1914, 6/8/1926, 7/29/1926, 9/7/1926, 9/7/1926, 11/3/1926, 1/13/1927, 7/9/1927, 9/13/1927, 5/14/1928, 10/11/1930, 11/4/1930, 12/31/1930, 9/17/1932, 3/2/1934, 4/13/1963, 9/19/1962.
[77] Stamford Advocate 7/18/1961, 8/2/1923, 7/6/1934.

Frank Moccia, Jeanette A. Corbo, Teresa P. Lopriore, Edith Lupinacci, Domenico Martella, and Michael DeAngelis.[78]

In 1935, Mariano Pimpinella was a member of the Socialist Town Committee that was endorsing a merit system for the city. The Italian American Real Estate Owners' Association with over 300 members endorsed the proposal. Dr. Rowell opposed it because it requested more jobs, not an efficient government.[79]

In 1936, Emiddio Iacuzio was a candidate for constable on the Democratic ticket. He lived at 63 Avery St. and was an active member of the West Side Italian American Democratic Club.[80]

In 1938, Dr. Peter J. Somma was elected to the Board of Education. In 1939, he pushed for the celebration of Columbus Day in schools. His term ended in 1944. Mr. Somma was elected to a term of the city's Board of Representatives from 1951 to 1953. He was a president of the Italian Center. He received his degree from the Philadelphia Dental College of Temple University. He resided at 36 Rachelle Ave. Born December 24, 1901, in Stamford to Donato and Maria Antonia. His father died as he was about to go to college, so Peter had to work to put himself through college. His son, Peter Junior remembers his father's office on Bedford Street in the building owned by the F.D. Rich Company, whom he was good friends with (it is located where McDonald's is now). He remembers the office had no elevator and it was quite a walk to get up to the top floor. Peter Jr. also remembers his father walking to work from Rachelle Ave., which was downhill, and then taking a bus back in the evenings (because it was uphill) with the Herald Tribune. One of his favorite memories of his father was going to ball games, Dr. Sloman a friend, was a good friend of Yankee announcer Mel Allen, who would often provide great tickets. Somma Sr. died just short of his 85th birthday on December 23, 1986. In Dr. Somma's obituary and press coverage it was noted that Dr. Somma was the longest serving Dentist at the time. Additionally, it was noted by another Italian dentist, Dr. Frank Sessa, that it was Somma who had encouraged him to pursue a dental career. Sessa met Somma when he was a 14-year-old messenger for a dental lab. Dr. Somma encouraged him to expand his horizons, apply himself at school and to become a dentist rather than a technician. One example of the many ways Italians looked out for each

---

[78] Stamford Advocate Tercentenary Edition Town of Stamford, CT 1641 – 1941. Supplement of the Stamford Advocate, Saturday, June 7, 1941, 31; Stamford Advocate 8/25/1936, 8/1/1936, 7/11/1936.
[79] Stamford Advocate 3/6/1935.
[80] Stamford Advocate 8/15/1936.

other and mentored other members of the Italian Colony; something they learned from the first Italian leaders in Stamford.[81]

Paul P. Pavia was an active member in the First Stamford Italian-American Republican Club and was named second selectman in 1934. In 1936, despite a Democratic sweep, Paul was elected third Selectman. He was a veteran of World War I, serving in the U.S. Navy on the U.S.S. Muscatine, member of the American Legion, Elks and was on the Board of Directors of the Italian Institute. Paul became a master electrician as member of Local 501 I.B.E.W., served as a member of the first Stamford Electrical Commission under appointment in 1928, and reappointed in 1952. In 1938, he was elected to his first of five terms as Second Selectman, earning a reputation for honesty. In 1940, Mr. Pavia was favorite to receive the Republican nomination for First Selectman; however, he was shockingly upset in what many interpreted as anti-Italian sentiment brought on by Mussolini and World War II. He attempted to become Mayor of Stamford in 1949 but was defeated. Later in 1954, he was appointed Acting Postmaster, and later in the same year, Permanent Postmaster. He was known as "Mayor of the West Side and well known for his participation in minstrel shows of the Sacred Heart Church."[82]

Peter De Rosa was elected member town committee 1931.[83] Frank W. Livolsi was elected representative to the general assembly in 1938. There was a movement in 1940 to support his candidacy for mayor.[84] Alfred A. Volante was an officer of the Small Claims Court 1937-39 and 1941-43. Attorney Charles Sessa was the clerk of the small claims court.[85] Charles Sessa was born in Morra De Sanctis, Avellino, Italy in 1894. He graduated from Stamford High School in 1914, and New York Law School in 1917. Sessa served in WWI in the Army (Carlevale, 363).

Carmine Preziosi was born in Calitri, Italy on October 6, 1899. He was a painter and owner of the Preziosi Painting Company. He was always active in political affairs. Carmine was elected corresponding secretary of the First and Third Ward Italian American Democratic Club in 1931. By 1934, he had changed affiliations. In June of 1934, Carmine was Chairman of the "Stamford Relief Workers' League. The group was an outgrowth of the organization of

---

[81] Stamford Advocate 9/26/1938, 10/1/1938, 10/12/1938, 6/28/1939, 9/13/1940, 10/15/1940, 12/24/1986.
[82] Stamford Advocate Tercentenary Edition Town of Stamford, CT 1641 – 1941. Supplement of the Stamford Advocate, Saturday, June 7, 1941; 29, Stamford Advocate 6/12/1933, 9/3/1936, 9/2/1991, 1/20/1962,
[83] Stamford Advocate 12/4/1931.
[84] Stamford Advocate Tercentenary Edition Town of Stamford, CT 1641 – 1941. Supplement of the Stamford Advocate, Saturday, June 7, 1941, 36; Stamford Advocate 8/21/1940.
[85] Stamford Advocate 6/5/1941, 6/30/1937.

(Civil Works administration) CWA workers. The CWA was a short-lived job creation program established by the New Deal during the Great Depression in the United States to rapidly create mostly manual-labor jobs for millions of unemployed workers. The jobs were merely temporary, for the duration of the hard winter of 1933–34. It advocated unemployment insurance legislation. In August of 1934, Carmine was nominated under the Communist Party for Mayor. His running mates included African Americans for councilman, and board of finance. Anthony Ribaudo and Mary Monaco were nominated for selectmen, and Rosario Ganino for town clerk. Their platform included: workers' right to organize in unions of their own choice, the ability to strike and picket, a graduated increase in income tax for incomes over $3,000 and a graduated decrease for incomes under $3,000, immediate cash relief of $10 weekly plus $3 for each dependent for unemployed workers, without discrimination as to race, nationality, citizenship, age or sex. Also included was an endorsement of the workers' unemployment and social insurance, complete political, social, and economic equality for African Americans and a maximum salary of $2,000 for all town and city officials. Mr. Preziosi came in last with 150 votes out of 14,182 cast votes, or about 1 percent. This did not prevent him from voicing his criticism of the Mayor in 1936, asking why Mayor Phillips had done nothing towards a solution of the relief program in Stamford, insisting that instead of giving his attention to the Democratic convention, he should think about constructive suggestions to offer.[87]

In 1934, Harry Socci ran for constable under the Socialist Party, getting 207 votes. Harry was a veteran who enlisted in the navy in October of 1920.[88]

In 1935, the following Italians were appointed special and temporary policemen: Patrick Aruzza, Jr., Stephen F. Belasco, Amato Boccuzzi, Louis DeMaio, Frank Demassa, Richard DeRubeis, Michael J. DeVito, Joseph Faugno, Philip T. Franchina, Joseph H. Franchina, Jr., Anthony Iannone, Emiddio Iscuzio, Joseph Itri, Anthony F. Marciano (also listed as a Justice of the Peace in the 1935 Stamford directory), Dominic Mazza, Samuel V. Morelli, Laurence Ottanio, Angelo V. Pace, Joseph Robertucci, Anthony Somma, Clemente DeLucia, Sebastian Grasso, Canio Sanseverino, and Gaetano Troisi.[89]

Clara Scala was a secretary of the Communist Party in Stamford. In 1936, she was a candidate for mayor. In a statement to the press, she indicates: "The Communist Party is the only party that will bring fundamental issues before the people of Stamford. These issues are the provision of adequate relief for

---

[87] Stamford Advocate 1/24/1931, 2/17/1977, 7/3/1936, 10/2/1934, 9/27/1934, 8/2/1934, 6/26/1934.
[88] Stamford Advocate 10/14/1920, 10/2/1934, 9/6/1934.
[89] Stamford Advocate 1/28/1935.

the unemployed, defending the right of workers to organize in trade unions for higher wages, shorter hours, and better working conditions, and to shift the burden of taxation from the poor to the rich." Her husband Louis was a candidate for the first selectman. Other nominations were: Councilmen, Rosario Ganino, Domenick Carella, Louis Testa; and constables, Emilio Mancuso and Marco DiBartolo. The party's platform included: opposition to any unemployment relief, the right of workers to organize, taxation of the rich (by removing the head tax, cigarette tax, and property tax in favor of an income tax), unrestricted freedom of speech, and full and equal rights for African Americans. Clara wrote several letters to the editor on behalf of the party extolling the Soviet recovery from the Depression and where she condemns local politicians for not confronting real issues, rather than jobs and security for workers, and protests the technique of identifying Communism with subversive activities. Clara ran for Congress for the fourth congressional district in 1938, garnering fifty votes to the winner's ten thousand.[90]

Nicholas Joseph Ottaviano was born in Stamford in 1909 to Theodore Ottaviano and Concetta Catino. In 1934, he ran as constable. In 1936 he was elected Justice of the Peace of Fairfield County. Attorney Joseph James Rinaldi was born in Stamford in 1906. Began his practice in Stamford in 1934 and began as Corporation Counsel for the City of Stamford in 1940 (Carlevale, 285, 328).

Another Stamford family's story encompasses a two generational transition from the hard life, and bias of the first generation to better conditions in the next generation is demonstrated in the Franchina family. Joseph J. Franchina, born in Stamford on October 22, 1906, was the son of Maria Grazia and Giuseppe Franchina. Giuseppe and Maria Grazia Franchina (Franchini) were born in Italy in 1876. They immigrated to the U.S. in 1901. Giuseppe was a shoemaker and lived on Garden St. Mr. Franchina graduated from Stamford High School in 1924, where he was on the wrestling and football teams. He attended Villanova College and, the University of Rome, New York University and Columbia Teachers College, where he majored in secondary school administration. His first full-time teaching job was at Burdick Junior High school. Mr. Franchina was appointed assistant principal of Rogers School in 1936 and in 1943 became principal of Rice and Elm Street Schools. He became school superintendent in 1960 and served until 1965. Mr. Franchina was described as tough but fair, and was quoted as saying: "Why do so many of us remember our 'tough' teachers most fondly? It is because they taught us something rather

---

[90] Stamford Advocate 1//8/1938, 6/25/1941, 11/5/1938, 8/30/1938, 7/27/1938, 6/9/1938, 1/30/1937, 9/9/1936, 9/8/1936, 9/5/1936.

than amusing us." Mr. Franchina left as superintendent after the Board of Education gave him a no-confidence vote after an anonymous letter alleged that he had a hand in changing grades of two students' transcripts that were then sent on to college. Mr. Franchina denied the charges and stated that it never was about the student transcripts, but about a group of North Stamford democrats on the board who wanted to oust him. Mr. Franchina was never charged with any wrongdoing. Instead, he submitted for retirement and then began a job with the Boston office of the Federal department of Health, Education and Welfare specializing in desegregation and financial aid programs.[92]

In 1940, Matthew J. Scinto ran for nomination to the Common Council on the Republican ticket. He graduated from Boston University where he played football and was on the boxing squad, and Fordham Law School. In a game for the championship of the New York and Connecticut metropolitan area he intercepted a pass and ran 75 yards for a touchdown. Stamford won seven to zero. He was awarded his varsity letter from Boston University at the age of 94. He was not allowed to play football as a senior because his status as amateur was violated. He had played in a professional summer football league in 1923.[93]

It would be some time before Italians would achieve higher offices such as Mayor of Stamford, indeed, beyond the period covered by this particular history.

Military Service

One path to assimilation has always been proving oneself in the military. The sacrifice and performance of foreign-born soldiers helped them earn the respect of non-foreign-born comrades. Under fire on the battlefield prejudice and stereotypes become irrelevant, all that really mattered was whether the person was a good soldier. Under these conditions, unbreakable bonds are formed regardless of race, or ethnic background. Italians made up about twelve percent of the men who joined the U.S. military during World War I, despite making up a much smaller percentage of the population.[94]

The U.S. declared war on Germany on April 6, 1917. More than 18 percent of the total U.S. Army was foreign-born. Many immigrants served honorably in WWI, often before they earned their American citizenship. Foreign-born members of the armed forces in WWI did not gain citizenship through military service alone. However, to encourage enlistments Congress passed

---

[92] Stamford Advocate 8/30/1948. 9/19/2002.
[93] Stamford Advocate 8/30/1940, 7/2/1995.
[94] See, Chris Wolf, and Anonymous.

laws to expedite military naturalizations. Under the Act of May 9, 1918, service members only needed proof of enlistment and testimony of two witnesses to naturalize (exempting them from the regular rules of 5 years of residency, fling declaration papers, speaking English, and taking history and civics exams). After the war, Congress passed a series of laws extending most of the benefits of military naturalizations to veterans. Eventually, more than 300,000 WWI soldiers became U.S. citizens under these laws.

Again, history is complicated and not linear. Military service definitely improved the regard of Italian Americans among native-born, but for several steps forward there are inevitable steps back. Often, after the war, when returning to civilian life, Italian Americans found that they were still last in line for the best jobs and were often considered "less than" in the eyes of fellow citizens and neighbors; often-regarded as just "wops" or "guineas."

Unlisted Italians showed patriotism by forming committees to sell Liberty bonds. In 1917, the hundreds of the Colony marched in a parade at the close of "Registration Day" headed by the Italian Band. One Italian leader declared, "It is a rare privilege that we are now fighting for the country of our adoption in alliance with the country of our birth in a common cause for a cause that appeals to every lover of human liberty." The committee in charge of this parade was Florida Cioveta, Alfredo Latte, Antonio Vitti, Angelo Cioveta, Amilcare Morone, Cesare Morone and Giuseppe DiPreta."[95] As part of the campaign to elevate the stature of Italians to native Stamfordites, the local societies were sure to celebrate war veterans and heroes. The Italian Institute invited an Italian war hero, Felice Crispi to a banquet in 1919. Private Crispi bore the scars of 148 wounds, one of his lungs was missing, he had a corked leg and one crippled hand. He was enlisted in the "death battalion" (an organization that had an international reputation for bravery, and the policy of which is to never surrender). He was one of eighteen Italians to receive the gold Medal of Honor (the highest award for bravery) from the Italian government. He was awarded this honor because despite being severely wounded in a mine explosion, buried to his waist in debris, he continued to fire on the enemy until relief came many hours later. He also was awarded the English D.S. Cross and the Croix de Guerre.[96]

During wartime, Italians were sure to celebrate Garabaldi's victorious entrance into Rome as part of Italian unification, with a parade, a banquet, a mass meeting in the High School assembly hall, and a street carnival on Pacific Street. They were also sure to invite Italian sailors from the Italian war vessel "Conti di Cavour" which was in New York Harbor to these celebrations.

---

[95] Stamford Advocate 4/25/1918, 6/6/1917.
[96] Stamford Advocate 6/17/1919.

Stamford Italians fought both for the U.S. and for Italy. Four Stamford Italian Americans lost their lives fighting in WWI for the U.S. (William Patrick Costello, Michael Gustav Dora, Michele Grillo, and Tomaso Foggetta). Henry J. Palo (Son of Tony Palo) Served in WWI. Unfortunately, he was 100% disabled and was honorably discharged on May 23, 1918. He died at 24 on September 19, 1923 and is buried in Woodland Cemetery. His brother, Sanford Francis Palo born November 11, 1896 died July 3, 1963, and served in World Wars I and II. A Stamford Italian American nurse (Mary Strollo) served during WWI.[97] The U.S. military rejected nurses who were immigrants for overseas service. Mary Strollo was born in New York, her parents were born in Italy. She was listed on the Honor Roll of the Stamford Hospital School of Nursing and graduated in 1916. In 1920, she became operating room supervisor (Updegraff, 22). An article in The Stamford Advocate indicates that Charles Geronimo (first family in Stamford) brother of Anthony Geronimo had enlisted.[99] Many of these veterans' stories were documented in the Stamford Advocate and follow.

Some Italians returned to Italy to fight in the Italian army. Guido Pia was featured in an article in The Stamford Advocate: "Pia of the 25th machine gun battalion of the Italian army (resident of Stamford, 26 West Avenue) received the Italian War Cross for bravery in action and was a member of the Association of the Order of Military Valor. On May 24, 1917, in the battle at Monte Vine, while operating a machine gun after all his company had fallen, he stood at his post, alone repulsing and killing many. He was wounded after having held the enemy at bay for hours. He was a native of Settefrati and went to Italy in 1914 to fight. He was wounded three times, and won a promotion to sergeant." It appears that Alberico Parrella served for Italy as a commander. Frank Pia, employed by the Advocate left in 1916 for Italy, where he had been called to join the army.[100]

Peter Arduino, a barber in Stamford, also joined the Italian Army. He was stationed as a telegraph operator between the firing lines for ten months, mostly at Mont Croce. He became ill with fever, which resulted in his discharge. He relayed messages from the supreme commander to various troops along the firing line. He escaped death once because he had been relieved by another operator shortly before his telegraph office was demolished by a bomb.[101]

This was a formative event for approximately, 150 Stamford Italian American residents who joined the armed forces during World War I. We can be proud of these service people and extend our gratitude for their sacrifice. There

---

[97] Stamford Advocate 6/22/1918.
[99] Stamford Advocate 12/12/1917.
[100] Stamford Advocate 4/30/1919, 5/23/1939, 11/22/1974, 10/28/1916.
[101] Stamford Advocate 4/17/1916, 8/12/1916.

were a total of three batteries engaged in WWI from Stamford. The term "battery" referred to a cluster of cannons in action as a group, either in a temporary field position during a battle or at the siege of a fortress or a city.

Battery D, 56th Artillery, originally part of the Connecticut Coast Guard as part of Battery F, Connecticut Field artillery that served in the Mexico expedition (though did not see active duty in Mexico) eventually became part of the 103d Field Artillery of the 26th Division. Battery F landed at Le Havre, France and then moved on to training. The regiment participated in six campaigns prior to the Armistice on November 11, 1918. The six campaigns were: Champagne-Marne, Aisne-Marne, St. Mihiel, Meuse-Argonne, Ile de France and Lorraine. On February 9th, 1918 Battery D, 56th Artillery took up position at Ostelt, France. The first shots were fired on February 14th, the position was held until March 18th, and on the 23rd a two-week march to Toul began. The battery made it to Vignot, and successfully occupied its positions until May 26th, when it was moved 25 kilometers to the west. On June 19, it was attacked by German gas. On June 28th, the battery was sent to the Chateau-Thierry front. The battery moved forward on July 18th and July 21st taking positions at Trugny. From there steady advances were made to Sergy, and onto Fismes on August 4th where they were relieved, as the second battle of Marne was won. In all a total advance of 25 miles was made by the battery with 7,000 rounds of ammunition fired. They were then sent on to the St. Mihiel sector after some rest, then on to Verdun on October 12th with steady advances until the Armistice was signed on November 13. Battery F had eighteen months of service abroad, spending 215 days in seventeen different active positions and fired 30,000 shells each weighing ninety pounds and covered thirty-seven miles.

Battery D, 56th Artillery, C.A.C. (recruited from the old 7th Company) also served in France. The Battery disembarked from the transport trip in Brest, France on April 5th, 1918. From April 9th to the 28th the regiment was stationed at Clermont-Ferrand undergoing gun drills. August 16th saw the first fighting at Lhuys. The Battery continued firing from this position until September 7th. They then moved on to the Argonne front at Meuse. From September 19th to Armistice the battery was engaged in the Argonne offensive. Battery D served in two major offensives (Fismes and Argonne-Meuse) in 87 continuous battle days and ten days of active service after the armistice.

Battery E arrived at Brest on April 5, 1918. After training, they saw their first real warfare on August 15 after receiving shell fire at Fismes. They began their first drive on September 26 at Verdun on the Argonne front. They remained there until Armistice was signed. What follows is a list of Italian names compiled from Connecticut state service records:

Joseph Abbazia
Rocco Abbruzese
Frank Accurso
Nicholas Adiletta
Domenico Agostino
Vito Aiello
Joseph Alebrande
Creste Aliterno
Francesco Altomura
Joseph Amaroso
Joseph Arciola
Angelo Bacco
Domenico Bacco
Giuseppe Badali
Domenico Barone
Rocco Barone
Gustave Belasco
John Edward Belasco
Steve G. Belasco
Joseph Bella
Stephen F. Bella, Jr.
Alex Benevelli
Attilio Berardelli
Frank Biase
Joseph F. Bissonette
Daniel Bivona
George Boccuzzi
Saverio Boccuzzi
Nicholas Bonaparte
Bartolemo Bonetti
John Bongiorno
Joseph Bonomo
Antonio Brancato
Joseph Brescio
John Joseph Briscoe
John Brucato
Dominick P. Bruneti
Rocco Bruno
Thomas Cacace
Giuseppe Calandrelli
John Campanile
Michael Campanile
Michael Cantillo
Angelo A. Caputo

Anthony Caputo
Tony Carbone
Nicholas Carlino
Joseph L. Carpinella
Vincenzo Caruso
Michele Casillo
Frank Cassario
Louis Cantanzaro
Alex Catino
John Catino
Michael Catino
Nick Catino
Joseph Cavalier
Alfonso A. Cavanna
John Cavanna
Luigi Cerreta
Raffaele Cerreta
John Cerritelli
Michele Cerbotte
Justino Cervi
Orazio Ciro Cesareo
Raffael Cestone
John C. Chiapetta
Florido Cioeta
Antonio Cipri
Angelo Cobelli
Vincenzo Cogliondro
Tony Colabello
Gaetano Coletta
Sam Coletto
Angelo R. Colucci
Joseph Colucci
William J. Colucci
Valerio Conterno
John M. Coperine
Patrick Coppola
Charles Corbo
Joseph M. Corso
Pietro A. Cosentini
Henry Costanzo
Ralph Edward Costanzo
John F. Costello
William Patrick Costello *
Joseph Coviello

Leonard Coviello
Rocco Peter Coviello
Joe Crea
Olympio Crescio
Michele M Crocco
James Henry Crosta
Joseph Crosta
Giuseppe Cundari
Fiore Cubaluzzi
Domenico D'Agostino
Frank D'Agostino
Albert D'Alessandro
Dominico D'Ambrosio
Paul D'Andrea
Luigi D'Aquila
Michael D'Aquila
Marino D'Aquila
Agustino Davrio
Michael De Angelis
Nicholas De Angelis
Andre Louis De Barbieri
Carmile De Francisco*
Victor Debarbrie
Carlo J. Debartolomeo
Giovanni DeBlasi
Dam Debrisco
Louis Dedda
Mauro Delfini
Michele Dellapinta
Luigi Demaio
Thomas Albert De Mar
Ernesto Demarchis
James Demartino
Casimer J. DeMott
Julius De Milla
Erberto De Nicola
Mike Denora
Lawrence Depaola
Circolamo Derosi
Louis Devesto
Nicholas Devito
John A. Dianni
Peter Dicarlo
Rocco Dicarlo

Antonio Difrancesco
Louis Difrancesco
Giuseppe Digiovanbattista
Francesco Dilerna
Angelo Dilesano
Attilo Dipreta
Thomas Dipietro
Giuseppe Dipreta
Vicenzo Disanto
Piere McKee Ditto
Paul Divosta
Michael Gustav Dora *
John Enginito
Joseph Fabbiano
Ciriaco Fabrizio
Michael Fabrizio
Joe Farenga
Frank Fedeli
Giambattista Ferrandino
Canio Ferrara
Sebastino Ferrollo
Pasquale Fiore
Tomaso Foggetta *
Paul P. Folco
Angelo Fonte
Augusto Fornaciari*
Savino Joseph Fortunato
Jerry Franchina
Domenico Gallaie
James Gallo
Nicholas M Gallo
Nicola Ganino
Sylvester J. Gardella
Guido Gardone
Ignazio Gasparro
Joseph Gaudio
Canio Genovese
Leo Gerardi
Vito Gerardi
Charles Geronimo
Joseph Giancola
James Giancoti
Joseph Giannitti
Enrico Giaquinto

Nick Ginolfi
Mikele S. Gofino
Allessando Golletto
Gaetano Grande
Emmanuelle Ernesto Granelli
Emilio Greco
Michele Grillo *
Angelo Guastanacchia
Giuseppe Gulla
Tony Iannone
Thomas Ignato
Salvo Interlaudi
Antonio Intrieri
Mariano Italiano
Frank Labbato
Patsy Labbadia
Joseph Labella
Michael Laggiora*
Donato Laginestra
Saverio Laguarda
Salvatore Laporta
Palma Laracco
Genaro Leone
Zita Leiberato
Patrick Leone(Lione)
Thomas J. Lionetti
Joseph Livolsi
Frank Loccisano
Pasquale Lomazzo
Ciro Lombardi
Joseph W. Longo
Sullivan W. Longo
Frank Lorenti
Giovanni Lorenti
Giuseppe Lorusso
Dominico Lucci
Attilo Lunghi
Leonardo Luongo
Emilio Lupinacci
William Lupinacci
Andrew Maiorano
John Malone
Jasper W. Namone
Lucien Marrucco

Guido E. Marschi
Dominick Marisco
Dominico Martinelli
Joseph Martinelli
William Martinelli
Joseph Martino
Santino Martinoli
Pietro Massimiani
Giorgio Mattera
John Dominick Mazza
Cesare Meda
Domenico Melchionno
John Melfi
Pasquale Melfi
Antonio Merolo
Luigi Metallo
Joseph Nino
Vincenzo Modaffari
Salvator Momeli
Joseph Monguse
Giovanni Montanese
Cesare Moroni
Rocco Muscatello
Clarence Muzzio
Nicholas Nardone
Camillo Natale
Charles Novella
Cesare Nosenzo
Frank Occulto
Anthony Ottano
Domenic Ottaviani
Canio Pace
Louis D. Paganetti
Anthony J. Palermo
John J. Palermo
Antonio Palmirie
Anthony Palo
Henry Palo
Joseph Palo
Sanford Francis Palo
Giuseppe Panaro
Antonio Parisi
Tony Pastore
Alessandro Pastrichelli

Filippo Pelazza
Antonio Perelle
Luigi Persiani
Leonard Piacenza
Michael Pierne
Dominick Piro
George Pope
Walter J. Porada
Chalres Edward Prangea
Neil D. Preziosi
Nicholas Preziosi
Nicola Puppo
John Quarracino
Clement Raiteri
Frank D. Recchia
Francis Reteare
James Rinalla
Jerry Ringi
Albert Robustelli
Antonio Roda
Camelo Roda
Salvatore Rosa
Joseph Rotante
Natale Rubino
Albert A. Russo
Giuseppe Russo
Antonio D. Sabia
Charles Sabino
Frank Salvatore
Panfilo Salvatore
Joseph Salzillo
Nicola Sanfelice
Frank Sapelli
Giuseppe Sassara
Jack Sassara
Alphonse Saumo
Jerry Saumo
Rocco Scalzi
Angelo Scaparotto
Giovanni Scollo
Mariano Sellini
Frank Sementini
Premavera Sente
Charles Sessa

Ernesto Severino
Frank Sico
Tony Simeone
Angelo Simonelli
Giuseppe Speranza
Domenick Sproviere
Frank J. Sproviero
Thomas Stefano
John Stefani
Mary Strollo @
Canio Summa
Salvatore Summa
Giovanni Tamburri
Paul Telesco
Angelo Telesco
John M. Teplica
Michele Torfino
Ralph Treglia
Joseph Trimboli
Giuseppe Truglia
Tony Tuccarone
Luigi Urbano
Antonio Uva
Tony Uvino
Sullivan Vaccaro
Tony P. Vaccaro
Michael Vagnone
Vincenzo Valenti
Peter Viggiano
Filippo Vitale
Antonio Vitti
Archie Volante
Tony Valante
Vito W. Zaccagnino
Rosario Zazzaro
Michael Zezima
Allesandro Zinicola

*killed in action
@nurse

The following veterans either moved to Stamford after service, or enlisted in different cities, and are listed in Stamford Town Soldier Discharge veteran records: Pvt. Francesco Liberatore born in Lareto, Italy, Battery D, 33rd artillery, CAC, Frank DeMott, from Stamford but discharged because of defective vision, Private first class Vito Engenito, Battery F, 303rd Field artillery, born in Eboli, Italy, served in the Toul sector (Marcheville, and Pintheville Butgneville, Bois de Harville offensives), Gun Captain Nicholas Edmund Iovanna was discharged with a physical disability from service in the Navy.

All of their lives were altered as a result of their service. Some of the soldiers were awarded honors, some gave their lives, but all were heroes. Some of their individual stories are highlighted here. Many of the stories are from letters written by young men from the front, which speak of being homesick, family, their patriotism for their country (sometimes adopted homeland), hopes for the future, fragility of life, and a glimpse of the experience of life at war with carefully chosen words designed not to worry their families. Often these letters demonstrate their naivety.

Even before actual combat, overseas Private Michael Fabrizio guarded the drawbridge of the New Haven Railroad in Bridgeport against attack by saboteurs. During one evening's watch, Eric Persen, despite orders to halt kept moving towards the mechanism that controlled the drawbridge. Fabrizzio arrested Persen. The Bridgeport police would not give details except to say that they knew him to be a "notorious character." Fabrizio would go on to serve at the second offensive of the Marne (August 15th, to September 6th, 1918), and Argonne Meuse offensive (September 24th to November 11th, 1918). Private Anthony Caputo, born in Stamford, of 34 West St. contracted typhoid pneumonia while guarding the bridge over the Connecticut River in Connecticut as part of the Ninth Company, Coast Artillery. He was close to death but rallied. He went on to be a Bugler for Battery E. 56th Artillery (CAC). Anthony served at the second offensive at Marne, and the Argonne-Muese offensive. As a Bugler, he was responsible for rousing the troops with reveille, last post, food calls, and so on. In battle, he would also be required to convey command signals via the bugle. To do so required him to stand tall and play the instrument with great force so all could hear over the rattling of machine guns and the explosions of artillery shells. Buglers were often the target of snipers as this would cut off lines of communication.[103]

Private Antonio Vitti of 29 Raymond Street joined the Army in June 1918 and was part of Company I, Third Battalion, 328th Infantry. He was reported missing on October 27, 1918. Taken prisoner by the Germans, he

---

[103] Stamford advocate 2/19/1917, 4/30/1917, 4/4/1917, 3/30/1917.

escaped after being a prisoner for ten minutes. Interestingly, when employed at the Yale and Towne Company, he was noted for his quickness, both in thought and action. He escaped by tripping his German guard and running. Vitti was wounded once and gassed once in the Argonne Forest. The gas laid him up in the hospital for a two-week period. His Christmas dinner was spent with Attilio DePreta of West Main Street near Chateau Thierry where they were part of the troops guarding the Rhine. He notes that the French provided the best macaroni and fresh eggs and treated them to the finest champagne and toasted them.[104]

Michael Zezima was born on October 31, 1896 in Settefrati to Loreto and Orazia Conetta Zezima and came to America in 1898. He returned to live again in Italy at age 12 with the rest of the family after his brother, Sando was killed by a trolley while playing baseball. Later he returned to Stamford, after his older brother Peter wrote and told him he could get a job in the subways. He lied about being 18 to get the job, but then as a result of this falsification, he got drafted. He tried to explain he was only 17, but the draft board retorted, "you said your age is 18, so that is your age." He won a Silver Star medal for bravery while serving in France. In a letter to Mayor Treat of Stamford in 1919, he described the fighting of his division (Company 1, 60th U.S. Infantry, 5th Division, A.P.O. 745 American F.F.): "The 5th Division was designated by General Pershing as a shock division. Early in June, we saw our first experience in the trenches in the Vosges. The 60th and 61st were in no less than six sectors, which brought us from the Franco-Swiss border as far north as Belgium. In the St. Mihiel offensive, the division gained fame, going over the top at 5 am September 12th, taking a number of prisoners." Men ordered to attack – or 'go over the top' – had to climb out of their trenches, carrying their weapons and heavy equipment, and move through the enemy's "field of fire" over complex networks of barbed wire, keeping low to the ground for safety. "This was the first independent undertaking by the American army in the war. The division was cited in the general orders for its work…. From the rest camp, we went into the Argonne-Meuse fight…. We suffered many casualties. The Germans gave us much trouble in crossing the Meuse. Our pontoon bridges were repeatedly destroyed by their fire. Finally, some of the men swam the river and silenced the machine guns. Then the bridges were built and the remainder of the division crossed." Later on back in Stamford, he was the owner of the Skipper Restaurant for more than 30 years until the property was sold to the Urban Redevelopment Commission. He lived at Shelburne Road in Stamford. Zezima

---

[104] Stamford Advocate 2/7/1919.

was a member of the Holy Name Society of Sacred Heart Church, the American Legion, the Veterans of Foreign Wars, the Settefratese Social Club, and the Richmond Park Republican Club.[105]

In 1918, Rocco Scalzi wrote a letter to his brother John Scalzi about his service with Battery F in France. In the letter, he tells of an engagement with the Germans, during which he and his Battery were under fire for 24 hours: "I have had a great experience. I was out on detached service for about three weeks, and I took part in a great battle. Believe me, if I ever live to tell you about it, you will be proud of me. It was something you never even saw in moving pictures. I was under German fire for about 24 hours and came out without a scratch. The Germans tried to break through our lines, but they found out we were more than willing to meet them at any point. They know now the Americans are not so "easy" as they expected them to be. Believe me, brother, we will bring victory to the good old U.S.A.—the only place in the world. As we were coming out of the battle on our way back to the lines, for a rest, we met one of our generals. He asked us a few questions, and he certainly was proud of us."[106]

Joseph Bonomo born in Stamford and Joseph Cavalier were in Battery F of the 303d Field Artillery, 151st Brigade, 76th Division and served nine months and six days duty in France. Battery F first landed in South Whales, and after two days rest they moved to Southampton to cross the Channel and landed in Havre, France. After three days and nights of traveling, they reached the training camp at Clermont Ferrand. Here there was hiking of ten, fifteen or twenty miles at a time and sleeping in the open air. It was a day and a half from the camp to the front. They saw eleven days of heavy fighting in November of 1918. Cavelier worked on Hotchkiss machine guns. Bonomo worked on the "Big Six French Guns." Bonomo fought at Toul near Metz. But for their gas masks, a heavy barrage and gas attack on the Toul sector might have finished things for these men. It was at two in the morning and the attack was one of the worst of his experience in battle. They took positions at Hannonville Woods, twenty-five kilometers northeast of St. Mihiel, and were under heavy fire. Privates Potratz, Cavalier, Bonomo and Engenito (all of Stamford) worked together on the big guns. They wheeled the guns into position to barrage the enemy so the infantry could move forward. Bonomo stated: "We spent many hours here under fire without any relief. We had very little to eat, besides a few sandwiches, which we had been given

[105] Stamford Advocate 6/19/1988, 3/27/1919.
[106] Stamford Advocate 5/22/1918.

at the start of the battle. We worked together, and we certainly did give Fritz all that was coming to him."[107]

Private John Cavanna of Company C 151st Machine Gun Battalion of the 42d Division went to France in March 2018 with the 41st Division and was sent to the Lorraine, France sector with other replacement troops. He received a bad case of mustard gassing in hard fighting at Sergy. Private Michael Laggiora of the 102d infantry was engaged in the attack on Trungy and Epieds on July 23rd, 1918. By nightfall they had forced the enemy to retreat, however, Private Laggiora was killed in the battle for possession of the two cities on July 23, 1918. The American forces Argonne-Meuse offensive followed St. Mihiel. The campaign had three phases and lasted 46 days. The first attack resulted in the advance of seven miles and ten thousand prisoners. In the assaults of the first phase, Private Augusto Fornaciari of Company G, 39th infantry, Fourth Division, was killed in action. Fornaciari had been on the firing line since July 1918. He was drafted from Stamford, on May 27th, 1918. He joined an infantry division. Before being inducted into the army he was employed by the New York, New Haven, and Hartford Railroad, and had been in the country for six years, and taken out his citizenship papers. Private Antonio Pastore of Company E, 39th Infantry was wounded in that first attack. Pastore was slightly gassed but was soon back in the trenches. He was also in the fighting along the Marne. On October 17, 1918, he was wounded in the leg by a machine gun bullet while in the thick of the fighting in the Argonne. Private Pastore volunteered in June 1917 and arrived in France in July 1918. He was in hospitals for some time and he was feared dead at one point.

On October 1, 1918, Private Gaetano Colatta of Company L, 28th Infantry, a First Division soldier was severely gassed. At the Verdun front, Company L was starting to go over the top for the third time. They stepped forward cautiously, after gaining 300 yards they were forced to dig down where they were. While in their trench the Germans sent out a heavy gas attack, and almost every man in the company stayed there, in serious condition for four days, until they were brought to the rear of the line and then to the hospital. Colatta was burned all over the body and his eyes were so badly burned that he was unable to see for about a month. Colatta was unable to speak for a number of days, and it was not until he returned to the United States that he could be understood fairly well. Even at that point, he spoke with difficulty and twitching. Upon returning to Stamford, he tried his old job at Yale and Towne but had to give it up. His physicians told him that he had to live in the open air, as his throat and lungs would be weak for some time as a result

---

[107] Stamford Advocate 3/22/1919, p 2, 5/6/1919.

of the impact of the gas. Of Colatta's company of 250, only 22 were able to stand up after the gas attack.

Nicholas Nardone of the 14th Machine Gun Battalion was severely wounded once the Fifth Division crossed the Meuse. Private Joseph Albonisio of Company 6, 125th Infantry, 32d Division was injured on October 14 in the fighting for Romagne losing a finger but escaping with his life. Private Enrico Giaquinto was wounded on October 31, 1918, at the fighting on the edge of the Argonne Forest. Private Florido Cioeta of Company G, 116th Infantry, 29th Division entered the service via draft in May 1918. His division went into action in the Argonne-Meuse offensive. On October 8, the first day of the 29th Division's operations east of the Meuse for possession of the wooded heights, Private Florido Cioeta of Company G, 116th Infantry was hit with shrapnel and seriously wounded. He had participated in three attacks before being hit in the hip with shrapnel. He recovered after being in the hospital for five months. Private Cioeta was an alien, who did not claim exemption from military service, but in fact requested to be called before his turn.

The final phase of the Argonne-Meuse campaign began on November 1, 1918. While helping to lay a bridge over the river, Private Carmile de Francisco of Company E, second engineers, was fatally wounded. Domenico Conetta was drafted but not yet in service when he was killed in an accident in Stamford on September 20, 1918 the day he was scheduled to leave for service. Domenico was engaged to be married to Nascienza Macari. William Costello in the U.S. Navy died in a hospital on May 21, 1917, he had been in the Navy since 1911. Michael Dora, carpenter, second class U.S. Navy, died of pneumonia at Marine Hospital, Staten Island, September 28, 1918. Private Tommaso Fogetta, Motor Transport Company 471 died of pneumonia in France, on January 13, 1919. Private Augusto Forniciari, Company G, 39th Infantry was killed in action on September 28, 1918. Augusto was twenty-three years old and was drafted on May 27, 1918. He was employed by New Haven Railroad at the time he entered service. He had come from Italy to the U.S. six years prior and was a citizen. Private Michael Lagiora, employed by contractor Frank Valerio at the time he was drafted was killed in action near Fere-en-Tardenois, France, on July 23, 1918, while a member of the 102d Infantry, 26th Division. He enlisted in Hartford and was with the Yankee Division during its push north from the Marne in June and July of 1918. Private Frank Lorenti was reported severely wounded. Emilio Lupinacci was reported as wounded, the degree not being determined. His parents received a letter from him indicating he was slightly wounded, but that he returned to the front again. No letter had been received from him for almost three months. Private Michael Catino, 19 years old of 63 Spruce Street was charged with desertion in June of 1917. Catino said he left because he was having trouble with his teeth and the dentist indicated that it would cost him $60 to treat. He did not have the money and could not stand the pain. He was perfectly willing to serve, but stated his teeth needed to be fixed and he did not have the money to pay for it. It appears that he eventually received treatment as he arrived in Brest, France and was in Battery 103d Field Artillery. Private Joe Farenga of 50 Liberty Street of Company A, 61st Infantry, 5th Division was at the front for six months and escaped without a scratch. The Advocate reported on his father's barbershop ("Colucci & Farenga") displaying German war souvenirs that Joe had sent.[108]

Private Leo Gerardi of 27 Virgil Street enlisted on January 30, 1918, and was attached to the Ambulance Service and assigned to Italy. Leo served with the Italian army in the Piave Offensive, from October 1, 1918, to the end of the war. He was almost constantly under fire during that time but escaped major injury. Private John J. Palermo was in Company A. 14th Engineers. His regiment was among the first American regiments to face hostile fire during the March 1918 offensive against the Germans. Private Palermo and eight Americans who were on detached duty were knocked flat by the explosion of a bomb dropped by a German airman on a British train. The bomb made a direct hit on the engine and killed a number of British engineers. John also saw service in the offensive at Verdun.[109]

Sanford F. Palo, second lieutenant in the 6th Regiment, Field Artillery wrote: "At the present moment I am up in an observation post in the infantry trenches. I have to see that our barrage does not fall short and hit our own men. Of course, it is impossible to say just where we are, but we are in the real big party of the year. Our boys are rapidly developing into experienced veterans, taking to the game like the proverbial duck to water. Last night we "pulled off" a surprise attack and caught the Boche (slang for German soldier), napping. Got away with three officers and 176 prisoners...It was the first time I had ever seen a real modern attack—if it can be called such, since there was very little hand-to-hand fighting. Our artillery just peppered the life out of them, so that they were "all in" when the real fight began." He also describes the truck he was riding to the front on being hit by artillery, demolishing the engine and causing he and his companions to walk a mile to their destination. In another letter he describes fighting in Bordeaux, France: "I am in a hospital,

[108] Stamford Advocate 6/8/1917, 12/27/1918, 2/1/1919, 10/11/1919, 1/13/1919, 2/15/1919, 2/17/1919, 3/24/1919, 7/28/1919, 1/31/1919, 3/1/1919, 10/12/1918, 11/25/1918, 2/27/1919, 12/19/1918, 12/9/1918, 12/18/1918, 2/27/1919, 6/16/1919, 4/12/1919; see also, U.S. Army Transport Service passenger lists, 1910-1939.
[109] Stamford Advocate 5/6/1919.

way down in the south of France. I am terribly unlucky: I didn't even get wounded. I have an abscess just like the one I had under my arm about five years ago…Now that I have a little time, I will tell you a few of my experiences…Well, mother, I can't tell you all I saw, but it was enough to make one feel terribly nervous for a while. Here we were in Picardy…The English had retreated in an orderly manner, and we were to be the reinforcements. It was all open warfare from the start. We swung into position over a shell-swept road, only losing two men and six horses. The Germans were coming over in mass formation. There were thousands of them. I don't remember anything except that there was artillery in that valley placed almost wheel to wheel, and the noise was terrific. I saw a division of French Algerian troops go swinging into the fight, singing a weird chant. They suffered terrible losses but finally held the Boche. For three days and four nights, we did nothing else but fire barrage after barrage. The fourth night there were so many dead Germans that they had to give it up. Immediately we started digging in, which took about a week of hard work. Well, Heine gave up trying to come through, and for a month we had a nice quiet time, living in deep dug-outs, and ducking an occasional shell…We then decided to pull off a little party of our own. So on May 28, we pushed the Heines back a mile and a half, and took the village of Cantigny…That party was the first attack the American troops made in France. It certainly was a splendid sight and I enjoyed every bit of it. We opened up about 4 a.m. with a raking fire of shrapnel all over the German lines. We kept this up till 6 a.m. Then there was a rest for half an hour for breakfast. You have to eat, no matter how much you fight. Then, at 6:40 we started the rolling barrage, and as our first shots fell, the infantry went over the top in three waves. I was with the third wave, as I had to string a telephone wire in back of me as I went along. The attack lasted 45 minutes. We swept right through Cantigny, and established our front lines about 400 yards."

In another letter, Sanford writes: "By the way, my division has been cited, seven times in general orders, so I think we probably will be used as shock troops hereafter. It certainly is the best job on the front, as you stay behind for months, then go up and make your big push, and come out again, the only objection being that you have fearful losses for the little while they you are in." Of the rush that swept the Germans out of the Narne, he writes: "I joined my regiment, which was on its way to the Soissons front, after getting out of Montdidier. We marched three days and three nights, and on the dawn of July 18, 1019, we went into action…Of course you know that this was the blow that turned the German victory into defeat. We advanced eight kilometers on the first day, and captured 3,500 prisoners and 68 guns. My battery lost a second lieutenant and twenty men…We went so fast that we lived on

German pickles and sausages, some coal-black German bread, and stale beer, for a few days…. I have been recommended for promotion, which I won on the battlefield, and I am waiting for it to come." In the next letter he writes: "I just received notice that I am promoted to a first lieutenant…The reason I value it greatly, is because I won it at the front, and not behind the lines, and also being only twenty-one years old. I think I am pretty lucky. We certainly have seen a lot of fighting this summer: in fact, we were in every big fight that was on. We are now classed as "shock troops." I have had quite a few hair-breath escapes, and there were times in this last drive of July 18 that I never expected to write another letter. The closest call happened on the third morning of the big push. Another officer and myself were sleeping, under a steep bank beside the road. I was as lazy as anything, and he after waking tried to arouse me, just fooling you know. Suddenly a shell passed over and hit the road. This poor lad was killed instantly, and I sent his last words home. So now I think it pays to be lazy once in a while." It was also reported that Sanford assisted in the burial of Ernest Sexton of Stamford, who had been shot in the head. Sanford later served eight months in Germany during the occupation. He was award four service stripes.[110]

James DeMartino of Battery F, 56th Artillery wrote a letter to a friend back home: "I am sitting on the edge of the wood where our camp is hidden, resting until this evening at 6, when I go on duty again. I received your many newspapers, magazines, and various other things that you sent me, and you have no idea how much I appreciate your kindness…. I'll never forget that first night, even though I may live to be a hundred years old. We were tied up on this crossroad. I had never seen real war before that time, and while we were waiting in the dark, I wondered what there really was to war. Suddenly the sky lit up in the direction of the dipper just like a Fourth of July celebration. Reports from huge guns that sounded like the rumbling of far-off thunder were then heard. There was a storm coming, and I said to my friend, I can't realize that we are at war; can you? Then the storm came. Something like a big firecracker exploded right at our feet it seemed, but it came nowhere near us. It is funny how a fellow does things without being taught. When that weird whistle of shrapnel begins to come your way, and vibrates your eardrums, you just naturally duck. You try to bury your nose in the hard road, or in the soft grass, or in the dirt of your dugout. It makes little difference where you happen to be." He goes on about the first night under fire: "There is a rumor that our battalion has been recommended for bravery for their cool-headedness under fire that first night. On my left, about 40 feet

[110] Stamford Advocate 6/22/1918, 7/17/1918, 8/24/1918, 9/28/1918, 12/18/1918, 1/30/1919, 7/31/1919.

from where I stood and not 20 minutes after the time I spoke to my friend, that loud whistle that I spoke of came first. Then followed a flash and excitement. The men began running to and fro, for they had never seen fire, and although they weren't afraid, they were quite excited. ...Old soldiers who had seen service for nearly a year said that this was the heaviest shelling they had seen in some time...We had some casualties, not many, and only three members of my gun crew. Since that eventful night, we have certainly give'm hell."

"Our first position was a swamp, and it took some maneuvering to get our guns in there...There is where I gave the command that sent the first shot from the "Kaiser's Misery"...The "Kaiser's Misery" is the name of my gun. I was a sick boy, with a bad case of cramps, that night, but I would not allow them to send me back to camp. I don't know how I ever received the commands and then issued them to my crew, but after I gave the order to fire, and after the powder had ignited, it must have sent my cramps with the projectile over to the Boche for I felt fine after that first shot. Say, but Guy Empey sure left a whole lot of things out in his first book." Guy Empey was an American soldier, author, actor, and filmmaker who served with the British Army during WWI, and upon his return wrote a popular autographical book. "We gave it to them and kept on giving it to them till they got our range, and then they made us duck their shrapnel and forced us to wear our gas masks, and finally drove us out of the position. Now we have another position, and we fooled them for it is a much better one...we pulled out of "Death Valley" as it was nicknamed by one of our boys, it took some fancy maneuvering to get us out. I worked steadily for 36 hours and changed two crews, to get this new position. Now I feel much better. Oh, its dandy, and we'll hammer the stuffin' out of those Huns before they find us this time. The band was just playing a one-step down in the woods, about a mile or so away, and the wind brought the music up to me fine. They are playing "Huckleberry Finn: now and oh, how fine it sounds. Well anyhow, tonight you will know that the Kaiser is catching hell for making us wear those gas masks, for gassing a couple of our men, for making us duck shrapnel. I really believe my neck is two inches shorter from ducking so much... I am still happy as ever, and sleeping in a dugout bothers me very little...Shells don't bother me much unless they hit me. I don't believe I will ever be bothered with shellshock, for some of them have come pretty close to me. How is Dr. Frank? I often think of him as a friend, although not very often as a minister. I wish we had him here as a chaplain. I am afraid I need to be chaplained a little, but when things all go wrong, and the Boche is firing gas and shrapnel, and your crew take shelter, and you don't really blame them, still you give them hell...You need something. I've a good crew. After the war, if there are any of us left, we are going to get together and have a banquet…In the distance, I can see a small village that the Boche is shelling with gas. But I hope this wind keeps up, for it is blowing the gas right back again. Many of the boys who had been sent to the hospital have returned to duty, and a few of those who had been shell-shocked also returned." Shell shock was a term coined in World War I by British psychologist Charles Samuel Myers to describe the type of post-traumatic stress disorder (PTSD) many soldiers were afflicted with during the war. "I must get my crew together now, for a 24-hour shift, and if I don't hurry, my day crew or the crew that is on now will get pretty hungry. I just finished a supper of some nice boiled beans, bread, and coffee, and now I guess I'll go down for my piece of chocolate. They give each of us a piece, about two inches square, and you ought to see the boys line up for it."

In another letter, he writes: "I bought an old mandolin on the way to the front when we passed a small village, and I have it with me now. Some great old times we have had with it. At the last position where we made the "big drive," I played the thing, and the boys all gathered around my gun after dusk, and we all sang. The French soldiers who were our neighbors also gathered around and they would sing and talk French with us. In this manner, we passed the time very quickly and pleasantly, in spite of the shells bursting all about us. Last night we fired a number of gas shells at the Boche, and then turned in for some sleep. But sleep we did not. It wouldn't have been so bad if the rain wasn't so cold, but I suppose that is all in the war. My gun, the "Kaiser's Misery," is entitled to several wound stripes, for she has several marks from bursting shells which fell almost directly in front of it. Good luck to us, no one was hurt. My corporal, who was lying on the gun, was hit on the wrist, getting away with only a slight scratch. I felt lucky. The gun was warm from firing, and it was cold. We generally sit on the rifle to keep warm, but somehow I couldn't pick myself up to go out. Then Bang! And there fell a shower of dirt on the tarpaulin. But we are firing the old baby just the same…All is quiet at the front today, and peace talk is "old stuff" by now. All the boys want to win the war with a royal flush and the Kaiser had better cut out his shenanigans. However, who can tell: We may be home by Christmas. Let's hope so at any rate. Hope that you will enjoy a happy Thanksgiving, and that we will all enjoy the next one together. Faintly from far away a bugler is blowing "taps." And you know what that means at the front."[111] Playing taps would mean a call to rest for the evening.

Nicholas DeVito wrote about his war experiences. "I am over in Germany now, camping at a convent school, and we are being treated well by

---

[111] Stamford Advocate 9/27/1918, 11/6/1918.

those who live here. We are to leave in the morning, headed for the Rhine. We have bad weather and talk about your mud! I think that, when I get on a cement walk, I don't know how to act…This was one of the fighting divisions all the way through, and we claim it is one of the best in the service. We went through all the hard battles. The Marines, the ninth and Twenty-third Infantry lost a number of men, but the artillery did not have many men killed. We passed on a good many fronts where the Germans were doing some heavy shelling but were lucky enough to get away without mishap. We were first sent to the St. Mihiel front, and then we stopped the Germans from going through to Paris, at Chateau Thierry. We remained there for a few weeks, and then went to Soissons, and again beat them back. We were then transferred to St. Mihiel again, and went to Champagne from there. The Argonne Forest was our next destination and we finished up on the Verdan front. DeVito was wounded in Champagne fighting. Nick, stationed in Ehrenbritstein, Germany, with Battery E, 17th Field Artillery, Second Division, wrote to his mother when the peace treaty was signed: Well mother, peace was signed yesterday, and, believe me, the soldiers went wild when they heard the news, after spending six months on the Rhine. It won't be long now, that we will have to remain here, and we will be glad to get back to God's country once more…It was two years ago, yesterday, mother that I left my happy home. I did not realize what I was doing, because I was only a young boy, but I found out what war is. It is all over now, and I am proud that I came overseas and did my bit as a regular soldier should do. I do not regret it, even though I did suffer a great deal of hardship. I know that you have suffered since I left you, and you have shed a good many tears, but now everything is all over, and we expect to leave soon. When you receive this letter, I may be on the way home…When I get out of the service, I will have a clean record on my discharge. We lived a life of misery for a while, and didn't know what rest was, while those at home had it easy, and everything they wanted was there. I will be free again soon, and I hope to enjoy life once again."[112]

Gennaro Leone, in Company I, 60th Infantry wrote his sister Rose Leone: "This is our third time at the front, and we were glad to get back. Tony Sabia is only about 30 feet away from me, with the Machine Gun Company, and when we haven't anything else to do we sit down and talk of the good old days in Stamford…I've been out in "No Man's Land" four times already. We go out mostly at night, to try to capture some Boches, but they never come near us, because someone in our bunch would happen to make some noise and that scared them away. We expect to remain here a little while longer,

---

[112] Stamford Advocate 1/28/1919, 3/14/1919, 4/47/1919.

and I hope we get a few of those Dutchmen before we are sent to the rear of the lines, to a rest camp."[113]

Corporal Thomas Stefano set sail for France on April 16, 1918, and arrived on May 1. His regiment spent two months training behind the lines and finished training in the Vosges Mountains, and later participated in battles at St. Mihiel and the Argonne Forest. On November 14th he became ill and had to part from other Stamford comrades in Company 1, 60th Infantry, Fifth Division, including Mike Zezima, Tony Sabia and Gennaro Leone. After spending two months in the hospital, he returned to the U.S. He mentions appreciation for the Red Cross, the Knights of Columbus and the WMCA, and says "I don't know what we would have done without these welfare societies, which were with us wherever we went." In another letter he wrote of the seasickness that he and many others in his transport experienced on their way to France. Corporal V.W. Zaccagnino, of Company M, 394th Infantry however wrote back that he did not have seasickness.[114]

Albert Robustelli of 258 State Street was on the U.S.S. Ophir, which was lost at the Strait of Gibraltar two days after the signing of the armistice when it caught fire carrying troops, gasoline and Trinitrotonuol. All but two of the crew were able to get out. For twenty-four hours, English and American sailors turned streams of water on the blazing gasoline, but could not extinguish the blaze. In October, the first day out a submarine attacked the ship, but the Ophir rammed the U-boat and sent it to the bottom.[115]

Antonio D. Sabia of Company A, 14th Machine Gun Battalion, wrote to Mayor John J. Treat from Luxemburg: "We are just beginning to learn that life is worth living, after all, for we are out of those shell-holes and dugouts, and know that we can rest without having shells bursting around us while we are trying to sleep." Antonio served at the St. Mihiel and Meuse Argonne offensives. Private Joseph Trimboli was impressed with Paris: "Well, I'm getting along very nicely now, only I'm just a little lonesome when I begin thinking of home and all the rest of the things there... You know this place must be just like your country because the people are so old-fashioned-that is the old people; but the younger set have really got the class. Well, we are having some pretty fine weather out here, and everything is very nice. The trees and flowers are all in bloom, and Paris looks beautiful."[116] He served at the St, Mihiel, and Meuse Argonne offensives and in the army of occupation.

---

[113] Stamford Advocate 9/19/1918.
[114] Stamford Advocate 4/8/1919, 4/8/1919, 6/28/1919, 8/14/1918.
[115] Stamford Advocate 1/11/1919, 12/17/1918.
[116] Stamford Advocate 1/10/1919, 6/17/1918.

241

Thomas Lionetti born March 27, 1899 in Stamford was the son of Raffaele and Giovanna Carpinella Lionetti. He graduated from Stamford High School in 1916 where he belonged to the History Club and a member of the Minstrel chorus. His nickname was "Galileo" and he attended Fordham. He was a veteran of both World Wars. He was a U.S. Army veteran of World War I and served as a chief petty officer with the U.S. Navy in World War II.[117]

Walter Longo born in Avigliano, Italy on July 6, 1895, graduated from Stamford High School in 1916 and wrote the class song. He played football (halfback) and baseball (third base); later playing semi-professional football and baseball in the area. He wrote the words of 1916's class song. He starred in the Minstrel show in high school and was famous for his rendition of "Old Bill Bailey." He attended Riverview Military Academy and American International College, graduating from the University of Maryland School of Dentistry. He was a veteran of World War I serving at Alsace. He was vice president of the Cavour Democratic Club in 1919. In 1917, he attempted to form a local basketball league. He died from a coronary thrombosis while he was driving to work as a dentist from his home on 239 Cold Spring Road.[118]

Military service was a way for Canio Genovese to break into the Irish-dominated police force in Stamford. While a few of the early leaders were "special officers," likely hired to provide translation services due to the influx of Italians, it was not until May 22, 1922, that supernumerary officer, Canio Genovese was assigned to regular patrol duties and became the first Italian American to join the Stamford Police Department.[119] Canio was born in Avigliano, Italy and immigrated to the U.S. in 1900 with his parents (Vincenzo and Carmela Buonovoglia). The family eventually settled at number 37 Liberty Street in Stamford. It was reported that he had an exemption for military duty in 1918, but for unknown reasons, he did serve during WWI.[120] He married Mildred Corbo in 1919.[121] His nickname was Kelly, so he fit in well with the Irish cops and was known as "Kelly the Irish WOP." He had an Irish partner, Bill Lynch, and their best friend was Herman ("Murphy") Fertig, the Jewish president of Hudson Paper Company. "Murph" loved to tag along with Kelly and Bill on police calls. Kelly Genovese eventually worked himself up from traffic cop to Detective Sargent. Every morning he would rise early, put on his work clothes, and tend to the garden before work. He would then

[117] Stamford Advocate 2/27/1979.
[118] Stamford Advocate 6/6/1916, 10/3/1916, 6/10/1919, 12/21/1957, 4/27/1916, 9/14/1917.
[119] Stamford Advocate 5/18/1922. 5/23/1922, 521/1947.
[120] Stamford Advocate 7/18/1918, 6/27/1918.
[121] Stamford Advocate 11/28/1919.

change for headquarters, go to work, come home for lunch at noon, work in the garden for a while, go back to work and come home for more gardening (Kelly, *passim*). It was reported in the Advocate that the singer Frankie Laine visited the home of Kelly Genovese on occasion and was crazy about Mildred's cooking.[123] When Kelly retired in 1963 he was given a testimonial dinner at the Italian Center.

Mr. Joseph LiVolsi ("Mr. Veteran") was born on May 27, 1896, in Cerami, Sicily, to Sebastian and Mattia Masseo LiVolsi. He arrived in Stamford as an eight-year-old. He began his military service in 1910 when he joined Stamford's Battery F of the Connecticut National Guard. When it was federalized in 1914, he went to the Mexican border as part of General Pershing's expedition against Pancho Villa. In World War I, he went on to fight with the 26th "Yankee" Division. Joseph served in the following battles: Toul Sector, Selphrey Defensive, Xivray Defensive, Alsne Marne defensive, Alene Offensive, St. Mihiel Offensive, Verdun sector, and Meuse Argonne. He returned to Stamford in 1919, the year after the armistice ended the fighting. LiVolsi served as a special police officer for the city of Stamford. For more than 30 years, he played a leading role in Stamford's patriotic observances. In 1955, he and others led a drive to change the name from Armistice Day to Veterans' Day so all veterans could be honored on November 11th. This culminated in a personal meeting with President Dwight Eisenhower and the successful passage of a bill from Congress to change the name. He coordinated and supervised the City's annual Veterans Day Parade. He was the City's veteran's representative and was often known to have driven veterans to the Veterans Administration Hospital in West Haven for treatment without compensation. He organized the Fairfield County Basketball League in 1926, and managed the Stamford Blues, the team, which took the championship three years in a row. A building contractor, he was awarded first prize at the New York World's Fair in 1939 for the construction of the first all-plywood house in the United States. An article in the Stamford Advocate regarding his death states: "If this community is more mindful today of the gratitude it owes its veterans, it is thanks to men like Joe LiVolsi, the boy from Italy with pride in his new country."[124]

Erberto DeNicola was born on December 10, 1896, in Calitri, Italy. He was a Navy WW I veteran, serving on the USS Orizaba, and received a commemorative medal for his service. He was a builder and member of the Carpenters Local N. 194. Erberto was a member of the American Legion for

---

[123] Stamford Advocate 4/23/1997.
[124] Stamford Advocate 12/22/1975, 12/26/1975, 7/8/1939, 8/4/1939, 8/7/1934, 11/20/1931, 8/26/1931, 12/8/1925.

sixty years and won both a local and national level award while a member. He was also a member of the Veterans of Foreign Wars (Toglia 2013, 348).

Cesare Meda, was a member of the First Air Park, USA. He served in France on the S.S. George Washington and was in Foreign Service for eighteen months. Cesare was discharged in October of 1919.[126]

The following was found in the Stamford Town Soldier Discharge records. Private Sebastino Ferrollo, born in Agua Vera-Debari, Italy of the 302 Salvage Unit (made repairs and salvaged equipment), Army served in France. Private Donato Laginestra, born in Genzano, Italy, Battery F, 303rd Field artillery served in the Toul sector at the Morcheville, Pintheville, Butgnetille, and Bois de Horville offensives. Fireman second class Ernest Mollozzi, served on the U.S.S. Idaho. Private Vito Gerardi, Company D, 74th Infantry was born in Avigliano, Italy. Private, 1st Antonio Brancato born in Sicily, received two Silver Service Chevrons. Private Joseph Colucci, born in Avigliano, Italy served in Battery E, 56th Artillery (CAC). Private Antonio Cipri was born in Italy, and served in Company G, 2nd Bri. Edgewood Arsenal. Private Attilio DiPreta, born in Settefrati, Italy served with 328th Infantry in medical detail. Attilio served in the Touls sector and Warbachs. Private Marino D'Aquillo served in Battery D, 68th Artillery, Coast Artillery, and was born in Stamford. Private Luigi D'Aquila served at Camp Hospital A.S.B. Norfolk, Va. Private Frank Fedeli of 333rd Supply Company, Army born in Rome, Italy served as an American Expeditionary Force leaving the U.S. on October 6, 1918 (the war ended November 11th, 1918). Private Ciriaco Fabrizio born in Sngilo, Italy, served with Company D, 74th Infantry. Private Ciro Lombardi born in Avellino, Italy served with the 19th Development Co, 154th Depot Brigade, Army. Private Rocco Muscatello (medical department) of the 59th Artillery (CAC) born in Messina, Italy served at the Meuse, and Argonne battles. Private 1st Class Camillo Natale born in Mont Avellino, Italy served with Battery D, 303rd Field Artillery at the Tould Sector, Marchville offensive, and Pinthaville, Bugneville Bois S. Harville offensives. Private Neil D. Preziosi, born in Calitri, Italy served with Company B, 12th Supply Train. Private James Rinaldi served with Company D of the Third Regiment of NY volunteers in 1898. Chauffeur Frank Tallerico was born in Naples, Italy was in flying school with the 10th Company, 152 D.B. Private Peter Vaccaro born in Hazleton, PA fought at Meusee-Argonne. Private Domenico Bacco, born in Potenza, Italy served with Company C Development Battalion. Private Nicholas Joseph Bonaparte born in Aoli, Italy served with Company A, 330 Bn Tank Corps, Army. Private Luigi Cerreta, born in Calitri, Italy served with 6th

---

[126] Stamford Advocate 10/18/1919, 5/14/1918, 1/23/1918.

Company, 2nd Bu. 151st Depot Bridgade. Musician 3rd Class Joseph Nico-angelo Corso born in Montemareno, Italy served with Headquarters company, 73rd Infantry. Private Gabuo Colletta, born in Rome served with Company L 28th infantry at Verdun, and St. Mihiel. Private Joseph Coviello, born in Avigliano, Italy served with Company D, 74th infantry. Private Dominick Marisco, born in Greenwich, CT served with Company P Dev. Bu. No 2. Corporal Albert D'Alessandro born in Ortona, Italy served with 1st Billeting and Supply Co 439th Sup Train Co. He served in the Vosges sector and Meuse Argonne. Private Luigi De Maio was born in Avellino, Italy, and served in France from August 14th, 1918 to June 20th, 1919. Private Peter Viggiano born in Stamford, served with Company 36, 9th Bu. 153rd depot. Corporal Clarence Muzzio of Hq Motor Supply Train served at the St. Mihiel and Meuse Argonne offenses. Private Joseph Palo of the 56th Regiment served at Marne and Argonne. Dominico Possidento born in Avellino, Italy of Company A 316th W.G. Br. Served at Meuse Argonne. Master Engineer Jr. Grade Joseph T. Preziosi Company M served at Meuse Argonne. Corporal Alfonso Russo born in Battipaglia, Italy of Battery E, 56th Artillery served at the Marne and Argonne Meuse offensives. Private Bartolomeo Rosa born in Avigliano, Italy served with the 14th Company, 4th Brigade 153rd Deport Brigade and Supply Company. Private Allesandro (Alexander) Zinicola was born in Santa Maria Infante, Italy, and served with Fourth Company, Convalescent Center, 151 Depot Brigade at St. Mihiel and Verdun. Sargent Joseph Abbazia, Battery E, 56 Artillery CAC served at the second offensive of the Marne, and the Argonne Meuse Offensive. Private John Bongiorno born in Cropoloto, Italy of Company C, 315th Infantry, Army served at Sector 304 defensive, the Meuse Argonne offensive, Grand Montagne, and the defensive Troyon Sector. Private Medical Corps Dominick P. Brunetti, born in Bari, Italy served as an American Expeditionary Force from September 26th, 1918 to July 27, 1919. Private Henry Costanzo, Battery D, 56 CAC was born in New Haven and served the Second Battle of Marne, Second Battle of Argonne, Rheim Soissons and Verdun. Private 1st Class Frank Cavaliere, born in Baraggiario, Italy with Company 5, 153 1st Battalion served in defensive sector 304, Meuse Argonne offensive (Montgaucon) and (Grand Montague) and the Troyon Sector defensive. Michael M. Crocco, born in Luzzi, Italy served at Champagne Foul Sector, Marlache sector, the St. Mihiel and Meuse Argonne offensives, and the Rioufalire offensive. Private 1st class Paul Divesta of Battery B, 56th artillery, born in Minturno, Italy served at the Second Battle of Marne, and Second Battle of Argonne. Private Santo Mancini served at the Tould Sector, at St. Mihiel and as army of occupation at Meuse Argonne. Private Frank Occulto, born in Naples, Italy with Company D, 59th Infantry served at Aisne, the Marne Offensive, St. Mihiel Offensive and the Meuse Argonne Offensive. Private Leonard Piacenza with 331st Supply Company 2 M.C. served as an A.E.F. from October 6th, 1918 through to July 11, 1919. Private Dominick Sproviere born in Picarno, Italy with 331 Butchery Co served as and A.E.F. Private First Class, Gaetana Santamaria, born in Mirabella, Italy of Company M 315th Infantry, served at Sector 304 defensive, Meuse Argonne offensive (Montgaucon), (Grand Montague), and the Troyan Sector defensive. Seaman 2c Joseph Giancola, served in the Navy.

A record of "Rural" Stamford veterans lists the following Italians: Ballista Cuzzupoli, son of Antonio Cuzzupoli, long ridge, R.F.D. 55. Enlisted in 1918 and assigned to infantry service. Giuseppe Espone, Riverbank Rd., Enlisted August 30, 1918, assigned to Camp Upton. Vincenzo Lofar, enlisted from Long Ridge Road, July 23, 1918. Assigned to Camp Upton. Charles Nosenzo, brother of Carlo Nosenzo, live with E.P. Brown, Webb's Hill, and enlisted in December 1917. Was engaged in construction work in France. Francisco Nucero, Mill Road, enlisted on June 24, 1918. Assigned to Camp Meade. Antonio Roda, enlisted on September 4, 1918, assigned to Camp Devens.[127]

Italians were able to elevate themselves by demonstrating their patriotism in their adopted land and exhibiting honor during their service to their new country. This allowed them to earn a better reputation in the community. Progress was slow but steady; Italians were displaying their capabilities and garnering respect and friendship in their new home.

---

[127] Stamford History Center IC 205 – WWI Documents, Newspaper Clips, Personal Records. "Welcome Home Reception to Rural Stamford's Soldiers" at Willard school, Thursday, August 28, 1919.

CHAPTER 8

Business

Il modo migliore per predire il futuro è crearlo.
(The best way to predict your future is to create it.)

The journey to the American dream took many paths for the diverse members of the Italian Colony. The majority of occupations (other than for self-employed persons) for Italians were for men: tunnel diggers, layers of railroad tracks, bridge, road and building construction and for woman, mill, clothing factory and seamstress work. For the self-employed, there was more variety in the businesses they owned. For the most part businesses with low barrier to entry were popular (e.g., barbers, grocery, butcher, baking and other food related businesses, junk dealers, and shoe repair). Professional fields were also widely held (e.g., doctors, dentists, banking, and pharmacists). Other services such as liquor sales, taverns, plumbers, etc. were popular as well. The following individuals are Italian Americans for whom I have found references of businesses during the period of 1860 through 1941, in Stamford through various sources and that have not been mentioned in previous chapters. It is not intended to be a complete list.

Some of the original documents of the City of Stamford's tax records are preserved at the Stamford History Center.[1] The 1896 ledger provides insight into the early Italian taxpayers, owners of property and their occupations. The ledger includes the following Italian American taxpayers: Paolo Acunto (taxable amount 165), Leonardo Buchicchio, a contractor and stone mason at West Stamford Avenue (taxable amount 1,000), Vito Carluccio (Carlucci), (taxable amount 495), Vito Nicola Colucci, (taxable amount 165), Leo Donatelli, one of early Italian leaders in Stamford (taxable amount 275), Nicolo Jacobi (taxable amount 330), Nicola Giancola, a baker who lived on Virgil St. (taxable amount 550), Meda and Vetriolo, merchants (taxable amount 550), John Muzzio, owner of a Ferris wheel amusement park (taxable amount 900), Michael Palo, brother of Tony Palo and early Italian leader of Stamford (taxable amount 400), Vito Prezioso, merchant who owned tenement buildings in Stamford (taxable amount 550), Louisa M. Ripetucci (taxable amount 1,600), Alfred Taliaferro, a merchant who went into business with his father-in-law (farmer and real estate investor, C.F. Brinkerhoff) (taxable amount 885), Andrea (and wife) Telasco

---

[1] Stamford Tax Records, 1996 preserved at Stamford History Center, collection IC-75; Stamford Advocate 3/2/1898, 4/13/1894, 12/6/1900, 7/15/1904, 10/19/1900, 2/2/1906, 12/1/1910, 11/11/1887, US Census 1900, 1910.

(taxable amount 440), C.A. Tinelli, who served in the Civil War (taxable amount 1,200), Frank Zanone (taxable amount 330), Charlie R. D'Antonio, Fausto DeAngelis, and Louis and Philip Donatelli (all paid the $2 military additional tax).

The Grocery business was a popular Italian American business. In 1898, Cuneo and Libano had a fruit store described as one of the longest-established and most extensive fruit stores in Stamford. It was owned by Antonio Cuneo and Giovanni Libano and was located at the corner of Main and Pacific Streets. The store was purchased by the owners in 1890. Cuneo came from Cincinnati where he was already a dealer in fruit and candy and Libano came from Genoa, where he had gained a reputation for the manufacture of candy. They also sold ice cream. Donato Corbo owned a saloon on Canal Street, a grocery store on Liberty Street and some real estate. Pietro Casareale, had a grocery and butcher shop at 136 W. Main St. Frank D'Agostino was a butcher at 97 Lockwood Ave. Patsy Conetta was an ice cream vendor in 1923.[3] Pasquale Carmine Schinto born in Castelfranco, Miscano Benevento, Italy in 1876, established his grocery store in Stamford, which at one time was the oldest and largest Italian American supermarket in Stamford (Carlevale, 359).

Caleaguo Gentile had a fruit stand on 98 Pacific Street in 1898 and 1899. Peter Zezima had a meat and grocery business on 189 West Main Street, which he sold to Albery De Nicola and Peter Conetta in 1921. Quintino Vetriolo (one of the initial members of the Vittorio Emmanuele Society) had a cigar and tobacco business at 157-159 Canal Street and sold wines and groceries that he imported from Italy (including olive oil). Quintono started the business in Stamford in 1894. He had a private banking business in partnership with Vito Pittaro and owned a bar on Canal Street. A fight broke out in the bar, during which, Vetriolo received a severed artery and required a tourniquet to stop the flow of blood. Fines aggregating $135 resulted from the melee. Vetriolo later bought a building at the corner of Main and Gay Streets intending it to be the new location of his bar, only to sell the new location as well. Instead, a restaurant (Stamford Café) was opened at the location. Vetriolo's brother-in-law Santino Envino was also a grocer. Santino died from pneumonia at 32 and left a widow and three children. Michele Caputo had a fruit and candy store on Henry Street that he sold to Domenico Viggiano. The Toglia Brothers had a grocery store on Pacific Street.[5] John Gardella was

---

[3] Stamford Advocate 12/1/1898, 3/18/1921, 5/10/1922, 4/27/1938, 12/23/1968, 4/10/1911, 3/17/1924, 8/18/1933, 7/7/1923.

[5] Stamford Advocate 2/5/1921, 4/1/1903, 2/27/1904, 1/3/1908, 4/14/1908, 10/23/1911, 4/17/1912, 8/5/1912, 9/14/1912 p 1, 3/7/1913, 4/23/1913, 10/8/1913, 12/16/1913, 5/4/1917, 8/13/1921, 1/3/1955, 5/9/1910, 6/14/1898, 9/9/1899, 7/27/1908. 3/4/1916.

born in Geneva Italy in 1874; he had a grocery and liquor business at 55 and 309 Atlantic Street. [6] Frank B. Tinelli Grocer on 90 Main St. is listed in the Stamford Directory for 1883. Mr. Tinelli also had a tea store. Mr. Tinelli was born in Brooklyn and served in the 90th N.Y. Regiment during the Civil War (His father was Colonel Lewis W. Tinelli of the regiment).[7] Giuseppe Strafaccio, a grocer on Foundry St., decided to give away a bottle of beer with each dollar's worth of goods bought in his store as a promotion. Unfortunately, the City Court fined him $25 for this promotion as it was illegal.[8] Frank Gallo was a grocer at 142 New Spruce Street. During a sugar shortage in 1919, he gave away sugar to poorer customers. Pietro Terenzio had a butcher shop on 95 Liberty St. in 1920. Vito Racaniello had a meat market, grocery, tea, coffee and Olive Oil business at 296 Pacific St. in 1912. The Meda Brothers' store on 197 Main St. sold imported goods including wine, liquor, olive oil, sardines, olives, pasta, and cheese. Elia Rinaldi had a fruit and vegetable business on Manhattan St. The Macari Meat Market was at 321 Atlantic St. Antonio and Angelo Macari were butchers there, and Gerry Macari also had the Stamford Beef Co. on 390 State St. In 1910, Charles Rosso owned a wholesale liquor and grocery store at 85 Main St. Lorento Zezima of 22 Rose Park Pl. had a grocery and butcher shop both in Stamford and New York City.[9]

The 1925 Stamford directory lists the following grocers: Rocco Lambrusco, 180 State St., Penachio Bros, 941 Hope St. Emiddio Roberti, 159 Myrtle Ave. fruit vendors, (he also had a store at 5 Atlantic St.).[10] Leonardo Accursi, 159 Stillwater Ave., Oreste Aliterno, 126 Spruce St., Benedetto Arena, 66 Canal St., Andrew Bartolomeo, 217 W. Main St., Isidore Beltrone, Belltown Road, and Leonard St., Antonio Bochicchio, 64 Liberty St., John Bongiorno, 195 Stillwater Ave, Michele Bria, 178 West Ave., Frank Caccavello, Camp Ave., Joseph Candelmo, 295 W. Main St., Agostino Capone, 12 Court, Luigi Caposella, 1083 Hope St., Fortunato Caputo, 14 Pacific St., Millie Carlucci, 18 Alden St., Joseph Catino, 8 Stillwater Ave., Pasquale Catino, 452 W. Main St., Cavanna Bros, 169 Canal St., Centenze and Cognetta, 325 Pacific St., Angelo Cianci, 41 Dean St., Julia Conetta, 156 Stillwater Ave., Generoso Coppola, 113 Stillwater Ave., Giuseppe DeYulio, 258 Pacific St., Antonetta DiGuardi, 229 Pacific St., Ferrando Bros, 349 Atlantic St., Canio Ferrara (WW I veteran), 76 and 101 Stillwater Ave., Rocco Frangione, 121 Stillwater Ave., Frank Galasso,

---

[6] Stamford Advocate 12/4/1913, 7/31/1951, 5/17/1941.
[7] Stamford Advocate 4/11/1884, 7/20/1883.
[8] Stamford Advocate 8/8/1907.
[9] Stamford Advocate 9/1/1910, 8/28/1944, 8/13/1945.
[10] Stamford Advocate 11/28/1919, 1/9/1920, 11/28/ 1899, 4/28/1903, 10/16/1902, 1/31/1912, 8/28/1931, 3/29/1940, 2/11/1922, 11/29/1905.

75 Spruce St., Peter Galasso 39 Virgil St., Francesco Gallo, 142 Spruce St., August Gargiulo, 117 Summer St. and 1 Bedford St., Michele Genovese, Victory St., Charles Gentile 72 Mill River (also operated Charles Gentile Poultry Market on 214 Pacific St.), Frank Gerardi, 267 W. Main St., Carmeno Gerbasi, 415 W. Main St., Nicandra Giancola, 56 Virgil St., Julia Giannattasio, 174 West Ave., Antonio Grancola, 92 Liberty St., Bruno Grineino, 257 Canal St., Sebastino Inzingo, 162 Lockwood Ave., Erasmo Iovino, 210 Pacific St., Felice Iovino, 466 State St., Paul Labella, 4 Virgil St., Frank Lacalandra, 6 Greenwich Ave., Domenico Lacerenza, 163 Stillwater Ave., Aniello LaGuardia, 85 Spruce St., Francesco Lionetti, 93 Spruce St., Augustus Lombardi, 240 Fairfield Ave., Michele Lopriore, 405 W. Main St., Frank Lorenti, 32 Tresser, Lorenti J. & Son, 80 Pacific St., Donata Lorusso, 213 W. Main St., Canio Lovello, 101 Stillwater Ave., Angelo Maffei, 410 State St. (also owned a cigar store on Cove Rd.), Joseph Maffei, 198 Canal St., John Malizia, 474 State St., Nicholas Marcucci, 273 Canal St., Thomas Marusco, 323 W. Main St., Biagio Masone, (meat market) 247 W. Main St., Ferdinand Mazzi, 34 Horton St., Meda & Bracchi, 545 Main St., Alexander Melfi, 932 Hope St., James Melillo, 45 Dean St., Vincenzo Parrillo, 1087 Hope St., Carmine Passero, 304 Pacific St., Penachio Bros, 941 Hope St., William Perillo, 17 Garden St., Ralph Portia, 14 Greenwich Ave., G. Possidento & Sons, 170 Stillwater Ave., Tony Rennella, 6 Lafayette, Vincenzo Rinaldi, 98 Stillwater Ave., Samuel Salerino, 266 Pacific St., Pasquale Sarni, 63 Spruce St., Giovanni Sessa 274 W. Main St., Rocco Sessa, 236 W. Main St., Vincenzo Sessa, 190 W. Main St. (he also had a restaurant at 296 Pacific St.), John Sibilio, 17 Stephen St., Louis Stabile, 41 Canal St., Antonio Suttile, Horton, Paul Telesco, 2 Virgil St., Angelo Telesco, 417 W. Main St., Michele Vaccara, 285 W. Main St., Rosina Veroni, 89 Spruce St., Pasquale Vigilio, 95 Stillwater Ave., and Laura Zaffino, 286 Pacific St. Pasquale Catino was not only a grocer but an inventor, and was awarded a patent for a lifesaving garment. The vest consisted of a rubber bag which fastened about the waist, by slipping it over the head, the arms being slipped through leather straps. The bag was then blown up with a small tube, with a patented closing valve. Giuseppe DeYulio's children (Victor Joseph DeYulio and Fannie DeYulio Bregialio) owned and operated the DeYulio Sausage Co., which was operated in Stamford for many years on Myrtle Ave. Canio Ferrara was born in Avigliano in 1890, a WWI veteran, and owner of Pure Food Market in Springdale. The following Italians had Meat Markets: Robert Cenami, 908 Main St., Salvatore Coppola, 24 Cove Rd., Anthony DeCarlo, 161 Jefferson, Felix Dumagala, 24 Cedar, Charles Lopriora, 123 Pacific St., Donata Lorusso, 213 W. Main St., Antonio Macari, 192 Canal St., Michael Pia (also a special police officer), 253 Pacific St., and Giovanni Sessa, 274 Main St. Frank Lorenti (WWI veteran) also

operated Lorenti's Tavern at 74 Pacific St. Margareta Poccia was a grocer at 177 West Main St. Giacinto DePiro was a grocer at 215 W. Main. St. Michael Pia was a private detective in 1922 and was president of the Retail Merchants Association organized in 1932. The organization lobbied for a tax on chain stores. He was also president of the Independent Retail Food Merchant's Association.[11] John Prizio was a poultry dealer in the 1930s. The 1935 Stamford directory lists the following poultry dealers: Luigi Frattaroli, 73 Pacific St., Michael A. Frattaroli, 188A W. Main St., Nicholas Frattaroli, 98 Virgil St., Mrs. Florence Gentile, 107 Pacific St., Raffaele Gentile, 436A, State St., Francesco Lionetti, 95 Spruce St., and Antonio Prizio, 17 Hazel St. The 1935 Stamford directory lists the following fruit vendors: Biondi's, 58 W Park Pl., John DiSette, 95 Stillwater Ave., Elizabeth Gragnelli, 276 State St., Michael LaRocco, 268 Greenwich Ave., David J. Marucco, 39 Rose Park Ave., Giacomo Pia, 267 W. Main St., Matthew Pocograno, 208 Pacific St., and Sotire Bros., 70 Richmond Hill Ave.

The 1935 directory lists the following grocers: Frank Pia, 91 West Ave., Fredrick Pocograno, 194 Pacific St., Carmelo Santaromito, 66 Hawthorne, Louis Semmentini, 41 Canal St., Rocco Sessa, 236 W. Main St. Vincenzo Sessa, 192 W Main St., Joseph Tedeschi, 54 W. Park Pl., Angelo Valenzano, 32 Rose Park Ave., Raffaele Vartulli, 144 Spruce St., Francesco Vento, 101 W. Broad St., Jerry Viggiano, 163 Stillwater Ave., William Viggiano, 32 Liberty St., Ralph Vitti, 24 Victory St., and Loreto Zezima, 194 W. Main St. The same directory lists Gus Scalfani as a grocery wholesaler. Additionally, the 1935 directory lists the following meat purveyors: Ralph Boccuzzi, 153 Spruce, Fortunato Caputi, 137 Myrtle Ave., Pietro Casareale, 77 W. Broad St., Ferdinand Cenami, 912 Main St., Florindo Conetta, 474-476 W Main St., J. Coppola & Bros., 24 Cove Rd, Cristede Bros., 615 Main St., Frank D'Agostino, 97 Lockwood, Giuseppe DeYulio, 256 Pacific St., Frank Gaudiosi, 40 Court, Carmino Gerbasi, 415 W Main St., Domenico Lacerenza, 177 W. Main St., Michele Lopriore, 405 W. Main St., Angelo Lorusso, 213 W. Main St., Lovallo Bros, 101 Stillwater Ave., Anthony Macari, 52 Pacific St., Benedetto Macari, 210 W. Main St., Concetta Marchiano, 258 Pacific St., Andrew Penachio, 1013 Hope St., Michael Pia, 245 Pacific St., Thomas Sessa, 91 Richmond Hill Ave., Vincenzo Sessa, 192 Canal St., and Raffaele Vartulli, 144 Spruce St. The same directory lists Angelo Moavero as a milk dealer.

According to family lore (as reported by Theresa Conetta Cucco), Frank Tripodi moved from New Jersey to Stamford to escape Mafia extortion. He

---

[11] Stamford Advocate 10/26/1911, 7/17/1913, 8/17/1991, 3/30/1923, 2/25/1947, 1/10/1986, 3/20/1971, 10/15/1966, 3/6/1913, 9/20/1978, 4/26/1930, 8/11/1916, 7/19/1932, 3/29/1933, 5/3/1933, 11/1/1933, 3/15/1922, 1/2/191, 1/2/1917, 1/26/1915.

built a home on West Broad St. and went into the Grocery business at the corner of West Broad St. and Boston Post Road. Frank went into business with his brother-in-law, Florindo Morone Conetta. Tripodi and Conetta Market did so well, they eventually purchased more property across the street and opened a small strip mall of stores.

In 1929, during the depths of the Depression Salvatore Cingari lost his job as a laborer paving roads in Stamford. He had to become creative to support his family. He bought an old, dilapidated school bus for less than $100 and filled it with pasta and produce that he bought on credit. He peddled the items on his bus on the outskirts of town. Soon he was a success thanks to the fact that his bus could cover more ground faster than other peddlers of his day who used horses and carriages instead. As a result, he could sell more and because of that volume, he could sell at cheaper prices. He was able to increase his inventory. Later on, the Grade A Market stores so familiar to Stamfordites opened up.

The confectionery business was also a popular one among Italians. Marco Guassardo born in Capriata D'Orba, Italy on April 25, 1883, to Peter and Mary Ponasso Guassardo owned the Springdale Star Confectionery on the corner of Main and Pacific, (he also did construction work). The Guassardos also owned a soda shop on Hope St. in Springdale, Star Tavern, and interestingly owned a pet bear that Guassardo gave to the State's Shade Swamp Sanctuary in Farmington in 1938. John Ballo had a confectionary store. Luigi Angelici had a soda water and confectionery store at 65 Richmond Hill Avenue that he sold to Quintino Vetriolo. The following are listed in the 1925 directory: John Ballo, Florence Candido, 94 W. Main St., Anthony Caputo (WW I veteran), 99 Franklin, Pasquale Connetta, 35 Liberty St., Nellie Costello, 199 Elm, Louis DeCarlo, on Wardwell, Frank Del Russo, 14 Cedar St., Giuseppe Epifanio, 533 Pacific St., Alfonso Esposito, 48 W. Main St., (Alfonso also previously had stores at 28 Pacific St., and 295 West Main St.), Nicholas Bervasio, 166 W. Broad St., Carlo Guasco, 71 Elm St., Marco Gussardo, 91 Hope St., Massoletti Inc., 51 Bank St., Ernest Mazza, 247 Main St., Rocco Mazza, 298 Elm St. (he also had a peanut stand at 481 Main St.), George Multello, 9 Chapel St., Andrew Raccaniello, 146 Broad St., Sabino Sabilia, 266 Pacific St. Michael Scatamarci, 50 Liberty St., Modesto Serra, 760 Elm St., Bennino Tedesco, 314 State St., and Ralph Treglia, 910 Main St. J.D. Nicholas Melatti is listed as a deli owner in the directory. Massoletti was also interested in education. J.D. along with J.M Wright was involved in the establishment of the trade school in Stamford and sponsored the Stamford

High School garden movement. Ferrando & Bosco owned the Star Confectionery at 481 Main St.[12] The 1935 directory lists the following confectionary businesses: Alfred Abbazia at 387 W. Main St., Luigi Cannella at 193 Stillwater Ave., Anthony Cerulli at 28 Pacific St., Gaetano Galasso, 24 Rose Park Ave., Marco Gussardo, 912 Hope St., Rose Mancuso, 133 W Main St., Angela J.Mazza, 386 Elm St., Ernest Mezza, 911 Main St., Giuseppe Morelli, 279 1/2 Cove Rd., Dominick Mosca. 98 Stillwater Ave., Josephine Nobile, 229 Pacific St., Giacomo Rizzi, 71 W. Broad St., Anna T. Russo, 191 W Main St., Canio M. Sanseverino, 2 Cove Rd. and 290 W Main St., Pasquale Sarni, 67 Smith St., Star Confectionary, 485 Main St., Joseph Tedeschi, 54 W Park Pl., and Ralph Treglia, 910 Main St. Francesco Vento, 101 W. Broad St. The same directory lists Dominick J. Mosca, 98 Stillwater Ave., and Canio Sanseverino, 204 Atlantic St., as news dealers, and Anna T. Russo, 191 W. Main St., as a stationary retailer.

Natale Candido had a bakery in 1907 at 68 Spruce Street, which he sold to Tommaso and John Sessa. They argued over the terms of the sale, the Sessa's indicating the price was $100 for a horse and two wagons, a stove, and six breadboxes. Candido, claimed that an additional $200 was due and never paid.[13] The 1935 Stamford directory lists the following bakers: Joseph Biancardi, 392 State St., Joseph Burriesci, 37 Holly Pl, Domenico Cassone, 60 Spruce St., Mariano Cipri, 86 Virgil St., Joseph Esposito, 242 Pacific St., Francesco Ganino, 71 Stillwater, Rose Mancuso, 133 W. Main, and Sabia Bakery 202 Stillwater Ave. Mariano Cipri born in Palmi, Reggio Calabri, Italy in 1897, was said to be among the originators of the custom-styled round pizza pie. Mariano was a soldier in the Italian army in WWI. Family history is that he escaped a German POW camp and fled to the United States to join his brother Philip.[14]

Cigar purveyors (Castello Gentile and Paul Comosino) were on Pacific Street in 1905. They were embroiled in a quarrel about the rights to sell certain brands and after assaulting each other were arrested and fined $10 each.[15] Joseph Bonomo and Giuseppe Mancuse had Cigar and Tobacco shops on 456 Atlantic St. and 290 W. Main St. The 1935 directory lists the following under Cigar and Tobacco purveyors: Egilio Giordano at 31 Bedford St. and Charles Sabia at 501 Atlantic St.

---

12 Stamford Advocate 7/3/1923, 8/30/1917, 8/03/1906, 6/11/1917, 12/6/191, 12/5/1915, 11/21/1908, 11/21/1908, 6/24/1909, 4/19/1910, 10/14/1903, 1/22/1904.
13 Stamford Advocate 9/18/1908.
14 Stamford Advocate 1/31/1972 p 6, 3/23/1988.
15 Stamford Advocate 7/31/1905, 8/1/1936.

The following are listed in the dry goods business in Stamford in the 1925 directory: Dominick D'Agostino, 115 Stillwater Ave., James DeSanto (Disanto), 175 W. Main St., Antonio Malazie, 229 Pacific St., Raffaele Rotante, 80 Stillwater Ave., Vito Tortora, 171 Stillwater Ave., Anna Ucciferri, 30 Virgil St. DeSanto was also a music teacher.[16] The 1935 Stamford directory lists the following in the dry goods business: Domenico D'Agostino, 115 Stillwater Ave., Sebastiano Insigna, 162 Lockwood Ave., Antonio Lopiano, 26 Orchard St., and Margarita Tortora, 171 Stillwater Ave.

The Moraio Brothers (Anthony Moraio managed the Stamford store) opened up a florist shop in Stamford after seven years of success at Rye, New York. Their business was local, but they also served customers throughout the country. In 1925 he opened a nursery, greenhouses, and a flower shop in Greenwich. He was a charter member of the Stamford Florist Club. Anthony Moraio was active in the Italo-American Business and Professional Men's Club. Joseph Trombetta sold vegetable and flower plants at 492 State St. He also owned a twelve-family tenement on Cardinal Place.[17] From 1932 through 1940, the Stamford directory lists William J. Cotta as officer of the Stamford Horticultural Society. John L. Racanello, born in Stamford in 1908, began his florist business, Racanello Florist Shop of Stamford, in 1936 (Carlevale, 318). The 1935 Stamford directory lists the following florists: James Melillo, 57 Sound View Ave., Ralph Poccia, 14 Greenwich Ave. and John L. Racanello, 95 Richmond Hill Ave.

The junk business thrived in Stamford on Canal Street. John Amarto at Canal St. near Railroad Ave. is listed as a "ragman" (junk dealer) in the Stamford Directory of 1883. The 1885 and 1887 directories list Michael Hamani and Joseph Qualano as junk dealers also on Canal Street. Rubino Brothers was founded in 1900 by Antonio Rubino as a one-man operation with only a horse and cart as equipment. As the years progressed, Antonio's sons, John, Samuel, Frank, and Michael came into the business. Their website indicates that through hard work and determination, they overcame the hard economic times of the early 1900s and persevered. The original location was on Cardinal Place (where the Stamford Marriott now stands). Their current location is on Canal St. The 1925 Stamford directory lists the following junk dealers: John D'Amato, 105 Worth, and John Manguso, Cardinal. John Anthony Ferro, born in Sassano, Salerno, Italy in 1885, moved to Stamford in 1925 where his business dealt in ferrous and non-ferrous metals (Carlevale, 175). The 1925 Stamford directory lists the following junk dealers: James Canino, 80 Hawthorne St., John D'Amato, 105 Worth, John A. Ferro, 20-26 Chapel St., John Galatro, 24

---

[16] Stamford Advocate 5/25/1945.
[17] Stamford Advocate 10/9/1920, 4/21/1932, 4/15/1968, 5/17/1909, 1/9/1914.

Cardinal St., Rubino Bros. 26 Cardinal, and Gennaro Rubino, 24 Cardinal St. The 1935 Stamford directory lists Leo Carlucci, 58 Victory St., and Donato Pace, 248 West Ave. as junk dealers ("scavengers").

Barbering was a popular occupation for Italian Americans. The State Board of Examiners came to Stamford to administer examinations to prospective barbers. Italians were listed as officers of the Master Barbers Association; in 1918 and 1919 this included D. S. Tarenga, secretary; and V. A. DeRosa, treasurer. In 1920, Domenico Farenga was listed as an officer. In 1923, Pasquale Coviello was listed. Francesco Gagliardi had a shop at Manhattan Street. T. Gagliardi has a shop in 1895 in the Advocate Building. Natale Candido had a shop on Pacific Street. The 1887 Stamford Directory lists Genoroso Tedesco as a barber at 16 Broadway. Marino Passero was born on August 5, 1881 in Italy, had a barbershop in 1907 on Atlantic Street, and became involved in a lawsuit that other barbers became interested in. A customer, William C. Rungee of Greenwich sued for $25 in damages to cover the loss of a $5 hat. Rungee was shaved in Passero's shop. He entered the shop with a brand new $5 hat, after his shave, as he was leaving, he noticed his hat was gone and a shabby one was left in its place. Rungee won the case with a judgement of $3 and this ruling was appealed to a higher court. Passero later ran for Justice of the Peace as a Democrat. He was defeated in 1916, but was elected in 1917. As justice of the peace, he performed the marriage ceremony for Antonio Mongillo and Adeline Infentile on June 25th, 1917. He then sold his barbershop to A. Claps and Carlo de Bartolemo in 1921. He garnered 7,849 votes in 1928 and remained active in the Democratic Party for many years. He later also became a real estate broker and is listed as a Justice of the Peace in the 1935 Stamford directory.[20] Vito A. DeRosa was a member of Barber's Local Stamford and had a shop at 195 Main St. and was a pupil of Crescenzo Tamburri. John Bello was a barber operating four shops: Ambassador Barber Shop at 60 South St., The Elite Barber shop at 199 Elm St., Jack's Barber Shop at 92 Manhattan St., and Bello's Barber Shop at 314 Canal St. Bello sued in 1936 requesting to be allowed to charge twenty-five cents per haircut, rather than the state regulated price of forty cents as prescribed by the State Barber Commission claiming the rule violated his constitutional rights. Other Barbers listed in the 1925 Stamford directory included: Charles Belline at 166 Atlantic St. Salvatore Cannizzano at 906 Main St, Harry Del Prete at 230 Atlantic St., Nicola Esposito at 314 Canal St. (who previously sold his half interest in a barbershop at 467 Pacific St. to Leonardo Sanarsiero in 1917), John Fallace at 330 State St., Autere Falcioni at

---

[20] Stamford Advocate 10/4/1907, 10/21/1907, 10/28/1907, 11/4/1907, 11/9/1907, 12/31/1908, 6/18/1912, 10/12,1914, 9/11/1916, 9/13/1916, 6/28/1917, 6/28/1917, 2/5/1921, 11/5/1924, 11/7/1928, 10/13/1930, 3/10/1934, 2/3/1957.

263 Cove Rd., Antonio Fedele at 128 Richmond Hill Ave., Francesco Gagliardo at 9 Manhattan St. (Gagliardo sold his barbershop in the Advocate building to Crescenzo Tamburri in 1898), Salvatore Gallo at 693 Atlantic St., John Grasso at 467 Pacific St., Emilio Greco at 368 Atlantic St., Frank Lasalandra at 176 State St., Vincent Mercadante at 97 Franklin St., Salvatore Pagano at 251 Pacific St., Pasquale Pastore at 251 Pacific St., Ralph Prinzi at 53 Oliver St., Louis Robustelli at 288 W. Main St., Frank Scalise at 268 Greenwich Ave., Francesco Scorese at 84 Park Pl., Gennaro Siriglia at 67 Manhattan St., Matteo Siriglia at 208 Pacific St., Vito Tortora at 171 Stillwater Ave., John Vento at 90 Stillwater Ave., and Vito Verrasto at 394 Main St. Joseph Mazella was a barber (with five children) who opened a speakeasy when his business fell off was sentenced to two months in jail, execution suspended and placed on probation for two years. He owned Park View Beauty Shoppe at 140 Atlantic St. in the Quintard Building. William Arduino had a barbershop on 41 Gay St. Vincenzo Boccarusso had a barbershop on Pacific Street in 1901. Giacomo Tarantino had a shop at 193 West Main St. and a grocery store (and liquor business) at 35 Shippan Ave (Toglia 2013, 352).[21] The 1935 Stamford directory lists the following barbers: Pasquale Auletta 40 Liberty St. Frank Avella, High Ridge, Vito Bafundi 49 Myrtle Ave., Mario Battiato 324 Greenwich, Thomas Bellantoni 425 W Main, Angelo Bello 314 Canal, Billone & Arancia 176 Myrtle, Michael Botticelli, 1082 Hope (Mr. Botticelli had a shop on 23 Camp Ave. that he bought from Jerry Lione in 1928)[22], Joseph S. Buccheri 695A Pacific, Peter Calitri 994 Hope, Louis Calanzaro 70 Pacific, Claps & Tartaglia 478 Atlantic, Ferdinando Colacchio 487 W Main, Angelo Colucci, 834 Main, Ricardo DeVartti, Long Ridge, Cold Spring, Joseph DeVito 20 Maple, Joseph DiChiara 92 Franklin, Domenic Farengo 84 W Park, Joseph Fiordelisi 34 Summer, Jerry Franchina 763 Elm, Nicholas Gagliardi 80 Main, Carmine Gandino 253 Hope, John Longo 495 Main, Matthew Lucipora 322 Main, Joseph Maffei 59 Hawthorne, Frank Martinelli 119 W Main, Louis Meli 281 Cove, Daniel Mercadante, 5 Main, Nicholas Camillo, 21 River, Antonio Pagano 412 Main, Marino Passero, 609 Atlantic St., Joseph Pennacchio, Beltown Rd, Joseph Rabita, 34 Worth, John Rosa, 289 Greenwich Ave., Daniel Santangelo, 609 Main, Michael Santo, 184 W Main, Giacomo Tarantino,73 Richmond Hill, Anthony Torentino, 299 Canal St., Felice Trimboli, 43 Pacific St., James Zito, Belltown Rd. Billone & Arancia are listed as a beauty salon at

---

[21] See also: 1925 Stamford Directory, Stamford Advocate 2/15/1936, 6/4/1929, 2/12/1932, 8/1/1907, 10/25/1916, 5/29/1917, 8/31/1895, 5/25/1898, 6/12/1899, 2/19/1921, 4/19/1917, 6/19/1903, 5/6/1901.
[22] Stamford Advocate 8/2/1928.

176 Myrtle Ave. Jerry Franchina served in WWI, serving in the cavalry.[23] The Coviello Brothers had two beauty salons in Stamford. Joseph Coviello born in Avigliano, Potenza, Italy in 1895, came to Stamford in 1912, he served in WWI oversaw the salon at 250 Bedford St. His brother, Pasquale also born in Avigliano, ran the salon at 180 Atlantic St (Carlevale, 107).

Shoe repair was also a popular occupation. George Grimaldi had a shop at 89 Broad Street at which his brother Gaètano conducted business while George was away. Unfortunately, George was away in Calabria in 1908 during the large earthquake and likely perished there. Pasquale Urbano was listed as a shoe repairer in the 1889 Stamford Directory. Philip Parillo had a cobbling shop on Hope St. Giuseppe Candelmo had a shoe repair at 180 West Main St. Samuel DeMarco, shoemaker had a shop on West Main St. Anthony Rubino owned a shop in 1938.[25] The 1935 Stamford directory lists M. Savina Genovese, 215 W. Main St., and Peter P. Latte, 389 W. Main St., as shoe dealers, and the following as shoe repairers: Ralph A. Altomare, 110 Broad St., Pasquale Aruzza, 310 Hope St., John Aulenti, 91 Spruce St., John Ballo, 279 Cove Rd., Antonio Bartolo, Belltown Rd., Rosario Caruso, 693 ½ Pacific St., Dominick Colucci, 115 North St., Salvatore Colucci, 855 Main St., Carmine Concillo, 252 Pacific St., Aniello Coppola, 59A Hawthorne, Thomas Coppola, 6 William, Louis D'Alessio, 1086 Hope St., John DeBlasi, 93 Woodside, Giuseppe Franchina, 447 Pacific St., Stefano Licastro, 19 Stillwater Ave., Joseph Lombardo, 156 Pacific St., James LoRusso, 73 W. Broad St., Francesco Merlino, 121 Stillwater Ave., Donato Miusciello, 163 Stillwater Ave., Joseph Morsa, 98 W, Main St., Umberto Mossa, 76 Stillwater Ave., Joseph Natale, 489 Glenbrook Rd., Vincent Pelosi, 374 Elm St., Antonio Porto, 351 Atlantic St., Gaetano Preziosi, 91 Richmond Hill Ave., Racaniello Co, 370 Atlantic St., Nicola Racaniello, 271 Summer St., Fillipo Bello, 754 Elm St., Salvatore Robustelli, 605 Atlantic St., Roma Shoe Repairing, 34 Summer St., John Sacco, 783 Elm, Biagio Salvatore, 417 W. Main St., Michele Santini, 343 Atlatnic St., Pasquale Savino, 55 Main St., Nicholas Tatano, 83 Stillwater Ave., Raffaele Venezia, 222 Elm St., and Rocco Venneri, 33 Selleck St. The same directory lists the following shoe shiners: Joseph Christiano, 520 Main St., Peter Colucci, 144 Atlantic St., and Racaniello Co, 370 Atlantic St.

The following are listed in Carl Lobozza's "Journey Through Time" and include photos: Passero Brothers Plumbing, 229 West Main Street, 1904; Clapes Brothers Garage (gas station and sold Star and Flint automobiles) in 1920s, Iovanno Grocery store, 210 Pacific Street 1924; DeNocenzo Tavern on Pacific Street. Paul Rosa is listed as a contractor in 1907. Paul Rosa died

---

[23] Stamford Advocate 3/13/1950.
[25] Stamford Advocate 12/31/1908, 1/11/1921, 1/15/1901, 10/31/1938.

at the age of 39 while working in Rhode Island working on a project laying sewer drains as part of the firm Alberto & Rosa in 1918. Mr. Rosa was also a member of the Elks and Foresters of America (Lobozza, 20, 62, 67, 74).

John Muzzio, a blue-eyed blond born in Italy in 1841 lived on Shippan Avenue. He was by trade an organ maker and was the proprietor of a carousal at Roton Point and Shippan. In 1890, Muzzio bought a merry-go-round in Asbury Park, New Jersey, and moved it to Shippan. It was located on the east side of Ocean Drive West near Rogers Road. In 1905, he purchased the East Side Rod & Fun Club. In 1910, Muzzio moved the merry-go-round to Roton Point. He operated the attraction there for about fifteen years and was a familiar figure to the patrons of the shore resort. He had four organs at Roton and used them to provide music for the carousal and draw crowds. At his death in 1914, his widow trucked the merry-go-round back to Seaview Ave. Shortly after, his children ran a boat yard business from the property in Shippan. In 1904, he was fined for violation of the Sunday Law, by operating the facility on Sunday, after neighbor complaints.[27]

P. Sabini & Son, furniture stores first located on Pacific Street then Shippan Ave. (Pellegrino Sabini born in Montegroffo Italy also owned a grocery store at 21 Pacific St., a pool hall, and a jewelry store/jewelry repair shop on Atlantic St.). His wife Mary operated a cigar store on 549 Main St.[28] Their children, David, Elbina, Joseph, John, Louis and Angelo continued the furniture business at 175 Pacific St. The 1925 Stamford directory lists that Paolo Marciano had a home furnishings store on 138 Pacific St. (he also had a shoe store and is listed in the 1935 directory as well) and Ralph Loglosco had a hardware store at 251 W. Main St. Gabriele Colbi, born in Forsato DeVico, Peruggia, Italy in 1896 settled in Stamford in 1924 establishing a jewelry business. He was the first Italian American jeweler in Stamford. Gabriele served in WWI (Carlevale, 185). The 1935 Stamford directory lists upholsterers Andrew J. Annunziato, 419 Elm St., and Louis Argenio, 164 Wardwell St.

Louis S. Croce was listed in the Stamford directory in 1925 as a furrier at 468 Main St. The 1935 directory lists Joseph Sorrento at 178 W Main St. and Carmela Summa at 449 W. Main St. as cleaners.

Luigi Frattaroli, born in Settefrati in 1881, of 45 Virgil St. came to Stamford in 1900 and had an ice business for over twenty-five years.[30] The 1935

---

[27] Stamford Advocate 9/9/1911, 6/31/1991. 5/4/1979, 4/27/1979, 6/22/1904, 8/22/1904, 8/30/1905, 10/16/1905, 11/14/1905, 5/15/1905,.
[28] Stamford Advocate 2/11/1910, 11/8/1934, 2/21/1924, 7/19/1917, 4/4/1916, 12/28/1915, 11/26/1910.
[30] Stamford Advocate 9/4/1940.

directory lists the following ice dealers: Angelo Conetta, 31 Liberty St., Tomasso Conforti, 162 Spruce St., Daniel DeGruttela, 29 Ardmore Rd., Domenico Forte, 38 Ann St., Camillo Natale, 29 Ann St., Antonio Rubino, 16 Cardinal Pl., and Ralph Uva, 43 Pressprich.

The Cappabianca Travel service began serving Stamford in 1908 and had offices on 115 Main St. The business was started by Zanetto F. Cappabianca.[31] The 1935 Stamford directory also lists Mr. Cappabianca as a steamship agent at 6 Greenwich Ave.

Some other Italian American owned businesses include the following. John Scalzi and his brother Daniel owned a Tavern/pool hall on Pacific Street (White Front Café). Billiards tournaments involving the Scalzi family were reported in the Advocate and appears to be a popular pastime/sport in the early 1900s; in 1910, there was a match between "Shakespeare, the one handed pool player" and "Big Boy", another match featured "Hotel" Riley of Stamford. John Scalzi and Joseph Colucci battled for the Italian championship of Stamford over several days in 1911. Scalzi emerged victorious.

The pool hall meant dealing with disorderly people, and complaints by those opposed to such establishments. In the early 20th Century, the temperance movement was active. Often the tavern business was their target. In 1912, Reverend Priddy of the First Methodist Church determined to clean up the city hired private detectives to help in the "crusade against the demon rum" and forwarded an affidavit to the Mayor of Stamford of wrongdoing at local taverns. Earlier in the year, the Reverend tried unsuccessfully to prevent the movement of a saloon into the Waterside section of Stamford (the church's district). Undeterred by this setback, he was instrumental in forming the "The Conservation Committee of the Men and Religion Forward Movement of Stamford" that wanted to limit new liquor permits in the city, which was called the "no-license" movement. The intent of the movement was to reduce the number of taverns in Stamford to one-third of the existing. It was under these circumstances that Scalzi's tavern got embroiled in Priddy's campaign. There were mass meetings at the Methodist Church (up to 1,200 people attending) where citizens listened to the anti-liquor call. Priddy's followers claimed that "the moral, mental and physical side of Stamford life had been made corrupt by the overwhelming influence of the saloon." As part of this crusade, reverend Priddy had undercover detectives surveil local establishments. The detectives presented "evidence" against several locals, including an officer who went into a bar while on duty, and Scalzi's tavern and leaked information to the Advocate. The mayor, along with the chief of police and an advocate reporter went to the

31 Stamford Advocate Tercentenary Edition Town of Stamford, CT 1641 – 1941. Supplement of the Stamford Advocate, Saturday, June 7, 1941, Stamford Advocate 10/30/1948, 3/16/1949.

Reverend's house to demand the evidence that backed up the affidavit. As the mayor pressed for proof, Priddy stated: "I am just as anxious to give you this evidence as you are to get it. It isn't in my possession at the present time, in detail. I can have it the next time I see the detectives."

Part of the complaint against Scalzi involved a woman drinking in the bar, with her arm around the neck of the man who she was drinking with. Rev. Priddy exclaimed the woman could have been arrested for loitering. The Mayor went to the bar, confronted the woman and asked her to leave. She refused. He then suggested to the bar's owner, Mr. Scalzi that it was bad judgement to have her there. Mr. Scalzi's showing himself as a fair man, responded (maybe because of naiveté or because he himself was probably subject to bias and didn't want to inflict it on someone else) that "he did not see why he should put her out when she was breaking no law." In my opinion, based on the social hierarchy of the time (and considering how Italians were perceived and treated), it would be unlikely that Mr. Scalzi would challenge the mayor, police and religious authority without feeling he was in the right. Although, an honorable act, Scalzi was not rewarded for his righteousness. The mayor actually confirmed that the woman did not have her arm on anyone when he was there. The Reverend told his congregation that the detectives had substantiated the charges, which was in contradiction of Mayor Rowell's statements about what he had witnessed. This despite reports that the private investigators often presented distorted evidence.

The Advocate reported that the officer in question had gone into the bar, but that it was attached to a grocery store and he had stopped in there for lunch. This was vouched for by the mayor. The Reverend was insistent and the mayor was forced to demonstrate in some way that he was doing his job. The mayor had to show some corrective action was being taken and a few days later, on that evidence, (her arm around a man, which was only evidenced by testimony of undercover detectives) Miss Annie Myres, better known as "Gold Tooth Annie," and John Scalzi were fined $25 and costs, and $100 and costs, respectively for loitering and allowing persons to loiter. Thus, Scalzi and some other establishments were caught up in the blowout of the movement and not as a result of proven unlawful activities. It is probable that this type of evidence would not result in a conviction under our current laws, and in fact would be in contrast to preserving the rights of accused citizens. It is likely that the proceedings would be determined to be biased. After an appeal, Scalzi was able to reduce his fine by $62.81, possibly due to the evidence. Scalzi attempted to move his tavern from Pacific Street to Canal Street but was denied. After this, John Scalzi declared that the saloon business did not pay and he decided to make a living painting instead. The

Reverend's desired results were achieved, if the saloon was not closed he was persuading owners to get out of the business. Scalzi sold his business to his brother Daniel (Donato) R. Scalzi.[32]

Scalzi Paint Store was established in 1910 by John A. Scalzi Sr. and Carmella Genovese Scalzi and was on 44 Pacific Street. He was also a painting contractor with sixteen painters in his employ but gave up the contract work to concentrate on the store in 1921, opening a wholesale business as well. They later relocated to 42 West Main and Pleasant Streets and again on Summer Street. The city purchased the store on Main Street to establish a greenbelt from Scalzi Park to the South End. The company later added the lumber business as well. John A. Scalzi (an independent) was named to the Park Commission. The company dissolved in 1987.[33]

The 1935 Stamford directory lists the following painters: John V. Cerulli, 68 Avery, Pasquale P. Esposito, 687 Elm St., Rudolph Gatti, 126 Spruce St., John J. Leone, 39 Beckley Ave., Frank Marro, 30 Raymond St., Michael Occhionero, 133 Sound View Ave., and John Sanfilippo, 32 Walnut St. The same directory lists Louis DeLuca, 190 Stillwater Ave. as a sign painter.

The 1935 Stamford directory lists the following billiards establishments: Philip LaPorte, 920 Hope St., Domenico Possidento, 170 Stillwater Ave., Johnnie Scalzi's, (also included bowling alleys) 184 Summer St., George Vaccaro, 298 W Main St.

G. Boccuzzi owned a bar as well at 66 Canal St. Prohibition began in 1922 and bar owners had to stop selling liquor. Italian Americans impacted and ceasing the sale of liquor included Joe Colucci, Quintino Vetriolo, Henry Bracchi, Lavallo, Mancusi, Varrichio, Rinaldi, Ben Arena, Sabias, Giancola, and Luiga Donatelli. Antonio Terenzio came to Stamford in 1890 from Settefrati, Italy where he was a police officer. Originally employed at the stove foundry and later at Yale and Towne, he later opened a saloon business as well and was active in the Societa Vittorio Emanuele. Antonio Genovese (who moved to Stamford in 1885) owned a saloon at 215 W. Main St. The Colucci Lupo Saloon was on 251 West Main St. Michele Vaccaro saloon was at 285 W. Main St.[34] The 1935 Stamford directory lists the following in the beverage/tavern business: Peter Latte, 389 W Main, Ralph Loglisci, 99 Richmond Ave., Leonard DiSessa, 479 Atlantic St., Rocco Rosati, 87 Stillwater

---

[32] Stamford Advocate 12/6/1910, 7/25/1911,8/21/1911,9/8/1911, 9/13/1911, 9/14/1911, 9/16/1911, 10/7/1912, 6/15/1912, 10/15/1912, 10/22/1912, 3/19/1913, 3/12/1914, 3/29/1915, 4/26/1915, 7/5/1915, 7/19/1915, 10/18/1916, 6/14/1917, 6/18/1917.
[33] Stamford Advocate 5/25/1928, 12/11/1961, 5/2/1989, 12/16/1992, 12/30/1992, 8/19/1915.
[34] Stamford Advocate 11/28/1911, 7/22/1922, 7/27/1910, 3/17/1915, 2/4/1933.

Ave., Michele Vaccaro, 63 Spruce St., Corbo Beverages (Anthony Corbo) as a wholesaler. The same directory lists the following taverns: Amadio Bocuzzi, 99 Stillwater Ave., Brass Rail Tavern, 124 Spruce St., Joseph G. Chiapetta, 454 W. Main St., Venturine DeNocenzo, 246 Pacific St., Alexander L. Melfi, 932 Hope St., Pasquale Sarni, 67A. Smith St., Mede Sementini, 71 Gay St., Sizone Tavern, 238 W. Main St., and Antonio Zezima, 70 Mill River.

The Italian-American banking business developed as a necessity because of the barriers to capital for Italians. Quentino Vetriolo, Aniello Palomba and Henry Bracchi were banking partners. Later the partnership ended and Palomba took over the whole business. At the twentieth anniversary of the bank, Louis Zezima indicated that the bank was one of only 12 similar banks throughout Connecticut, which was able to survive the Depression and show progress through the lean thirties. Luigi Zezima born in Settefrati in 1889, came to Stamford in 1906 at 17 to work at Yale and Towne. In 1926, he left Yale and Towne to become a John Hancock Insurance agent. Luigi (Louis) Zezima was an insurance salesman for John Hancock Life Insurance Co. for 28 years. He was one of the founders of the Settefratese mutual benefit society, and member of the Sons of Italy. All the while, he dreamed of elevating the community by freeing them of the whims of the local banks. In 1926 Attorney Frank Rich, Louis Zezima, Joe Mastrich, Matteo Pisano, Michael Gandia, Gettulio Marini, Ciciaco Iovanna, Antonio Sansone and Louis Donatelli incorporated the "Italian Loan Association, Inc." with capital of $50,000 with offices at 509 Atlantic Street. The bank started in 1920 under the name Italian Loan, with just $2,000. In 1929, the officers were Louis Zezima, president; Frank Rich, vice-president, Matthew Pisani, secretary; Joseph Mastrich, treasurer. He later founded Atlantic National Bank (which then became Connecticut National Bank). He was born in Settefrati, Italy to Cesido and Carmella Zezima.[35] Matteo Pisano was born in 1886 in Altrani, and married in 1922 but only after 7 months his wife, Concettina Cardone passed away.[36] Catherine (Kay) Sessa was born on November 20, 1915, to Michael and Margaret Sabia Claps. After graduating from Stamford High School in 1933, she began a 40-year career in banking. She worked her way from an entry-level position at the Italian Loan to become the first woman Vice President in the banking industry in the State of Connecticut, at Atlantic National Bank on Bedford St. She also held the position of Corporate Secretary for the bank. Kay dedicated her life to helping people. She was a lifelong member of Sacred

---

[35] Stamford Advocate 4/26/1946, 3/4/1920.
[36] Stamford Advocate 3/3/1920, 7/9/1926, 7/9/1928, 1/8/1929, 6/15/1926, 1/8/1929, 2/7/1931, 4/8/1940, 1/12/1922. See also, *Il Progresso degl'Italiani nel Connecticut*, G. Chiodi Barberio, New Haven Connecticut 1933.

Heart Church, where she was a member and officer of the Rosary Alter Society and a member of the parish council. She and her husband, Al Sessa served as foster parents in the Fresh Air fund program.[37] The 1935 Stamford directory lists Paul Bacco as in the banking business and Francis Z. Cappabianca, 6 Greenwich Ave., and Maddelena Paloma, 3 Main St. as foreign exchange businesses.

Pasquale Gasperino was a dentist and lived at 64 Club Road. He was born in Stamford on May 5, 1903, to Joseph and Ann Caruso Gasperino. He graduated from Temple University School of Dentistry in 1927 and opened an office at 105 Bedford St. in 1928. He was a member of the American Dental Association, Connecticut Dental Association and the Stamford Dental Association (of which he was president). Louis J. Genesse and S. Walter Longo are listed as dentists in the 1925 Stamford directory.[38]

Pharmacist was a popular occupation as well. Emilio Bria born in Rose, Cosenza, Italy, in May of 1890, had a pharmacy at 177 West Main St. (Bria's Pharmacy) for 12 years. He was a committee member of the "field day" put on for the Stamford Children's Home in 1936 and sponsored by the Italian Newspaper "La Tribuna." The Field Day was five hours long and included lunch, refreshments, sports, music, and entertainment for forty children. This was an annual affair. In 1936, the event included the WPA band, under the direction of Pasquale Zuffino, a guitar duo by Anita Pezzi and Mary Ann Latte. Anthony L. Gaudio was chairman of the event. Other committee members included: Dr. Dominic A. Zaccardo, Pauline Altomaro, Yolanda Vescio, Pauline Turso-Vescio, Fanny Fulco, Representative Vincent Giampietro, S. B. Esposito, Russell Gaudio, Vincent Botticelli, Michael Scatamacchia, Frank W. LiVolsi, Vincent J. Laino, Alfred A. Sessa, Patsy Chiappetta, Neil Preziosi and Peter P. Vescio. Ferrante's pharmacy was on 113 West Main St. and 791 Main St. and was owned by D. A. Ferrante, born in Buenos Aires, Argentina in 1898. Argentina was also a major destination for Italian immigrants. In 1921 he got his degree from Brooklyn College of Pharmacy and moved to Stamford in 1925.[39] Victor Emanuel Centonze, proprietor of the Temple Pharmacy was born in Stamford in 1909, to Giovanni A. Centonze and Raffaela Guarniera. Mr. Centonze graduated from Stamford High School in 1929, and Temple University School of Pharmacy in 1934. In 1941 he owned his own drug store at 113 West Main St (Carlevale, 84). The 1935

---

[37] Stamford Advocate 12/15/1965, 2/2/1965, 2/11/1963; Stamford Daily Voice 5/6/2013.
[38] Stamford Advocate 12/5/1973, 1/20/1949.
[39] Stamford Advocate 11/27/1931, 6/26/1931, 6/26/1936, 6/28/1935, 6/29/1935, 5/10/1924, 7/1/1940 p 2; Il Progresso degl'Italiani nel Connecticut.

directory includes Ferdinand Cenami, 113 W. Main St. and Peter E. Dadonna, 124 Pacific St. as druggists.

A registry of medical practitioners in Stamford for the periods 1893 through 1938 found at the Stamford History Center lists the following names: Anchise Grossi (age 29), registered on March 15th, 1906, attended the University of Naples. No specialty is provided for Mr. Grossi. On December 17th, 1906, Angelo Biondi, age 38 is listed as graduating from Eclectic Medical School. On November 23, 1906, Eduardo Sollima age 31 is listed as graduating from Bologna Medical College. On December 13, 1907 Josephine Ferrara, 26 years old, graduating from Women's Infirmary and Maternity Home. On August 5, 1909, A. Preziosi, 23 years old is listed as graduating from the College of Physicians and Surgeons. On April 8, 1918, Melchisedec A. Barone, 24 years old born in Foggia, Italy is registered as graduating from College of Physicians and Surgeons, with a specialty in obstetrics and gynecology. Melchisedec was the son of Rev. Alfredo Barone (Barone, 35, 80). On July 9, 1918, Phillipina Blancato, age 49 is listed as a mid-wife who attended the University of Catania. She was located at 70 Pacific St.[42] On April 7th, 1921, Ralph E. Costanzo, 33 born in New Haven, Ct, graduated from Loyola University, and was a general practitioner. He was the brother of Dr. J. J. Costanzo. Ralph resided at 18 Broad St. and was a captain in the U.S. Medical Corps Reserve after active service in 1917 and 1918 during World War I, serving with the 148th (R.N.) Field Ambulance, Drake Battalion, Anson Battalion, and Hood Battalion. He was appointed lieutenant in the Medical Corps in June 1917, and stationed at the Old Mill Military Hospital at Aberdeen, Scotland, after which he served attached to the British Expeditionary Force. He was promoted to captain in 1918. He also served in WW II. He provided free vaccinations for children administered in the city court room in 1922.[43] Anthony R. Campo is listed both in 1921 and 1922 (when he was 28). Dr. Campo graduated with high honors from Trinity High School in NYC. He received a gold medal and a four-year scholarship to Trinity College, he then attended Baltimore Medical College for three years and then finished his senior year at St. Louis College of Physicians and Surgeons, where he graduated. He was a general practitioner. In January 1924, his license to practice was revoked by the Connecticut Eclectic Medical Examining Board, which claimed that the schools he attended were not legitimate schools. He continued to practice until 1929 and appealed this to every court in the state and the United States Supreme Court. In an interview in 1935 he states: "But what hurts most …is that these kids should be in college…I don't

---

[42] Stamford Advocate 7/5/1918.
[43] Stamford Advocate 4/22/1941, 8/8/1917, 2/3/1922, 3/3/1936,, 12/27/1946,.

care for myself, but for their futures." He was referring to his five children. As a result of the revocation, he was forced to turn to other ways of earning a living and was unable to send his children to college, although their academic records warranted it. In July of 1935, he received a writ of mandamus ordering the State Department of Health to restore his license. However, he lost this in June of 1936 when the judge in the Superior Court granted a motion to quash the mandamus. Finally, after much litigation, Dr. Campo's license to practice medicine was restored in 1938 by a judge in Superior Court. He was fined $110 for practicing medicine while his license was revoked in 1940. In July of 1926, he was arrested after Federal prohibition agents and Darien police discovered several stills and five thousand gallons of liquor in an old house on the grounds of the Noroton Relief Hospital. Dr. Campo was head of the private hospital at the time. He faced charges three times, as twice before juries disagreed in the case. At the third trial, he pled guilty and was sentenced to fifteen days in jail.[44] On December 15, 1922 Marie F. Esposito, age 25 is listed as graduating from the Bellocine School for Midwifery. On June 17, 1925, Santa Musco age 50, born in Italy is listed as a midwife licensed as of 1911. On June 21, 1928, Alfred J. Sette, age 28 is listed as graduating from George Washington University and was a general practitioner. On June 17, 1929 Antonio Paolillo, age 45, is listed as graduating from the Chicago College of Chiropractors. He is listed in the 1935 Stamford directory as a naturopathic physician. On July 5th, Vincenzo Leggiardo, age 34 is listed as graduating from the University of Naples and is a general practitioner. On January 12, 1933, Alfred F. DiMilia, age 29 is listed as graduating from Laval University and is listed with a specialty in Allopathic medicine. On April 21, Deonis M. Lupo is listed as graduating from Jefferson Medical College, interned at Baltimore City Hospital, and was a general practitioner. He was a Captain and then promoted to Major in the Medical Corps, of the U.S. Army in WWII, and appointed chief of orthopedic surgery. He later was also a gynecologist.[45] On June 5, 1933 Lindo Peter DiFrancesco, age 26 is listed as graduating from Tufts College of Medicine and was a general practitioner. Dr. DiFrancesco is listed in the 1935 Stamford directory at 54 River St. On November 6, 1936 William B. DeBellio, age 48 is listed as graduating from Middlesex College, and was a general practitioner. On April 22, 1937, James John Cognetta, age 26 is listed as graduating from the University of Vermont, and listed as a general practitioner and surgeon.[46] On May 5th, 1938 Daniel

[44] Stamford Advocate 1/11/1924, 2/19/1924, 3/30/1927, 4/29/1927, 9/16/1927, 9/20/1927, 3/31/1933, 7/6/1935, 8/25/1938, 5/1/1939, 2/1/1940.
[45] Stamford Advocate 6/11/1931 p 23, 2/6/1942, 9/25/1942, 4/16/1994.
[46] Stamford Advocate 8/8/1964.

Joseph Sabia, 28 is listed as graduating from Marquette Medical School and was a general practitioner. He was promoted to Captain in WWII. Upon returning to Stamford he had an office at 65 South St. and was also a surgeon.[47] William Francis Bria born in Greenwich in 1908, graduated from Stamford High School in 1926, interned at the Stamford Hospital and was a member of the Italian Center (Carlevale, 50). The 1935 Stamford directory lists Alfred F. deMilia as a physician in Stamford.

The 1935 Stamford directory lists the following nurses: Sylvia Caputo, 36 Windsor Rd., Irene Fekete, 26 Holly Pl., and Stephanie Polimeni, 756 Elm St.

Frank J. Sprovieri born in Stamford in 1892 was a chiropractor with an office in Bridgeport and was a member of the Taxation Board for the City of Stamford (Carlevale, 372).

The Stamford Medical Society Board minutes reflects the following Italian names: Dr. Sorgi, Dr. J.J. Costanzo, Dr. R.E. Costanzo, Dr. Frank D'Andrea, Dr. Lindo D.F. Di Francesco, Dr. A.J. Sette, Dr. James Cognetta, and Drs. DeMelia, and Campo (who may have been practicing without a license, see Dr. Campo's ultimate victory in court above). In a meeting of 1939, Dr. James J. Costanzo was elected to the committee for St. Joseph's Hospital, and Dr. D'Andrea is treasurer.[50] Dr. James Cognetta was born in Stamford in 1910, to Vincenzo and Marietta Centonze Cognetta. He graduated from Stamford High school in 1929, and the University of Vermont School of Medicine in 1936, interning at Stamford Hospital. His office was at 366 Atlantic St (Carlevale, 97).

Dr. Aniello Preziosi died at 24 years of age, engaged to be married. His eulogy was as follows: "A few years ago, there came to Stamford, from Italy, a lad. He knew not American customs nor any of our manners. He was merely a little immigrant boy, with all the chances against him. In due time he was enrolled among the pupils in the West Stamford School.... Principal Sipsco Stevens became interested in him, and to the principal's formative influences the little Italian boy nobly responded.... French American Institute at Springfield, medical school in Baltimore. He returned to Stamford. To the credit of the Stamford medical fraternity, the physicians gave the young doctor their sympathy and any advice he needed. Patients had confidence in him, and in increasing numbers applied to him for aid. As a young doctor, he had achieved

---

[47] Stamford Advocate 3/25/1938, 3/11/1944, 8/7/1957.
[50] Stamford Medical Society Board Minutes, Stamford Historiy Center, collection number RG-17, Sept 30 1902-Jan14, 1918 p. 99, 101, 103; Feb 12, 1918 – Jan 8, 1935 p 49, 83, 84, 125, 128, 141, 180, 181, 183, 192; Feb 7, 1935-April 4, 1939 p 81, 85; May 1939-Feb 9, 1954 p 1, 7; see also: Stamford advocate 1/11/1924, 6/27/1925, 7/19/1926.

the beginning of his ambition-was a success-and was happy. Weighted down with great handicaps at the start, he might have been satisfied to become a mere laborer; but, because he was truly heroic, he lifted himself out of his poor environment and walked up a highway, which only the brave can tread. Not the least formative influence in determining the boy's future manhood, was that imparted by his faithful, patient Bible-school teacher, Miss Ella Davis, who became his friend when he was twelve years of age. This consecrated teacher watched over the Italian lad, thoroughly taught him not only our American ways and manners, but also our sturdy Christian faith."

Joseph DeMino was in the Stamford High School graduating class of 1913; among the few Italian Americans who graduated from high school in the early 1900s. He was a star tackle on the football team and participated in theater. As a high school student, he worked with younger boys by taking lead in running the Stamford Boys' Club. Joseph went on to study medicine. He was one of fourteen children born to Leonardo and Lena DeMino who lived at 65 Canal Street. Leonardo was a butcher with a shop on Canal St. DeMino went on to study medicine in Washington D.C. and after becoming a doctor relocated there.[52]

The 1935 Stamford directory lists Paul Buccheri as a podiatrist at 366 Atlantic St. Michael L. Sabia was a podiatrist, graduating from the First Institute of Podiatry (Long Island University) in New York in 1936. He was also a member of Stamford's Board of Education and Taxation. He was born in Stamford on August 8, 1914.[53] He was the son of Vito and Angela Maria Romano Sabia, and married Marie Annita Salvatore. Ambrose P. Vezina is listed in the 1935 Stamford directory under physician exchange.

Alberico Parrella was an Italian teacher and lived at 179 West Broad St. He was born in San Leucio in Benevento, Italy on April 21, 1898, to Ignazio and Carmella Parrella. He got a teaching degree in 1926. He operated the Alberico Parrella Insurance and Real Estate Agency at 270 Pacific St. He was a member of the Loyal Order of Moose, the Italian Center, and the Connecticut Realtor Board. He served in WWI and received the Croix de Guerre and other medals. His three daughters, Irma, Theresa, and Mary Carmela died in 1966 after battling half their lives against muscular dystrophy. Irma was head of the Histology Department of Stamford Hospital while immobilized by the disease. A research fellowship was established in their names by the Muscular

---

[52] Stamford Advocate 5/11/1907, 10/23/1911, 5/27/1913, 9/16/1913, 10/16/1941, 12/8/1906.
[53] Stamford Advocate 6/11/1936, 6/4/1982, 12/21/1983.

Dystrophy Association of America.[54] James F. Stramaglia and Vuono Realty Co. are listed under real estate in the 1935 Stamford directory.

Pasquale Chiapetta was born on October 16, 1887 in Rose, Italy. At 16, he immigrated to Stamford in November 1903 joining his father who was already there. He worked in a shirt factory for 15 years. In 1918 opening his own factory. He began Lindy Dress Mfg. Co. being the first Italian to break the foreign monopoly of woman's clothing manufacturing in Stamford, with his factory making women's blouses. He was president of Chiapetta's Inc. (formed in 1947) and a director of the Greater Blouse Association of New York. He was an honorary member of the Italian Center's Board of Directors. He lived at 47 Clinton Ave. Pasquale was one of the first to start Sons of Italy in Stamford. He filed for bankruptcy in 1938.[55]

Peter Anthony Rosa was born in Avigliano, Italy, on January 12, 1891, to Dominic and Margaret Rosa. He was orphaned at 16 and immigrated to America in 1907. He began as an apprentice cutter, with his future father-in-law Pasquale Chiapetta. With Chiappetta, he opened a blouse factory at 336 and 338 West Main Street. This was the first such factory founded by Italians in Stamford, employing sixty workers, with a daily production of fifty dozen. Peter was a former member of the Republican Town Committee and president of the Italian Center Board of Governors for six years, president of the Federation of Aviglianese Society, and active in the Community Chest (now United Way) work. On August 23, 1933, he was honored by the Italian government with the title Cavalier to the Crown of Italy for his work among the Italian people of Stamford. He was president of the Stamford Waist Co. He died on October 15, 1943.[56]

Tommaso Tella came to Stamford in 1909 and was a head cutter in women's apparel factories, and for a brief time opened his own factory. He was very active in fraternal organizations, such as the Italian Institute (of which he was vice president) and the Sons of Italy.[57]

Anna (Antonia) Macari Tamburri moved from New York City to Stamford to open her apparel company. Based on family lore (relayed by Theresa Conetta Cucco), Anna moved to escape threats from the mafia against her business and lived on 22 Fairfield Ave. Seeking a place to relocate she boarded the train from New York City and exited at Greenwich, Ct. There she inquired about available property and the person she met suggested that she would get a better price in Stamford. This is how she eventually made her way to the city.

---

[54] Stamford Advocate 2/12/1924, 6/30/1967, 5/19/1969; *Il Progresso degl'Italiani nel Connecticut.*
[55] Stamford Advocate 6/24/1960, 4/21/1947, 12/6/1938; *Il Progresso degl'Italiani nel Connecticut.*
[56] Stamford Advocate 10/16/1943; *Il Progresso degl'Italiani nel Connecticut.*
[57] *Il Progresso degl'Italiani nel Connecticut.*

Anna married Michele Tamburri and had four children Julia, Julian, Michael Ubaldo, and Francis (Filomena). She opened her first shop in Stamford in 1923 remarkably at the age of 19, with Mrs. Mary Macari Fabrizio (her sister). Her other sister Theresa Macari Chiriani was "floor lady" at the shop. The Anna Costume Company filed its certificate of incorporation in Connecticut in December of 1927. The incorporators were Anna Tamburri, Mary Fabrize (Fabrizio), and Julia Tamburri. She later owned the Flora Dress Company. Anna employed hundreds of women immigrants from Settefrati in her factories. Jerry Pia, a tailor, also worked at the factory, as did her brother-in-law Daniel Chiriani, also a tailor. Anna was very successful in business and was not impacted significantly by the Depression. She purchased two homes next to the factory with her earnings, for her children.[58]

There was a Macari Dress Shop on 487 Atlantic St. in 1934 with union employees.[59] The 1925 Stamford directory lists Frances Engenito (33 Stephen St.) and Angelina Tozzola (49 Hazel St.) as dressmakers, and E Anna Laureno as a milner at 469 Atlantic St. Mrs. L. T. Rustici had a baby apparel and art goods shop located at the Strand Arcade in the 1920s.[60] The 1935 directory includes Madelyn Robustelli at 117 Myrtle Ave. as a dressmaker, Germaine Rustici as a knit goods salesperson on Long Ridge Rd. and LaMode Millinery at 5 Bank St.

Joseph Santarsiero born in 1900 in Avigliano, came to America at 10 in 1910. He began Stamford Service Stations, Inc. in 1924, on the intuition that there would be great demand for such companies in the future, and by 1929 had 9 service stations (State St. and Guernsey, 235 Greenwich Ave., 53 Myrtle Ave., 53 West Main. St., Canal and Pacific St., Luther St. Sound Beach Ave., Mianus, and Hope St., and Camp Ave.). He was also made a special policeman in 1931. Joseph was involved with City Loan Association of Stamford, which had officers as follows in 1932: Michael A, Genovese, president; Joseph Santarsiero, vice president; Antonio Sabia, treasurer; Isabella D. Genovese, secretary. Ralph Cerreta was part owner of the Federal Filling station on Federal Street.[61]

In the 1925 Stamford directory the following are listed as garages: Nicola D'Aquilla (WW I veteran) at 94 Avery St., and Antonio DeMarco at Wardwell. In 1927, Rosino Socci who operated The Village Garage and Service Station at Forest Street and Locust Ave. became an agent for Chandle automobiles. In 1928, Rosino signed up as a dealer with General Motors Corp.'s

---

[58] Stamford Advocte 10/12/1949, 12/3/1927; Vitti (26,70).
[59] Stamford Advocate 6/8/193.
[60] Stamford Advocate 3/6/1924.
[61] Stamford Advocate 10/31/1925, 1/8/1931, 3/18/1931, 2/1/1932, 3/20/1926.

Pontiac and Oakland automobiles.[62] The 1935 directory lists the following Gas Service Stations: Ralph Altomare, 480 W Main St., Angelo's Gas Station, High Rd and Cedar Heights, Ralph Lupinacci, 211 Stillwater Ave., John Mazzola, Long Ridge Rd., Dominick Pinto, 76 Camp Ave., and Bonfiglio Preli, Long Ridge Rd. The 1935 directory lists Joseph Gardella, auto rental at 6 Sheridan, Anthony Claps at 433 W. Main, Frank Muzzio, 847 Main as auto repair shops, and Alexander D'Andrea, auto wreckers at 6 Dryden. The directory also lists the following notaries: Andrea Cappabianco, at two Greenwich Ave., Joseph Leone (who is also listed under real estate), at 109 Atlantic St., Anniello Palomba at 1 Main Harold Bossa, 293 Main St., Zanetto Cappabianca, 6 Greenwich Ave., Alonzo Maffucci, 29 Main St., Vito Pittaro, 125 Washington Ave., and Charles Sessa, 115 Atlantic St. Also listed in the directory is Vincent Caruso, photographer, at 249 Main St. Italo A. Marchetti was a repairman at 332 Oak St.[63] The 1935 Stamford directory lists Pasquale Bongo, 270 Atlantic St., and Vincent Caruso, 135 Main St., as photographers.

Leonardo Santarsiero was assistant superintendent of Prudential Life Insurance Company, the only Italian at that time in Stamford to reach that level. He emigrated at 17, from Avigliano, Italy and moved to Stamford in 1923. He was a barber for three years.

Antonio D. Sabia born in Stamford in 1894 to Vito and Angela Maria Romano Sabia. He was active in many civic and fraternal organizations. In 1921, he founded the Genovese Supply Company, one of the most widely known building supply companies in the area, with Rocco Genovese. He was the treasurer of the Genovese Block Co. and the Peoples Oil Co. and was a founder of the Builders Supply Credit Association. Mr. Sabia was treasurer of the City Loan Association (formerly Loan Aviglianese). He was a member of the board of directors of the J.M. Wright Technical School. Antonio served in World War I. He was an honorary life member of the St. Augustine Council No. 41 of the Knights of Columbus and was a holder of the fourth degree.

The Italians excelled in the construction industry almost from the outset of their immigration to Stamford. Rocco Savino Genovese born in 1877 in Avigliano, came to the U.S. with his parents, brothers, and sisters at the age of nine (1886) and settled on the west side of Stamford. According to legend the forefathers in Italy owned a desirable piece of land that bandits demanded and when refused, burned the home and the elder Genovese perished. The rest of the family scattered and settled elsewhere. Rocco's family moved to the U.S. He married Rosa Maria Labella (the first president of the Rosary

---

[62] Stamford Advocate 5/7/1927, 4/12/1928.
[63] Stamford Advocate 12/22/1934.

Society at Sacred Heart Church) in Stamford in 1899. Rosa Maria's father had a small woodworking shop. Rocco and his brothers Michael and Antonio started a construction company (Genovese Brothers). They built the Richmond Hill Bridge in Stamford. In 1923 they formed the Genovese Coal Yard on Davenport Street. They also established the Genovese Coal and Mason's Material Company. The company supplied coal, coke, wood, gasoline, range and fuel oils, mason's materials, concrete and glass blocks and ready mixed cement. In 1941, the officers were Rocco Genovese, president; Antonio D. Sabia vice president/treasurer; and Nicola A. Caruso, secretary. Over the years as it grew, it became known as the Genovese Supply Co. They built a cement block company and bought an oil company (Peoples). The companies later became known as Genovese Industries. In 1996 the company was sold to O&G Industries.[64]

Frank Palmer was born on July 16, 1876, in San Fili, Italy and moved to Stamford in 1909. He and his wife Margherita had ten kids. He was a construction contractor who was awarded many city contracts for sewers, sidewalks, and roadwork. In fact, many of the roads and buildings (pre-urban renewal) were built by him. He also worked on improving the Mill Pond Park. No embellishments were involved, just tearing down the old damn and rebuilding a new one and retaining walls on each side of the river.[65]

There is a street in Stamford, called Cerretta St. The street is named after a Vincenzo Cerreta (spelled with one t), who was a stonemason from Calitri, Italy. He built homes on the street during the period of 1915 through 1926. He was listed in the 1897 Stamford directory as "stoneman." He had eleven children, whom one by one he brought to America. Catello Cacace, Ralph Cappellieri, Luigi Draghi (a farmer), Michael Genovese, Alexander Melfi, and Gayton Poppalardo are listed as contractors in the 1925 Stamford directory. John Ucciferri was a painter and decorator. Peter J. Vescio is also listed as a farmer (Toglia 2007, 299).[66]

Emil Albert (Recchia) Rich was a founder, director and senior vice president of the F. D. Rich Company. Mr. Rich directed operations on major construction projects nationwide and helped lead the company from a small local contracting firm to one of the largest development and construction companies in Connecticut, and one of the largest in the country. He became a recognized leader in defense department construction. Notable military

---

[64] Notes by Rosemarie (Marrucco) Blosio, as told by "Aunt Jennie Genovese Mancusi and "Aunt Missie: Geneovese Sementini.
[65] Stamford Advocate 3/28/1911, 4/8/1911, 6/27/1911, 7/14/1911, 1/25/1912, 1/16/1913, 5/14/1914, 8/29/1916, 6/10/1922.
[66] Stamford Advocate 2/20/1907, 9/9/1915.

projects included the construction of the prototype double cantilever hanger for bomber-type aircraft, a secret weapons storage facility for the Air Force, and he built the complex for the forerunner to NASA. He was also known for medical facility construction worldwide and built hospital facilities in Stamford.

Frank D. (Recchia) Rich was Emil's brother and cofounder of the construction company that bore his name. Rich was born in Casalveiri, Italy on August 23, 1894. He came to the U.S. in 1903, through Boston to Stamford, where his father came to work on the railroad for ten cents an hour. The rest of the family came over one by one, settling on Liberty St. He worked as a mason. At 23, he enlisted and served as American Expeditionary Forces from July 8, 1918 to July 10th, 1919. Frank D. was a veteran of WWI, a corporal in the 155 Company Transportation Corp. The F. D. Rich Company started in 1920, when a contractor he was working for asked him to take on a job that he, the contractor, could not handle. The first job was a fireplace. From there he and his brothers, stonemasons started building walls, fireplaces, and foundations. They built the general contracting business by taking on a range of local projects in the 1930s and 1940s. Rich Sr. recalled getting up every morning very early, packing his mason's tools and walked from his home on Stillwater to wherever they were working because they couldn't afford a horse and wagon. This included a job on Cedar Heights Road (i.e. four miles each way on top of a full day's worth of manual labor). He was in demand to do special jobs, because he was good at "five-point stone cutting" where a stone is chosen from a pile and then cut to fit with others. Eventually, the company got into real estate development as well and became one of the largest construction companies on the Eastern seaboard and reshaped the city of Stamford.[67]

Frank Mercedes (Construction Contractor) was born April 3, 1902, in Gravina di Puglia, the son of Nicholas and Theresa Mercede. He was second oldest in a family of 11 children. When yet a boy, having barely finished the 4th grade, he gave up school to follow his father on his construction jobs, thus making himself very useful by contributing with his labors to the many needs of his large family. At 18 years old, he landed in New York on December 24th, Christmas Eve. Unfortunately, upon his arrival he felt lonely in a strange land. On a solitary Christmas, away from his family, he was not even a free man in the great land of opportunity, because for a while he was quarantined and eventually sent to Ellis Island, which was known at that time of as the "Island of Tears." When he was finally released from Ellis Island, he was put on a train that was to take him to Stamford, Connecticut, to join his

---

[67] Stamford Advocate 11/21/1999, 5/19/1999, 11/18/1990, 11/17/1990, 11/11/1990.

uncle's family. He felt lost, and even more so when he arrived at the railroad station to find no one waiting for him. He didn't know how to get to his relative's residence. After many attempts at finding worthwhile work, he moved to New York for a brief time. He returned to Stamford, and in 1926, a building company from Greenwich sublet small contracts to him. Thus the Mercede Construction Company was born. It would later become one of the largest building contractors in Fairfield County. The buildings they constructed in Stamford include: The Harry Bennett branch of the Ferguson Library, the Church of the Archangels, New Hope Towers, The Advocate Building, Stillmeadow and Davenport Ridge schools, and the Edgehill Senior Assisted Living Complex (Mercede).

Henry Vacca is listed as a mason contractor at 54 West Avenue in the 1930s. He signed onto the President's reemployment Program in 1933. In response to the Depression, the President's Reemployment Agreement (PRA) of 1933 directed firms to reduce workweeks so existing jobs could be spread into additional employment opportunities. The Depression was hard on Mr. Vacca, who filed for bankruptcy in 1936, showing assets of $1, and claims of $2,307.38. He would later go on to continue his career with the Merchant Marines as a Lieutenant Commander. He was born in Settefrati in 1893 and was a resident of Stamford for seventy years.[69] The 1935 Stamford directory lists the following masons: Frank Caccavello, 88 Camp Ave., Enrico D'Aprile, 86 Avery, Michael DeAngelis, 39 Highview Ave. John A Ferro, Inc., 26 Chapel St., and Lovallo Bros., 101 Stillwater Ave. The same directory lists Rosario Curto of 96 Myano Lane as a quarry owner.

In 1936, DeLuca Construction was founded by Patrick A. DeLuca who was also the Chairman of the Italian Center campaign in 1940. The company built the Willard School on Vine Road, and the First Presbyterian Church ("fish church"). DeLuca started out as a timekeeper in construction firms in New York, learning the business from the ground up. He came to Stamford in 1927 and started his own business in 1936. He served in WW I.[70] J. Corbo was a well digging contractor in 1894. He later became bar owner (Joseph Corbo's Hall on Stillwater Avenue). In 1906, Joseph worked to get Anthony Geronimo elected.[71]

John Rotante (250 Pacific St., 41 Cottage St.) was a mason contractor. The Passaro Brothers were plumbers and locksmiths with a business at 433 Main Street. Angelo Arcade was a carpenter on 203 Pacific St. Joseph Valen-

---

[69] Stamford Advocate 11/2/1936, 8/15/1933, 10/4/1943, 12/4/1969.
[70] Stamford Advocate 12/31/1938, 3/22/1940, 1/22/1972.
[71] Stamford Advocate 9/10/1894, 11/2/1906.

tino was a carpenter at 26 Chapel St. Ralph Treglia was in the trucking business.[72] The 1935 directory lists the following trucking businesses: Alexander Benevelli, Travis Ave., Benjamin Brondo, 380 Elm St., Alexander Coletto, 74 Palmer Ave., Dominick Danna, 40 St. John's Pl., Rocco DeCarlo, 673 Elm St., August P. Foligno, 35 East Ave., Peter Gallo, Newfield, Charles Gerbasi, 19 Oak Hill, John Gerbasi, 328 Atlatnic St., Gaspero A. Girardi, 211 Fairfield Ave., Joseph Iacovo, 57 Hubbard Ave., Dominick Ienner, 48 Stillwater Ave., Francis Liberatore, Francis Ave., Pasquale Ofiero, 72 Dean St., John L. Orrico, Roosevelt Ave., Michael F. Perna, Orlando, Anthony Roda, 82 Camp Ave., John Sacco, 117 Clinton Ave., Thomas Stefano, 21 Mannin, Ralph Treglia, 38 Wilson St., and Antonio Tufaro, 49 Wardwll. The 1935 Stamford directory lists the following contractors: Nicola Cognetta, 17 Greenwood Hill, Anthony P. Coviello, 23 Shelburne Rd., Genovese & Rich Inc., 270 Atlantic St., Joseph Lionetti, 94 Noble St., Charles Lupinacci, 182 Stillwater Ave., Massare & Ferrara, 41 Aberdeen St. Carlo Mesotti, 109 Atlantic St. Carmine Montanaro, 252 West Ave., George Muldello, 13 Chapel St., Peter Muti, 131 W Broad St. Angelo A. Preli, Webbs Hill Rd. and Chestnut Hill Rd., Vito Stolfi, 145 Selleck St., Nunziato Tamburri, 70 Revonah Ave., Henry Vacca, 54 West Ave., Salvatore Vavala, 116 Virgil St., Angelo Arcade, (carpenter) 262 Pacific St., and Domenico Ioli, (carpenter) 125 West Ave. Gaetano Iovino, 4 Cardinal Pl. is listed as a floor surfacing contractor.

Amedee A, Arduino an electrical contractor at 20 Winthrop St. (along with P.W. Arduino) were awarded a patent in 1906 for a electric lamplighter. Amadee was also active in the Red Cross authoring an article in Italian and English in the Stamford Advocate in 1918 requesting that citizens contribute to the Red Cross during World War I.[73] The 1935 Stamford directory lists the following as electrical contractors: Pasquale Russo, 841 Hope St., Canio M. Sanseverino, 290 W Main St., and Samuel Terenzio, 2 Railroad Ave. The same directory lists the following plumbers: Domenico Agostino, 798 Atlantic St., Louis Caporizzo, 183 Fairfield Ave., Philip Pelazza, Long Ridge Rd., Salvatore Rosa, 146 Fairfield Ave., and Charles Trantanella, 39 Beal, 316 South St.

Luigi Persiani was born in Catignano, Italy in 1890 and lived at 176 Shippan Ave. Mr. Persiani was a veteran of World War I in the U.S. Army, a member of the American Legion, the Italian Center, Elks, Eagles and past president of the Quarter Century Club. He owned Luigi's by the Sea Restaurant at 75 Shippan Ave. and was an officer of the Southwestern Full Permit Restaurant Association of Connecticut. In 1932, he was fined $300 and

---

[72] Stamford Advocate 10/22/1924, 7/29/1911, 1/9/1902, 6/7/1920, 12/13/1937.
[73] Stamford Advocate 8/30/1919, 5/23/1918, 1/25/1906.

served 60 days in jail for the operation of a speakeasy (during prohibition) and was arrested again in 1948 for violation of state liquor laws.[74]

Luigi Serafino was born in Isernia, Italy on June 27, 1889, and lived at 34 Fairfield Ave. He was in real estate. He was a director of the Italian Institute (the Italian Center). He was also president of the Society Campenella, and a supreme delegate of the Sons of Italy. He was active in Republican politics.[75]

Joseph Gerli was born in Milan Italy and was known as "Uncle Joe". In 1894, he came to the U.S. as part of his brother's silk importing business (E Gerli and Co.), after the death of his brother in 1934 he became president of the company. He relocated to Stamford in 1912. He purchased six acres of land on Weed Ave., then adding more acreage to give to his daughters as wedding presents, until he had a section of about 30 acres. He later donated some land to the city to be used as a park (Gerli Park).[76]

Salvatore Francis Apicella Sr. was born in Maiori, Italy on December 15, 1895 to Francesco and Maria Apicella. After becoming an apprentice, he became the owner of the Arrow Upholstery Company in New York and New Jersey and later purchased the Nothnagle's Furniture store in Bridgeport. He is most famous for the brick mansion built in the late 1930s at 631 Long Ridge Road, called the "castle" because of its turrets, reported secret passageways, slate roof, and terraced gardens. The mansion was sold to developers and was slated for demolition until a neighborhood preservationist association made a plea, the developers decided to maintain some of the original building. The building had previously survived a fire and the great flood of 1955.[77]

Peter P. Vescio founded the local Italian newspaper, *La Tribuna* in 1933. He was born in Rose, Italy on October 16, 1901 to Pasquale and Angelina De Rose Vescio and lived at 26 Main Street in Stamford. He also worked to bring opera presentations to Stamford at affordable prices, including "La Traviata." He was a member of the Italian Center and Moose Lodge of Stamford, and Loggia Operaia No 159 (Sons of Italy). He worked in real estate and insurance and owned the Stamford Real Estate Company in partnership with Frank J. Terenzio. Additionally, he had a shoemaker shop and patented a process for

---

[74] Stamford Advocate 12/29/1932, 4/21/1950, 12/9/1955.
[75] Stamford Advocate 3/3/1913, 1/15/1914, 9/12/1923, 2/24/1930, 2/13/1947.
[76] Stamford Advocate Tercentenary Edition Town of Stamford, CT 1641 – 1941; Supplement of the Stamford Advocate, Saturday, June 7, 1941.
[77] Stamford Advocate 10/6/1964, 10/7/1964, 5/19/1961, 11/15/2003, 5/17/2004, 10/22/1955.

waterproofing footwear. He also participated in theatrical events at the Alahambra Theater as part of the Stamford Italian Club and at the Italian Center as part of the Paganini Santa Celia Music Club.[78]

Felix LiVolsi, born in Cerami, Sicily in 1897, was a tailor at 477 Atlantic Street. He was active in the Business and Professional Men's Club of the Italian Center and was part of the reorganization when he was director of the Italian Center in 1939. Felix was named to the All-state semi-pro football team in 1922. In 1926, he organized and participated in a semi-pro baseball team. He was also a great coach, vice president of the Twilight League and even had an annual baseball trophy named in his honor. He later became vice president and general manager of the People's Oil Co., which carried fuel oil and oil heating, air conditioning, and cooling equipment.[79]

Jerry A. Pia and Sons Tailor and Dry Cleaning started at 237 West Main Street. Born in Settefrati, Italy in 1897 to Gaetano and Teresa Vagnone Pia, was brought to America in 1898, and then returned to Italy for 12 years, where he learned the tailor trade in Rome. He began his business in Stamford in 1916 (Carlevale, 307). Michele (Michael) Lombardo was a tailor in Springdale at 1091 Hope St. He had to take out an advertisement in the Advocate in 1919, explaining he was not charged with any crime, because a Joseph Lombardo of Mulberry St. was charged with counterfeiting and people were confusing the names. This seemed to have worked because he worked until he passed away at the age of 95 in 1979. M. DeRosa was a tailor at 197 Main St. Frank Macari was a tailor and also a member of the Richmond Park Republican Club and Settefratese Social Club.[81] D'Alessando, Bros., tailors were at 342 Atlantic St. The 1935 Stamford directory lists the following tailors: Thomas Abate, 182 State St., Frank Canella, 193 Stillwater Ave., Hugo DeFrancesco, 611 Main St., Peter Delle Donna, 489 Glenbrook Rd., Michael DeRosa, 67 Summer St., Frank Dorrico, 62 South St., James Farfaglia, 466 Atlantic St., Joseph Farina, 193 Stillwater Ave., Vito Gerardi, 193 W. Main St., Antonio Giordano, 695B Pacific St., Nicola Grimaldi, 911 Main St., Luca Improta, 253 W. Main St., Angelo Lombardo, 248 Cove Rd., Michele Lombardo, 1091 Hope St., Otto & DeVita Inc., 32 Worth, Jerry Pia, 237 Main St., Gilbert Rosilla, 765 Elm, Charles C. Sabatini, 70 Summer St., Salvatore Sagnelli, 262 Hope St., and Florence Sotire, 267 Greenwich Ave. The same

---

[78] Stamford Advocate 3/28/1938, 5/20/1940, 2/23/1923, 3/11/1919, 9/18/1919, 8/30/1920, 8/30/1920, 12/2/1922, 10/11/1935.

[79] Stamford Advocate 04/19/1940, 1/16/1939, 5/26/1938, 3/9/1938, 5/11/1937.

[81] Stamford Advocate 6/18/1926, 1/10/1934, 7/14/1915, 12/8/1979, 7/12/1929, 12/27/1919, 2/11/1915, 2/5/1929, 10/9/1964.

directory lists the following tailor-merchants: D'Alessandro Bros., 148 Bedford, Thomas Sova, 487 Main St., and Zemo Bros., 82 Main St.

Stolfi's radio shop was at 217 West Main Street and later became Stolfi's appliances.[82] Vito Colucci was a coal merchant and operated the Colucci Coal and Fuel Company.[83] M. Rossi was an architect.[84] Rocco Alfredo Davino, born at Frigento, Avellino, Italy in 1881 graduated from Yale and then the New York State University of Architecture, was an architect and engineer and was the first Italian American in the state in the architecture field. Davino served in WWI. He opened an office in Stamford in 1932 (Carlevale, 121). The 1935 Stamford directory lists the following fuel dealers: Antonio Boccuzzi, Amedeo Mancini, 500 Glenbrook Rd., Jerry Petrizzi, 380 Elm St., Joseph Pustari, 140 Washington Ave., Giuseppe Scarella, 10 Burr St., and Frank Tamburino, 35 Wright Ave. The 1935 Stamford directory lists Maddaloni & Co. as an insect screen manufacturer.

Some local businesses found in advertising in the Italian newspapers (La Sentinella, La Tribuna) include the following: Generi Alimentari, Joseph De Julio, 256 Pacific St., Farmacia Colucci, corner of Cottage and Pacific Sts. Nunziato Tamburri, Builder & Contractor, 72 Revonah Ave., Rosetti & Lenoci, Jewelers at 189 Main St. Caffe Napoli, Giuseppe Esposito, 242 Pacific Street, Dr. D. A. Zaccardo, dental surgeon, 280 Atlantic St., Pittaro Civic League, 252 Pacific St., D. Martella's Commercial Real Estate Agency, Lakeside Dr., Stamford Stationary & Music Store, P. Zaffino, 157 Canal St., La Pittaro Real Estate, 125 Washington Ave., Diamond Fire Works Co, Joe Calandrelli, 132 Richmond Hill Ave., Angelo Panapada Car Sales, 880 Main St., Sabino Pellegrino Furniture, 157 Pacific St., James Rinaldi Real Estate, 454 State St., Dr. Germano 514 Main St., Gordon, Walter & Persiani, selling grapes Canal St., P. Sabini Jewelers 205 Main St., Farmacia Italiana, J. Champagne 67 Main St., The Yale, J. Paulino warehouse at the corner of Atlantic and Cottage Sts., Giuseppe Leone Bar 436 State St., Macchine Parlanti Italian Record Store 590 Main St., Borg Bros & Co Grocers Corner of Main and Greyrock.[86]

Anthony J. Penachio was the founder of the Springdale Laundry.[87] Elita Donatelli did hemstitching at 366 Atlantic St. Michael Mascia was an engineer, and was an officer of the Connecticut Society of Professional Engineers in 1935 and 1936. Mr. Mascia was also active in the Italian Institute and the

---

[82] Stamford Advocate 7/15/1940.
[83] Stamford Advocate 4/19/1984.
[84] Stamford Advocate 2/11/1913.
[86] *Bridgeport La Sentinella*, 11/16/1929, 9/13/1930, 9/20/1930, 10/26/1929, 8/9/1930, 12/7/1929, 2/8/1930; *Bridgeport La Tribuna Del Connecticut* 7/28/1906.
[87] Stamford Advocate 1/23/1982.

Boy Scout troop affiliated with that organization.[88] The 1935 Stamford directory lists Louis Bacco, 1 Atlantic St., and Francis Z. Cappabianca at 6 Greenwich Ave., as engineers.

Joseph E. Rustici, born in Settefrati in 1887, was an inventor who held a patent for the JER Food Grater invented in 1922. His obituary indicates that he worked as a supervisor at the Bliksenderfer Typewriter Company of Stamford and was instrumental in developing the rotating ball typewriter, and helped develop postage meters, the mailomat and the cigarette tax imprinting machine for Pitney-Bowes Corporation.[89]

The 1935 Stamford directory lists the following lawyers: Herbert A. DeLima, 545 Bedford St., Frank J. DiSessa, 303 Main St., Lawrence Epifanio, 322 Main St., and Charles Sessa, 115 Atlantic St.

Other businesses found in Stamford directories include: Sapelli Brothers and Hertz Engineers and Contractors, in the Gurley building, who did work in concrete, flag stone, tennis courts, rented pumps, and compress mixers; Mooraio Brothers Florists and 325-327 Atlantic St.; Esposito Funeral home and embalmer at 43 West Main St., Anthony Lacerenza funeral director at 180 West Main St., Aj Angevine Co. Inc. sold furniture and carpets at 481 Atlantic St.; Realtors Alonzo Maffucci at 29 Main St, and C.D. Tarantino at 1 Bank St., Thomas Abate, tailor at 182 State St., Joseph Abbazia, plumbing at 58 Avery St., Augustine Abronzeno, shoe repair at 351 Atlantic St., Leonard Accursi, Grocer at 159 Stillwater Ave., Peter Accusta plumber at 181 Stillwater Ave., chauffeurs Jeremiah Adiletti and Dominick Albonizio, Domenic Agostino proprietor at Luders Marine Construction at 39 Henry St., Frank Agostino, grocer at 44 Walnut St., Francesco Allevato, gardener at 202 Stillwater Ave. Rocco Ambruso, fruit vendor on Garden St., Amedeo Buongiorno, baker, painters Joseph Amente and Anthony Anastasia, Domenico Annetta, huckster, Andrew and Felix Annunziata upholsterers, John A. and Joseph U. Arancia, barbers, Antonio Bevacqua shoe repair at 71 Main St., Casimer DeMott proprietor of Post Road Wrecking Co. Used Parts at 914 East Main St., John Vitti, huckster at 231 West Ave., Shoemakers Domenico Pugliese and Ambrose Racaniello at 191 Main and 71 Gay St., and Anthony Tenaglia proprietor at New England Blacksmith & Iron Works at 254 Canal St. Charles Burriesci, William Caicca, and Louis Persiani had billiard and bowling establishments at 324 Pacific St., 315 Atlantic St. and 265 Pacific St. Joseph Christiano, Peter Colucci, James Marcetti, and Vito Racaniello had shoeshine businesses at 520 Main St., 144 Atlantic St., 461 Pacific St., and 370 Atlantic St. Maurilio D'Agostino of 75

---

[88] Stamford Advocate 2/23/1934, 1/18/1934.
[89] Stamford Advocate 1/7/1978.

Pacific St. was an undertaker in 1918.[90] The 1935 Stamford Directory includes Jerry Franchini as a dance teacher on 424 Main St. and Stanislao Esposito, 43 W. Main St., and Anthony Lacerenza, 8 Schuyler Ave., as embalmer/undertakers. The 1935 directory lists the following who rented rooms: Louise Colline, 51 Suburban Ave., Hazel Gagliardi, 578 Summer St, and Clementino Raiteri, 324 Pacific St.

Italian American merchants who sold and displayed Wrigley's chewing gum that were included in advertising in 1940 included: Leo Accurso, 159 Stillwater Ave., Rocco Ambruso, 14 Garden St., Domenick Anneta & Son, 335 W. Main St., D. Bevino, 64 Liberty St., Angelo M. Bittetto, 17 Stephen St., Ralph Boccuzzi, 153 New Spruce St., Bondi's 38 West Park Place (Bondi was the largest whole-sale fruit dealer in Stamford), Joseph Burriesci, 52 Holly Pl., Mrs. A. Capone's Grocery, 12 Court St., Caputo's Market, 137 Myrtle Ave., Cenami Pharmacy, 113 W. Main St., Joe Christiano, 518 Main St., Cianci's Grocery, 41 Dean St., Joe Colucci, 18 Alden St., Frank Conte, 23 West Ave., William Covino, 39 Victory St., J. De Francesco, 32 Shippan Ave., Mrs. M. Dellaventura, 41 Chapel St., Angelo Fucarino, 45 Liberty St., Peter Galasso, 94 Virgil St., John Gardella, 349 Atlantic St., August Gargiulo, 237 Summer St., Frank Gerardi, 247 W. Main St., E. Iovino, 212 Pacific St., Felix Iovino, 466 State St., Lombardo's Conf, 154 Stillwater Ave., The Lovallo Bros. Inc. 161 Stillwater Ave., C. Lupinacci, 211 Stillwater Ave., D. Magliero, 230 W. Main St., Ernest Mallozzi, 39 Rose Park Ave., J. Marchiano, 258 Pacific St., Giovanni Matteis, 164 Stillwater Ave., R Mazza, 386 Elm St., John Miceli, 21 Chapel St., Nick's Neighborhood Store, 165 Stillwater Ave., Frank Nobile, 229 Pacific St., F. Pocograno, 219 West Ave., Raiteri's Restaurant, 247 Main St., John Rendos, 523 S. Pacific St., A. Riggio Pastry Shop, 160 Pacific St., Joseph Santaromita, 66 Hawthorne, M. Scatamacchia, 175 W. Main St., A. F. Serrafin, 240 Fairfield Ave., Rocco Sessa, 236 W. Main St., Michele Tarantino, 121 Stillwater Ave., Tripodi & Conetta, 476 W. Main St., M. Vaccaro, 63 Spruce St., Angelo Valenzano, 32 Rose Park Ave., R. Vartuli, 160 Stillwater Ave., WM Viggiano, 32 Liberty St., and Julio Zezima, 194 W. Main St.[91]

Restaurants in the 1935 Stamford directory include: Nicholas Colucci at 267-269 Pacific St., John Coppola, 24A Cove Rd., Mary Giancola, 90 Liberty St., Rocco J. Grosso, 12 Beckley Ave., Anthony Ianazzi, 30 Worth, Vito D. Longo, 414 State St., Frank Mancuso, 135 W. Main St., Filomena Martinelli, 432 W. Main St., Napoli Restaurant, 201 Pacific St., Paradiso Restaurant, 239 Main St., Raiteri Bros, 324-326 Pacific St., Raiteri's Restaurant, 247 Main St., and Johhny Scalzi's Academy, 184 Summer St.

---

90 Stamford Advocate 1/4/1918.
91 Stamford Advocate 7/30/1940, 7/22/1907, 8/3/1914.

Final Thoughts

I have always loved the city I grew up in and have been proud of my Italian heritage just as a matter of fact. Now, after researching this rich history, and even though I have only scratched the surface of the Italian-American experience in the city, with more clarity I understand why I am so full of pride. The strength and focus of Italians today in Stamford are so easily understood when considering the life and struggles of the early Italians in Stamford documented in this history: their strength not only in terms of physical, exhibited by the hard work that many of them endured is inspiring, but so is their emotional strength. This emotional strength is demonstrated not only by the fortitude to change and adapt to a new language and culture, but also by the power to retain, pass along, and demonstrate the importance of their own culture and traditions in the face of overwhelming opposition. Also admirable is the intensity within which they live life and share as much with others. All of this became possible when they united to accomplish their goals and changed life in Stamford for the benefit of all.

The accomplishments of the anonymous majority of Italians relocating to Stamford in pursuit of their American dream — who made a difference just by working hard, prioritizing their families, and retaining their customs, while still becoming patriots of their new home — have been lasting. Thankfully, they encountered allies along their journey. For the most part, Italians were proud of their heritage but, equally, were patriots of the U.S. and considered the United States the best country in the world in spite of how difficult life was for them. Perhaps it is because of Italian culture, which is infused with an Italian concept of grace, that they had immense gratitude for all they received by moving to the United States. Certainly, it is thanks to their intellect, creativity, and joy of love and life exemplified by the Italian mantra "life is beautiful." Italians have so much to be proud of in what they have accomplished and provided to this city and its citizens.

The presence of these ancestors is visible externally everywhere you look in Stamford; in the skyline, in the parks on the baseball diamonds, football fields, and bocce courts, at downtown theaters, in the churches, on memorials to the fallen, and on statues and plaques throughout the city to name a few. Look deeper and you will see it in the foods we eat, the restaurants and other businesses we frequent, the laws and regulations that govern, the music and rituals of our town, in the homes with gardens growing Italian vegetables, grapevines, and other fruits. Most of all you will see it in the faces of a large portion of the population and feel it in their warm welcoming embrace.

Thank you to our ancestors. *Grazie di cuore*. How could we ever thank you enough? Other than doing our part, to follow your lead in continuing to assimilate in our ever-changing society, in elevating our Colony, retaining and passing on our evolving culture and heritage, maintaining unity, and endeavoring to leave a lasting positive impact for future generations.

BIBLIOGRAPHY

Arrighi, Antonio. *The Story of Antonio, the Galley Slave.* New York: Fleming H. Revell Company, 1911.

Barberio, G. Chiodi. *Il Progresso degl'Italiani nel Connecticut.* New Haven Connecticut: Maturo's Printing and Publishing, 1933.

Barone, Dennis, *Beyond Memory, Italian Protestants in Italy and America.* Albany: SUNY Press, 2016.

Blosio, Rosemarie (Marrucco), Notes provide to Kim Harke, *As Told by Aunt Jennie Genovese Mancusi and Aunt Missie-Genovese Sementini,* no date provided, available at Stamford History Center.

Bolanowski, Lawrence J. *The Golden Years never ended, the history of the Parish of St John the Evangelist Stamford, CT.* Stamford, CT: St. John's Roman Catholic Church, 2012. https://stjohnbasilica.org/parish-history. Accessed November 12, 2023.

Boyd, W. Andrew. *Boyd's Stamford and Norwalk General Directory (Directory of Fairfield County) 1881-1182.* Washington, DC: W. Andrew Boyd, 1881.

Bridgeport La Sentinella, Bridgeport, CT, (1929, October 26, November 16, and December 7), p. 4, 4 and 5, (1930, February 8, August 9, September 13, and September 20), p. 5, 5, 4 and 5,.

Carlevale, Joseph William. *Who's Who Among Americans of Italian Descent in Connecticut.* New Haven, CT: Carlevale Publishing Co. 1942.

Cicero, Frank Jr. *Relative Strangers: Italian Protestants in the Catholic World.* Chicago: Chicago Review Press, 2011.

City of Stamford, *City of Stamford tax records, 1896* available at Stamford History Center, Collection IC-75. 1896.

City of Stamford, *Stamford Town Soldier Discharge veteran records,* available at Town Hall vault. Stamford, CT various years.

City of Stamford, *Stamford's Welcome to the Soldiers and Sailors of the Great War,* City of Stamford, October 1919.

Crumpton, Emily M., *"Murder Becomes Her: Media Representations of Murderous Women in America from 1890-1920"* (2017). All Graduate Theses and Dissertations. 6634. https://scholarworks.umb.edu/masters_theses/154. Accessed November 12, 2023.

DiGiovanni, Stephen Michael, *The Catholic Church in Fairfield County 1666-1961,* New Canaan, CT: William Mulvey Inc., 1988.

Genovese, John.Kelly, *On Liberty Street: A portrait of the Genoveses of Stamford, Connecticut*, Stamford, CT, John Kelly Genovese, 1986 available at Stamford History Center.

Gesualdi, Louis, *The Arinese, an Italian American Community in Stamford, Connecticut*, New York, NY, John D. Calandra Italian Institute, 2000.

Gravinese Mutual Aid Society, *Gravinese Mutual Aid Society 75th Anniversary Booklet*, Gravinese Mutual Aid Society, 1996.

Harke, Kim, *Italian American Recollections in Stamford, Connecticut*, Old Greenwich, CT, Harke Strategic Communications, Inc., 2020.

Historic Neighborhood Preservation Program, *Historic West Main Street*, Stamford, CT Historic Neighborhood Preservation Program, Stamford, CT., 1982, available at Stamford History Center.

Janis, Mark Weston, "Connecticut 1818: From Theocracy to Toleration" 2021, *Connecticut Law Review*. 486. https://digitalcommons.lib.uconn.edu/lawreview/486, (accessed November 12, 2023).

Johnson, Paula, *A History of Christ Church*, New Haven 1853- to 1962. New Haven, Society of Christ Church Parish, 2019.

Limone, Carmine, *An American Tradition, The Italian Center/Italian Institute History*, Stamford, CT, The Italian Center, 2004.

Lobozza, Carl, *Journey Through Time*, Stamford, CT, Stamford Historical Society, 1971.

Lyon, Deaconess Josephine A., *Project Canterbury, The Chronicle of Christ Church*, New Haven CT Quinnipiack Press. No date.

MacDonald, John S., and Leatrice D. MacDonald. *"Chain Migration Ethnic Neighborhood Formation and Social Networks."* The Milbank Memorial Fund Quarterly 42, no. 1 (1964): 82–97. https://doi.org/10.2307/3348581. (accessed November 12, 2023).

Marcus, Ronald. *Stamford, Connecticut--a bibliography: an annotated, indexed compilation of books, pamphlets, special editions of newspapers, atlas, articles in periodicals, and motion picture film, containing information relating to the history of Stamford, Connecticut*. Final ed. Stamford, CT: Stamford Historical Society, 2012.

McCann, Richard Daniel, *The Trials and Triumphs of New York's Italian Catholic Immigrant Community in the Struggle for Equality*, New York, https://oldcathedral.org/historians-corner. (accessed November 12, 2023).

Mercadante, Linda A. *Italian-American Immigrants and Religious Conversions*. Pastoral Psychol 60, 551–561, 2011.

Mercede Corp., 2023, *Continuing a legacy*, GoDaddy, https://mercedecorp.com/
frank-mercede-%26-sons, accessed 11/2/2023.

Morin, David, *The Yankee Volunteer, A Virtual Archive of Civil War Likenesses collected by Dave Morin*, https://dmorinsite.wordpress.com/, accessed 11/2/2023.

Morris, Richard, *Research on First Italian Baptist Church,* Stamford, CT, Richard Morris, no date provided, available at Stamford History Center.

Office of the Adjutant General, State Armory, 1941. *Service records: Connecticut Men and women in the armed forces of the United States during World War, 1917-1920*. Vol. 3 Hartford, CT, 1941.

Piccoli, Giuseppe, *Italian Immigration in the United States* (Master's thesis, Duquesne University), 2014 https://dsc.duq.edu/etd/1044, (accessed November 12, 2023).

Puleo, Stephen*, "From Italy to Boston's North End: Italian Immigration and Settlement, 1890-1910"* 1994, Graduate Masters Theses. Paper 154. https://scholarworks.umb.edu/masters_theses/154, accessed November 12, 2023.

Rich, Frank D. Jr. *Recollections, Reflections, with assorted Chronicles of Small Beer*, Deerfield Beach, FL, Biography For Everyone, 2007.

Rich, Lance, *Magic in Bloom: From Seed to Stage*, Youtube presentation by magician Lance Rich https://youtu.be/6ta_BIBGIy4, accessed November 12, 2023.

Rinaldi, Mary Lou, *The Italian American Experience, The History of the Founding of Sacred Heart Church*, Stamford, CT, UNICO, Stamford Chapter. no date provided, available at Stamford History Center

Sacco/Mercede Families, *Eating Italian with the Sacco & Mercedes Families,* Philadelphia, Goodway Printing, 2008.

Sacred Heart Parish *Sacred Heart Church, Stamford, CT Golden Jubilee 1923-1973*, Stamford, CT, 1973, https://www.stamfordsacredheart.org/wp-content/uploads/2019/12/Sacred-Heart-Golden-Jubilee_reduced.pdf (accessed November 12, 2023).

Sidore, Timothy, *International Students at Dickinson College Snapshots II profiles*, https://chronicles.dickinson.edu/studentwork/engage/foreignstudents/snaps2.htm, accessed 11/2/2023.

St. John Presbyterian Institutional Church, *Building a Better Community, St. John Presbyterian Institutional Church*, Chicago, St. John Presbyterian Institutional Church, no date provided.

St. John Presbyterian Institutional Church, City, Country, Family, Church, *A Story of St. John Presbyterian Institutional Church*, Chicago, St. John Presbyterian Institutional Church, 1936.

Stamford Advocate, *Stamford Advocate Tercentenary Edition Town of Stamford, CT 1641 – 1941 Supplement of the Stamford Advocate* , Saturday, 1941.

Stamford Information Directories, New Haven, The Price and Lee Company, various years, available at Stamford History Center.

Stamford Old Timer's Association, *Stamford Old Timer's Annual Dinner Programs*, Available at Stamford History Center. Various years.

Stave, Bruce M., Sutherland, John F. and Alerno, Aldo *From the Old Country, An Oral History of European Migration to America*, Univ Pr of New England; First Edition, 1999.

The Italian Institute Inc. Silver Anniversary Committee, *Twenty-Five Years of Progress 1910-1935*, Stamford, CT., The Italian Institute Inc. 1935.

Tamburri, C. (1907, October 19), p. 4, (1907, November 2), p. 4, (1907, July 13), p. 4, (1906, September 15), p. 2, (1906, July 28), p. 3, Bridgeport, CT., Bridgeport La Tribuna Del Connecticut.

Toglia, Mario, *Celebrating The Heritage*, Bloomington, IN., Xlibris, 2015.

Toglia, Mario, Josephine Galgano *"Preserving Our History,"* Bloomington, IN., Xlibris, 2013.

Toglia, Mario, *They Came By Ship: The Stories of the Calitrani Immigrants in America*, Bloomington, IN., Xlibris, 2007.

U.S. Census Bureau, *Connecticut Occupation Statistics 1900*, https://www2.census.gov/library/publications/decennial/1900/occupations/occupations-part-10.pdf, (accessed November 12, 2023).

U.S. Census Bureau, *Connecticut Occupation Statistics 1900*, https://www2.census.gov/library/publications/decennial/1900/occupations/occupations-part-8.pdf, (accessed November 12, 2023).

U.S. Census Bureau, *Connecticut Occupation Statistics 1930*, https://www2.census.gov/library/publications/decennial/1930/population-volume-4/41129482v4ch03.pdf, (accessed November 12, 2023).

U.S. Census Bureau, *United States Census*, various years, FamilySearch. https://familysearch.org: 2023, (accessed November 12, 2023).

U.S. Citizenship and Immigration Services (USCIS), *Connecticut US Naturalization Records*, various years, FamilySearch. https:// familysearch.org: 2023.

Vitti, Mario, *Una Nuova E Piu Grande Settefrati Sul Suolo D'America*. New Fairfield, CT: Casa Lago Press, 2023.

Woolf, Chris, "A brief history of America's hostility to a previous generation of Mediterranean migrants—Italians" 2015, https://theworld.org/stories/2015-11-26/brief-history-america-s-hostility-previous-generation-mediterranean-migrants. (accessed November 12, 2023)

Appendix A

Towns from which Stamford Italian Americans immigrated
(Not intended to be a complete list)

Alessandria	Itri
Avellino	Picinisco
Avigliano	Roccasecca
Arena	Genoa
Bari	Genzano
Battapaglia	Gravina
Borrunio	Martone
Bovino	Minturno
Calitri	Naples
Capriata D'orba	Palermo
Casalvieri	Rose
Cerami	Roseto Valfortore
Cosenza	Salerno
Dasa	San Fele
Faeto	San Mango
Foggia	Settefrati
Genzano	Torino
Isernia	

APPENDIX B

ST. JOHN'S CEMETERY
WALKING TOUR

288

Family, respect, and honor are extremely important to Italians and Italian Americans, not only for the living but for the dead as well. In addition to praying for the deceased, Italians visit and take care of their graves and share stories with younger generations so that our heritage can be passed on. In that vein, this walking tour is intended to assist in passing along Stamford Italian heritage. Some of the Italians described in this history have been included in the tour (also included are some non-Italian famous Stamfordites). As you take the tour, please do look around and discover other Italians who have contributed to Stamford and not mentioned here, as they deserve acknowledgement and thanks as well.

Entering through the second entrance of St. John's Cemetery in Darien off Hoyt Street, in Section 14 (see map) you find three graves:

A. Andy Robustelli, Hall of Fame Professional Football Player. For fourteen seasons (1951 to 1964), he played at the defensive end position in the National Football League with the Los Angeles Rams and New York Giants. Section 14 lot 8W Gr 10. There is only a marker, not a headstone. (Adjacent graves are Galasso, D'Aquila, Dedda, Iovino).

B. From the road look for Mazza grave, next to this is Fred Dugan, Professional Football Player. For six seasons (1958 to 1963), he played at the offensive end/tight end positions in the National Football League with the San Francisco 49ers, Dallas Cowboys and Washington Redskins. Section 14 Lot 267, Gr 1 (Not Italian but famous Stamfordite).

C. Two rows back, on other side of section you will find Luigi Donatelli (Early Leader, brother of Lelio, involved with Italian Republican Club) Section 14, Lot 755 Gr 3.

Moving to Section 10, across from the Mausoleum Building, you find:

D. Vito Sabia, involved with Aviglianese Political Club, and Italian Institute. Section 10, Lot 656 ½ Gr. 3.

Next to Section 6, to the left of the Ferro Mausoleum, you find:

E. John and Rosalind Geronimo (First Italian-American family that remained and planted roots in Stamford, parents of Anthony Geronimo, politician) Section 6, Lot 737 1/2 Gr C&D.

Next to Section 8 you find:

    I.   Crescenzio Tamburri Section 8 – "Secretary General" of Stamford, early leader active in many Italian-American Organizations.

At Section 12 you will find:

    J.   Mary and Charles Vuono, of Vuona Construction (one of first construction companies) and Palace Theater female owner.

Next, exiting the cemetery at Hoyt Street, taking a left on Camp Avenue, enter cemetery. In the first row on the left, you find:

    F.   Dr. Anthony Sorgi (Early leader, signed petition for Charles Pasquale Esposito, involved with Italian organizations) Block Row 1, Lot 17, Gr 2.

Further in on left in Block 23 you find:

    G.   Gerardo Metallo Stamford actor and magician, involved with early educational circle organizations. Block 23, Lot 12 Gr 2.

Across at Block 50 through 55 you will find:

    H.   Giovanni Sacco one of the founders of Società Gravinese Mutuo Soccorso.

You can also find the following at the cemetery:

Zone Z:

Mike Sandlock PLOT Zone Z, Lot 20, Grave 1 Major League Baseball Player. For five seasons (1942, 1944 to 1946, and 1953), he played at the catcher, shortstop, and third baseman positions with the Boston Braves, Brooklyn Dodgers, and Pittsburgh Pirates.

Homer Lee Wise World War II Medal of Honor Recipient Zone Z, Row 7, Lot 9 Gr 1

Section 6: Alex Raymond Cartoonist. Section 6 Lot 179 F H Gr 1.

Appendix C

Typical Foods of Towns

Food has always been a major component of the Italian American experience. The diversity of Italians is evident also in the foods from the various regions. It is not intended to be a complete list.

Avellino – Noicole, and castagne (philbert nuts and chestnuts), spaghetti with black truffle, Fiano di Avellino, Aglianico, Greco di Tufo and Taurasi wines, 'capocollo', 'soppressata', bacon and the 'fiocco di prosciutto', Pecorino Carmasciano, Pecorino Bagnolese, Ricotta Laticauda, torrone.

Bari – Orecchiette alle cime di rapa (little ear shaped pasta with turnip tops)

Faeto – Prosciutto, bread, and cheese. The bread is baked in a wood-fired oven, giving it a unique flavor and texture. Faeto is also known for its cheese, particularly the local pecorino cheese. Made from sheep's milk, the cheese has a rich, tangy flavor.

Gravina – Orecchiette with broccoli rabe and sausage, Cavatelli with red sauce, pasta fagioli, "orucule" pizza dough pastry with raisins, onions, pignoli nuts, and black olives, anisette cookies, and pignoli cookies.

Isernia – crjoli (pasta alla chitarra), cavatelli with tomato and pork, the laganelle with beans (a sort of lasagna), roasted turcinelli, a recipe based on very elaborate lamb interiors, sausage and sopressata, mozzarella and scamorze Molisana, stracciata, burrino and pecorino. Cannellini beans and onions ("cipolla di San Pietro"). Typical desserts are the calzoni stuffed with chocolate, chickpeas, cinnamon, pine nuts and honey, i pepatelli (with almonds), and caggiunitti (donuts filled with chestnuts). Biferno and Pentro wine, poncho and limoncello liqueurs

Itri – Pasta e Fagioli (pasta with beans), Polenta with Sausage Ragu, Risotto with Porcini Mushrooms, Linguine with Asparagus, grilled, roasted or sauteed wild game (such as wild boar, jackrabbit, pheasant, quails, and other local wild birds), and the delicious Marzolino cheese.

Marcianise – fried frogs and eels, pettole and beans and then sea cuoppo, panini, sausage, and broccoli.

Minturno – Ricotta cheese and sheep, buffalo mozzarella, Saute, tripe, sausage, zucchini flowers stuffed Artichokes, fried artichokes, soup Cicerchie, Chicory with Beans, Broccoli and Sparnocchie Saffron, beans and octopus, Polenta with Telline, arrecanate Anchovies, Anchovies fried, razor clams au gratin and Telline to scottadito Pumpkin and Shrimp dumplings Scialatielli Broccoli and Chickpeas and Sausage with potatoes Tracchie Oranges and Persimmons with Vanilla Struffoli.

Potenza – Lucania's Sausage, Ciambotta (vegetable stew), Piatto d'Erbe alla Lucana, cotechinata, fried pork, peperonata with pork or sanguinaccio, orecchiette, cavatelli, strozzapreti, strascinate or fusilli, pecorino burrata, provola, manteca and cacioricotta.

Rose – Baccala made with tomato sauce topped with breadcrumbs and anchovies (pasta nudriga), "pitulipre" like zeppoli, dough made with potatoes and anchovies and fired, 'nbiliu, pin-wheel pastry with raisins, nuts, honey. Cruspilla, scalige.

San Mango – Fig of San Mango, Red Chestnut of San Mango, Caciocavallo, Taurasi Wine. Pastiere (made with eggs, macaroni, and ricotta), Taralli.

Settefrati – Sagne e fagioli, Polenta con salsice, Pane a molle, gnocchi, roasted lamb, salume (prosutto, salami, etc.), trippa, tartuffo.

Turin – Grissini (Breadsticks), pasta include tajarin and agnolotti, Carnaroli, Baldo and Arborio rice, Brasato al Barolo, carne cruda all'albese, cheeses, Robiola, Castelmagno, Raschera and the Piedmontese variety of ricotta known as seirass.

Appendix D

PATRON SAINTS OF TOWNS

Every town in Italy has a patron saint. The practice of adoration of saints is important in Italian culture to this day and is particular to the Italian manner in observing Catholicism. This practice led to bias against Italians by other peoples of faith. Passing on this aspect of Italian heritage to future generations is important. Here is a list of some of the patron saints of towns from which Stamford Italians immigrated.

Arena – Santo Michele, Madonna Della Grazie, and Santo Rocco.

Avellino - St. Modestinus. Modestinus and his assistants, were successful in their preaching, converting and baptizing many in Itlay, including the Avellino area. They were arrested, imprisoned and tried by an envoy of the Emperor Maxentius and taken to the place called the "Praetorium" where they suffered Martyrdom wrapped in red-hot robes and burned to death.

Avigliano – Saint Vitus (Vito), according to legend, died during the Diocletianic Persecution in AD 303.

Bari - Saint Nicholas's legendary habit of secret gift-giving gave rise to the traditional model of Santa Claus.

Calitri – Saint Canius refused in the presence of the prefect Pigrasius to worship idols and to acknowledge the divinity of the Emperor. He was thereupon put to torture and then imprisoned, on the assumption that hunger and his injuries would erode his resistance. He continued nevertheless to proclaim the Gospel and with his words and long-suffering converted to Christianity all who came near him. When the prisoner's resistance was reported to him the prefect ordered him to be decapitated. A violent storm accompanied by an earthquake scattered the soldiers, and in the confusion Canius, with some of the faithful, was able to escape in a boat to Volturno.

Cosenza – Our Lady of the Pillar is the name given to the Blessed Virgin Mary in the context of the traditional belief that Mary, while living in Jerusalem, supernaturally appeared to the Apostle James the Greater in A.D. 40 while he was preaching in what is now Spain. Those who adhere to this belief consider this appearance to be the only recorded instance of Mary exhibiting the mystical phenomenon of bilocation. Among Catholics, it is also considered the first Marian apparition, and unique because it happened while Mary was still living on Earth.

Faeto – Saint Prospero. According to leggend, he was a noble Roman soldier who converted to Christianity, abandoning the worldly life and donating his wealth to the poor, renouncing all positions of prestige and power.

Genoa – St. John the Baptist was an ascetic Jewish prophet known in Christianity as the forerunner of Jesus. John preached about God's Final Judgment and baptized repentant followers in preparation for it. Jesus was among the recipients of his rite of baptism.

Gravina – Michael the Archangel, is an archangel, a spiritual warrior in the battle of good versus evil. He is considered a champion of justice, a healer of the sick, and the guardian of the Church. St. Philip Neri was a Christian missionary and founder of the Congregation of the Oratory, a community of Catholic priests and lay brothers.

Isernia – Pope Celestine V was head of the Catholic Church and ruler of the Papal States for five months from 5 July to 13 December 1294, when he resigned. He was also a monk and hermit who founded the order of the Celestines as a branch of the Benedictine order.

Itri – Madonna della Civita; The Sanctuary of Our Lady of Civita in the territory of Itri, of the Archdiocese of Gaeta, is the oldest Marian temple in the world consecrated to the Mary Immaculate. Popular tradition narrates that the sacred painting representing the image of the Madonna was found in the 8th century by a deaf and mute shepherd, who was looking for a missing cow on Mount Civita. Upon discovering the painting, the mute shepherd fell to his knees, prayed, and miraculously was able to hear and speak for the first time in his life. He went back to the town to share his discovery with the Itrani, who were shocked and amazed to witness that the shepherd could now hear and speak. The institution of the annual feast day of 21 July dates back to 1527 when the Virgin from the Civita freed all the inhabitants of the surrounding villages from the plague.

Marcianise – St. Michael. (see above).

Minturno Madonna Della Grazie – Devotion to the Virgin Mary. According to legend, in 1412, the Blessed Virgin Mary appeared to a local woman, holding broken arrows symbolizing protection against God's wrath and promised an end to the plagues.

Picinisco – Saint Lawrence. (see above).

Potenza - Gerard was born in Piacenza into a noble family. He travelled into southern Italy in search of holy sites, but when he reached Potenza he decided to dedicate himself to the apostolic life. Such was his drive that when the bishop died, the people and clergy chose Gerard as his successor. He was proclaimed bishop at Acerenza and was in post for eight years. After Gerard's death Pope Callixtus II declared him a saint viva voce in 1120. His relics are kept in a sarcophagus in Potenza Cathedral, which is dedicated to him.

Rose – Saint Lawrence or Laurence was one of the seven deacons of the city of Rome under Pope Sixtus II who were martyred in the persecution of the Christians that the Roman Emperor Valerian ordered in 258.

Roccasecca – St. Thomas Aquinas was born at Roccasecca in 1225. Thomas Aquinas was an Italian Dominican friar and priest, who was an immensely influential philosopher, theologian, and jurist in the tradition of scholasticism.

San Mango Sul Calore St. Teodoro d'Amasia – St. Theodore was a military recruit in the Roman Army who protested paganism by setting fire to the Temple of Cybele (the local mother-goddess of Amasea. He was condemned to death, tortured and thrown into fire.

Settefrati Madonna di Canneto – Devotion to the Virgin Mary. According to legend Our Lady of Canneto appeared to a shepardess, and told her to go tell the priest to build a church dedicated to her. The girl responded she could not leave her sheep for she had to lead them to water. The lady touched the cliffs with her fingers and out sprang water for the sheep allowing the Silvana to go to town and tell the priest.

St. Stephen Protomatyr – first martyr of Christianity was, according to the Acts of the Apostles, a deacon in the early Church at Jerusalem who angered members of various synagogues by his teachings. Accused of blasphemy at his trial, he made a speech denouncing the Jewish authorities who were sitting in judgment on him and was then stoned to death.

Torino – St. John the Baptist (see above).

Appendix E

Anthony Pellicci Corner (Intersection of Stillwater Ave. and Smith St.)

Bocuzzi Park (200 Southfield Ave)

Boyle Stadium (Stamford High School)

Carpinella Park (Hoyt Street and Strawberry Hill Ave)

Columbus Park (Main St.)

Columbus Statue at Columbus Park (Main St.)

Cubeta Stadium (Scalzi Park)

James J. De Preta Park (Cove Road)

Joseph Gerli Park (Weed Avenue and East Main St.)

Plaque for John "Sharkey" Laureno (Scalzi Park)

Lione Park (Merrell Ave.)

Palace Theater (Atlantic St.)

Stamford Center for the Arts (Atlantic St.)

Scalzi Park (97 Bridge St.)

The Stamford Lincoln
(Dedicated to Frank D. Rich, intersection of Atlantic and Main St.)

Stamford Veterans Memorial (intersection of Atlantic and Main St.)

Stamford Veterans Monument (intersection of Grove St. and Main St.)

Plaque for Frank, Angelo, Ann, Lynn, and Linda Torelli at Cove Island Park

Representative Philip J. Giordano Playground at Hart School (Adams Ave.)

Appendix F

WALKING TOUR OF STAMFORD'S
EARLY ITALIAN AMERICAN RELIGIOUS LIFE

Religion is an important topic in the Italian American experience. In Stamford, bias required Italians to practice Catholicism in the basement of St. John's church until they built their own church, Sacred Heart. In addition, there was a competition among Christian denominations in Stamford for the newly arrived immigrants, the Baptist church (now One Way Church of Christ) was an Italian language mission built by Italians. Also, included in the tour due to proximity, is the home of the first family to come to Stamford and stay.

Start at SACRED HEART CHURCH, 37 Schuyler Ave, Stamford, CT 06902 (A church built by and for Italians, so that they were no longer relegated to the basement for services and could celebrate mass in their native tongue).

Head south on Schuyler Ave toward Smith St for 0.1 mile, and turn right onto Smith St for 446 ft, then turn left onto Stillwater Ave for 0.2 mile, turn left onto W Main St for 217 ft, turn right onto Greenwich Ave for 0.2 mile, and turn right onto Richmond Hill Ave. The Destination will be on the left in about 331 ft.

ONE WAY CHURCH OF CHRIST, 98 Richmond Hill Ave, Stamford, CT 06902 (This was the Baptist Church built by and for Italians under the leadership of Reverend Pasquale De Carlo).

From here, head east on Richmond Hill Ave toward Greenwich Ave for 0.2 mile, then turn left onto Washington Blvd for 0.2 mile, then turn right onto Tresser Blvd for 0.1 mile, turn left onto Atlantic St. The destination will be on the left in 390 ft.

BASILICA OF SAINT JOHN THE EVANGELIST, 279 Atlantic St, Stamford, CT 06901 (First Catholic Church in Stamford for Italians, although they were only allowed to worship in the basement.).

From here, head north on Atlantic St toward Bell St for 72 ft., and turn left onto Bell St for 0.1 mile, then turn right onto Washington Blvd for 0.5 mile, turn left onto North St. The destination will be on the right in 0.2 mile.

2 North St. HOME OF THE GERONIMO FAMILY, first Italian American Family in Stamford. Head west on North St toward Adams Ave for 0.1 mile, then turn left onto Adams Ave for 0.2 mile, then turn left onto W. Broad St. for 36 ft.

To return to the beginning of the tour, turn right onto Schuyler Ave, the destination will be on the left 0.1 mile, SACRED HEART CHURCH, 37 Schuyler Ave, Stamford, CT 06902.

Appendix G

First Italian-American to reside in Stamford	Joseph Shamish 1860
First Italian-American Family to come and stay	John and Rosalind Geronimo 1877
First Italian-American Special Police Officer	Dominico Palo, 1898
First Italian-American Fulltime Policeman	"Kelly" Genovese 1922
First Italian-American elected to public office	Romolo D'Aloia 1904
First Italian weekly newspaper	"La Liberta" edited by Alfonso Tamburri 1898
First Italian-American Column in Stamford Advocate	1903 "Della Colonia Italiana"- Vito Pittaro
First Italian Society/Organization	Società fra Tommaso Campenella 1894
First Regional Society	Società Aviglianesi 1905
First Musical Band Formed	1907, Professor Pittaro Lelio Donatelli, Passero and Maestro E. Pumpo, Stella D'Italia Brass Band.
First Italian-American Baptist Minister in CT	Reverend Pasquale De Carlo 1897
First Italian-American Home Church – Catholic	Sacred Heart Church Built 1924
First Italian-American Home Church –Baptist	1903 Richmond Hill Avenue and Mission Street
First Celebration of Columbus	1911
First Woman's Society formed	1913 Loggia Adelaide Cairoli
First Wedding Motorcade	Joseph Bruno, 1905

First Medical Professional	Anchise Grossi 1906
First Female Medical Professional	Josephine Ferrara 1907 (midwife)
First Woman Vice President Banker in CT	Catherine Sessa
First Pizza Fritta served in area	At "Festoon" Gravinese Society Feast 1947
First Italian-American Selectman	Anthony Geronimo 1932
First Italian-American Birth in Stamford	Pauline Hemenway Altrocchi

Appendix H

STAMFORD BUILDINGS BUILT BY ITALIAN CONTRACTORS

Italian Center – Mercedes

Harry Bennett branch of the Ferguson Library – Mercedes

New Hope Towers– Mercedes

The Advocate Building – Mercedes

Stillmeadow and Davenport Ridge schools – Mercedes

First Presbyterian Church of Stamford (Fish Church) – DeLuca Construction

Old Stamford Town Hall – Vuono Construction

Stamford Mall – F. D. Rich

Landmark Square – F.D. Rich

Trump Tower – F. D. Rich

Stamford Hospital – F. D. Rich

Avon Theater – F. D. Rich

Various Merritt Parkway Overpasses – Bacco Construction

Appendix I

Abate	Arrigassi	Bongiorno
Abbario	Arrigoni	Boniso
Abbatemarco	Astone	Bonomo
Abbazia	Auletta	Borea
Abbruzese	Bacco	Borio
Abronzeno	Badali	Botticelli
Accousti	Bafundi	Bracchi
Accursi	Ballo	Brancato
Accurso	Barone	Brescio
Accusta	Bartolomeo	Bria
Acunto	Battiato	Briscoe
Adesso	Belasco	Brucato
Adiletta	Beliatore	Bruneti
Agostino	Bella	Bruno
Aiello	Bellantoni	Buccheri
Albonisio	Belline	Buchicchio
Alebrande	Bello	Burriesci
Aliterno	Beltrone	Buzzeo
Altieri	Benedetto	Cacace
Altomura	Benevelli	Caccavello
Amaroso	Berardelli	Caica
Amarto	Bervasio	Calandrelli
Amato	Biancardi	Calanzaro
Amente	Biase	Calitri
Angelici	Billone	Campanile
Angevin	Bissonette	Candelmo
Arancia	Bivona	Candido
Arcade	Blancato	Cangiano
Arcano	Boccarusso	Cannizzano
Arciola	Bocchichio	Cantanzaro
Arduino	Boccuzzi	Cantillo
Arena	Bonaparte	Cantore
Argeaneis	Bonetti	Caperino

Capocci	Chiapetta	Corbo
Capone	Chiriani	Corso
Caporino	Chirillo	Cosentini
Caposella	Christiano	Costanzo
Capossela	Cianci	Costello
Cappabianca	Cianciulli	Coviello
Cappellieri	Cianculo	Crea
Cappielo	Cicali	Crescio
Caputo	Cilfoni	Cristiani
Carbone	Cingari	Crocci
Cardone	Cioeta	Crocco
Carella	Cipri	Croce
Carlesimo	Ciriaco	Crombetta
Carlino	Clapes	Crosta
Carlucci	Claps	Cubaluzzi
Carluccio	Cobara	Cucui
Carpainni	Cobelli	Culaccio
Carpinella	Coco	Cundari
Carpinelli	Cogliondro	D'Agostino
Caruso	Cognetta	D'Alessandro
Casareale	Colabella	D'Ambrosi
Casillo	Colabello	D'Ambrosio
Cassario	Colacchio	D'Andrea
Cassone	Colangelo	D'Antonio
Casta	Colarossi	D'Aquila
Catino	Coletta	D'Aquila
Cavaliere	Coletto	D'Egreorio
Cavanna	Collini	D'Elia
Centenze	Colucci	D'Orba
Centonze	Comosino	D'Acunto
Cerbotte	Conetta	D'Amato
Cerreta	Conforte	Davrio
Cerritelli	Conforti	De Angelis
Cerrutu	Conterno	De Barbieri
Cervi	Coperine	De Carlo
Cesareo	Coppera	De Julio
Cestone	Coppola	De Mar

De Marco	Dicamillo	Ferrando
De Milla	Dicarlo	Ferrara
De Nicola	DiChiara	Ferrari
De Rosa	Difrancesco	Ferrollo
De Yulio	Digiovanbattista	Figlioli
Debarbrie	Diguardi	Fiordelisi
Debartolomeo	Dilerna	Fiore
DeBlasi	Dilesano	Fiorentino
Debrisco	DiNardo	Fiorillo
DeCostanzo	Dinecola	Foggetta
Dedda	Dipietro	Folco
Del Pianto	Dipompa	Follo
Del Prete	Disanto	Fonte
Delfini	Ditto	Fornaciari
Dellapinta	Divosta	Fortensato
Dellarocca	Donatelli	Fortunato
Delprete	Dora	Franchina
Delrusso	Draghi	Frangione
Demaio	Dumagala	Franklin
Demarchis	Enginito	Frate
Demartino	Envino	Frattaroli
Deminno	Epifanio	Fresco
DeMott	Esposito	Fuda
DeNocenzo	Fabbiano	Fulvo
Denora	Fabrizio	Furilli
Depaola	Falcioni	Gagliardi
Depiro	Fallace	Galasso
Derosa	Fallamal	Gallaie
Derosi	Farenga	Gallo
DeRubeis	Farina	Galtano
DeSanto	Fastiggi	Gandia
Devartti	Fauci	Gandino
Devesto	Faugno	Ganino
Devito	Fedele	Gentile
Di Preta	Fedeli	Gerardi
Dianni	Feglinoli	Gerbasi
Diaspro	Ferrandino	Geronimo

Gervasio	Intrieri	Loppittoli
Gesso	Inzingo	Lopriore
Gettulio	Ioli	Lorenti
Giampietro	Iovanna	Lorusso
Giancola	Iovino	Lotte
Giancoti	Italiano	Lovello
Giannattasio	Itri	Lucci
Giannetri	Izzi	Lucipora
Giannitti	Labbadia	Lunghi
Giaquinto	Labbato	Luongo
Ginolfi	Labella	Lupinacci
Gira	Lacerenza	Macari
Giuffre	Laginestra	Macchio
Gofino	Laguarda	Maddaloni
Golletto	Lambrusco	Maffei
Grancola	Laporta	Maffucci
Grande	Laracco	Maggi
Granelli	LaRocca	Magliano
Granese	Lasalandra	Maiorano
Grasso	Latte	Malazie
Graziano	Laureno	Malizia
Greco	LaValle	Mallozzi
Grillo	Leiberato	Malone
Grimaldi	Leone	Mancini
Grineino	Libano	Mancuse
Grippo	Lione	Mancusi
Grossi	Lionetti	Mangufi
Guasco	Livolsi	Manguso
Guastanacchia	Loccesano	Marcetti
Guerber	Loccisano	Marciano
Gufliano	Loco	Marcucci
Gulla	Loglisi	Marena
Gussardo	Lomazzo	Margotta
Hamani	Lombardi	Marisco
Iannone	Lombardo	Marrucco
Ignato	Longo	Marschi
Interlaudi	Lopiano	Martinelli

Martini	Morucco	Parente
Martino	Mottola	Parisi
Martinoli	Multello	Parrella
Massaro	Muscatello	Parrillo
Massimiani	Muzzio	Pascarelli
Massoletti	Namone	Pasquirao
Massone	Nardone	Passero
Matrich	Nardozza	Pastore
Mattera	Nardozzi	Pastrichelli
Mazza	Nastri	Patricelli
Mazzella	Natale	Pavia
Mazzi	Nino	Pecora
Meda	Nizzardo	Pelazza
Media	Nosenzo	Pellen
Melatti	Novella	Pellicci
Melchionno	Occulto	Penachio
Melfi	Operando	Pensiero
Meli	Orsino	Perella
Melillo	Ottano	Perelle
Mercadante	Ottaviani	Perrillo
Merolo	Ottaviano	Persecchini
Metallo	Otto	Persiani
Micile	Ozella	Petrilli
Milone	Pace	Petrosino
Minero	Paganetti	Pia
Moavero	Pagano	Piacendo
Moccia	Pagliarulo	Piacenza
Modaffari	Palermo	Piallige
Momeli	Palmer	Pierni
Monguse	Palmiere	Pieta
Montanese	Palmieri	Pimpanella
Moraio	Palo	Pinonto
Moreno	Palomba	Pinza
Mori	Panapado	Piro
Moroni	Panaro	Pisani
Morro	Paolini	Pittaro
Morsa	Parchi	Poccia

Pombi	Rosasco	Sente
Pompa	Rossi	Serafino
Pope	Rosso	Serra
Poppalardo	Rotante	Sessa
Porada	Rotunno	Sette
Portia	Rubino	Severino
Possidento	Ruserick	Shamish
Potito	Russo	Sibilia
Prangea	Sabia	Sibilio
Preziosi	Sabilia	Sico
Prinzi	Sabini	Sileo
Prizio	Sabino	Simeone
Prunotto	Sacci	Simonelli
Pugliano	Sacco	Siriglia
Qualano	Salerino	Sisto
Quarracino	Saltarelli	Socci
Racaniello	Salvatore	Sollima
Raina	Salzillo	Sorgi
Raiteri	Samdello	Spagnoli
Rambo	Sandelli	Speranza
Recchia	Sanfelice	Spoviero
Rennella	Sansone	Sproniero
Restaino	Santaserio	Sproviere
Reteare	Santasero	Spruriero
Rich	Sapelli	Stabile
Rinaldi	Sarni	Stefani
Rinalla	Sassara	Stefano
Ringi	Saumo	Strafaccio
Riodi	Scalise	Strollo
Ripetucci	Scalzi	Summa
Rizzi	Scaparotto	Suttile
Rizzo	Scatamarci	Taddone
Roberti	Scollo	Tamburri
Robustelli	Scorese	Tamburro
Roda	Sellini	Tarantino
Romano	Sementini	Tartaglia
Rosa	Senese	Tartora

Tedesco	Tuccarone	Vetriolo
Telasco	Ucciferri	Vetti
Telesco	Urbano	Viggiano
Tella	Urso	Vigilio
Teodora	Uva	Vitale
Teplica	Uvino	Vitti
Terenzio	Vacca	Volante
Tiani	Vaccaro	Volpe
Tinelli	Vagnone	Votto
Tinglese	Valante	Vozzella
Toglia	Valenti	Vuona
Torbora	Valentine	Vuono
Torfino	Valentino	Zacarola
Tornillo	Varrichio	Zaccagnino
Tortora	Vazella	Zaffino
Tosone	Vento	Zanone
Tozzola	Ventre	Zazzaro
Treglia	Venturini	Zezima
Trimboli	Vergilo	Zinicola
Tripodi	Veroni	Zinnie
Trombetta	Verrasto	Zita
Truglia	Vescio	

Appendix J

Take a step back in time and imagine what life was like for Italians in Stamford in the early 1900s. The West Side of Stamford became synonymous with the Italian Colony, an area that after WWI was majority Italian residents and businesses. The heart of the West Side would include the following streets: West Main St., West Ave., Liberty St. Virgil St., Fairfield Ave., Stillwater Ave. ("Black Road"), Finney Lane, Rose Park, and Waverly Place. About 800 Italian families were residing here by the 1920s. The streets were bustling with activity. Businesses in the area would have included poultry markets, grocery stores, dry goods stores, shoemakers, barbers, tailors, dress factories, bakeries, saloons, restaurants, and pharmacies. Fraternal organizations were also headquartered in the area. Here is a walking tour of some buildings, either built by Italians, or housing Italian businesses that remain.

Starting by parking at Mill River Playground, walk over to 135 West Main Street (on the north side of West Main). This is a wood frame structure with a brick front, built in 1802 by Reuben Smith, in 1920 its commercial occupant was Luigi Sciglimpaglia, shoe repair, in 1940, John DiMarino, baker, and Frank Mancuso restaurant.

From here head west on W Main St. toward Stillwater Ave. 144 feet to 182 W. Main St. This is a four-story brick building built in 1914 by Vito Sabia. In 1920, its commercial occupants were Luigi Serafini, real estate. In 1940, Joseph Corona shoe repair, Frank Epifanio, beverages, and the Stillwater Athletic Club.

From here head southwest on W Main St toward Rose Park Ave. 43 feet to 186 West Main St. This three-story cut stone building was built by Benjamin Malozzi in 1908 and was primarily residential.

From here head southwest on W Main St toward Rose Park Ave 66 ft Turn left onto Rose Park Ave.

The destination will be on the right, 188 West Main Street. This one-story frame commercial structure was built in 1910 by Scofield and Hoyt. In 1920, it was the Sessa Brothers grocery store, and in 1940 Nicholas Frattaroli poultry store.

From here head north on Rose Park Ave toward W Main St 49 ft Turn left onto W Main St 89 ft to 208 W. Main Street. This is a one-story brick row of stores built in 1928 by Loreto Zezima. In 1940, its occupants were Loreto Zezima Grocer, DiSette Brothers Fruit, and Benedetto Macari Meat.

To the rear, a two-story frame flat-roofed house was built in 1922 by Vincenzo Mercadante.

From here head southwest on W Main St toward Ann St 266 ft. to 228 West Main Street. This is a two-story frame structure with a brick front built in 1928 by Peter Zezima. In 1940 it was Brown's Tavern and Restaurant.

From here head southwest on W Main St toward Spruce St 154 ft to 274 West Main Street. This is a two-story frame structure built in 1850 by Robert Stevens and moved in 1904 (when sold to the Genovese Brothers) from the corner of Spruce Street to the northeast corner of its lot in order to make way for the Genovese building. In 1920, it was the Loreto Lazaro grocery store.

From here head southwest on W Main St toward Spruce St 69 ft to 290 West Main Street. This is a four-story brick structure with a pressed metal cornice, built in 1905 by Genovese Brothers. In 1920 it housed Genovese Brothers Saloon and Louis Robustelli, barber.

From here head northeast on W Main St toward Spruce St Destination will be on the right 85 ft, 298 West Main Street. This is a two-story frame house with a one-story commercial addition, built in 1860 by Michael Sullivan. In 1920 it was Francesco Vaccaro's Confectionary and in 1940 Sullivan Vaccaro beverages.

From here head southwest on W Main St toward Fairfield Ct 108 ft to 302 West Main Street. This is a two-story building with a fieldstone first floor and a shingled flat roofed second floor. It was built in 1921 by Francesco Vaccaro.

From here head southwest on W Main St toward Fairfield Ave 56 ft to 300 West Main Street. This is a one-story brick building built in 1921 by R&M Genovese. It was originally known as the Stamford Waist Co.

From here, head southwest on W Main St toward Fairfield Ave for .3 mi. You will pass the Yerwood Center on the left (this used to be Steven's School, Italian children on the west side would have attended here, adults would have attended English classes at night here as well). Continuing you will pass Jackie Robinson Park also on the left. Also pass Liberty St. on the right, and turn right onto Virgil St.

The destination will be on the right 299 ft. The Settefratese Social Club, 23 Virgil St. Italians created many mutual benefit societies, that later became social clubs as they became integrated into other organizations that included a more diverse population. This organization, "La Società Mutuo Soccorso fra Settefratesi "Capitano Alessandro Venturini" di Stamford" was organized in 1916.

From here, Head north on Virgil St toward Dryden St. 207 ft. Turn left onto Minor Pl 0.1 mi Turn right onto West Ave 52 ft. to the San Manghese Social Club, at 107 West Ave. The "Società Italiana Di M.S.S. Teodoro Martire, fra I Cittadedini di S. Mango Sul Calore" was organized in 1906. Many may remember the annual "Feast" held on these grounds in late August in honor of the town's patron saint, Saint Theodore.

From here, Head south on West Ave toward Minor Pl. 52 ft. Turn left onto Minor Pl 0.1 mi Turn left onto Virgil St 0.2 mi. Turn right onto Stillwater Ave. Destination will be on the right 0.1 mi. This is the corner of Stillwater and Finney Lane, and important spot where the first public celebration of St. Vito occurred. Important for Italians, creating pride in their culture, as these practices had been looked down upon by other ethnic groups.

From here, head east on Stillwater Ave toward Finney Ln. 440 ft. At the corner of Fairfield Avenue and Stillwater, at 1 Fairfield Avenue, you will see a group of stores, this was once the Anna Dress Company owned by Anna Tamburri. There are two houses behind the building on Fairfield where the daughters and sons of Anna Tamburri lived.

From here you can find your way back to your car at Mill River, whether following Stillwater Ave down, or crossing at Spruce St to West Main.

Appendix K
POLITICAL WARDS

FIRST WARD includes: Beginning at the junction of Broad and Gay Streets; through the center of Gay Street to Main Street; then through the center of Atlantic Street to Stamford Harbor; then along the harbor and waters of Long Island Sound to the point of the boundary between Greenwich and Stamford, then along the westerly boundary of Stamford to the point which intersects the center line of West Main Street, then along the center of West Main Street to Richmond Hill Avenue, then through the center of Richmond Hill Avenue to Mill River; thence through the center of Broad Street to the point of beginning.

SECOND WARD includes: Beginning at Stamford Harbor at the foot of Atlantic Street, through the center of Atlantic Street and along the boundary of the First Ward to the point at which it intersects the center line of Main Street, then through the center of Main Street to Elm Street, then through the center of Elm Street to the Cove Road, then through the center line of Cove Road to the eastern boundary of Stamford, then along the waters of Westcott's line of Cove Road to the eastern boundary of Stamford, then along the waters of Westcott's Cove, Long Island Sound and Stamford Harbor to the point of beginning.

THIRD WARD includes: Beginning at the point of intersection of the center lines of Bedford and Summer Streets, then through the center of Bedford Street to Broad Street, then through the center of Broad Street to Mill River, then along Mill River to Richmond Hill Avenue, then through the center of Richmond Hill Avenue and West Main Street to the western boundary of Stamford, then along the western boundary of Stamford to a point in said boundary formed by the westerly prolongation of a line drawn from a point formed by the intersection of the center lines of Strawberry Hill Avenue and Belltown Road to a point formed by the intersection of the center lines of Summer and Bedford Streets, then along that line to the intersection of the center lines of Summer and Bedford Streets (the beginning point).

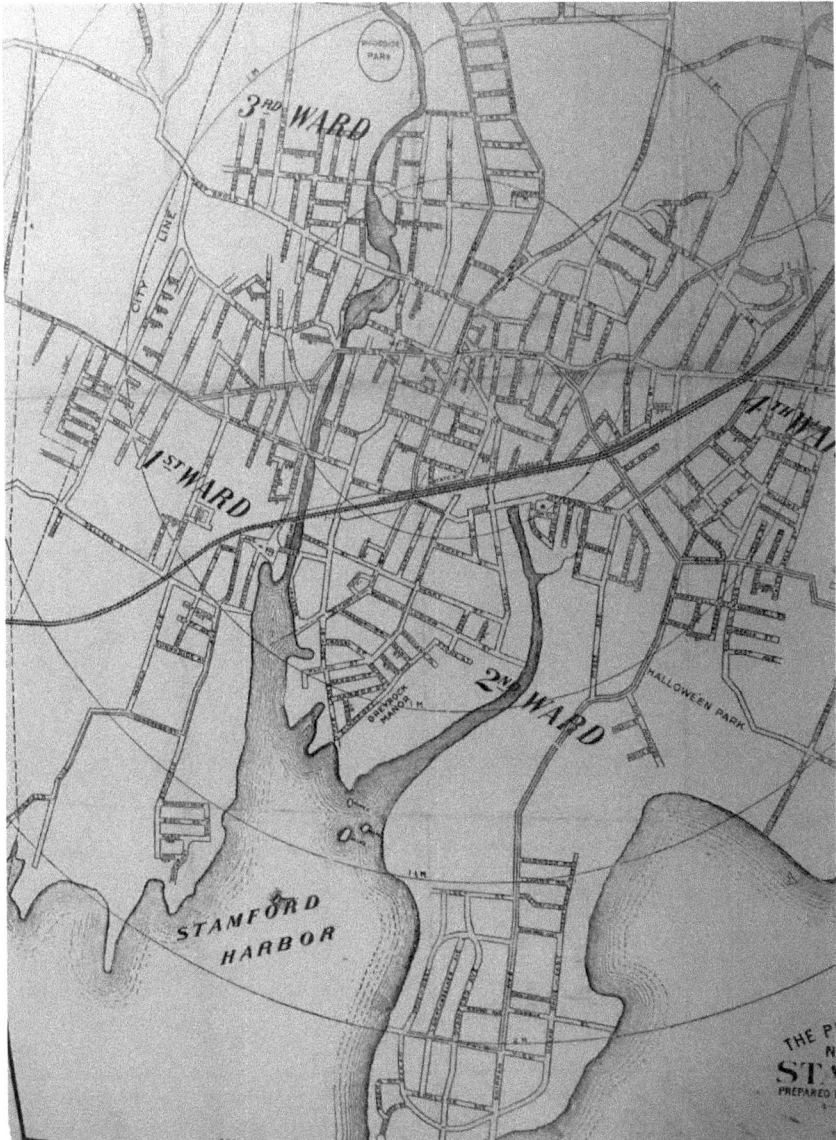

Map courtesy of Stamford History Center

Depaola, Lawrence 227
DeRosa, Vito 255
Derosi, Circolamo 227
DeSanto, James 254
DeSilva, Fernando 8
DeVartti, Ricardo 256
Devesto, Louis 227
DeVito, Joseph 90, 98, 102, 256
Devito, Nicholas 239-240
DeYulio, Giuseppe 249-251
Di Nardo, Raffaele 134
Di Preta, Antonio 15
Di Vivo, Vincenczo 71
Di Nardo, Orazio 133
Dianni, John A. 227
Dicamillo, Vincenzo 22
Dicarlo, Peter 227
Dicarlo, Rocco 227
DiChiara, Joseph 256
Difrancesco, Antonio227
Difrancesco, Louis 227
Digiovanbattista, Giuseppe 227
Dilerna, Francesco 227
Dilesano, Angelo 227
Dipietro, Thomas 138, 227
DiPompa, Michael 22
Dipreta, Attilo 227
Dipreta, Giuseppe 227
Disanto, Vicenzo 227
DiSessa, Frank J. 152, 156, 278
DiSessa, Leonard 261
DiSette, John 251
Ditto, Piere McKee 227
Divosta, Paul 227
Donatelli, Elita 277
Donatelli, Leo 21, 33-36, 40, 44, 247
Donatelli, Louis 262
Dora, Michael Gustav 224, 234
Draghi, Luigi 271
Dumagala, Felix 250

East Side 45, 86
Engenito, Frances 269
Epifanio, Giuseppe 128, 252
Epifanio, Lawrence 153, 214, 278
Epifanio, Louise 46
Esposito, Alfonso 252
Esposito, Antonio 22
Esposito, Eduardo 113
Esposito, Francisco 22
Esposito, Joseph 253
Esposito, Nicola 255
Esposito, Pasquale 11, 27-31, 89, 93, 200, 290
Esposito, Stanislao 104, 147, 279
Fabbiano, Joseph 227
Fabrizio, Ciriaco 227
Fabrizio, Michael 227

Fairfield Ave. 44-45, 91, 152, 250, 268, 274-275, 279, 309
Falcioni, Autere 255
Fallace, John 255
Farascinoe, Emilio 48
Farenga, Joe 160, 235
Farengo, Domenic 256
Fastiggi, Gaetano 98
Fastiggi, Vincenzo 23
Fastiggi, Vito 23, 102, 105-106
Faugno, Francesco 134
Faugno, Giovanni 133
Faugno, Giuseppe 133
Faugno, Raffaele 134
Fedele, Antonio 113, 256
Fedeli, Frank 227, 244
Fekete, Irene 266
Ferrandino, Giambattista 227
Ferrando Bros 249
Ferrando, Carlo 113
Ferrara, Canio 160, 227, 249-250
Ferrara, Donato 130-131
Ferrara, Gaetano 107
Ferrara, Raffaele 113

Gerardi, Leo 227, 235
Gerardi, Mollie 45
Gerardi, Vito 227, 244, 276
Gerari, Giuseppe 131
Gerbasi, Carmeno 250
Gerbasi, Carmino 251
Geronimo, Anthony 85, 103, 112,
  138-139, 141, 151, 184, 203-205,
  210, 273, 289, 298
Geronimo, Charles 4, 224, 227
Geronimo, John 1-2, 6, 8-10
Gervasio, Antonio 113, 139
Gesso, Gioacchino 113
Giacomo, Martinelli 131
Giancola, Joseph 160, 227, 246
Giancola, Louis 181
Giancola, Nicandra 250
Giancoti, James 227
Giannattasio, Julia 250
Giannetri, Nurianto 22
Giannitti, Angelo 133-134
Giannitti, Enrico 134, 143
Giannitti, Joseph 227
Giannitti, Nunziante 133
Giannitti, Pietro 134
Giannitti, Sabato 133
Giaquinto, Enrico 227, 234
Ginolfi, Nick 228
Giordano, Egillio 253
Giordano, Phil vii, 50-51, 296
Gironimi, John 1
Giuffre, Rocco 23
Glenbrook 16-18,
Gofino, Mikele S. 228
Golletto, Allessando 228
Gragnelli, Elizabeth 251
Grancola, Antonio 250
Grande, Gaetano 228
Granelli, Emmanuelle Ernesto 228
Granese, Salvatore 23
Grasso, John 256
Grasso, Luciano 22

Grasso, Samuel 22
Gravina 51, 154, 272, 291, 294
Gravinese vii, 146, 154, 283, 290,
  300
Graziano, Carmine 108
Greco, Emilio 150, 228, 256
Grillo, Michele 224, 228
Grimaldi, Achille 113, 257
Grimaldi, Francisco 101
Grineino, Bruno 250
Grosso, Berardino 131
Guasco, Carlo 140, 252
Guastanacchia, Angelo 228
Guerber, Sopha 2-3
Gufliano, Pietro 113
Guglielmi, Domenico 131
Gulla, Giuseppe 228
Gussardo, Marco 252

Iannone, Tony 228
Ignato, Thomas 228
Insigna, Sebastiano 254
Interlaudi, Salvo 228
Intrieri, Antonio 228
Inzingo, Sebastino 250
Ioli, Domenico 274
Iovino, Erasmo 250, 279
Iovino, Felice 250, 279
Iovino, Gaetano 274
Italian Center vii, 13, 50, 53, 60,
  82-83, 89, 94, 115-127, 141-142,
  145, 155, 157, 179, 187, 193,
  205-207, 211, 214, 216, 218, 243,
  266-268, 273
Italian Loan and Brokerage Assn.
  216, 262
Italian Political and Benevolent
  Club 94, 102-103, 132, 212, 289
Italian Republican Club 20, 78, 88,
  101
Italian Social Club 104
Italiano, Mariano 228

Marschi, Guido E. 228
Marsico, Vittoria 27
Martinelli, Andrea 23, 107, 131
Martinelli, Dominico 154, 228
Martinelli, Francesco 131
Martinelli, Frank 256
Martinelli, Joseph 228
Martinelli, William 228
Martino, Domenico 134
Martino, Joseph 228
Martino, Nicola 134
Martino, Raffaele 134
Martino, Rosario 28-9, 92, 99-100, 134-135
Martino, Salvatore 100, 134-135
Martino, Venanzio 134
Martinoli, Santino 228
Marucco, David J. 155, 251
Marucco, Joseph 67
Marucco, Pasquale 56
Masi, Francesco 131
Masone, Biagio 250
Masone, Patsy 156-157
Massare & Ferrara 274
Massaro, Nicola 23
Massimiani, Pietro 228
Massoletti Inc 252
Mattera, Giorgio 228
Mazza, Ernst 203, 228
Mazza, John Dominick 220, 228, 253
Mazza, Rocco 252, 279
Mazzi, Ferdinand 250
Mazzola, John 270
Meda Brothers 249
Meda & Bracchi 250
Meda, Albino 93, 113, 182
Meda, Alfonso 113
Meda, Cesare 228, 244
Meda, Evasio 113, 126
Meda, Fortunato 93
Melatti, Nicholas 252

Melchionno, Carmine 134
Melchionno, Domenico 228
Melchionno, Giovanni 133
Melchionno, Teodoro vii, 135
Melfi, Alexander 139, 250, 262, 271
Melfi, John 228
Melfi, Pasquale 228
Meli, Louis 256
Melillo, Domenico 142, 185
Melillo, James 127, 250, 254
Mercadante, Daniel 256,
Mercadante, Vincent 154, 256, 310
Merolo, Antonio 228
Mesotti, Carlo 274
Metallo, Gerardo 105-106, 179, 181-182
Metallo, Josephine 45
Metallo, Luigi 114, 182
Metti, B. 3
Mezza, Ernest 253
Miceli, John 279
Micile, Pietro 107
Milone, Domenico 134
Minero, Joseph 23
Minturnese vii, 142-143, 155, 180, 292
Minturno 136-137, 155, 177, 245
Moavero, Angelo 251
Moavero, Vincenzo 111, 114
Moavro, Vincenzo 23
Moccia, Generoso 134
Modaffari, Vincenzo 228
Momeli, Salvator 228
Monaco, Sabatino 181
Monguse, Joseph 228
Montanaro, Carmine 129, 147, 174, 274
Montanese, Giovanni 228
Moraio Brothers 254
Morelli, Giuseppe 253
Moreno, Michael 22

Mori, Henry 23
Moroni, Cesare 228
Morucco, Pasquale 22
Mosca, Dominick J. 253
Mosca, Dominick 253
Mottola, Giovanni 134
Muldello, George 274
Multello, George 252
Muscatello, Rocco 150-151, 228, 244
Muti, Peter 274
Muzzio, Clarence 228, 245
Muzzio, Frank 270
Muzzio, John 247, 258

Namone, Jasper W.
Napoletano Brothers 58, 188-189
Napoletano, JoAnn vii, 58
Nardone, Nicholas 228, 234
Nardozza, Donato 130-131
Nardozza, Paolo 29, 119, 124, 131-132
Nardozzi, Paul 28, 132, 141
Nastri, Carmine 22
Natale, Camillo 228, 244
Nobile, Felice 279
Nobile, Josephine 253
Nosenzo, Cesare 228
Nosenzo, Charles 246
Nosenzo, Eugene 140
Novella, Charles 228
Nurra, Raffaele 45

Occhionero, Michael 261
Occulto, Frank 228, 245
Operando, Petro 6
Ottano, Anthony 228
Ottaviani, Domenic 228
Ottaviano, Angelo 134
Ottaviano, Lorenzo 134
Ottaviano, Michele 134
Ottaviano, Pasquale 134
Ottaviano, Raffaele 23

Ottaviano, Sabino 134
Ottaviano, Teodoro 22, 28, 134
Ottaviano, Theodore 93, 135, 160. 221
Otto, Max 22
Otto, Oscar 23
Otto, Paul 22
Ozzella, Ruciano 22

Pace, Canio 228
Pacific Street 1, 3, 8, 13-14, 17, 20, 22-3, 26, 44-45, 47, 53, 65, 69, 79, 81, 84, 86, 90-93, 96, 98-9, 106-7, 115, 117, 127, 139, 152, 160, 164-166, 169, 182-184, 201, 205, 210, 223, 248-58, 261-262, 264, 267, 269, 273-274, 276, 277-279
Paganetti, Elvira Theresa 70
Paganetti, Louis D. 228
Pagano, Antonio 256
Pagano, Salvatore 256
Pagliarulo, Aneslmo 107
Palemaro, Concesso 41
Palermo, Anthony J. 179, 228
Palermo, John J. 179, 228, 235
Palladino, Vito 131
Palmatier, Alvie 23
Palmiere, Gerardo 22
Palmieri, Gerardo 113
Palmirie, Antonio 228
Palo, Anthony 77, 179, 228
Palo, Antonio 76, 78-79, 99, 101-103, 105, 119, 179, 184, 200
Palo, Henry 228
Palo, Joseph 76-77, 160, 179, 224, 228, 245
Palo, Sanford Francis 70, 228, 235
Palo, Tony 9, 76, 79, 89, 104, 111, 224, 247
Paloma, Maddalena 263
Palomba, Anniello 262, 270

Panaro, Giuseppe 228
Paolillo, Antonio 265
Parchi, Aerger 28
Parisi, Antonio 228
Parisi, Mary 45
Parrillo, Vincenzo 250
Pascarelli, Michael 22
Pasquarelli, Giuseppe 102
Pasquirao, Phinelo 7
Passero, Angelina
Passero, Angelo
Passero, Carmine 128, 139
Passero, Charles 151
Passero, Frank 111
Passero, Gennaro 28-29, 111, 114,
   119, 127, 203
Passero, Marino 102
Pastore, Michalangelo 107, 113
Pastore, Pasquale 256
Pastore, Tony 228
Pastrichelli, Alessandro 228
Patricelli, Antonio 107
Patricelli, Giovanni 107
Patricelli, Michele 107
Pavia, Michele 102
Pavia, Nicola 45, 98-99, 139
Pavia, Paul 48, 147, 160, 179, 219
Pelazza, Filippo 229
Pelazza, Philip 274
Pellicci, Antonio 103, 107
Pellicci, Vincenzo 23
Pellien, Pasquale 22
Penachio Bros 249-50,
Penachio, Andrew 217, 251
Penachio, Joseph 217
Pensiero, Benedetto 108
Perelle, Antonio 229
Perrone, Stanley 131, 153
Persecchini, Raffaele 108
Persiani, Louis 278
Persiani, Luigi 229, 274
Petrilli, Antoinette

Petrilli, Antonio 113
Petrilli, Salvatore 113
Petrizzi, Jerry 277
Petrone, Joseph 71, 177
Pia, Elia 23, 111, 184
Pia, Frank 224, 251
Pia, Giacomo 251
Pia, Guido 71, 145, 224
Pia, Michael 250-1
Pia, Orazio 144-145, 184
Pia, Palmerino 102
Pia, Raffaele 23
Piacendo, Leonardo 22
Piacenza, Leonard 160, 229, 246
Piacenza, Leonardo 107, 130-131,
   149
Piacenza, Luigi 23, 130-1, 149
Piacenza, Michele 131
Pierne, Michael 229
Pierni, Giovanni 134
Pierni, Michele 134
Pieta, Antonio 22
Pinonto, Frank 22
Piro, Dominick 229
Pittaro, Vito 13, 28-9, 82-3, 94-95,
   98, 100, 102-3, 105-123, 126-
   127, 142-143, 203, 205, 248, 270,
   299
Plase, Vito 44
Poccia, Ralph 254
Pocograno, Fredrick 251, 279
Pocograno, Matthew 251
Polimeni, Stephanie 266
Pombi, Joseph 23
Pope, George 229
Poppalardo, Gayton 271
Porada, Walter J. 229
Portia, Ralph 250
Possidento, Domenico 250, 261
Possidento & Son 250
Potito, Antonio 134
Potito, Giovanni 134

Tamburro, Giuseppe 23
Tarantino, Charles D 156, 175, 178, 278
Tarantino, Giacomo 256
Tartora, Francesco 23
Tedeschi, Joseph 251, 253
Tedesco, Bennie 23
Tedesco, Bennino 252
Telesca, Domenico 131
Telesca, Donato 130
Telesca, Francesco 131
Telesca, Vincenzo 131
Telesco, Angelo 185, 229, 250
Telesco, Daniel 44, 180
Telesco, Paul 229, 250
Teodora, Giovanni 23
Teplica, John M. 229
Terenzio, Antonio 22-23, 107, 261
Terenzio, Emilio 145-146, 161
Terenzio, Ermenegildo 22
Terenzio, Giuseppe 144-145
Terenzio, Frank J 275
Terenzio, Pietro 22, 249
Terenzio, Samual 274
Terlizzo, Pasquale 43
Tiani, Laviero 102
Tinglese, Giuseppe 23
Tolla, Giovanni 130
Torbora, Francesco 22
Torentino, Anthony 256
Torfino, Michele 229
Tornillo, Luigi 105-106
Tortora, Francesco 108
Tortora, Giuseppe 131
Tortora, Margarita 254
Tortora, Vito 127, 150, 254, 256
Tosone, Generoso 134
Tozzola, Angelina 269
Trantanella, Charles 274
Treglia, Ralph 126, 143, 229, 252-3, 274

Treglia, Thomas 127, 136, 138, 142-143
Triacca, Charles 9
Trimboli, Felice 99-100, 103, 107-111, 113-114, 123, 184, 256
Trimboli, Joseph 229, 241
Truglia, Giuseppe 229
Tuccarone, Tony 229

Ucciferri, Anna 254
Ucciferri, Giovanni 113
Unione Manovali 28
Unione Muratori 28
Urbano, Antonio 22
Urbano, Capto 22
Urbano, Luigi 229
Urso, Frank 124
Uva, Antonio 229
Uva, Ferdinando 133
Uva, Giovanni 134
Uva, Giuseppe 133
Uva, Raffaele 134
Uva, Ralph 259
Uva, Teodoro 23, 134
Uvino, Tony 229

Vacca, Alfonse 15-16, 151-152, 159
Vacca, Elaine vii, 169, 185
Vacca, Henry 273-274
Vacca, Vincenzo 15, 22, 43, 169
Vaccara, Michele 23
Vaccaro, Donato 131
Vaccaro, Francesco 131, 310
Vaccaro, George 261
Vaccaro, Michele 108, 131-132, 149, 250, 261-262, 279
Vaccaro, Sullivan 229, 310
Vaccaro, Tommaso 131
Vaccaro, Tony P. 229
Vaccaro, Vito 130-131, 149
Vagnone, Marie 14
Vagnone, Michael 229

ABOUT THE AUTHOR

ANTHONY SOCCI, the son of Italian immigrants, grew up in Stamford, Connecticut, surrounded by Italian culture, which engendered his deep admiration and respect for Italy, Italians, and their culture.

As a writer with a passion for preserving history for future generations, he became inspired when he was unable to find a comprehensive history of Stamford's Italian Americans among the existing historical reading materials pertaining to the subject matter at the Stamford History Center's (SHS) collection; even though fifteen percent of the city's population has Italian roots. At the encouragement of the team at SHS, he launched his mission to honor and tell the stories of Italians in his home city. The research has been a labor of love, and infinitely rewarding. He hopes through telling these stories, he can spark a renewed engagement of pride and inspiration for not only the local community but beyond. Nonfiction is not his only means of expressing his passion for storytelling.

Anthony has written several plays, two of which have been published (*Bottom of the Ninth*, which was produced in Norwalk, CT after winning a local competition, and *Dreamkeepers*). Anthony has a Bachelor of Science degree in Accounting from the University of Connecticut, and a Master of Business Administration in Taxation from Pace University and has used his creativity while working in these areas. In the end, nothing is as satisfying, creatively, for him than reaching audiences through written word.

Antonio Vitti – Immigrated from Settefrati in early 1900s working as an Iceman, only to return to Italy, "Ritornati."

Corrente Family, Francesco and Lucia Corrente lived on Cerreta St. Photo Courtesy of Lucille D'Acunto Limone.

Gennaro Passaro – third from the left, front row, Officer of Società Operaia Italiana di Mutuo Soccorso, Italian Institute and Italian American History Center. Photo Courtesy of The Stamford Historical Society.

John Geronimo was among one of the first Italians to come to Stamford and remain. Photo Courtesy of The Stamford Historical Society.

Crescenzo Tamburri – The earned the moniker "Secretary General" of Stamford because of membership in many organizations including: Societa Operaia, Sons of Italy, Societa Campanella, Soccieta Vittorio Emanuale and the Italian Social and Political Club. In his eulogy, it was noted "Crescenzo Tamburri made the town better because he lived in it; he made these societies better and stronger because he worked in them, and he has left a pleasant memory with all who knew him.

Vito Pittaro – Mr. Pittaro was the editor of the first Italian newspaper in Connecticut, author, teacher, banker, and a leader of the Italian community in Stamford from 1894. He was another founder of the Italian Social Institute (later became the Italian Center) and historian of the Italians in Stamford. Photo Courtesy of The Italian Center of Stamford.

LELIO DONATELLI

ANTONIO PALO

REV. P. DE CARLO

Various early leaders. Photo Courtesy of The Italian Center of Stamford.

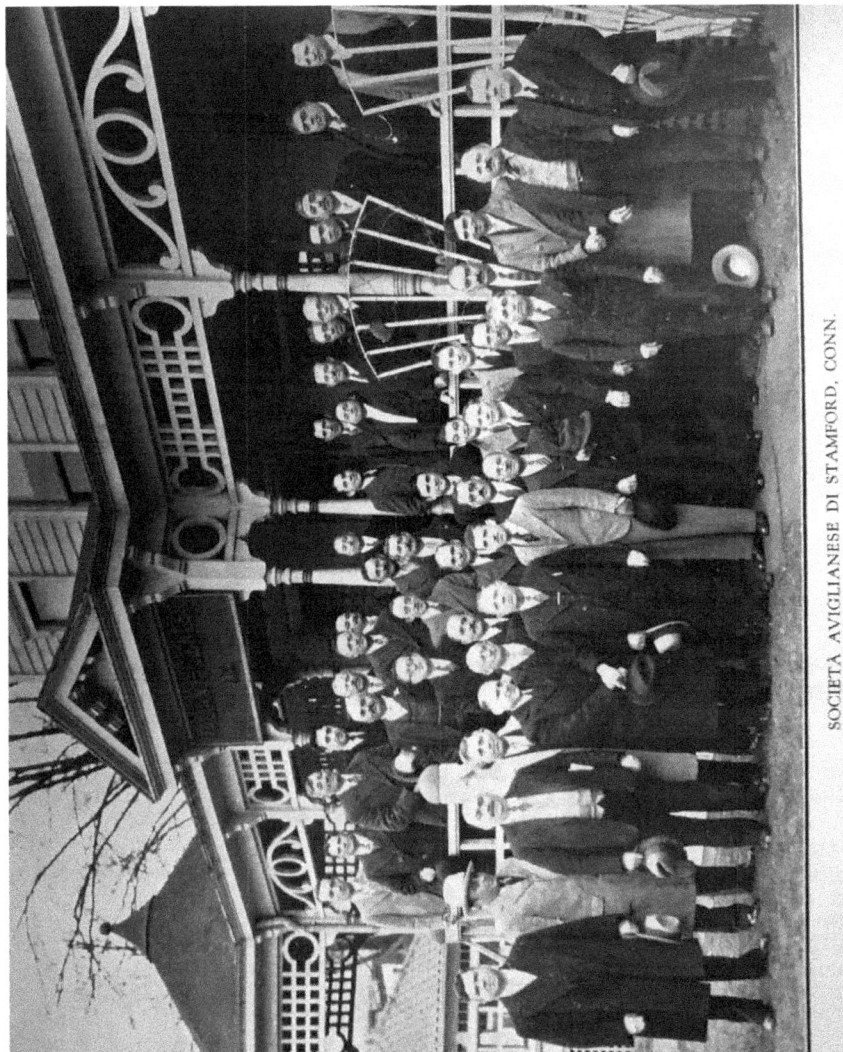

Società Aviglianese di Mutuo Soccorso – Founded with 75 members and incorporated with the State of Connecticut on August 18, 1905, this organization appears to be the first regional (Italians and their descendants from Avigliano, Italy) mutual aid society. Photo Courtesy of The Italian Center of Stamford.

The first Italian organization in Stamford, "Società di Mutuo Soccorso Fra Tommaso Campenella" a mutual aid society was formed in 1894 to create a social backstop for the Italian workforce. Photo Courtesy of The Italian Center of Stamford.

Donatelli leading parade in Stamford in 1898 with members of Società di Mutuo Soccorso Fra Tommaso Campanella. Photo Courtesy of The Stamford Historical Society.

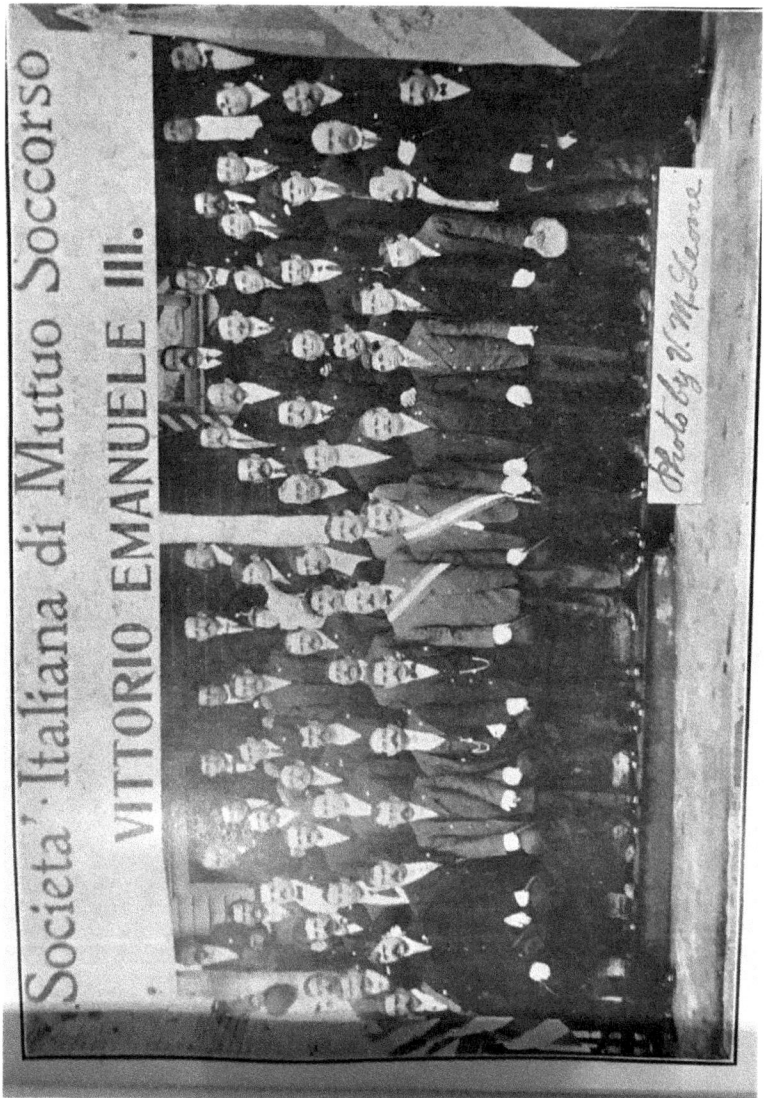

Società di Mutuo Soccorso Vittorio Emanuele III - Società di Mutuo Soccorso Vittorio Emanuele III was incorporated under the laws of Connecticut on April 30, 1901, and was a mutual self-insurance group. To aid, help and assist members of the Society in cases of sickness, death, and other distress, and to elevate their civil, moral, and social standing, and to disseminate general knowledge among them. Photo Courtesy of The Italian Center of Stamford.

Italo American Republican Club. Vito Sabia lower left, Joseph Carpinella top middle. Photo Courtesy of Sabia Family.

SOCIETÀ SAN MANGHESE ... SAN TEODORO MARTIRE

The society was incorporated in June 28th, 1906 and was for Italians and their descendants from San Mango Sul Calore, Italy. The articles stated that the objects of the society are to aid, help and assist the members of the society in case of sickness, death, or other distress, and to elevate their civil, moral and social standing, and to disseminate general knowledge among them. The society offered a health insurance policy to new immigrants and helped them get settled in Stamford. Photos Courtesy of The San Manghese Social Club of Stamford.

The West Side Athletic Club filed articles of association with the secretary of state on July 15, 1926. The subscribers were Louis DeLuca, William V. Mancusi, Leo J. Possidento, Tony Delupica, Alfred A. Ferretto and Thomas A. Ferretti. The club put on amateur boxing matches, and baseball games. Photo Courtesy of Attorney Peter Somma.

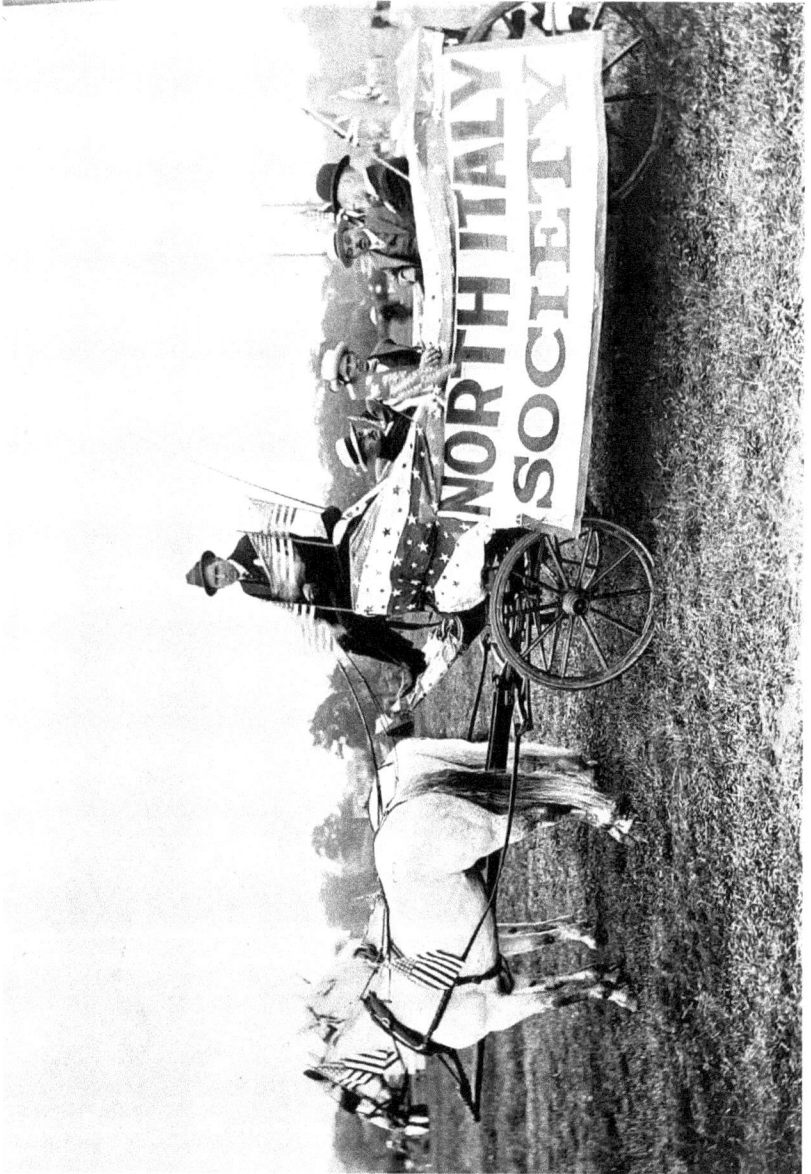

North Italy Mutual Benefit Society – The North Italy Mutual Benefit Society was formed in 1913 to encouraging the social, civic, and moral welfare of its members and to help each other in case of sickness or need. Quintino Vetriolo riding in carriage. Photo Courtesy of the Vetriolo family.

Pietro Rosa – Co-founded first clothing factory founded by Italians in Stamford. Member of the Republican Town Committee and president of the Italian Center board of governors for six years, president of the Federation of Aviglianese Society and active in the Community Chest (now United Way). Honored by the Italian government with the title Cavalier to the Crown of Italy. Photo Courtesy of The Italian Center of Stamford.

Businessman club – Joseph Vuono, Vito Sabia, Joe Carpinella. Photo Courtesy of the Vetriolo family.

Albino Meda – Treasurer of Italo-American Educational Circle (Circolo Educativo), partner of Quintino Vetriolo, father of Cesare Meda. Photo Courtesy of the Vetriolo family.

Cesare Latte – Leader of Italian political clubs, Societa di Mutuo Soccorso
Vittorio Emanuele III, Building Laborers' Union, Society of Saint Vito
Martire and Marie S.S. Del Carmine, Inc., and La Societa Mutuo Soccorso fra
Settefratesi "Capitano Alessandro Venturini" di Stamford. Photo Courtesy of
the Latte family.

Reverend Barone and family (including son Melchisedec) – Baptist missionary in Stamford founded Alpha and Omega Assembly after leaving church. Melchisedec was a physician in Stamford. Photo Courtesy of the Barone family.

Colonial Band in 1912. Marching band at many Italian parades. Photo Courtesy of The Stamford Historical Society.

Michael F (Mickey) Lione was a policeman (starting in 1939) and star football player at Georgetown, where he later was an assistant coach in the early 1930s. He also played semi-professional baseball and professional football, but was most famous in Stamford as a Coach. Photo Courtesy of The Stamford Historical Society.

John A. Scalzi (an independent) was named to the Park Commission. Scalzi Park is named for him. Member of Italian Center. John was awarded the Joseph A. Wilner Trophy as Georgetown's most valuable player by vote of the student body. He also played baseball and basketball there. His ability attracted major league scouts who signed him for a cash bonus with the Boston Braves in 1931. Photo Courtesy of The Stamford Historical Society.

Cesare Meda - was a member of the First Air Park, USA. He served in France on the S.S. George Washington and was in foreign service for eighteen months. Married Eda Vetriolo. Photo Courtesy of the Vetriolo family.

Sanford Palo – One of first Italians to graduate from Stamford High School. WW I and WW II veteran. Photo Courtesy of The Stamford Historical Society (Stamford High School Yearbook).

Charles Corbo. WW I veteran. Photo Courtesy of The Stamford Historical Society.

Cesare Meda – World War I veteran, outside Carlo Rosso grocery store. Photo Courtesy of the Vetriolo family.

Frank Mercede, founder of Mercede Construction Company. Photo Courtesy of Sacco & Mercedes Families.

Vincenzo Vacca

25MAY1867–24MAY1930

Vincenzo "James" Vacca - About 1884, Vincenzo "James" Vacca came to Stamford, with a group of stonemasons who were recruited from New York City to build the North Stamford Reservoir. Principal employers of stonemasons in the town. Photo Courtesy of the Vacca and DiPreta families.

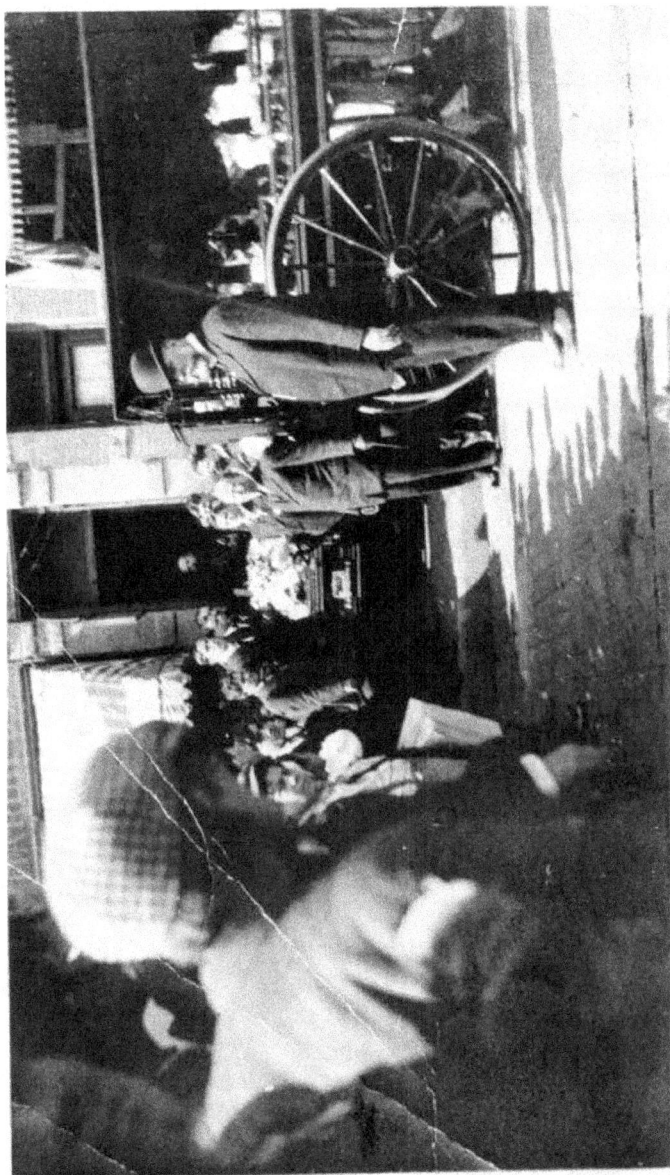

Dr. Aniello Preziosi died at 24 years of age, one of the doctors serving the mutual benefit societies, who worked his way out of poverty to become a doctor. Photo Courtesy of The Stamford Historical Society.

Giovanni Sacco, founding member of Società Gravinese di Mutuo Soccorso, was a shoemaker. Photo Courtesy of Sacco & Mercedes Families.

Marco Gussardo owned a confectionary store, and owned a pet bear. Photo Courtesy of The Stamford Historical Society.

Mike Sabia, podiatrist, son of Vito Sabia (WW II veteran), Sabia family. Photo Courtesy of Sabia Family.

Carmella Genovese Scalzi holding Patricia Scalzi. Photo Courtesy of Scalzi Family.

John Scalzi Sr. – Scalzi Paint Store. Photo Courtesy of Scalzi Family.

Quintino Vetriolo (second from left) early Italian leader and Virginia Cavanna Vetriolo (fourth from left). Photo Courtesy of Vetriolo Family.

Virginia Cavanna – Virginia assisted in running the husband Quintino Vetriolo's grocery and liquor store, and steamship business. She counseled immigrants on saving money, acted as an interpreter when they had problems, and even went to Ellis Island welcoming and escorting new immigrants. Virginia was the founder of the first woman's society, Adelaide Cairoli. Photo Courtesy of Vetriolo Family.

Vito Salvatore, president of Aviglianese Society. Photo Courtesy of The Stamford Historical Society.

Vito Toglia – One of first Italians to graduate from Stamford High School, was well respected at school and written about in the Advocate for his studies. Later graduated from Harvard. Photo Courtesy of Mario Toglia.

Antonio DiPreta. Early immigrant mason. Photo Courtesy of DiPreta Family.

Attilio DiPreta. WWI veteran. 328 Infantry Medical detail. Attilio at 28 years. Photo Courtesy of DiPreta Family.

Italian 3rd Ward Republican Club 1929. Joe Carpinella in second row, third from left. In 1929, officers included: Joseph L. Carpinella, president; S. B. Esposito, vice president; Ralph Lionetti, Jr., secretary; Peter P. Zezima, treasurer; and John Rose, Louis Caporizzo and Frank Lacerenza, trustees. Charles Vitti was also a member. Photo Courtesy of The Stamford Historical Society.

Joseph Colucci. WW I veteran, sheriff, court interpreter. Photo Courtesy of
The Stamford Historical Society.

Paganini Society – The Santa Cecilia Paganini Music and Dramatic Club was organized in 1931 by Aniello Preziosi and performed at the Italian Center and various other venues in Stamford and surrounding towns. Courtesy of The Stamford Historical Society.

Peter Colucci, bootblack Courtesy of The Stamford Historical Society.

Settefratese Club picnic 1929. La Società Mutuo Soccorso fra Settefratesi "Capitano Alessandro Venturini" di Stamford was formed on April 15, 1916 and incorporated under the laws of Connecticut on April 25th, 1916. Courtesy of The Stamford Historical Society.

Diaspora

As *diaspora* is the dispersion or spread of people from their original homeland, this series takes its name in the intellectual spirit of willful dispersion of subject matter and thought. It is dedicated to publishing those studies that in various and sundry ways either speak to or offer new methods of analysis of the Italian diaspora.

Carmelo Fucarino. *Two Italian Geniuses in New York: Broken American Dreams.* ISBN 978-1-955995-05-4. 2023.

Anthony Julian Tamburri, ed. *Re-Thinking* The Godfather *50 Years Later.* ISBN 978-1-955995-06-1. 2024.

www.ingramcontent.com/pod-product-compliance
Lightning Source LLC
Chambersburg PA
CBHW070541270326
41926CB00013B/2162